Viewing Positions

Rutgers Depth of Field Series

Charles Affron, Mirella Affron, Robert Lyons, Series Editors

Edited and with an introduction by
Linda Williams

Viewing Positions

Ways of Seeing Film

Rutgers
University
Press

*New Brunswick,
New Jersey*

Library of Congress Cataloging-in-Publication Data

Viewing positions : ways of seeing film / edited by Linda Williams.
    p.   cm.—(Depth of Field series)
    Includes bibliographical references and index.
    ISBN 0-8135-2132-7 (cloth)—ISBN 0-8135-2133-5 (pbk.)
    1. Motion pictures. 2. Motion picture audiences. I. Williams, Linda, 1946– .
II. Series.
    PN1995.V437   1994
    791.43—dc20   94-14071
                                                                                      CIP

British Cataloging-in-Publication information available

For Quinn, my favorite viewing companion.

Contents

Viewing Positions

Linda Williams

Introduction

> *In the average European oil painting of the nude, the*
> *principal protagonist is never painted. He is the spec-*
> *tator in front of the picture and he is presumed to be*
> *a man. Everything is addressed to him. Everything*
> *must appear to be the result of his being there. It is for*
> *him that the figures have assumed their nudity. But*
> *he, by definition, is a stranger with his clothes still on.*[1]

Though perhaps not as often quoted within the field of film studies as
Laura Mulvey's 1975 pronouncement that the gaze of the classical
Hollywood cinema is male,[2] this passage from John Berger's *Ways of
Seeing* could stand as the earliest and most accessible single statement
of a whole generation's turn toward a commentary on a hypothetical
spectator's relation to the visual image. Berger's insight that there is a
"way of seeing," structured into visual representations and the way those
representations address spectators, would be elaborated in a wide variety
of ways throughout the 1970s and into the 1980s by such influential
poststructuralist film theorists as Metz, Heath, Baudry, Mulvey, Silverman, and Doane.[3]

What all these theorists shared was the belief that in the most
seemingly natural or beautiful of visual images, there is an invisible
ideology that affords the gaze that surveys it both mastery and equilib-
rium. In Berger's passage, as later in Mulvey's famous formulation of the
visual pleasure of the masculine gaze at cinematic narrative, that hypothetical spectator was male. For other theorists, the hypothetical spectator was nominally male but more frequently reduced, as Vivian Sobchack
has noted, to a kind of giant, disembodied set of eyes,[4] as in Christian
Metz's description of

[S]pectator-fish taking in everything with their eyes, nothing with their bodies: the institution of the cinema requires a silent, motionless spectator, a *vacant* spectator at once alienated and happy, acrobatically hooked up to himself by the invisible thread of sight.[5]

Similarly, in Jean-Louis Baudry's influential essay on the apparatus of cinema, the analogy between film spectators and the chained, immobile prisoners of Plato's cave offered a picture of spectatorship as pure absorption into the projected, illusory world of image and sound. For Baudry, the projected "representations experienced as perceptions"[6]—that is, representations that spectators would forget were representations, so immediately perceptual did they seem—were simply the perceptual lures of what Metz would soon after call the cinema's "imaginary signifier."[7]

In her remarkably influential 1975 article "Visual Pleasure and Narrative Cinema," cited earlier, Laura Mulvey argued that the mainstream, classical cinematic narrative constructs an Oedipal subject of desire engaged in the twin perversions of voyeurism and fetishism in order to master the potentially fragmenting and castrating threats of the body of the woman in the film. In this formulation, perverse forms of visual pleasure, especially sadistic mastery and voyeurism, are, in effect, normalized by the vision of classical cinema.

Thus a classical cinema, and a classical cinematic apparatus, seen as the continuous extension of Western idealism, seemed to produce a hegemonic, masculine, Oedipal, bourgeois spectator, who was subject to its vision but who gained an illusory power and coherence in that very subjugation. The singularity of this dominated and dominating spectator—positioned and subjected by the text, yet in paradoxical command of all he surveyed—was appealing as a focus of what was wrong with the suspect pleasures of a homogenizing classical cinema.

It is important to understand the extraordinary appeal of such a paradigm. Without necessarily blaming individual men in the audience, this condemnation of a sadistic-voyeuristic male gaze nevertheless provided something akin to a popular villain whose specter has haunted the field of visual representation ever since. Even though many feminist critics were uncomfortable with such a totalizing concept and began to seek exceptions to the dominance of the gaze—originally in "women's films" and more recently in horror films—the very notion that such works *were* exceptions to the dominance of the gaze left the totalizing concept intact.[8]

Although the hegemony of a masculine-bourgeois-white-Eurocentric classical gaze was eventually challenged by a range of diverse positionalities not only of gender but also of class, race, sexual orientation, and ethnicity, those challenges did not themselves add up to a newly coherent formulation of spectatorial relations. Rather, they tended to add up to an interesting list of exceptions to a dominant mainstream whose typicality went largely unchallenged.[9]

By the late 1970s, it had become a kind of orthodoxy of much feminist and ideological film criticism that all dominant cinema was organized for the power and pleasure of a single spectator-subject whose voyeuristic-sadistic gaze became a central figure of visual domination. Soon it seemed that only those productions that worked to subvert or destroy that gaze's domination were worthy of scrutiny. For Berger, this subversion occurred within the category of what he called "exceptional nudes"—for example, nudes by Reubens and Rembrandt, which had been painted with such love that the women in them did not become voyeuristic spectacles. For Mulvey, however, exceptions occurred only in avant-garde films that could frankly destroy spectatorial pleasure and return viewers to a material awareness of the medium. Everything else was complicit with a suspect ideology that lured spectator-subjects into identifications with false images.

It was perhaps predictable that historically grounded studies of cinematic reception, along with cultural studies aimed at delineating the complex interactions between audiences and texts, would challenge some of the foregoing notions. The variable experiences of actual viewers, who are in possession of many more "ways of seeing" than Berger, Metz, Mulvey, or Baudry could have imagined, have recently challenged a more monolithic account of the "gaze." The aforementioned motionless, bodiless, vacant gaze cited by Metz has come to seem both oversimplified and ahistorical. Although that gaze once taught us much about the workings of power and pleasure in images that would never again seem so innocently natural, it has become, as Hansen puts it in her contribution to this collection, as outmoded as bell-bottom jeans. (Of course, now that bell bottoms have returned as postmodern pastiche, Hansen's figure of outmodedness has now itself become outmoded. Perhaps the more pertinent point, as we shall see, is that these spectatorial positions have now become like bell-bottoms, one among many possible costumes, or roles, to be taken on.)

The singular, unitary spectator of what I will, for purposes of abbreviation, call gaze theory has gradually been challenged by diverse viewing positions. Whereas 1970s and 1980s film theory tended to posit, despite Berger's title, a *unitary* way of seeing, contemporary discussions of spectatorship emphasize the plurality and paradoxes of many different, historically distinct viewing positions. The issue that now faces the once influential subfield of spectatorship within cinema—and indeed all visual—studies is whether it is still possible to maintain a theoretical grasp of the relations between moving images and viewers without succumbing to an anything-goes pluralism.

This volume is dedicated to the proposition that many of the insights into what I am calling gaze theory are still relevant to film studies. There is still the need for a theoretical understanding of relations between films and viewers. No amount of empirical research into the sociology of actual audiences will displace the desire to speculate about the effects of visual culture, and especially moving images, on hypothetical viewing subjects. Berger's insight that spectators are somehow "in" the work remains valuable.

However, the concept of a singular, dominating, voyeuristic male spectator-subject is in as much need of revision as that other stereotype: the spectator as passive subject, as pure absorber of dominant ideology. It would have been possible for this volume to have included essays written in the name of a wide variety of audience constituencies— straight women, lesbians, gays, African-American men, African-American women, Chicanos, Chicanas, and those who are part of the complex networks of subcultural affinities that have been articulated in reception studies and cultural studies. However, I have decided instead to include articles that maintain a focus on some of the traditional concerns of a hypothetical spectator's relation to visual texts and apparatuses. The essays collected here seem to me to have carried the general debate about relations between spectators and films in important new directions without opting to speak only for the interests of specific audiences. Although many of the essays concentrate on periods that either precede or follow the conventionally accepted dates of the hegemony of classical cinema, the very interest in these preclassical and postclassical moments has become a means to question the orthodoxies of a classical spectatorship without abandoning the fundamental insight that there is something to be learned from the moving picture and its apparatus about the spectators who gaze at it, look at it, glance at it, or avert their eyes from it.

The essays collected in this volume, some reprinted from journals, some that were chapters in books, some written especially for this collection, offer important challenges to certain of the more familiar axioms of spectatorship as promulgated by film theory of the 1970s and 1980s, yet most of them remain concerned with the institutional, apparatical, and textual effects of cinematic moving images on spectators. They represent some of the best new thinking about the crucial relation between visual representations and human subjectivity.

The volume is organized into three clusters. The first, Vision and the Apparatus, centers on the crucial role of apparatically mediated visions within cinematic and other visual apparatuses of modernity, in essays by Jonathan Crary, Vivian Sobchack, and Anne Friedberg. The second section, Precinema, Early Cinema, and Late Cinema, examines the historical context of the emergence of the specific apparatus of cinema, as well as the parallels between early and late cinema, in essays by Vanessa R. Schwartz, Tom Gunning, and Miriam Hansen. A final cluster of topics, Paradoxes of Spectatorship, concentrates on gender- and sexuality-based challenges to a homogeneous classical theory of spectatorship, in essays by Judith Mayne, Carol J. Clover, and Rhona J. Berenstein. In this section we see how analysis of a supposedly exceptional genre—the horror film—may end up offering the most comprehensive analysis of gender and sexuality in spectatorship in general.

Vision and the Apparatus

The essays in this section challenge the classical model of spectatorship by asking whether there really has ever been such a thing as a continuous tradition of a centered, unitary, distanced and objectifying gaze or whether, as Crary and Friedberg suggest—though in very different ways—there had not already been an important rupture of that spectatorial tradition, which the apparatus of cinema, along with a great many other devices for mediated viewing, continued.

Crary's "Modernizing Vision" offers an overview of ideas worked out at greater length in his book *Techniques of the Observer*. Crary's thesis is that theories of vision have been wedded to the model of continuous Western visual tradition at the expense of important discontinuities in that tradition. Although Crary does not mention Baudry or cinematic apparatus theory by name, his argument is diametrically opposed to Baudry's notion that the cinematic apparatus represents the culmination of the Western philosophical tradition of a transcendental idealist subject.

Baudry argued that the centered, transcendental subject of vision posited by the camera obscura and Renaissance perspective had simply been extended in the cinematographic apparatus of cinema. In both, subjects experience themselves as the basic source of meanings centered in their visual field. To Crary, however, there is little continuity between the ideological effects of the camera obscura—as discursive model of vision—and the technical photographic—and later cinematic—apparatus. Crary argues that by the 1820s and 1830s, the model of the camera obscura had already been displaced by very different notions of vision. Thus the invention of the photographic camera during this period did not simply extend the camera obscura model of vision, as Baudry argues. Crary thus distinguishes between the philosophical and ideological model of a centered, ideal, disembodied vision—which reigned roughly from the late 1500s to the end of the 1700s in the writings of Descartes, Locke, and Leibniz and in the science of Kepler and Newton—and the collapse of that model in the early nineteenth century.

The camera obscura model of vision had guaranteed access to an objective truth about the world based on the secure positioning of an immaterial self within the empty interior space of the camera, from which perspective a secure knowledge could be founded. But such access to truth was based on the notion of a privatized, isolated subject whose sensory experiences are subordinated to an external, pregiven world of objective truth. Crary argues that the most crucial way in which that model collapsed in the early nineteenth century was through "the insertion of a new term into discourses and practices of vision: the human body, a term whose exclusion was one of the foundations of classical theories of vision and optics."[10]

In the early nineteenth century, a number of researchers began to view the body as the key producer—rather than neutral registerer—of images. When that happened, the entire distinction between inner and outer upon which the camera obscura depended collapsed. Vision was seen to be subjective, an unfolding of processes within a body whose senses had an almost innate capacity to misperceive—that is, to be affected by sensations that have no necessary link to an external referent. A new modernity of vision was thus grounded, Crary argues, not in the modernist art of the late nineteenth century but already in the early part of the century in the creation of a new type of observer, whose vision had a new "carnal density" in place of the invisible, disembodied spectator of the camera obscura.

Against the familiar teleology of the birth and gradual perfection of the camera obscura—first as concept, later as technical means of reproduction—Crary maintains that the camera obscura and the nineteenth-century models of vision belong to two fundamentally different visual regimes. Thus for Crary the fragmented, subjective vision so evident in modern art was already taking place earlier in the century in philosophical toys such as the kaleidoscope and the thaumatrope, which were usually associated with the rise of cinema and the extension of the camera obscura.

Crary's argument has profound implications for the conventional notion that a continuous tradition of classical mimetic representation leads from the camera obscura through Renaissance perspective to cinema. Perhaps most significantly for apparatus theory, it radically alters the standard division of twentieth-century art into a classical mimesis and an elite, avant-garde modernism that is supposedly alone in its capability of returning the spectator to an awareness of the effects of an apparatus. Crary claims that the spectator (he prefers the Foucauldian term *observer*) within one regime is not so different from the spectator within the other. Both were plunged into a "newly corporealized" immediacy of sensations.

It is this notion of the "corporeality of vision" that I find most useful in Crary despite some difficulties with his model.[11] The classical model of spectatorship—whether psychoanalytic or ideological—presumed a distanced, decorporealized, monocular eye completely unimplicated in the objects of its vision. Crary, on the other hand, offers a model in which the boundaries between body and image on the one hand, and body and machine for viewing on the other, are blurred. The body is implicated, in some ways even assaulted, in vision in a way that was inconceivable in the classical model of the camera obscura's ideological mastery. And that implication and assault are not dependent on any avant-garde rupture; it is simply how vision was conceived and experienced in the early nineteenth century.

Crary's Foucauldian approach to the discontinuities of the history of vision provides an important context for all the essays in this volume. Many of these essays share the important notion that there have been more ruptures in the history of vision than any classical theory of spectatorship can explain. When Crary argues that modernist discourses and technologies constructed newly corporealized bodies of observers with no precedent in the disembodied regime of the camera obscura, he suggests that a long tradition of mind/body dualism that has treated the bodily sensations provoked by images as suspect has already ended. He thus begins to speak of spectatorship without invoking the judgment against its bodily implications that have been in effect since Plato: that the image's seduction of the body is to be defended against by models of vision that emphasize control, mastery, and knowledge rather than pleasure, implication, and assault.

In "Cinema and the Postmodern Condition," Anne Friedberg extends the debate about the nature of modernist vision into ongoing debates about the postmodern condition. Friedberg says that many of the arguments about the detemporalized and despatialized experience of postmodernity are applicable to modernity as well. Thus, like Crary, she stresses the importance of a rupture with the classical, centered, unitary forms of vision. Unlike Crary, however, she does not seek to locate that rupture precisely. Rather, she posits "a gradual and indistinct epistemological tear along the fabric of modernity, a change caused by the growing cultural centrality of a feature that is integral to both cinema and television: a mobilized gaze that conducts a *flanerie* through an imaginary other place and time."

The traditional flaneur—the urban male dandy who distractedly wandered the city arcades of the nineteenth century—has been described by Walter Benjamin as the quintessential modern subject. The mobilized gaze of this literal, pedestrian wanderer, epitomized by Baudelaire's distracted observations and dreamlike reveries, was typical of a certain gender (and class). Friedberg borrows from Mulvey and others the concept of a gendered gaze and links it not to vision in general but to a specific moment in modernity when a certain class of men could exercise the power of their gaze by wandering the public spaces of big cities. Instead of either the eternal male gaze of the 1970s feminist film theory or the strangely neuter observer of Crary's modernized vision, however, Friedberg introduces a historically specific figure: the mid-nineteenth-century *flâneur*—to stand for one aspect of the mobilized gaze of modernity. Immediately afterward, however, and in contrast to earlier feminist theorizing about the singular male gaze, she introduces another figure of modernity: the *flâneuse*—the woman shopper of the *grands magasins* who by the late nineteenth century had become a socially acceptable fixture of bourgeois leisure.

Friedberg's approach to the modernization and postmodernization of vision thus takes a gendered and commodified direction, different from Crary's description of scientific discourses of vision. However, like Crary, Friedberg sees cinema as simply one of many ways in which vision has been enlisted in both modern and postmodern life. Whether in the mobilized, strictly gendered gaze of the actual *flâneur* or *flâneuse* (in arcades, *grands magasins*, or shopping malls) or in the mobilized, and perhaps less strictly gendered, virtual gaze of the various apparatuses (whether dioramas, panoramas, cinemas, malls, or VCRs), Friedberg emphasizes the social and economic constraints that accompany actual, and virtual, looking.

Vivian Sobchack is a phenomenologist writing under a very different philosophical influence from both Crary and Friedberg. In her book *The Address of the Eye: A Phenomenology of Film Experience*, from which her chapter "Phenomonology and the Film Experience" is excerpted, Sobchack argues that the human body has been the forgotten term in all theories of spectatorship, especially in the three most influential models of cinema: the formalist model of the frame, the realist model of the window, and the contemporary poststructuralist model of the mirror.[12]

In an elegant summary of the operation of these three metaphors for the spectator's experience of film, Sobchack shows how each has privileged one part of the cinema experience: expression is privileged in formalist models, perception in realist models, and the confusion of perception and expression (Baudry's "representations mistaken for perceptions") in the contemporary apparatical model. In the last model, signification is seen to be predetermined either by the apparatus and ideology or by fixed psychic structures that cause spectators to confuse their vision with that of the camera. Sobchack argues that each of these approaches has privileged one part of the film experience while ignoring the correlated whole. Instead, she advocates a formulation accommodating both perception and expression. Film is not just an object of the viewer's vision; it is also a "viewing subject"—not that film is human but that it is an act of vision with both a subjectivity that views and a view that is seen:

> it possesses sense by means of its senses, and it makes sense as a "living cohesion," as a signifying subject. It is as this *signifying subject* that it existentially *comes to matter* as a *significant object*, that is, can be understood in its *objective* status by others as sensible and intelligible.[13]

In this way Sobchack breaks down the traditional oppositions between subject and object, mind and body, the visual act and the visible object in order to argue that the film experience has always been a "dialogical and dialectical" engagement of two viewing subjects. As with Crary, Sobchack challenges the classicism of a model of spectatorship, with the viewer on one side and the object of view on the other, to encourage instead a model of more fluid exchange. But where Crary challenges the disembodied camera obscura model in the name of scientific discourses of modernist vision that gave vision a historically new "carnal density," Sobchack argues for a specifically cinematic embodied vision that challenges all previous models of film theory in the name of a phenomenological experience.

Here, then, are three new ways of thinking about spectatorship: Crary and Sobchack eschew the disembodied, distanced control and mastery of a classical gaze and reenvision vision as bodily implicated in what it sees. Crary also posits a historical rupture with the fixed model of classical spectatorship, and Friedberg maintains a gradual slide into postmodernity. There are many differences between these models and no doubt many difficulties in each. Taken together, however, I believe these essays go a long way toward challenging the notion of the persistent classical model of spectatorship as a fixed subject.

Precinema, Early Cinema, and Late Cinema: Historians View Spectators

In this section, we turn from apparatical models of spectatorship to historical investigation of the period when film spectatorship began to arise. If cinematic spectatorship has not always been the same, then it is important to see what different things it has been. Film historians have often traced the history of cinema in technologically deterministic terms: that is, once the technological apparatus was invented, cinema as we know it could be seen to follow. The essays in this section show first that much more than technology was involved in the invention of cinema, and second that the cinema as we know it was not necessarily what audiences of early cinema saw. At issue in each of these articles is thus a description of the historical audience viewed as constituting a particular kind of collectivity or public.

In "Cinematic Spectatorship before the Apparatus: The Public Taste for Reality in Fin-de-Siècle Paris," Vanessa R. Schwartz examines specifically the pattern of spectacular visual amusements that reigned in the fin-de-siècle Paris that was one important locale for cinematic invention. Schwartz argues that many forms of public life in Paris were increasingly being experienced as a show at the same time as visual spectacles became more like real life. Offering the kind of detailed history of mass cultural visual amusements that only a social historian can provide, Schwartz investigates three sites of popular Parisian spectatorship—the spectacular display of bodies at the Morgue, the wax museum, and the panoramas—to show how those sensational visual spectacles were linked to the as yet unillustrated popular press.

Whereas the Morgue, with its lines of spectators, its corpses dressed and seated on chairs, and its windows and curtains, offered, until 1907, a highly theatrical tableau of real, albeit dead, bodies linked to unusual crimes or mysteries, the wax museum of the Musée Grevin, whose second-order representations survive to this day, offered yet another tableau illustration of the newspapers' *actualités*. Schwartz shows that the wax museum, seen in its day as a kind of "animated newspaper," augmented its reality effect with the use of authentic accessories such as Marat's bathtub and Hugo's pen. The hunger for historical facsimile so important, for example, to the art of D. W. Griffith, is here seen in an even purer form.

Through these wax tableaux, spectators began to identify with the private, intimate moments of public personages as well as with the narrative stages of sensational actions, as in the seven-tableaux mixture of serial novel and *fait divers* showing the progression from crime to punishment: "l'Histoire d'un Crime." Finally, in the case of the panoramas of the 1890s, Schwartz shows how traditional landscape panoramas gave way to urban representations of Parisian modern life or scenes from past wars, as represented in the press or in history books.

Schwartz's essay shows the diversity of precinematic attractions reigning in Paris on the eve of the invention of cinema. Though the audiences Schwartz describes are certainly more mobile and possibly more distracted than the first cinema audiences, it is clear that those sensations have more in common with the sensations experienced by early cinema audiences than they do with the narrative absorption of later cinema. Tom Gunning's "An Aesthetic of Astonishment: Early Film and the (In)Credulous Spectator," the second essay in this section, offers a portrait of early cinema audiences whose sensationalism and shock are not unlike the precinematic real-life shows described by Schwartz. Gunning points out that even when early cinema tells a story, the attraction of the film lies more in the exhibitionistic display of events and actions than in the expression of a narrative.

Gunning's timely description of the difference between early cinema's spectatorial relations and those of classical narrative has recently begun to vie with Laura Mulvey's classic formulation of the spectatorial relations of classical cinema as one of the most frequently cited concepts in the field.[14] The reason, I suspect, relates not only to the undeniable importance and relevance of this concept to the attractions of early cinema, as well as to the attractions cited by Schwartz, but also to its ability to point to aspects of spectatorial relations that have been ignored under the dominance of the gaze paradigm and that are perfectly applicable to all forms of spectatorship, not only those early sensations. Gunning's notions of *attraction* and *astonishment* have caught on, in other words, because, in addition to being apt descriptions of early cinema, they describe aspects of all cinema that have also been under-valued in the classical paradigm.

Scholars have been drawn to early cinema for its exhilarating variety of spectatorial relations so radically different from diegetic ab-sorption and voyeuristic looking on. The spectatorial lessons of early cinema, as Miriam Hansen's essay so well explains, may have more to do with our own, postclassical and postmodern, sense of existing as heterogeneous spectators in an era of fragmented and diverse spectacles that have more affinity to early cinema than to a cinema of classical spectatorship. Hansen's essay, "Early Cinema, Late Cinema: Transfor-mations of the Public Sphere," points to that affinity while going on to assert the important changes that have taken place in the postmodern and postclassical public sphere.

Hansen points out, for example, that 1970s gaze theories of classical spectatorship were promulgated at precisely the moment that the dominance of classical narrative and classical spectatorship began to crumble. Not only is cinema no longer the primary means of moving-image entertainment, but even when movies are the primary focus, their reception context, as Friedberg, too, notes, in mall or living room, breaks the spell of classical diegesis: "an aesthetics of the 'glance' is replacing the aesthetics of the 'gaze.'" Today's postmodern, globalized culture of consumption operates more through diversification than homogeniza-tion. We have returned, then (but did we ever entirely leave?), to the phenomenon of attractions that, as Hansen sibilantly puts it, "assault the viewer with sensational, supernatural, scientific, sentimental or otherwise stimulating sights."

What do we learn from the affinity between early and late cinemas and from the spectatorial relations obtaining within them? To Hansen what we learn is not that they are the same but that both moments mark important transitions in the development of a process through which "social experience is articulated, interpreted, negoti-ated and contested in an intersubjective, potentially collective and oppositional form." Historically, early cinema and late cinema are moments in which the public sphere has opened up to more diverse forms of social experience. The public sphere has been an important concept to the Frankfurt School tradition of cultural critique—most recently in the work of Jurgen Habermas, Oskar Negt, and Alexander Kluge. The critical project of that tradition has been to register the role of cinema—and mass culture in general—in the structuration of subjectivity.

Drawing on Negt's and Kluge's critique of Habermas, Hansen argues that the concept of the public sphere needs expansion from the enlightenment concepts of free speech and free association to a more comprehensive notion of the whole social horizon of experience in material, psychic, and social re-production. The political task of such critique is thus to make connections between isolated fragments of experience—across segregated domains of work and leisure, fiction and fact, and past and present—to identify intersections among diverse and competing publics.

If we think of the public sphere as consisting of fluid, competing ways of organizing social experience with room for unpredictable collisions and opportunities, then we begin to see the value of thinking of the cinema—and of mass culture in general—in terms of an expanded notion of the public sphere. Such thinking, Hansen adds, means considering not only sociological determinants but also a range of multiple and conflicting identities and constituencies activated by mass culture. The cinema and mass culture can be catalysts for new forms of community and solidarity, as was early cinema for immigrant audiences. Early cinema and late cinema both give spectators greater room to interact with the film, along with a greater awareness of exhibition and cultural intertexts, and they draw upon socially marginalized and diverse constituencies. This does not mean that spectators are not also seduced and manipulated by films; it means simply that the forms of seduction and manipulation are more diverse than assumed under the classical paradigm.

The final advantage of seeking affinities between early and late, preclassical and postclassical, cinema may be to remove some of the appearance of inevitability of the classical paradigm. Even more important, "classical cinema may itself no longer look quite as classical as the study of its dominant mode suggests." It is possible that the homogeneity of classical cinema and of classical spectatorship will one day seem more like the aberration than the norm of cinematic history.

Paradoxes of Film Spectatorship

If it is no longer possible to assume that the classical model of spectatorship has been in continuous operation throughout Western history, then concerns about gendered power and gendered pleasure in vision do not, as Friedberg has shown, simply go away. Rather, it means that the classical model of spectatorship, which too easily assumed fixed ideological and psychic effects on spectators, needs to be viewed, as Judith Mayne puts it in the lead essay of the next section, as a more complex set of paradoxes. In "Paradoxes of Spectatorship"—a chapter from her recent book *Cinema and Spectatorship*[15]—she turns to cinematic spectatorship specifically to detail some of those paradoxes.

Mayne begins with the assertion that there is no simple division between a cinema that functions as an instrument of dominant ideology and a cinema that challenges such ideology. This is her first, and most important, paradox: the competing claims of a cinema viewed as a homogeneous institution (as in 1970s apparatus theory) and the heterogeneity of different spectators (of different races, classes, genders, socializations, and subcultural affinities) who engage with it. Mayne points out that if the cinematic apparatus had been as fully saturated with idealist ideology and Oedipal desire as apparatus theory had argued, then nothing in cinema would ever have changed. Because cinema has changed, she proposes to examine the tension between homogeneity and heterogeneity—the in-between of the competing claims of domination and resistance.

Mayne first examines the gap between cinematic address—the way a text addresses spectators and in so doing assumes certain spectatorial responses—and cinematic reception—the actual conditions of reception that may, or may not, facilitate those responses with actual viewers. Where *address* concerns an ideal viewer, *reception* concerns a real viewer. As Mayne puts it, "it is one thing to assume that cinema is determined in ideological ways . . . to assume that is, that the various institutions of the cinema *do* project an ideal viewer, and another thing to assume that those projections *work*." Her point is not that apparatus theories are wrong but that they are incomplete. Mayne is careful to note, however, that reception studies of real audiences can be just as incomplete as well. She is suspicious, for example, of a certain return to sociological analysis taking place under the influence of cultural studies in which readers and viewers are seen to challenge dominant ideology through their everyday appropriations of ostensibly conventional works. For all their emphasis on the real reader or spectator, such studies often idealize in turn the contestatory capabilities of these real people.

The second in-between Mayne examines is the realm of fantasy. In fantasy, Mayne finds the best reasons to retain some elements of the psychoanalytic model of spectatorship, for psychoanalytic theory provides a useful model of the relation of the spectator to the image-discourse of cinema. The crucial lesson of fantasy, as Elizabeth Cowie, Constance Penley, and others have pointed out, following the work of Laplanche and Pontalis, is that the fantasist, like the spectator, does not necessarily identify in any fixed way with a character, a gaze, or a particular position but rather with a series of oscillating positions that fantasy's mise-en-scène of desire facilitates.[16] Fantasy is, most importantly, an imaginary scene—a place for the staging of desire. In this it is like the cinema. But it is not necessarily the enactment of a single character's desire. Its pleasures are the pleasures of mobility, of moving around among a range of different desiring positions. However, that mobility does not make a particular film or genre automatically liberatory.

Mayne also points out that most discussion of fantasy tends to assume that sexual difference is the ultimate binary out of which all fantasy proceeds, thus collapsing what would seem to be the varieties of desire into a master code of heterosexual desire. In other words, fantasy can engage with the complex effects of spectatorship, but we need a better understanding of how the categories of sexual difference, and desire itself, are culturally variable.

The third item that encapsulates the in-between homogeneity and heterogeneity of film spectatorship is negotiation. Cultural studies uses the term to describe a reader or viewer's often ambivalent engagement with the so-called dominant ideology of a text. To Stuart Hall negotiated readings stand midway between dominant readings, which are consistent with the ideology of a text, and oppositional readings, which go totally against it. The social formations of audiences are usually seen as determining the ways in which a text will be negotiated so as to shape mass culture to their own needs. Mayne is highly suspicious of the liberatory effects of such negotiation. She insists, however, that *negotiation* is an important term so long as we remember that no negotiation is inherently oppositional and that the identities conducting the negotiation are, as Christine Gledhill puts it, contradictory and changing. Mayne concludes, "the challenges to apparatus theory described in this chapter return to the problem of identification, as if to suggest that however mobile and multiple subject positions may be, spectatorship still engages some notion of identity."

The two essays completing this section prove the continued importance of "some notion of identity" even as the stability of this identity is questioned. They also continue Mayne's examination of the paradoxes of spectatorship through horror cinema—a genre deeply engaged with fantasy. In Carol J. Clover's concluding chapter—taken from her groundbreaking study of contemporary horror film, *Men, Women and Chain Saws: Gender in the Modern Horror Film*[17]—and Rhona J. Berenstein's chapter—taken from her forthcoming book on classic horror film, *The Attack of the Leading Ladies*—we see how important genre study has been to the ongoing thinking about cinematic spectatorship. Horror cinema is an especially useful example because so much work has been done on it and because it is a classic genre that has not only survived the supposed demise of classical cinema but, like many of the zombies and monsters its depicts, flourished with that supposed death. It is important as well because horror, like pornography, has often been cited as an extreme and obvious example of the sadistic, voyeuristic, and mastering male gaze of apparatus theory. In other words, if in even *this* genre the gaze does not operate as presumed, then the implications for the whole of classical cinema would be far-reaching.

Clover begins her study of the modern horror film with the assumption that the "majority viewer" of such films is a young male whose fascination and pleasure lie in the abject terror: the gendered feminine of the genre's frequent "female victim-heroes." Her assumption is that the pairing of this off-screen, on-screen couple can teach us a great deal not only about spectatorship but also about the politics of criticism and theory. "The Eye of Horror," the conclusion to Clover's study of modern horror, is the chapter in which she draws together the insights about spectatorship gained throughout the book.

Although Clover assumes that the important spectator of modern horror is male, she does not assume that his pleasure resides in identification with voyeuristic mastery. Rather, her close observation of the form leads to some surprising conclusions about the almost systematic function of "failed gazing" in horror cinema: "whenever a man imagines himself as a controlling voyeur—imagines, in Lacanian terms, that his 'look' at women constitutes a gaze—some sort of humiliation is soon to follow." Clover's point is not that horror always forecloses voyeuristic pleasure but that the real investment in this genre is in the reactive or introjective gaze that vaginally takes in and absorbs what comes at it. Feminine masochism—meaning the masculine enjoyment of the passive and introjective feminine position—is thus for Clover the key pleasure of a horror cinema that "openly trades in fear and pain."

Even though Clover's conclusions emphasize the dominance of masochistic pleasure in horror cinema, the larger significance of her argument, as she goes on to stress, lies in its corrective of the blind spots of theories of spectatorship advocated by Metz and Mulvey. Here, I think, the lesson for spectatorship, and for cultural criticism in general, extends far beyond the realm of horror: Clover argues that Metz, Mulvey, and a host of followers have been blind to the obvious masochistic pleasures of masculine identification with a feminine position because such identification would challenge the entrenched, and often politically useful, cliché that men *are* sadists. The capacity for sadistic violence in men has frequently been used as a kind of bottom line of feminist criticism, from Mulvey[18] to Brownmiller[19] (Clover's examples), to Dworkin[20] and MacKinnon[21] (my examples). While not discrediting feminism's fundamental advocacy for women, Clover does censure a concept of the male gaze that has often worked as much against feminism as for it.

This lesson of horror cinema could easily extend beyond the genre to an understanding of how all cinematic narrative provides, but at the same time covers up, a male investment in female masochism. To put it simply, horror shows that one of the most important pleasures of film viewing resides in the journey made by one gendered identity (the male viewer) into the position of another gendered identity (the female victim-hero). Identity, as Mayne noted, is important to spectatorship, but it encompasses mobile and multiple positionalities.

In the final essay in this section, Rhona J. Berenstein expands on the mobile and multiple notion of the identity of spectators by criticizing the limitations of a binary model of identificatory positions: masculine/feminine and sadistic/masochistic. In "Spectatorship-as-Drag: The Act of Viewing and Classic Horror Cinema," Berenstein extends Clover's argument to maintain that spectators, as well as the horror genre itself, invest in the pleasures of both masochism and sadism—pleasures that are transgressive not only for male spectators but also for female spectators, whom Berenstein shows to have been much in evidence at classic horror as well. Using Freud's famous essay on children's beating fantasies, Berenstein asserts the significance—muted in Freud—of the fantasizing female child's cross-sex identification with a sadistic adult along with the more familiar masochistic identification. Her point is that one need not, like Freud, impose a heterosexual, Oedipal framework on these fantasies. Such fantasies, like classic horror films, allow for a fluid conceptualization of identificatory positions based on sex, gender, and sexual orientation. Because the monster is at once an aggressor, an object of desire, and a figure of identification, we need to see how sadism *and* masochism as well as identification *and* desire operate in horror films.

Berenstein thus proposes a more fluid model of the negotiation of spectatorial positions based on the way sex and gender roles are performed in drag. Drawing on the importance of performance in recent gay and lesbian theory—especially Judith Butler's important pronouncement that "gender is a kind of imitation for which there is no original"—Berenstein argues that the central figure of the monster in classic horror embodies this notion of gender performance as imitation rather than core identity. Not only are most horror monsters sexually ambiguous figures, but spectators (even, and perhaps especially, female spectators) may first cringe with fear at "his" appearance and then identify with and/or desire "him."

Pointing to the heterosexual biases that have prevented feminist film theorists from acknowledging the power of same-sex desire, Berenstein notes the particular power and pleasure for gay and lesbian viewers of identifying with a socially marginalized monster. Even more important, however, she criticizes the dominance of theories that describe viewing pleasures via similarities and sexual drives (e.g., that women only identify with heroines and only desire the opposite sex). Identification-in-opposition, in which viewers escape conventional social, racial, sexual, and economic identities, may be an equally important pleasure, permitting viewers to flaunt sexual roles as performances that contrast with everyday identity.

It is significant that Berenstein does not argue for the progressive or liberatory impact of her transgressive model of spectatorship as drag. Although drag is transgressive of more "conventional spectatorial positions," the transgression is carried out, Berenstein states, borrowing a phrase from Mayne, within the "safe zone" of the darkened theater. Nevertheless, the significant lesson to be learned about this safe zone, from all three contributors, is how putatively "conventional spectatorial positions" are much less conventional and fixed than previously thought—without being, however, totally fluid.

Perhaps the final lesson offered by all these essays is that any theory of spectatorship must now be historically specific, grounded in the specific spectatorial practices, the specific narratives, *and* the specific attractions of the mobilized and embodied gaze of viewers. There are a great many viewing positions, a great many "ways of seeing" in classical, modernist, and postmodernist spectatorship. Neither is it clear which way predominates in any of those highly debatable periods. What is clear is that although gaze theory certainly erred in its figurations of a far too limited way of seeing, it was gaze theory that first maintained that spectatorship mattered in an era of both visual narrative and visual attractions. It remains for historians and theorists to work together to specify the many forms that spectatorship takes.

NOTES

Special thanks to Lia Hotchkiss for help in all stages of this volume.

1. John Berger, *Ways of Seeing* (New York: Penguin Books, 1972), p. 54.

2. Laura Mulvey, "Visual Pleasure and Narrative Cinema," *Screen* 16:3 (1975), 6–18.

3. Jean-Louis Baudry, "Ideological Effects of the Basic Cinematographic Apparatus" and "The Apparatus: Metapsychological Approaches to the Impression of Reality in Cinema," in Philip Rosen, ed., *Narrative, Apparatus, Ideology* (New York: Columbia University Press, 1986), pp. 286–98 and 299–318. Stephen Heath, *Questions of Cinema* (Bloomington: Indiana University Press, 1981). Kaja Silverman, *The Subject of Semiotics* (New York: Oxford University Press, 1983). Christian Metz, *The Imaginary Signifier: Psychoanalysis and the Cinema*, trans. Celia Britton, Annwyl Williams, Ben Brewster, and Alfred Guzzetti (Bloomington: Indiana University Press, 1982). Mary Ann Doane, *The Desire to Desire: The Woman's Film of the 1940's* (Bloomington: Indiana University Press, 1987), and "Film and the Masquerade: Theorizing the Female Spectator," *Screen* 23(1982): 3–4, 74–88. Laura Mulvey, "Visual Pleasure and Narrative Cinema," pp. 6–18.

4. Vivian Sobchack, *The Address of the Eye: A Phenomenology of Film Experience* (Princeton, N.J.: Princeton University Press, 1992), p. 269.

5. Metz, *The Imaginary Signifier*, p. 97.

6. Baudry, "The Apparatus," p. 314.

7. Metz, *The Imaginary Signifier*, p.

8. Many feminists critics, myself included, began in the 1980s to examine films that were addressed specifically to women and in which such a male gaze might be questioned. If a biologically female spectator were addressed by a film in her social and psychic role as a woman, as occurred in the classic women's films of the 1930s and 1940s, then perhaps the gaze was not as uniform and unified as the theory of classical spectatorship had posited. See, for example, my "'Something Else Besides a Mother': *Stella Dallas* and the Maternal Melodrama" (*Cinema Journal* 24:1 (1984), 2–27). In another approach, Hansen examined the phenomenon of women's desiring gaze at male objects of desire in "Pleasure, Ambivalence, Identification: Valentino and Female Spectatorship" (*Cinema Journal* 25:4 (1986), 6–32). Still others began to look at the oscillations and ambivalences of even so classic and voyeuristic a director as Hitchcock. See Modleski's *Women Who Knew Too Much: Hitchcock and Feminist Theory* (New York and London: Methuen, 1988).

9. Thus, despite the variety of challenges brought to the uniform way of seeing that are inscribed within gaze theory, the one challenge that seemed never to be posed in all the discussion had to do with the homogeneity of the classical cinema itself. Despite many

exceptions to that homogeneity, the basic concepts of classical cinema and accompanying classical spectatorship have persisted.

10. Jonathan Crary, *Techniques of the Observer: On Vision and Modernity in the Nineteenth Century* (Cambridge, Mass.: Massachusetts Institute of Technology Press, 1992), p. 33.

11. One of these difficulties is the total absence of how gender may influence an observer.

12. Sobchack, *The Address of the Eye.*

13. Ibid., p. 23.

14. At the 1992 Society for Cinema Studies conference in New Orleans, the frequent quotation of this phrase by those on panel after panel became a kind of standing joke that attested, I would argue, to the hunger for a new paradigm of spectatorial relations. References were made to Gunning's first use of the term *cinema of attractions* in an essay in *Wide Angle.* The essay reproduced here is a much fuller treatment of that concept.

15. Judith Mayne, *Cinema and Spectatorship* (London and New York: Routledge, 1993). Mayne's study offers a highly nuanced description of the perpetual tension in the study of spectatorship between the analysis of viewers—the real people who watch movies—and the analysis of what theorists have called spectator-subjects—the hypothetical people subjected to the cinema's institutional and textual effects.

16. Jean Laplanche and J. B. Pontalis, "Fantasy and the Origins of Sexuality," in Victor Burgin, James Donald, and Cora Kaplan, eds., *Formations of Fantasy* (London and New York: Methuen, 1986), pp. 5–34.

17. Carol J. Clover, *Men, Women, and Chain Saws: Gender in the Modern Horror Film* (Princeton, N.J.: Princeton University Press, 1992).

18. Mulvey, "Visual Pleasure and Narrative Cinema."

19. Susan Brownmiller, *Against Our Will: Men, Women, and Rape* (New York: Simon and Schuster, 1975).

20. Andrea Dworkin, *Pornography: Men Possessing Women* (New York: Perigee Books, 1979).

21. Catherine MacKinnon, *Only Words* (Cambridge, Mass.: Harvard University Press, 1993).

Vision and the Apparatus

Jonathan Crary

Modernizing Vision

My starting point is the various ways in which vision and the techniques and discourses surrounding it have been periodized historically. It is interesting that so many attempts to theorize vision and visuality are wedded to models that emphasize a continuous and overarching Western visual tradition. Obviously at times it is strategically necessary to map out and pose the outlines of a dominant Western speculative or scopic tradition of vision that is continuous or in some sense effective, for instance, from Plato to the present, or from the Quattrocento into the twentieth century, or to whenever. My concern is not so much to argue against these models, which have their own usefulness, but rather to insist there are some important discontinuities that such hegemonic constructions have prevented from coming into view. The specific account that interests me here, one that has become almost ubiquitous and continues to be developed in a variety of forms, is that the emergence of photography and cinema in the nineteenth century is a fulfillment of a long unfolding of technological and/or ideological development in the West in which the camera obscura evolves into the photographic camera. Implied is that at each step in this evolution the same essential presuppositions about an observer's relation to the world are in place. One could name a dozen or more books on the history of film or photography in whose first chapter appears the obligatory seventeenth-century engraving depicting a camera obscura, as a kind of inaugural or incipient form on a long evolutionary ladder.

These models of continuity are used in the service of both, for lack of better terms, the right and the left. On the one hand are those who

From *Vision and Visuality*, ed. Hal Foster (Seattle: Bay Press, 1988). Reprinted by permission of the author and Bay Press.

pose an account of ever-increasing progress toward verisimilitude in representation, in which Renaissance perspective and photography are part of the same quest for a fully objective equivalent of "natural vision." On the other are those who see, for example, the camera obscura and cinema as bound up in a single enduring apparatus of power, elaborated over several centuries, that continues to define and regulate the status of an observer.

What I want to do are essentially two related things: (1) to briefly and very generally articulate the camera obscura model of vision in terms of its historical specificity and (2) to suggest how that model collapsed in the early nineteenth century—in the 1820s and 1830s—when it was displaced by radically different notions of what an observer was and of what constituted vision. So if later in the nineteenth century cinema or photography seem to invite formal comparisons with the camera obscura, or if Marx, Freud, Bergson, and others refer to it, it is within a social, cultural, and scientific milieu in which there had already been a profound rupture with the conditions of vision presupposed by this device.

For at least two thousand years it has been known that, when light passes through a small hole into a dark, enclosed interior, an inverted image will appear on the wall opposite the hole. Thinkers as remote from each other as Euclid, Aristotle, Roger Bacon, and Leonardo noted this phenomenon and speculated in various ways how it might or might not be analogous to the functioning of human vision.

But it is crucial to make a distinction between the empirical fact that an image can be produced in this way (something that continues to be as true now as it was in antiquity) and the camera obscura as a socially constructed artifact. For the camera obscura was not simply an inert and neutral piece of equipment or a set of technical premises to be tinkered upon and improved over the years; rather, it was embedded in a much larger and denser organization of knowledge and of the observing subject. If we want to be historical about it, we must recognize how for nearly two hundred years, from the late 1500s to the end of the 1700s, the structural and optical principles of the camera obscura coalesced into a dominant paradigm through which were described the status and possibilities of an observer.

It became a model, obviously elaborated in a variety of ways, for how observation leads to truthful inferences about an external world. It was an era when the camera obscura was simultaneously and inseparably a central epistemological figure within a discursive order, as in Descartes's *Dioptrics,* Locke's *Essay on Human Understanding,* and Leibniz's critique of Locke, *and* occupied a major position within an arrangement of technical and cultural practices, for example in the work of Kepler and Newton. As a complex technique of power, it was a means of legislating for an observer what constituted perceptual "truth," and it delineated a fixed set of relations to which an observer was made subject.

What I will argue is that very early on in the nineteenth century the camera obscura collapses as a model for an observer and for the functioning of human vision. There is a profound shift in the way in which an observer is described, figured, and posited in science, in philosophy, and in new techniques and practices of vision. Here I want briefly and very sketchily to indicate a few important features of this shift.

First, a bit more about the camera obscura in the seventeenth and eighteenth centuries. Above all, whether in the work of scientists or artists, empiricists or rationalists, it was an apparatus that guaranteed access to an objective truth about the world. It assumed importance as a model both for the observation of empirical phenomena and for reflective introspection and self-observation. In Locke, for example, the camera is a means of spatially visualizing the position of an observing subject.[1] The image of the room in Locke takes on a special significance, referring to what it meant in the seventeenth century to be *in camera,* that is, within the chambers of a judge or person of title.[2] Thus he adds onto the observer's passive role a more authoritative and juridical function to guarantee and to police the correspondence between exterior world and interior representation and to exclude anything disorderly or unruly.

Richard Rorty has pointed to Locke and Descartes as key figures in establishing this conception of the human mind as "an inner space in which clear and distinct ideas passed in review before an inner Eye . . . an inner space in which perceptual sensations were themselves the objects of quasi-observation."[3] For Descartes, the camera obscura was a demonstration of how an observer can know the world "uniquely by perception of the mind." The secure positioning of the self with this empty interior space was a precondition for knowing the outer world. Its enclosedness, its darkness, its categorical separation from an exterior incarnates Descartes's announcement in the Third Meditation, "I will now shut my eyes, I shall stop my ears, I shall disregard my senses."[4] If part of Descartes's method implied a need to escape the uncertainties of mere human vision, the camera obscura is compatible with his quest to found knowledge on a purely objective view of the world. The aperture of the camera corresponds to a single mathematically definable point from which the world could be logically deduced and re-presented. Founded on laws of nature—that is, geometrical optics—the camera provided an infallible vantage point on the world. Sensory evidence that depended in any way on the body was rejected in favor of the representations of this mechanical and monocular apparatus, whose authenticity was placed beyond doubt.

Monocular, not binocular. A single eye, not two. Until the nineteenth century, binocular disparity, the fact that we see a slightly different image with each eye, was never seriously addressed as a central issue. It was ignored or minimized as a problem, for it implied the inadmissible physiological and anatomical operation of human vision. A monocular model, on the other hand, precluded the difficult problem of having to reconcile the dissimilar and therefore provisional and tentative images presented to each eye. Monocularity, like perspective and geometrical optics, was one of the Renaissance codes through which a visual world is constructed according to systematized constants, and from which any inconsistencies and irregularities are banished to insure the formation of a homogeneous, unified, and fully legible space.

Finally, to wind up this extremely compressed outline, it should also be suggested how closely the camera obscura is bound up with a metaphysic of interiority. It is a figure for the observer, who is nominally a free sovereign individual but who is also a privatized isolated subject enclosed in a quasi-domestic space separated from a public exterior world. It defined an observer who was subjected to an inflexible set of positions and divisions. The visual world could be appropriated by an autonomous subject but only as a private unitary consciousness detached from any active relation with an exterior. The monadic viewpoint of the individual is legitimized by the camera obscura, but his or her sensory experience is subordinated to an external and pre-given world of objective truth.

What is striking are the suddenness and thoroughness with which this paradigm collapses in the early nineteenth century and gives way to a diverse set of fundamentally different models of human vision. I want to discuss one crucial dimension of this shift, the insertion of a new term into discourses and practices of vision: the human body, a term whose exclusion was one of the foundations of classical theories of vision and optics as I have just suggested. One of the most telling signs of the new centrality of the body in vision is Goethe's *Theory of Colours*, published in 1810, which I have discussed at length elsewhere.[5] This is a work crucial not for its polemic with Newton over the composition of light but for its articulation of a model of subjective vision in which the body is introduced in all its physiological density as the ground on which vision is possible. In Goethe we find an image of a newly productive observer whose body has a range of capacities to generate visual experience; it is a question of visual experience that does not refer or correspond to anything external to the observing subject. Goethe is concerned mainly with the experiences associated with the retinal afterimage and its chromatic transformations. But he is only the first of many researchers who become preoccupied with the afterimage in the 1820s and 1830s throughout Europe. Their collective study defined how vision was an irreducible amalgam of physiological processes and external stimulation, and dramatized the productive role played by the body in vision.

Although we are talking about scientists, what is in question here is the discovery of the "visionary" capacities of the body, and we miss the significance of this research if we don't recall some of its strange intensity and exhilaration. For what was often involved was the experience of staring directly into the sun, of sunlight searing itself onto the body, palpably disturbing it into a proliferation of incandescent color. Three of the most celebrated students of vision of this period went blind or permanently damaged their eyesight by repeatedly staring at the sun: David Brewster, who invented the kaleidoscope and stereoscope; Joseph Plateau, who studied the so-called persistence of vision; and Gustav Fechner, one of the founders of modern quantitative psychology. Fechner's biography provides an account of the almost addictive fascination with which he persisted in this activity. At the same time in the late 1830s and early 1840s we have the visual expression of these attempts in the late paintings of Turner, in which there is that piercing confrontation of eye and sun, paintings in which the strictures that previously had mediated and regulated vision are abandoned. Nothing now protects or distances the observer from the seductive and sensual brilliance of the sun. The symbolic confines of the camera obscura have crumbled.

Obviously afterimages have been noted and recorded since antiquity, but they had always been outside or on the margins of the domain of optics. They were considered illusions—deceptive, spectral, and unreal. In the early nineteenth century such experiences that previously had been an expression of the frailty and the unreliability of the body now constituted the positivity of vision. But perhaps more important, the privileging of the body as a visual producer began to collapse the distinction between inner and outer upon which the camera obscura depended. Once the objects of vision are coextensive with one's own body, vision becomes dislocated and depositioned onto a single immanent plane. The bipolar setup vanishes. Thirdly, subjective vision is found to be distinctly temporal, an unfolding of processes within the body, thus undoing notions of a direct correspondence between perception and object. By the 1820s, then, we effectively have a model of autonomous vision.

———

The subjective vision that endowed the observer with a new perceptual autonomy and productivity was simultaneously the result of the observer having been made into a subject of new knowledge, of new techniques of power. And the terrain on which these two interrelated observers emerged in the nineteenth century was the science of physiology. From 1820 through the 1840s it was very unlike the specialized science that it later became; it had then no formal institutional identity and came into being as the accumulated work of disconnected individuals from diverse branches of learning. In common were the excitement and wonderment at the body, which now appeared like a new continent to be mapped, explored, and mastered, with new recesses and mechanisms uncovered for the first time. But the real importance of physiology lay in the fact that it became the arena for new types of epistemological reflection that depended on new knowledge about the eye and processes of vision. Physiology at this moment of the nineteenth century is one of those sciences that stand for the rupture that Foucault poses between the eighteenth and nineteenth centuries, in which man emerges as a being in whom the transcendent is mapped onto the empirical.[6] It was the discovery that knowledge was conditioned by the physical and anatomical structure and functioning of the body, and, in particular, of the eyes. At the same time, as Georges Canguilhem has noted, for the new sciences in the nineteenth century the body was *a priori* a productive body: it existed to be set to work.[7]

Even in the early 1820s the study of afterimages quickly became the object of a more rigorous and *quantitative* scientific research throughout Europe. Studied were the persistence and modulation of afterimages: how long they lasted, what changes they went through, and under what conditions. But instead of recording afterimages in terms of the lived time of the body, as Goethe had generally done, they were studied as part of a comprehensive quantification of the irritability of the eye. Researchers timed how long it took the eye to become fatigued and how long dilation and contraction of the pupil took, and they measured the strength of eye movements. They examined convergence and accommodation in binocular vision and the relation of image to retinal curvature.

The physical surface of the eye itself became a field of statistical information: the retina was demarcated in terms of how color changes hue depending on where it strikes the eye. Also measured were the extent of the area of visibility and of peripheral vision, the distinction between direct and indirect vision, and the location of the blind spot. Classical optics, which had studied the transparency of mechanical optical systems, gave way to a mapping of the human eye as an opaque territory with varying zones of efficiency and aptitude and specific parameters of normal and pathological vision. Some of the most celebrated of these experiments were Joseph Plateau's calculation, in the 1830s, of the average duration of an afterimage, or persistence of vision, which was about one-third of a second, and later, Helmholtz's measurement of the speed of nerve transmission, which astounded people by how slow it was, about ninety feet per second. Both statistics heightened the sense of a temporal disjunction between perception and its object *and* suggested new possibilities of intervening externally in the process of vision.

Clearly this study of the eye in terms of reaction time and thresholds of fatigue and stimulation was not unrelated to increasing demand for knowledge about the adaptation of a human subject to productive tasks in which optimum attention span was indispensable for the rationalization of human labor. The economic need for rapid coordination of hand and eye in performing repetitive actions required accurate knowledge of human optical and sensory capacities. In the context of new industrial models of factory production the problem of visual inattention was a serious one. But what developed was a notion of vision that was fundamentally quantitative, in which the terms constituting the relation between perception and object became abstract, interchangeable, and nonvisual. One of the most paradoxical figures of the nineteenth century is Gustav Fechner, whose delirious and even mystical experiences with solar after-images led to his mathematization of perception, in which he established a functional relation between stimulus and sensation.[8] Sensory perception was given a measurable magnitude solely in terms of the known and controllable magnitudes of external stimulation. Vision became studied in terms of abstract measurable regularities, and Fechner's famous equations were to be one of the foundations of modern stimulus-response psychology.

Another dimension of the collective achievement of physiology in the first half of the nineteenth century was the gradual parcelization and division of the body into increasingly separate and specific systems and functions. Especially important were the localization of brain and nerve functions and the distinction between sensory nerves and motor nerves. Finally, by 1826, it was determined that sensory nerves were of five distinct types, corresponding to the five senses. All of this produced a new "truth" about the body, which some have linked to the so-called "separation of the senses" in the nineteenth century, and to the idea that the specialization of labor was homologous to a specialization of sight and of a heightened autonomous vision, something that Fredric Jameson develops briefly but provocatively in *The Political Unconscious*.[9] I believe, however, that such a homology doesn't take account of how thoroughly vision was reconceived in the earlier nineteenth century. It still seems to pose observation as the act of a unified subject looking out onto a world that is the object of his or her sight, only that, because the objects of the world have become reified and commodified, vision in a sense becomes conscious of itself as sheer looking.

But in the first major scientific theorization of the separation of the senses, there is a much more decisive break with the classical observer, and what is at stake is not simply the heightening or isolating of the optical but rather a notion of an observer for whom vision is conceived without any necessary connection to the act of looking at all. The work in question is the research of the German physiologist Johannes Müller, the single most important theorist of vision in the first half of the nineteenth century.[10] In his study of the physiology of the senses, Müller makes a comprehensive statement on the subdivision and specialization of the human sensory apparatus; his fame was due to his theorization of that specialization: the so-called "doctrine of specific nerve energies." It was a theory in many ways as important to the nineteenth century as the Molyneux problem was to the eighteenth century. It was the foundation of Helmholtz's *Optics*, which dominated the second half of the 1800s; in science, philosophy, and psychology it was widely propounded, debated, and denounced even into the early twentieth century. (Also, I believe Marx was paraphrasing this work when he discussed the separation of the senses in his *1844 Manu-*

scripts.[11]) In short, this is a major way in which an observer was figured in the nineteenth century, a way in which a certain "truth" about sight was depicted.

The theory was based on the discovery that the nerves of the different senses were physiologically distinct. It asserted quite simply— and this is what marks its epistemological scandal—that a uniform cause (e.g., electricity) would generate utterly different sensations from one kind of nerve to another. Electricity applied to the optic nerve produces the experience of light, applied to the skin the sensation of touch. Conversely, Müller shows that a variety of different causes will produce the *same* sensation in a given sensory nerve; in other words, he describes a fundamentally arbitrary relation between stimulus and sensation. It is a description of a body with an innate capacity, one might even say a transcendental faculty, to *misperceive*, of an eye that renders differences equivalent.

His most exhaustive demonstration concerns the sense of sight, and he concludes that the observer's experience of light has no necessary connection with any actual light. Müller enumerates the agencies capable of producing the sensation of light. "The sensations of light and color are produced wherever parts of the retina are excited (1) by mechanical influences, such as pressure, a blow, or a concussion; (2) by electricity; (3) by chemical agents, such as narcotics, or digitalis; (4) by the stimulus of the blood in a state of congestion."[12] Then, last on his list, almost begrudgingly, he adds that luminous images also can be produced by "the undulations and emanation which by their action on the eye are called light."

Again the camera obscura model is made irrelevant. The experience of light becomes severed from any stable point of reference or from any source or origin around which a world could be constituted and apprehended. And of course the very independent identity of light had already been undermined as a new wave theory of light became part of a science of electro-magnetic phenomena.

Sight here has been separated and specialized certainly, but it no longer resembles any classical models. The theory of specific nerve energies presents the outlines of a visual modernity in which the "referential illusion" is unsparingly laid bare. The very absence of referentiality is the ground on which new instrumental techniques will construct for an observer a new "real" world. It is a question of a perceiver whose very empirical nature renders identities unstable and mobile, and for whom sensations are interchangeable. And remember, this is roughly 1830. In effect, the doctrine of specific nerve energies redefines vision as a capacity for being affected by sensations that have no necessary link to a referent, thus threatening any coherent system of meaning. Müller's theory was potentially so nihilistic that it is no wonder that Helmholtz and others, who accepted its empirical premises, were impelled to invent theories of cognition and signification which concealed its uncompromising cultural implications. But what was at stake and seemed so threatening was not just a new form of epistemological skepticism about the unreliability of the senses but a positive reorganization of perception and its objects. The issue was not just how does one know what is real, but that new forms of the real were being fabricated and a new truth about the capacities of a human subject was being articulated in these terms.

The theory of specific nerve energies eradicated distinctions between internal and external sensation, so that interiority was drained of the meanings it once had for a classical observer, or for the model of the camera obscura. In his supposedly empirical description of the human sensory apparatus, Müller presents the subject not as a unitary "tabula rasa," but as a composite structure on which a wide range of techniques and forces could produce a manifold of experiences that are all equally "reality." If John Ruskin proposed reclaiming the "innocence of the eye," this was about as innocent as one could get. The observer is simultaneously the object of knowledge and the object of procedures of stimulation and normalization, which have the essential capacity *to produce experience for the subject.* Ironically the notions of the reflex arc and reflex action, which in the seventeenth century referred to vision and the optics of reflection, begin to become the centerpiece of an emerging technology of the subject, culminating in the work of Pavlov.

In his account of the relation between stimulus and sensation, Müller suggests not an orderly and legislative functioning of the senses, but rather their receptivity to calculated management and derangement. Émile Dubois-Reymond, a colleague of Helmholtz, seriously pursued the possibility of electrically cross-connecting nerves, enabling the eye to see sounds and the ear to hear colors, well before Rimbaud. It must be emphasized that Müller's research and that of psychophysics in the nineteenth century are inseparable from the resources made available by contemporary work in electricity and chemistry. Some of the empirical evidence by Müller had been available since antiquity, or was in the domain of common-sense knowledge. However, what is new is the extraordinary privilege given to a complex of electro-physical techniques. What constitutes "sensation" is dramatically expanded and transformed, and it has little in common with how it was discussed in the eighteenth century. The adjacency of Müller's doctrine of specific nerve energies to the technology of nineteenth-century modernity is made particularly clear by Helmholtz:

> Nerves in the human body have been accurately compared to telegraph wires. Such a wire conducts one single kind of electric current and no other; it may be stronger, it may be weaker, it may move in either direction; it has no other qualitative differences. Nevertheless, according to the different kinds of apparatus with which we provide its terminations, we can send telegraphic dispatches, ring bells, explode mines, decompose water, move magnets, magnetize iron, develop light, and so on. *The same thing with our nerves.* The condition of excitement which can be produced in them, and is conducted by them, is . . . everywhere the same.[13]

Far from the specialization of the senses, Helmholtz is explicit about the body's indifference to the sources of its experience and of its capacity for multiple connections with other agencies and machines. The perceiver here becomes a neutral conduit, one kind of relay among others to allow optimum conditions of circulation and exchangeability, whether it be of commodities, energy, capital, images, or information.

The collapse of the camera obscura as a model for the status of an observer was part of a much larger process of modernization, even as the camera obscura itself was an element of an earlier modernity. By the early 1800s, however, the rigidity of the camera obscura, its linear optical system, its fixed positions, its categorical distinction between inside and outside, its identification of perception and object were all too inflexible and unwieldy for the needs of the new century. A more mobile, usable, and productive observer was needed in both discourse and practice—to be adequate to new uses of the body and to a vast proliferation of equally mobile and exchangeable signs and images. Modernization entailed a decoding and deterritorialization of vision.

What I've been trying to do is give some sense of how radical was the reconfiguration of vision by 1840. If our problem is vision and modernity we must look first at these early decades, not to modernist painting in the 1870s and 1880s. A new type of observer was formed then, and not one that we can see figured in paintings or prints. We've been trained to assume that an observer will always leave visible tracks, that is, will be identifiable in terms of images. But here it's a question of an observer who takes shape in other, grayer practices and discourses, and whose immense legacy will be all the industries of the image and the spectacle in the twentieth century. The body which had been a neutral or invisible term in vision now was the thickness from which knowledge of vision was derived. This opacity or carnal density of the observer loomed so suddenly into view that its full consequences and effects could not be immediately realized. But it was this ongoing articulation of vision as nonveridical, as lodged in the body, that was a *condition of possibility* both for the artistic experimentation of modernism and for new forms of domination, for what Foucault calls the "technology of individuals."[14] Inseparable from the technologies of domination and of the spectacle in the later nineteenth and twentieth century were of course film and photography. Paradoxically, the increasing hegemony of these two techniques helped re-create the myths that vision was incorporeal, veridical, and "realistic." But if cinema and photography seemed to reincarnate the camera obscura, it was only as a mirage of a transparent set of relations that modernity had already overthrown.

NOTES

1. John Locke, *An Essay Concerning Human Understanding* (New York: Dover Publications, 1959), vol. 2, pp. xi, 17.

2. Ibid., vol. 2, pp. iii, 1.

3. Richard Rorty, *Philosophy and the Mirror of Nature* (Princeton, Princeton University Press, 1979), pp. 49–50.

4. René Descartes, *The Philosophical Writings of Descartes*, trans. John Cottingham et al. (Cambridge: Cambridge University Press, 1984), vol. 2, p. 24.

5. Johann Wolfgang von Goethe, *Theory of Colours*, trans. Charles Lock Eastlake (Cambridge, Mass.: Massachusetts Institute of Technology Press, 1970). See my "Techniques of the Observer," *October* 45 (Summer 1988).

6. Michel Foucault, *The Order of Things* (New York: Pantheon Books, 1971), pp. 318–20.

7. Georges Canguilhem, "Qu'est-ce que le psychologie," in his *Études d'histoire et de philosophie des sciences*, 5th ed. (Paris: J. Vrin, 1983), pp. 377–78.

8. See Gustav Fechner, *Elements of Psychophysics* trans. Helmut E. Adler (New York: Holt, Rinehart & Winston, 1966).

9. Fredric Jameson, *The Political Unconscious: Narrative as a Socially Symbolic Act* (Ithaca, N.Y.: Cornell University Press, 1981), pp. 62–64.

10. See Johannes Müller, *Handbuch der Physiologie des Menschen* (Koblenz, Germany: Holscher, 1838); *Elements of Physiologie*, trans. William Baly (London: Taylor & Walton, 1848).

11. See Karl Marx, *The Economic and Philosophic Manuscripts of 1844*, ed. Dirk J. Struik, trans. Martin Milligan (New York: International Publishers, 1964), pp. 140–41.

12. Müller, *Hanbuch de Physiologie des Menschen*, p. 1064.

13. Hermann von Helmholtz, *On the Sensations of Tone as a Physiological Basis for the Theory of Music*, 2nd ed., trans. Alexander J. Ellis (New York: Dover Publications, 1954), pp. 148–49.

14. Michel Foucault, *Discipline and Punish: The Birth of Prison*, trans. Alan Sheridan (New York: Vintage Books, 1975), p. 225.

Vivian Sobchack

Phenomenology and the Film Experience

> *In a sense the whole of philosophy . . . consists in restoring a power to signify, a birth of meaning, or a wild meaning, an expression of experience by experience, which in particular clarifies the special domain of language. And in a sense . . . language is everything, since it is the voice of no one, since it is the voice of the things, the waves, and the forests.*[1]

What else is a film if not "an expression of experience by experience"? And what else is the primary task of film theory if not to restore to us, through reflection upon that experience and its expression, the original power of the motion picture to signify? However, when Maurice Merleau-Ponty wrote the above lines shortly before his death in 1961, it is unlikely that the cinema was in his thoughts. Rather, his overarching concern was with the living exchange of perception and expression, with the sensuous contours of language, with meaning and its signification born not abstractly but concretely from the surface contact, the fleshly dialogue, of human beings and the world together making sense sensible. Yet it is precisely this emphasis on the material and carnal foundations of language that makes the above fragment of *The Visible and the Invisible* particularly relevant to the semiotic and hermeneutic questions posed by the medium of cinema. The passage suggests not only the primordial and unprivate nature of language, but also the physically

From *The Address of the Eye: A Phenomenology of Film Experience* (Princeton, N.J.: Princeton University Press, 1992). Reprinted by permission of the author and Princeton University Press.

concrete "reversibility" of perception and expression that constitutes both the moving picture and our experience of it.

More than any other medium of human communication, the moving picture makes itself sensuously and sensibly manifest as the expression of experience by experience. A film is an act of seeing that makes itself seen, an act of hearing that makes itself heard, an act of physical and reflective movement that makes itself reflexively felt and understood. Objectively projected, visibly and audibly expressed before us, the film's activity of seeing, hearing, and moving signifies in a pervasive, primary, and embodied language that precedes and provides the grounds for the secondary significations of a more discrete, systematic, less "wild" communication. Cinema thus transposes, without completely transforming, those modes of being alive and consciously embodied in the world that count for each of us as *direct* experience: as experience "centered" in that particular, situated, and solely occupied existence sensed first as "Here, where the world touches" and then as "Here, where the world is sensible; here, where I am."[2]

In an unprecedented way, the cinema makes visible and audible the primordial origins of language in the reversibility of embodied and enworlded perception and expression. However, as Merleau-Ponty points out in a continuation of the passage quoted above, "What we have to understand is that there is no dialectical reversal from one of these views to the other; we do not have to reassemble them into a synthesis: they are two aspects of the reversibility which is the ultimate truth."[3] That is, the reversibility of perception and expression is neither instantiated as a thought nor synthesized from discrete and separate acts of consciousness. It is *given* with existence, in the simultaneity of subjective embodiment and objective enworldedness. Using the term *chiasmus* to name this reversibility ("the ultimate truth"), Merleau-Ponty characterizes it as that "unique space which separates and reunites, which sustains every cohesion."[4] That unique space is both the lived-body and the experienced world.

Indeed, the cinema uses *modes of embodied existence* (seeing, hearing, physical and reflective movement) as the vehicle, the "stuff," the substance of its language. It also uses the *structures of direct experience* (the "centering" and bodily situating of existence in relation to the world of objects and others) as the basis for the structures of its language. Thus, as a symbolic form of human communication, the cinema is like no other. At the end of his two-volume *Esthétique et psychologie du cinéma* (and sounding very much like Merleau-Ponty), Jean Mitry articulates both the medium's privileged nature and the problem it poses for those who would discover the "rules" governing its expression and grounding its intelligibility:

> These [cinematic] forms are . . . as varied as life itself and, furthermore, as one hasn't the knowledge to regulate life, neither has one the knowledge to regulate an art of which life is at one and the same time the subject and object.
>
> Whereas the classical arts propose to signify movement with the immobile, life with the inanimate, the cinema must express life with life itself. It begins there where the others leave off. It escapes, therefore, all their rules as it does all their principles.[5]

In a search for rules and principles governing cinematic expression, most of the descriptions and reflections of classical and contemporary film theory have not fully addressed the cinema as life expressing life, as experience expressing experience. Nor have they explored the mutual possession of this experience of perception and its expression by filmmaker, film, and spectator—all *viewers viewing,* engaged as participants in dynamically and directionally reversible acts that reflexively and reflectively constitute the *perception of expression* and the *expression of perception.* Indeed, it is this mutual capacity for and possession of experience through common structures of embodied existence, through similar modes of being-in-the-world, that provide the *intersubjective* basis of objective cinematic communication.

Insofar as the embodied structure and modes of being of a film are like those of filmmaker and spectator, the film has the capacity and competence to signify, to not only *have* sense but also to *make* sense through a unique and systemic form of communication. Indeed, to the extent that any film can and does signify in some fashion to a viewer who is communicatively competent (that is, already aware that perception is expressible), and that any film—however abstract or "structural-materialist"—presupposes that it will be understood *as* signification, as conveying meaning beyond the brute material presence of light and shadow on a plane surface, the cinema assumes and assures its own intelligibility (even if it assumes and assures no single interpretation).[6] That intelligibility is also assumed by filmmaker and spectator. The film experience, therefore, rests on the mutual presupposition of its intersubjective nature and function, based on the intelligibility of embodied vision. Its significance emerges from a shared belief and from shared evidence that the substance and structure of cinematic perception and expression (however historically and culturally qualified) are inherently able to "reflect the universality of specific scopes of experience."[7]

This presupposition remains to be explored in the following chapters. Yet, immediately, it indicates that any semiotics and hermeneutics of the cinema must return to radically reflect on the origins of cinematic communication in the structures and pragmatics of existential experience. Such a semiotic and hermeneutic enterprise, undertaking this radical turn toward existence and away from secondary and abstract formulations, becomes a *semiotic phenomenology*—taking, as it does, signification and significance as immanent, as given with existence.[8] Such a phenomenology of human meaning and its representation attempts to describe, thematize, and interpret the structures of communication as they radically emerge in the structures of being. This phenomenology's aim, however, is not to arrive at "essential" and proscriptive categories but to address the "thickness" of human experience and the rich and radical entailments of incarnate being and its representation. To accommodate itself to experience, its method is responsively dialectical and informed by no particular *telos*.

The aim of this simultaneously empirical and philosophical study, then, is to serve as a prolegomenon to a lived logic of signification in the cinema. The focus here will center on the radical origin of such a logic in lived-body experience, that is, in the activity of embodied consciousness realizing itself in the world and with others as both visual and visible, as both sense-making and sensible. The entailment of incarnate consciousness and the "flesh" of the world of which it is a part will be described as the basis for the origination of the general structures of cinematic signification, structures that are themselves produced in the performance of specific modes of existential and embodied communication in the film experience (that is, in the activity of vision intersubjectively connecting film and spectator with a world and each other).

In no way is the following effort meant to deny the extra-cinematic, empirical, and contingent conditions that limit and affect the specific shape of actual (not merely possible) cinematic communication, systematically distorting it either spontaneously or willfully for ideological, rhetorical, and poetic purpose. Indeed, as indicated in the Preface, this study itself is necessarily situated within and distorted by its own theoretical context, and, so situated, it must always and necessarily entail the ideological, rhetorical, and poetic in-formation of its own historicity. Nonetheless, what follows is not intended as remedial. This is no idealist attempt to "cure" cinema or to uncritically embrace the "critical theory" of the Frankfurt school in general (or Habermas in particular).[9] It does not take as its focus the exposure of "distorted" cinematic communication and, in fact, refuses the idealism that yearns for communication (an *existential* phenomenon) made completely rational, somehow "purged" of historical and cultural prejudice or "distortion," somehow "cleansed" of the contingencies and specificity of biased existence that make communication not only necessary but also possible.[10] Similarly, although this study must be informed necessarily by rhetorical force and poetic linguistic praxis, it is not intended as a rhetoric or poetics of cinematic communication. Rather, its phenomenological project is to radically reflect upon the general structures that always emerge particularly and contingently as the entailment of the lived-body and the world in cinematic acts of perception and expression. These primary structures, founded in existence and constitutive of conscious experience, produce themselves in the world as a systemic "cinematic communicative competence," against which the secondary (but always present) notion of systematic "distortion" can be identified and, indeed, from which it can be constituted as ideology, rhetoric, and poetics.

The Embodied and Enworlded Eye: Perception and Expression

When we sit in a movie theater and perceive a film as sensible, as making sense, we (and the film before us) are immersed in a world and in an activity of visual being. The experience is as familiar as it is intense, and it is marked by the way in which significance and the act of signifying are *directly* felt, *sensuously* available to the viewer. The embodied activities of perception and expression—making sense and signifying it—are given to us as modalities of a single experience of being in the presence of and producing meaning and diacritical value. What we look at projected on the screen—whether Merleau-Ponty's "the things, the waves, and the forests," or only abstract lines and colors—addresses us as the expressed perception of an anonymous, yet present, "other." And, as we watch this expressive projection of an "other's" experience, we, too, express our perceptive experience. Through the address of our own vision, we speak back to the cinematic expression before us, using a visual language that is also tactile, that takes hold of and actively grasps the perceptual expression, the seeing, the direct experience of that anonymously present, sensing, and sentient "other."

Thus, the film experience is a system of communication based on bodily perception as a vehicle of conscious expression. It entails the visible, audible, kinetic aspects of sensible experience to make sense visibly, audibly, and haptically. The film experience not only *represents* and reflects upon the prior direct perceptual experience of the filmmaker *by means* of the modes and structures of direct and reflective perceptual experience, but also *presents* the direct and reflective experience of a perceptual and expressive existence *as* the film. In its presence and activity of perception and expression, the film transcends the filmmaker to constitute and locate its own address, its own perceptual and expressive experience of being and becoming. As well, the film experience includes the perceptive and expressive viewer who must *interpret* and *signify* the film *as* experience, doing so through the very same structures and relations of perception and expression that inform the indirect representational address of the filmmaker and the direct presentational address of the film. As a communicative system, then, what is called the "film experience" uniquely opens up and exposes the inhabited space of direct experience as a condition of singular embodiment and makes it accessible and visible to more than the single consciousness who lives it. That is, direct experience and existential presence in the cinema belong to both the film and the viewer. (As noted, the filmmaker's presence in that experience is indirect and only re-presented.[11])

As perception-cum-expression that can be perceived by another, as a communication of the experience of existence that is publicly visible, the anonymous but centered "Here, where *eye (I) am*" of the film can be doubly occupied. "Decentered" as it is engaged by an other in the film experience, it becomes the "Here, where *we see*"—a *shared* space of being, of seeing, hearing, and bodily and reflective movement performed and experienced by both film and viewer. However, this "decentering," this double occupancy of cinematic space, does not conflate the film and viewer. The "Here, where eye (I) am" of the film retains its unique situation, even as it cannot maintain its perceptual privacy. Directly perceptible to the viewer as an anonymous "Here, where eye am" simultaneously available as "Here, where we see," the concretely embodied situation of the film's vision also stands *against* the viewer. It is also perceived by the viewer as a "There, where I am not," as the space consciously and bodily inhabited and lived by an "other" whose experience of being-in-the-world, however anonymous, is not precisely congruent with the viewer's own. Thus, while space and its significance are intimately shared and lived by both film and viewer, the viewer is always at some level aware of the double and reversible nature of cinematic perception, that is, of perception *as* expression, of perception as a process of *mediating* consciousness's relations with the world. The viewer, therefore, shares cinematic space with the film but must also negotiate it, contribute to, and perform the constitution of its experiential significance.

Watching a film is both a direct and mediated experience of direct experience as mediation. We perceive a world both *within* the immediate experience of an "other" and *without* it, as immediate experience mediated by an "other." Watching a film, we can see the seeing as well as the seen, hear the hearing as well as the heard, and feel the movement as well as see the moved. As viewers, not only do we spontaneously and invisibly perform these existential acts directly for and as ourselves in relation *to* the film before us, but these same acts are coterminously given to us *as* the film, as mediating acts of perception-cum-expression we take up and *invisibly perform* by appropriating and incorporating them into our own existential performance; we watch them as a *visible performance* distinguishable from, yet included in, our own.

The cinema thus transposes what would otherwise be the invisible, individual, and intrasubjective privacy of direct experience as it is embodied into the visible, public, and intersubjective sociality of a language of direct embodied experience—a language that not only refers to direct experience but also uses direct experience as its mode of reference. A film simultaneously has sense and makes sense both for us and before us. Perceptive, it has the capacity for experience, and expressive, it has the ability to signify. It gives birth to and actualizes signification, constituting and making manifest the primordial significance that Merleau-Ponty calls "wild meaning"—the pervasive and as yet undifferentiated significance of existence as it is lived rather than reflected upon. Direct experience thus serves double duty in the cinema. A film presents and represents acts of seeing, hearing, and moving as both the *original structures of existential being* and the *mediating structures of language.* As an "expression of experience by experience," a film both constitutes an original and primary significance in its continual perceptive and expressive "becoming" and evolves and regulates a more particular form of signification shaped by the specific trajectory of interests and intentions that its perceptive and expressive acts trace across the screen.

The spontaneous and constitutive significance, the "wild meaning" that grounds the specificity and intelligibility of cinematic communication, is itself grounded in and borne by embodied existence in its relation to and within a world. Having the bodily capacity to perceive and express and move in a world that exists both for us and against us, we are, as Merleau-Ponty points out, "condemned to meaning."[12] From the first, we are engaged in a living dialogue with a world that sufficiently exceeds our grasp of it as we necessarily intend toward it, a world in which we are finitely situated as embodied beings and yet always informed by a decisive motility. Thus, the need and power to signify are synonymous with embodied existence in the world. As evoked by the passage that opens this chapter, that original need and power are first encountered everywhere and in everything, neither ascribable to a single source nor consciously differentiated in their range or application. Before the ascriptions, differences, and systems of exchange articulated in and by what we call "natural language" (the discrete instrumentality and systematic objectification of experience abstracted from experience for general use), we are always first immersed in the more primordial language of embodied existence.

This primordial language is not systematic and regulative but systemic and constitutive, arising in the process of being-in-the-world and in the living reversibility of perception and expression exercised by the lived-body as it materially and finitely shares the "flesh" of the world it inhabits. That is, both the *material nature* and the *finite situation* of embodied existence always already constitute a *diacritical system* that primordially signifies through the lived-choices of existential movement and gesture. From the first, embodied existence inflects and reflects the world as always already significant. Thus, long before we consciously and voluntarily differentiate and abstract the world's significance for us into "ordinary language," long before we constrain "wild meaning" in discrete symbolic systems, we are immersed in language as an existential system. In the very movement of existence, in the very activity of perception and its bodily expression, we inaugurate language and communication.

The moving picture, too, perceives and expresses itself wildly and pervasively before it articulates its meanings more particularly and systematically as this or that kind of signification, that is, as a specific cinematic trope or figure, a specific set of generic configurations, a specific syntactical convention. Indeed, before it is fragmented and dissected in critical and theoretical analyses, before the reified shorthand of formalist, realist, semiotic, structuralist, neo-Marxist, and psychoanalytic terminology abstracts aspects of the cinema's "wild meaning" into discrete codes governed by montage, mise-en-scène, syntagmatic categories, binary and oppositional structures, and particular ideological and poetic pathologies, a film makes sense by virtue of its very ontology. That is, its existence emerges embodied and finitely situated. It comes into being (becomes) as an ongoing and unified (if always self-displacing) situation of perception and expression that *coheres* in relation to the world of which it is a material part, but in which it is also materially and diacritically differentiated. As a medium that articulates the unified, if ever-changing, experience of existence, that expresses the original synonymity of existence and language, of perception and its expression, the cinema is a privileged form of communication. A film is given to us and taken up by us as perception turned literally inside out and toward us as expression. It presents and represents *to* us and *for* us and *through* us the very modes and structures of being as language, of being as a system of primary and secondary mediations through which we and the world and others significantly communicate, constituting and changing our meanings from the moment of our first lived gesture. Thus, in its modalities of having sense and making sense, the cinema quite concretely returns us, as viewers and theorists, to our senses.

What is suggested by this general, philosophically inflected, and preliminary description of the structure that is the film experience is that cinematic "language" is grounded in the more original pragmatic language of embodied existence whose general structures are common to filmmaker, film, and viewer. Even though the film differs from the other two in the material and mode of its embodiment, for each "the perceiving mind is an incarnated mind."[13] It is this mutuality of embodied existence and the dynamic movement of its perceptual and expressive relations with and in the world that provide the common denominator of cinematic communication. Situated, finite, and—by virtue of being a body— "centered" in a world, embodied existence is constituted as and marked by the intrasubjective and intersubjective exchange between perception and expression. In a film, as in our direct and immediate experience, perception functions as a modality of expression, and expression as a modality of perception, both aspects of a synoptic "reversibility" and lived "directionality" that is the movement of existence, both thus subject to directional reversals that allow them to appear as either spontaneously prereflective and "operational" or as reflective and reflexive.

As two modalities of significant and signifying existence, perception and expression are interwoven threads, the woof and warp that together form a seamless and supple fabric, the whole cloth of existential experience from which specific forms of signification can be fashioned to instrumentally suit specific functions. Thus, in a film as in life, perception and expression—having sense and making sense—do not originally oppose each other and are not separated or differentiated as distinctly binary constructs and practices. Rather, they are complementary modalities of an original and unified experience of existence that has long been fragmented and lost to those interested in the ontology of the cinema and its structures of signification.

Film Theory and the Objectification of Embodied Vision

The reversibility of cinematic perception and expression is the "enabling structure" of cinematic communication.[14] In semiotic terms, it constitutes what Umberto Eco calls an "s-code": the system-code that "makes a situation comprehensible and comparable to other situations, therefore preparing the way for a possible coding correlation."[15] Without such a systemic exchange of cinematic perception and expression (one comparable to and comprehensible as such an exchange in the human situation), other secondary and more systemic cinematic coding correlations would not be possible and comprehensible. There could be no narrative codes, no codes of subjective vision, no editorial codes, and their like. Nonetheless, the cinematic system-code constituted by the exchange and reversibility of perception and expression has been almost completely neglected by the respective analytic and synthetic emphases of classical and contemporary film theory.[16]

Three metaphors have dominated film theory: the *picture frame*, the *window*, and the *mirror*.[17] The first two, the frame and the window, represent the opposing poles of classical film theory, while the third, the mirror, represents the synthetic conflation of perception and expression that characterizes most contemporary film theory. What is interesting to note is that all three metaphors relate directly to the screen rectangle and to the film as a static *viewed object*, and only indirectly to the dynamic activity of viewing that is engaged in by both the film and the spectator, each as *viewing subjects*. The exchange and reversibility of perception and expression (both in and as the film and spectator) are suppressed, as are the intrasubjective and intersubjective foundations of cinematic communication.

Most often identified with the binary poetics of a sufficiently opposed but necessarily linked *formalism* and *realism*, classical film theory has argumentatively and analytically severed expression from perception in its inquiries into the "true nature" or ontology of the cinema. That is, cinematic "language" (here we might think of montage) and cinematic being (and here of mise-en-scène) have been contrasted categorically and set against each other as opposing poles of a single, digital, two-valued system—each, in opposing the other, affirming it by implication and dependent upon it by necessity. The formalists, seeking to transform and restructure the "brute" referentiality and "wild" meaning of cinematic images into personally determinate and expressive signification (hence the metaphor of the frame), acknowledge the camera's perceptive nature as they celebrate the artist's triumph over it. On the other side, the realists, seeking to reveal and discover the world's expression in all its "wild" meaning (hence the metaphor of the window), acknowledge the camera's expressive nature in its selective and shifting vision, even as they celebrate the medium's perceptual purity and openness. For the most part, however, this dependence on and suppression of one of the necessary conditions for the existence of a film has not been overtly articulated as the infrastructure that binds formalism and realism into a single theoretical system.[18] Instead, the emphasis has been on a dual poetics—one valorizing cinematic expression and the other, cinematic perception.

Opposing each other, both formalist and realist arguments converge in their assumption that meaning is located in the text as a significant object and in their assumption of that text's transcendence of its origin and location either in the world or in persons. The metaphor of the frame is emblematic of the *transcendental idealism* that infuses classical formalism and its belief in the film object as *expression-in-itself*—subjectivity freed from worldly constraint. In contrast, the window as metaphor is emblematic of the *transcendental realism* that informs realist film theory and its belief in the film object as *perception-in-itself*—objectivity freed from entailment with the prejudicial investments of human being. The first belief leads to the formalist celebration of what phenomenology criticizes as "subjective psychologism," the second to the realist celebration of what it decries as "objective empiricism."[19]

In an attempt to correct this tidy theoretical opposition and its contradiction by actual cinematic practice, contemporary theorists have tended to synthesize perception and expression, categorically collapsing and confusing them in an analogue relation in which they are distinguishable only by degree, not by modality. The nature of film is considered as neither perceptive nor expressive. Rather, both modalities of existential experience are conflated as a synthesis of the *refractive, reflexive,* and *reflective* (hence the metaphor of the mirror). Drawing primarily upon linguistically oriented psychoanalytic and neo-Marxist paradigms (the former already privileging the metaphor of the mirror for its own purposes), the resultant theories of cinematic communication have emerged not as a celebratory poetics, but as a critical rhetoric, charging cinematic communication with some equivalent to sophistry.

That is, contemporary theory (most of it feminist and/or neo-Marxist in approach) has focused on the essentially deceptive, illusionary, tautologically recursive, and coercive nature of the cinema and on its psychopathological and/or ideological functions of distorting existential experience. Such theory elaborately accounts for cinematic representation but cannot account for the originary activity of cinematic signification. Thus, it is hardly surprising, if poignant, that, attempting to liberate female spectatorship and spectators of color from linguistically determined psychic structures and colonial discursive structures, psychoanalytically based feminist film theory and ideologically based film theory so often bemoan the impossibility of a "new" language to express the specificity of their excluded experience and the lack of an uncolonized "place" from which to speak. Articulated in various ways and amid a number of highly sophisticated arguments, what contemporary film theory stresses and decries in its variations on the metaphor of the mirror is the totalitarian transcendence of either psychic or ideological structures over the signifying freedom of individual viewers in their concrete, contingent, existential situation. As perception and expression are confused with each other in the deceptive processes of the cinematic apparatus and the seamless and conventional unfolding of a privileged (if reviled) "classical narrative cinema," the possibility of dialogic and dialectical communication is suppressed and the film experience is seen as grounded in a false and sophistic rhetoric that essentially distorts the possibility of any "real" communication.

Thus, the metaphor of the mirror entails a critical judgment of the cinema that is as damning as it is descriptive. It condemns the very ontological being of cinema as substitutive (rather than expansive) and deceptive (rather than disclosing). It reflects the viewer only to point to his or her subjection to signs and meanings produced by an always already dishonest and subjugating "other." Idealist in its utopian longings for liberatory signification while losing itself in a labyrinth of representation, contemporary film theory is informed by a *transcendental determin-*

ism—based on the belief in the film object as *mediation-in-itself*. In the one instance, signification and significance are seen as always predetermined by apparatus and ideology; the film object as it is experienced invisibly and rhetorically interpellates the spectator and speaks the culture, producing cinematic language and its norms of usage as a *given*. In the other instance, signification and significance are predetermined by psychic structures; the camera's and spectator's vision are confused and bound together in a false and distorted primary identification that cannot be denied, only disavowed. In sum, in most contemporary theory, viewing in the cinema leads to no good—or, at best, to the remedial practice of demystifying the cinema's material, structural, and ideological pathology and, at worst, to a pleasure that is guilty and must be adjudged "perverse."

In most of its classical and contemporary articulations, then, film theory has focused not on the *whole correlational structure* of the film experience, but has abstracted and privileged only one of its *parts* at a time: expression-in-itself, perception-in-itself, and mediation-in-itself, respectively. Although the next section of this chapter will introduce the reader to phenomenology as the philosophy and research procedure that informs the remainder of this study, film theory's abstraction and fragmentation of the correlational structure that is the film experience can be criticized against the main phenomenological theme of *intentionality*: the invariant, pervasive, and immanent correlational structure of consciousness. Intentionality is "the unique peculiarity of experiences 'to be the consciousness *of* something.'"[20] That is, the act of consciousness is never "empty" and "in-itself," but rather always intending toward and in relation to an object (even when that "object" is consciousness, reflexively intended). The invariant correlational structure of consciousness thus necessarily entails the *mediation* of an *activity* and an *object*. If we substitute the specificity of the film experience as a reversible structure correlating the activity of perception and expression and commuting one to the other, the whole of the structure could, and later will more elaborately, be mapped as follows: *the perception* (act of consciousness) *of* (mediation) *expression* (object of consciousness) *and/as the expression* (act of consciousness) *of* (mediation) *perception* (object of consciousness). In relation to my previous thematization of classical and contemporary film theory, formalist theory can be linked to a focus on the cinematic *expression* (of perception)—perception here represented as the suppressed part of the entire relation; realist theory to a focus on the cinematic *perception* (of expression)—expression here represented as the suppressed part of the entire relation; and contemporary theory to a focus on the mediating copula (perception) *of* (expression)—with perception and expression represented as the suppressed part of the entire relation.

Whatever their respectively different foci, classical and contemporary film theory have pursued their inquiry into the nature of cinematic signification sharing three crucial and largely uninterrogated presuppositions. First, film theory has presupposed *the act of viewing.* Certainly, there have been some considerations of the anatomical, mechanical, and psychic aspects of vision that characterize and differentiate the human and camera eyes.[21] As well, a major portion of contemporary film theory dwells on the psychoanalytic aspects of the spectator's visual engagement with the cinema. Nonetheless, film theory has generally assumed as given the act of viewing in its totality, that is, as *the constituting condition of the film experience* in each and all of its aspects and manifestations, and as the nexus of communication among the filmmaker, film, and spectator.

Second, film theory has presupposed the cinema's and spectator's *communicative competence.* Discussions of cinematic codes and their entailments are all based on the assumption that a film is intelligible as the imaging and expression of experience—something that "counts" and has a particular kind of significance above the random projection and play of brute light and shadow. That is, although film theory has attempted to describe and explain cinematic signification or "language" in great detail, it has assumed the cinema's power to signify and the spectator's power to see this signification as significant. It has assumed *the fundamental intelligibility of the film experience.* Whether fragmenting its analyses of cinematic semiosis into a syntactics (primarily revealed in the formalist emphasis on structuring), a semantics (primarily revealed in the realist emphasis on content), or a pragmatics (primarily revealed in the contemporary theorist's emphasis on relational functions), film theory has assumed rather than accounted for the film experience's intrasubjective and intersubjective nature and its transitive function or performance.

Third, film theory has presupposed that a film is a *viewed object.* Whether it has been considered the aesthetic and expressive object of the formalist; the empirical and perceptive object of the realist; or the cultural, rhetorical, and reflexive object of the contemporary theorist, the film has been regarded as merely, if complexly, a vehicle through which meaning can be represented, presented, or produced; a visible object in the manner of the frame, the window, and the mirror. That a film, as it is experienced, might be engaged as something *more* than just an object of consciousness is a possibility that has not been entertained.

These three presuppositions have informed almost all film theory and directed its fragmented course and conclusions. That the act of viewing constitutes cinematic communication, that communication occurs, and that the communication is effected by a viewed object on a viewing subject (despite contemporary theory's objectification of the viewing subject as the predicate of cinematic vision)—these are the givens of the film experience and the ground upon which various theories of film base themselves and from which they proceed.

However, these presuppositions are themselves open to investigation and, indeed, require it if we are to understand the original power of the cinema to signify, its genesis of meaning and ability to communicate, its "expression of experience by experience." In this regard, both classical and contemporary theory have provided us only partial descriptions and abstract formulations that have detached cinematic signification from its origin in concrete sense and significance. As Dudley Andrew points out:

> We can speak of codes and textual systems which are the results of signifying processes, yet we seem unable to discuss that mode of experience we call signification. More precisely, structuralism and academic film theory in general have been disinclined to deal with the "other-side" of signification, those realms of pre-formulation where sensory data congeals into "something that matters" and those realms of post-formulation where that "something" is experienced as mattering. Structuralism, even in its post-structural reach toward psychoanalysis and intertextuality, concerns itself only with that something and not with the process of its congealing nor with the event of its mattering.[22]

Previous discussion has introduced the exchange or reversibility of perception and expression in the film experience as the commutative basis for the emergence of cinematic signification and significance. Focus on this exchange is a focus on both the process that constitutes "something that matters" and the "event of its mattering." It points to and describes the radical and existential ground for both a theory of sign production and a theory of meaning as they are always entailed in the lived-body experience. Thus, relative to cinema, the *existential and embodied act of viewing* becomes the paradigm of this exchange of perception and expression. That is, the act of viewing provides both the necessary and sufficient conditions for the commutation of perception to expression and vice-versa. It also communicatively links filmmaker, film, and spectator by means of their respective, separate, and yet homeomorphic existential performance of a shared (and possibly universal) competence: the capacity to localize and unify (or "center") the invisible, intrasubjective commutation of perception and expression and make it visible and intersubjectively available to others.

Filmmaker, film, and spectator all concretely use the agency of visual, aural, and kinetic experience to express experience—not only to and for themselves, but also to and for others. Each engaged in the visible gesture of viewing, the filmmaker, film, and spectator are all able to commute the "language of being" into the "being of language," and back again. Dependent upon existence and embodiment in the world for its articulation as an activity, the act of viewing as the commutation of perception and expression is both an intrasubjective and intersubjective performance equally performable by filmmaker, film, and spectator.

This suggests, therefore, the possibility that a film may be considered as more than a merely visible object. That is, in terms of its performance, it is as much a *viewing subject* as it is also a *visible* and *viewed object*. Thus, in its existential function, it shares a privileged equivalence with its human counterparts in the film experience. This is certainly *not* to say that the film is a *human* subject. Rather, it is to consider the film a *viewing* subject—one that manifests a competence of perceptive and expressive performance *equivalent* in structure and function to that same competence performed by filmmaker and spectator. The film actualizes and realizes its ability to localize, unify (or "center") the "invisible" intrasubjective exchange or commutation between the perception of the camera and the expression of the projector. As well, it makes this exchange visible and intersubjectively available to others in the expression of its perception—in the visible commutation between the perceptive language of its expressive being (the prereflective *inflection* of its "viewing view" as the *experience of consciousness*) and the expressive being of its perceptive language (the *reflection* of its "viewed view" as the *consciousness of experience*).

In the act of vision, the film transcends its existence as a merely visible object reducible to its technology and mechanisms, much as in similar acts of vision, the filmmaker and spectator transcend their existence as merely visible objects reducible to their anatomy and physiology. All are not merely objects for vision, but also subjects of vision. Thus, Merleau-Ponty's description of the structured, centered, inherent "co/herence" of human experience in the world as not only for others, but also for itself, seems just as applicable to the *visual being* of the *visible film:*

> Just as . . . when I walk round an object, I am not presented with a succession of perspective views which I subsequently co-ordinate thanks to the idea of one single flat projection, . . . so I am not myself a succession of "psychic" acts, nor for that matter a nuclear *I* who brings them together into a synthetic unity, but one single experience inseparable from itself, one single "living cohesion," one single temporality which is engaged, from birth, in making itself progressively explicit, and in confirming that cohesion in each successive present. . . . The primary truth is indeed "I think," but only provided we understand thereby "I belong to myself" while belonging to the world. . . . Inside and outside are inseparable. The world is wholly inside and I am wholly outside myself.[23]

The intrasubjective or implicit (what in phenomenological terms shall later be explored as the "introceptive") and the intersubjective or explicit are thus modalities of a single experience of being-in-the-world. Similarly, the invisible activity of viewing and its visible productions are both modalities of the single experience of vision-in-the-world. Understood as a viewing subject that—by virtue of the particular nature of its embodied existence—can also be viewed, the film no longer merely contains sense, significance, meaning. Rather, it possesses sense by means of its senses, and it makes sense as a "living cohesion," as a *signifying subject.* It is as this signifying subject that it existentially *comes to matter* as a *significant object,* that is, can be understood in its *objective* status by others as sensible and intelligible.

The direct engagement, then, between spectator and film in the film experience cannot be considered a monologic one between a viewing subject and a viewed object. Rather, it is a dialogical and dialectical engagement of *two* viewing subjects who also exist as visible objects (if of different material and in different ways to be elaborated further). Both film and spectator are capable of viewing and of being viewed, both are embodied in the world as the subject of vision and object for vision. Zygmunt Bauman tells us, "All signification starts from the establishing of an affinity between its subject and object; or, rather, between two subjects, standing respectively at the beginning and the end of communication."[24] In the film experience, all signification and all communication start from the "affinity" that is the act of viewing, coterminously but uniquely performed by both film and spectator. This act of viewing, this *"address of the eye,"* implicates both *embodied, situated* existence and a *material* world, for to see and be seen, the viewing subject must be a body and be materially in the world, sharing a similar manner and matter of existence with other viewing subjects, but living this existence discretely and autonomously, as the singular embodied situation that makes this existence also a unique matter that matters uniquely.

Most theoretical reflection abstracts the act of viewing, the "address of the eye," from its *double* embodiment and *double* situation in—and as—the specific relations of vision that constitute the film experience. The existential, embodied nature of vision and its signifying power are elided. So, too, is the lived sense that cinematic vision in the film experience is articulated by *both* the film *and* the spectator simultaneously engaged in *two* quite distinctly located visual acts that meet on shared ground but never identically occupy it. The theorist, abstracted from his own embodied experience in the movie theater, describes cinematic vision as the essential entailment of a *viewing subject* and a *viewed object* in what is thought of, rather than lived through, as a *single* and *disembodied* act of vision and signification.

Yet everything about my experience at the movies denies such description. The film for me is never merely a viewed "thing," that is, visible images that my vision sees, appropriates, and incorporates as "my own." No matter how I give myself up to the play of images I see and sounds I hear in the theater, those images and sounds are always to some degree resistant to my incorporation of—or by—them. Indeed, there would be no "play" were there not this mutual resilience and resistance I feel, this back-and-forth exchange I experience, in the encounter between myself and a film. Materially embodied, particularly situated, and informed by an intending consciousness that has its own "projects" in the world, I am never so vacuous as to be completely "in-formed" by even the most insinuating or overwhelming film. My experience at the movies is never lived as a monologic one, however easy and even often lazy my participation (or the film's) seems to be. There are always two embodied acts of vision at work in the theater, two embodied views constituting the intelligibility and significance of the film experience. The film's vision and my own do not conflate, but meet in the sharing of a world and constitute an experience that is not only intrasubjectively dialectical, but also intersubjectively dialogical. Although there are moments in which our views may become congruent in the convergence of our interest (never of our situation), there are also moments in which our views conflict; our values, interests, prospects, and projects differ; something is not understood or is denied even as it is visible and seen. Cinematic vision, then, is never monocular, is always doubled, is always the vision of *two viewing subjects* materially and consciously inhabiting, signifying, and sharing a world in a manner at once universal and particular, a world that is mutually visible but hermeneutically negotiable.

It is the embodied and enworlded "address of the eye" that structures and gives significance to the film experience for filmmaker, film, and spectator alike. The embodied eye materially presents and represents intending consciousness: the "I" affirmed as a subject of (and for) vision not abstractly, but concretely, in lived-space, *at* an address, *as* an address. Vision is an *act* that occurs from somewhere in particular; its requisites are both a *body* and a *world*. Thus, *address*, as noun and verb, denotes both a location where one resides and the activity of transcending the body's location, originating from it to exceed beyond it as a projection bent on spanning the worldly space between one body-subject and another. The address of the eye also forces us to consider the *embodied* nature of vision, the body's radical contribution to the constitution of the film experience. If vision is not regarded as transcendental (even if its address toward objects in the world transcends its originating and permanent if mobile residence in a "home body"), then two bodies and two addresses must be acknowledged as the necessary condition of the film experience.

Resonant with the body's other senses (particularly those of touch and sound), the "address of the eye" in the film experience expresses both the *origin* and *destination* of viewing as an existential and transcendent activity. It names a *transitive relationship* between two or more objective body-subjects, each materially embodied and distinctly situated, yet each mutually enworlded. Constituted from this transitive relation is a third, *transcendent* space, that is, a space exceeding the individual body and its unique situation yet concretely inhabited and *intersubjective*.

When the object of the eye's address is not only visible but also capable of vision, visual activity and its intentional projects are doubled and describe a semiotic/hermeneutic field. The visual activity of this doubled "address of the eye" (objectively invisible) calls to mind those strip comics and cartoons in which the characters' gazes literally "dash" themselves across space as hyphenated lines of force, crisscrossing each other in a complex circumscription of the space they both share. Such a circumscription of mutually lived space, such an intersection and connection of visual activity (neither fully convergent nor fully separate) creates a shared address whose semiotic ambiguity and existential richness cannot be reduced to geometry.

We are thus called to a radical reflection upon those presuppositions that inform classical and contemporary film theory. Instead of going forward in an ungrounded investigation of cinematic signification as it secondarily emerges fragmented into a syntactics, semantics, or pragmatics, we must now turn back to the origins of cinematic signification as it originally emerges in the systemic act of viewing, the address of the eye. Merleau-Ponty suggests the concerns of such a journey: "It is at the same time true that the world is *what we see* and that, nevertheless, we must learn to see it—first in the sense that we must watch this vision with knowledge, take possession of it, say what *we* and what *seeing* are, act therefore as if we knew nothing about it, as if here we still had everything to learn."[25]

Beginning again and radically reflecting on the origin of cinematic signification in the embodied act of viewing, in the "address of the eye," we ground this investigation, appropriately, in the philosophical context and method of existential—and semiotic—phenomenology.

NOTES

1. Maurice Merleau-Ponty, *The Visible and the Invisible,* ed. Claude Lefort, trans. Alphonso Lingus (Evanston, Ill.: Northwestern University Press, 1968), p. 155.

2. This manner of reference to the "centering" of embodied existence is used frequently within the context of phenomenological inquiry but has a slightly different emphasis than that currently used to discuss—and disparage—the notion of the "centered subject." For phenomenological usage, see particularly Maurice Merleau-Ponty, *Phenomenology of Perception,* trans. Colin Smith (London: Routledge & Kegan Paul, 1962); Erwin Straus, *The Primary World of the Senses: A Vindication of Sensory Experience,* trans. Jacob Needleman (London: Free Press of Glencoe, Collier-Macmillan, 1963); and Richard M. Zaner, *The Problem of Embodiment: Some Contributions to a Phenomenology of the Body,* 2d ed. (The Hague: Martinus Nijhoff, 1977).

3. Merleau-Ponty, *The Visible and the Invisible,* p. 155.

4. Maurice Merleau-Ponty, "Eye and Mind," trans. Carleton Dallery, in *The Primacy of Perception,* ed James M. Edie IEvanston, Ill., Northwestern University Press, 1964).

5. Jean Mitry, *Esthétique et psychologie du cinéma,* vol. 2 (Paris: Éditions Universitaires, 1965), pp. 453–54. My translation from the following:

> Les formes . . . sont . . . aussi variées que la vie elle-même et, pas plus qu'on ne saurait réglementer la vie, on ne saurait réglementer un art dont elle est à la fois le sujet et l'objet.
>
> Tandis que les arts classiques se proposent de signifier le mouvement avec de l'immobile, la vie avec du non-vivant, le cinéma, lui, se doit d'exprimer la vie avec la vie elle-même. Il commence là où les autres finissent. Il échappe donc à toutes leurs régles comme à tous leurs principes.

6. What is suggested here is that even at its most abstract and materially reflexive, the cinema is not understood as *merely* its brute material unless it is *secondarily* coded as such. Thus, in "structural-materialist" films, the materiality of the film is, and must be, *signified* in order to be understood on a material basis. In sum, the young infant (not yet communicatively competent because only preconscious of its own production of vision as both a viewing view/moving image) sees the play of light and shadow and color of *any* film as only its brute materiality, whereas the communicatively competent, self-conscious viewer sees *no* film in that manner, unless it is secondarily coded as materially significant. That is, to the baby the film is not yet a film, but to the mature viewing subject, the film is always *more* than its material presence and play before it can be seen as anything *less*.

7. Jürgen Habermas, quoted in T. A. McCarthy, "A Theory of Communicative Competence," in *Critical Sociology*, ed. Paul Connerton (London: Penguin Books, 1976), p. 472. On "communicative competence," see also Jürgen Habermas, *Communication and the Evolution of Society*, trans. Thomas McCarthy (Boston: Beacon Press, 1979).

8. This relation between existential phenomenology and semiotics is first made explicit and recognized as a "semiotic phenomenology" in Richard L. Lanigan, *Speaking and Semiology: Maurice Merleau-Ponty's Phenomenological Theory of Existential Communication* (The Hague: Mouton, 1972), pp. 51–96. This relation is summarized: "Existential phenomenology posits the *sign as given*, not as the synthetic product of a phenomenalism (or objective principium) or the synthetic product of an existentialism per se (or subjective principium)" (p. 75).

9. For a general yet thorough introduction to the "critical theory" of the Frankfurt school and Habermas, see David Held, *Introduction to Critical Theory: Horkheimer to Habermas* (Berkeley and Los Angeles: University of California Press, 1980). Held summarizes my own reservations about critical theory and its utopian idealism when, in a closing section on critical theory's "unresolved problems," he asks, "How can the possibility of critique be sustained, if the historical contextuality of knowledge is recognized? Or, to put the question somewhat differently, how can critical theory at once acknowledge its historicality and yet be critical?" (p. 398).

10. "Systematically distorted communication" is a concept used by Habermas and relates to his theory of communicative competence. See Jürgen Habermas, "Systematically Distorted Communication," in *Critical Sociology*, pp. 348–62.

11. The term *filmmaker* is used here and throughout (except where otherwise stipulated) as naming not a biographical person and his or her style or manner of being through cinematic representation (a focus found in Gilles Deleuze's *Cinema 1: The Movement-Image* and *Cinema 2: The Time-Image*), but rather the concrete, situated, and synoptic presence of the many persons who realized the film as concretely visible for vision. Thus, the term is also not equivalent to the textual function identified as the "implied author" in Wayne C. Booth, *The Rhetoric of Fiction* (Chicago: University of Chicago Press, 1961), pp. 71–76.

12. Merleau-Ponty, *Phenomenology of Perception*, p. xix.

13. Maurice Merleau-Ponty, "An Unpublished Text by Maurice Merleau-Ponty: A Prospectus of His Work," trans. Arleen B. Dallery, in Merleau-Ponty, *The Primacy of Perception*, p. 3. The use of the word *mind* here may seem problematic to the reader at this point, because the attribution of mind to a film (i.e., a consciousness) is yet to be demonstrated and seems at first highly unlikely. However, as shall be discussed at great length, insofar as the consciousness of another as well as of oneself is known in its manifest form as *embodied intentionality*, then a human and a film can both be said to articulate consciousness, or, in this instance, "mind."

14. The phrase *enabling structure* is borrowed from Wolfgang Iser, *The Act of Reading: A Theory of Aesthetic Response* (Baltimore: John Hopkins University Press,

1978), p. 230. The reader is also directed to Iser's discussion of "negativity" (pp. 225–31), which parallels Merleau-Ponty's discussion of reversibility or the "chiasm" in *The Visible and the Invisible*, pp. 130–55.

15. Umberto Eco, *A Theory of Semiotics* (Bloomington: Indiana University Press, 1979), pp. 40, 43–44.

16. In the following paragraphs, I thematize the work of traditional and contemporary film theorists too numerous to cite. The reader unfamiliar with the field who wishes to follow the arguments advanced here is urged to seek out specific theorists and their texts with the help, perhaps, of J. Dudley Andrew, *The Major Film Theories: An Introduction* (New York: Oxford University Press, 1976) and *Concepts in Film Theory* (New York: Oxford University Press, 1984). Andrew's two volumes are hardly exhaustive (and occasionally exclusive), but they do provide a place to begin.

17. This formulation was first emphasized in Charles F. Altman, "Psychoanalysis and Cinema: The Imaginary Discourse," *Quarterly Review of Film Studies* 2 (August 1977), pp. 260–64. Examples of other metaphors that have not had the same impact as the three mentioned here are the film as *dream* and the film as *consciousness*. The metaphor of dream tends to intertwine itself with the metaphor of the frame insofar as it is personal, subjective, autonomous, and connected with the artist/filmmaker; however, it is also connected with the metaphor of the mirror insofar as it is a deceptive structure needing disclosure and decoding or deconstruction in the psychoanalytic situation. See Janet Jenks Casebier and Allan Casebier, "Selective Bibliography on Dream and Film," *Dreamworks* 1 (Spring 1980), pp. 88–93, and John Michaels, "Film and Dream," *Journal of the University Film Association* 32 (Winter-Spring 1980), pp. 85–87. The metaphor of consciousness is to be distinguished from the thrust of the present study insofar as consciousness in this work is (1) not considered apart from its embodiment in a person and (2) not used as a metaphor but to denote an empirical function of being. Consciousness as a metaphor for film, however, can be found throughout George W. Linden, *Reflections on the Screen* (Belmont, Calif.: Wadsworth, 1970), and it provides a focal point for Bruce Kawin, *Mindscreen: Bergman, Godard, and First-Person Film* (Princeton, N.J.: Princeton University Press, 1978).

18. One of the earliest explicit statements of this systemic interdependence appears in Jean-Luc Godard, "Montage My Fine Care," in *Godard on Godard*, trans. Tom Milne (New York: Viking Press, 1972), pp. 39–41. It also pervades Mitry's many discussions of editing throughout both volumes of his *Esthétique et psychologie du cinéma*. Also of relevance here is a subtle and nuanced overview of the history and practice of literary theory (with references to film theory) found in Catherine Belsey, *Critical Practice* (New York: Methuen, 1980), particularly her use of the term *expressive realism* to nominate the single theoretical system that opposes and differentiates itself as formalism and realism.

19. For basic description and phenomenological critique of the limitations of "subjective psychologism" and "objective empiricism," see the preface to Merleau-Ponty, *Phenomenology of Perception*, pp. vii–xxi. This preliminary discussion is deepened in chapters 1–3, pp. 3–51.

20. Edmund Husserl, *Ideas: General Introduction to Pure Phenomenology*, trans. W. R. Boyce Gibson (New York: Collier 1962), p. 223.

21. See, for example, Barbara Anderson, "Eye Movement and Cinematic Perception," *Journal of the University Film Association*, 32 (Winter-Spring 1980), pp. 23–26. As well, most contemporary introductory aesthetics and histories contain mechanical and anatomical dissections of the camera and process of human vision and "perception." For a brief but comprehensive example, see the first two chapters in George Wead and George Lellis, *Film: Form and Function* (Boston: Houghton Mifflin, 1981), pp. 3–53.

Vivian Sobchack

22. J. Dudley Andrew, "The Neglected Tradition of Phenomenology in Film Theory," *Wide Angle* 2:2 (1978), pp. 45–46.

23. Merleau-Ponty, *Phenomenology of Perception*, p. 407.

24. Zygmunt Bauman, *Hermeneutics and Social Science* (New York: Columbia University Press, 1978), pp. 27–28.

25. Merleau-Ponty, *The Visible and the Invisible*, p. 4.

Anne Friedberg

Cinema and the Postmodern Condition

> *Our taverns and our metropolitan streets, our offices
> and furnished rooms, our railroad stations and our
> factories appeared to have us locked up hopelessly.
> Then came the film and burst this prison-world asun-
> der by the dynamite of the tenth of a second, so that
> now, in the midst of its far-flung ruins and debris, we
> calmly and adventurously go travelling.[1] (Empha-
> sis added.)*

In this well-traveled "passage," from Benjamin's now-canonical essay on
modernity, "The Work of Art in the Age of Mechanical Reproduction,"
Benjamin offers a hyperbolic image of the changes wrought by the
explosive advent of "the film." With a weight of near-biblical drama, the
film is poised to release despondent captives from the "prison-world" of
nineteenth-century architectural space. For Benjamin, "the dynamite of
the tenth of a second" sent a temporal charge that tore at the spatial
materials of modernity; its brickworks, pavements, window glass, and
iron girders were "burst...asunder." The film was privileged as the agent
of this rupture, an epistemological TNT. And in its wake, the *flâneur*
remained, left with a different yet "calm and adventurous" way of
"travelling."

The above "passage" is embedded in a discussion of the close-up,
followed by the frequently-cited maxim: "With the close-up, space expands;

Originally appeared as "Les Flâneurs du Mal(l): Cinema and the Postmodern Condition,"
published in *PMLA* 106:3 (May 1991). This is a slightly altered and reconstituted version
of that essay. Reprinted by permission of the author and the Modern Language Association
of America.

with slow motion, movement is extended. The enlargement of a snap-shot does not render more precise what in any case was visible, though unclear: it reveals *entirely new formations of the subject*"[2] (emphasis added). Benjamin attempts to measure the various cultural effects of photography and the cinema, of mechanical reproduction and the loss of aura, the impact of an "unconscious optics." In this essay, I extend his "entirely new formations of the subject" to include the postmodern subject.[3]

Rather than proclaim a single distinct moment of rupture—when the modern ended and the postmodern began—I suggest a gradual and indistinct epistemological tear along the fabric of modernity, a change caused by the growing cultural centrality of a feature that is integral to both cinema and television: a mobilized virtual gaze. I introduce this compound term in order to describe a gaze that travels in an imaginary *flânerie* through an imaginary elsewhere and an imaginary "elsewhen." The mobilized gaze has a history, which begins well before the cinema and is rooted in other cultural activities that involve walking and travel. The virtual gaze has a history rooted in all forms of visual representation (back to cave painting), but produced most dramatically by photography. The cinema developed as an apparatus that combined the mobile with the virtual. Hence, cinematic spectatorship changed, in unprecedented ways, concepts of the *present* and the *real*.

The gradual shift into postmodernity is marked, I argue, by the increased centrality of the mobilized and virtual gaze as a fundamental feature of everyday life. While social formations of modernity were increasingly mediated through images, this gaze was initially restricted to the public sphere (within high culture in painterly views, theatrical experiences; or within low culture in the arcade, the department store, the diorama or panorama).[4] During the mid-nineteenth century, the coincident introduction of department store shopping, packaged tourism,[5] and protocinematic entertainment began to transform this gaze into a *commodity,* sold to a consumer-spectator. In postmodernity, the spatial and temporal displacements of a mobilized virtual gaze are now as much a part of the public sphere (in, for example, the shopping mall and multiplex cinema) as they are a part of the private (at home, with the television and the VCR). The boundaries between public and private, already fragile in modernity, have now been more fully eroded. The mobilized virtual gaze is now available in the video markets of Katmandu and other outposts of the imperial web of technoculture.[6]

To describe adequately the role of the cinema in postmodernity, one must detail the effects of two forms of proliferation: *spatial* (mass distribution and its flip side, mass reception) and *temporal* (repetition—the metonymic aspect of mechanical reproduction). The mechanical (and now electronic) capacity to manipulate time and space—essential features of cinematic and televisual apparatuses—has produced an increasingly detemporalized subject. And at the same time, the ubiquity of those simulated experiences has fostered an increasingly derealized sense of presence and identity. Cinema and television become readable not just as symptoms of a "postmodern condition," but as contributing causes. Seen in that context, descriptions of a decentered, derealized, and detemporalized postmodern subject form a striking parallel to the subjective consequences of cinema and televisual spectatorship. The most profound symptoms of the postmodern condition diagnosed by theorists as diverse as Lyotard, Jameson, and Baudrillard—the disappearance of a sense of history, entrapment in a perpetual present, and the loss of temporal referents—have been caused at least in part by the implicit time travel of cinematic and televisual spectation.[7]

This chapter is, then, a route, an itinerary. It begins by situating the origins of a mobilized gaze and identifying it with that fundamental paradigm of modernity, the *flâneur*—the male dandy who strolled the urban streets and arcades in the nineteenth century. As the department store supplanted the arcade, the mobilized gaze was implemented in the service of consumption, and the space opened for a female flâneur—a *flâneuse*—whose gendered gaze became a key element of consumer address. And such spatial and temporal mobility led to a unique apparatical sequel: the moving virtual gaze of the cinema.

Les Flâneurs du Mal (1)

Baudelaire's collection of poems on Parisian *flânerie, Les Fleurs du Mal* (*Flowers of Evil*), is the cornerstone of Benjamin's massive and uncompleted work on modernity, his study of the Paris arcades.[8] For Benjamin, the poems record the ambulatory gaze that the flâneur directs on Paris, "the Capital of the Nineteenth Century." The flâneur, "who goes botanizing on the asphalt,"[9] was the quintessential paradigm of the subject in modernity, wandering through urban space in a daze of distraction.[10] Benjamin traces this figure from the arcades into the department store: "the construction of the department store [which] *made use of flânerie itself in order to sell goods.* The department store was the flâneur's final coup"[11] (emphasis added). Traffic and the decline of the arcade may have killed the *flâneur*. But his perceptual patterns—distracted observation and dreamlike reverie—became a prototype for the consumer, whose style of just looking is the pedestrian equivalent of slow motion.

The mobilized gaze could hardly have assumed the importance it did without strolling the arcades. Yet it was men who were at home in this privatized public space. As Susan Buck-Morss has detailed, if women roamed the street, they became streetwalkers, prostitutes, carnal commodities on sale alongside other items in the arcade.[12] Women were objects for consumption, objects for the gaze of the flâneur or for the poet who, like Baudelaire, would notice women as mere *passersby*.[13]

The Flâneuse

The female flâneur was not possible until a woman could wander the city on her own, a freedom linked to the privilege of shopping alone. Certainly the late-nineteenth-century development of shopping as socially acceptable leisure activity for bourgeois women—as a pleasure rather than a necessity—encouraged women to be peripatetic without escort.[14] Department stores became a central fixture in the capitalist city in the mid-nineteenth century. Bon Marché opened in Paris in 1852, and Macy's in New York in 1857, and others followed. Gradually these *grand magasins* began to employ female salesclerks, thus allowing the female to be both buyer and seller.[15] To Benjamin, as to Baudelaire, women in public spaces were "seller and commodity in one,"[16] not observers but objects in the panopticon of the sexual market. A poem from *Les Fleurs du Mal* provides illustration:

> Your eyes, lit up like shops to lure their trade . . .
> Or fireworks in the park on holidays,
> insolently make use of borrowed power
> and never learn (you might say, "in the dark")
> what law it is that governs their good looks.[17]

It was not until the closing decades of the century that the department store became a safe haven for unchaperoned women. The department store may have been the flâneur's last coup, but it was the flâneuse's first.[18]

Shopping, like other itinerancies of the late nineteenth century—museum and exhibition going, packaged tourism, and, of course, the cinema—relied on the visual register and helped to ensure the predominance of the gaze in capitalist society. The department store, like the arcade before it, "made use of flânerie itself in order to sell goods,"[19] constructing fantasy worlds for itinerant lookers. But unlike the arcade, the department store offered a protected site for the empowered gaze of the flâneuse. Endowed with purchasing power, she was the target of consumer address. New desires were created for her by advertising and consumer culture;[20] desires elaborated in a system of selling and consumption that depended on the relation between looking and buying and on the indirect desire to possess and incorporate through the eye.

Zola's 1883 novel about a *grand magasin*—*Au Bonheur des Dames*—makes apparent the purpose of the department store: for the pleasure of women. The novel describes the transformation of Denise, a young woman of twenty who comes to Paris from the country town of Valognes. In her first moments in the teeming metropolis, fresh from the Saint-Lazare railway station, Denise becomes transfixed in front of the windows of a great store, Bonheur des Dames. For Zola, the store window makes the equation between women and the commodity quite explicit. The mannequins "peopl[ed] the street with these beautiful women for sale, each bearing a price in big figures in the place of a head."[21] Even before Denise goes to work in the store, she "began to feel as if she were watching a machine working at full pressure communicating its movement even as far as the windows. . . . with mechanical regularity, quite *a nation of women pass[ed] through the force and logic of this wonderful commercial machine*"[22] (emphasis added).

The store's owner, Mouret, arranges displays of umbrellas and silks and woolen mantles, aware that they produce an almost mesmerizing effect on the women who pass by them:

> Mouret's unique passion was *to conquer woman.* He wished her to be queen in his house, and he had built this temple to get her completely at his mercy. *His sole aim was to intoxicate her with gallant attentions, and traffic on her desires, work on her fever*[23] (emphasis added).

While these merchandising changes were transforming the bourgeoise in Paris, in other capitalist cities such as New York, Chicago, London, and Berlin the department store was also becoming a common temple of consumption, a "cathedral of modern commerce."[24]

L. Frank Baum edited The Show Window, *a monthly journal of practical window trimming, from 1897 to 1902.*

The shop window was the proscenium for this visual intoxication, the site of seduction for consumer desire. In 1900, in addition to writing *The Wizard of Oz*, Baum published a treatise on window display, entitled *The Art of Decorating Dry Goods Windows*.[25] In it, he describes a variety of techniques for catching the eye of window-shoppers and turning them into absorbed spectators:

> How can a window sell goods? *By placing them before the public in such a manner that the observer has a desire for them and enters the store to make the purchase.* Once in, the customer may see other things she wants, and no matter how much she purchases under these conditions *the credit of the sale belongs to the window*[26] (emphasis added).

One of Baum's recommended techniques was what he called an illusion window, which would be "sure to arouse the curiosity of the observer."[27] A window display called the vanishing lady used a live female model who, at intervals, would disappear into a drapery-covered pedestal and reappear after changing her hat, gloves, or shawl.

Baum's conception of the show window seems to bear a clear analogy to the cinema screen. The window frames a tableau; placing it behind glass and making it inaccessible arouses desire. Cinematic spectation, a further instrumentalization of such consumer gaze, produced paradoxical effects on the newfound social mobility of the flâneuse. From the middle of the nineteenth century, as if in a historical relay of looks, the shop window succeeded the mirror as a site of identity construction, and then—gradually—the shop window was displaced by the cinema screen. Window-shopping becomes an apt paradigm for cinematic and televisual spectatorship.[28] The newly conjoined *mobilized and virtual* gaze of the cinema answered the desire not only for temporal and spatial mobility but for gender mobility as well. The spectator-shopper—trying on identities—engages in the pleasures of a temporally and spatially fluid subjectivity. Theories of spectatorship that imply a one-to-one correspondence between the spectator position and gender, race, or sexual identity—as if identity were a constant, consistent continuum unchallenged by the borrowed subjectivity of spectatorship—do not consider the pleasures of escaping that physically bound subjectivity. Isn't cinema spectatorship pleasurable precisely because new identities can be "worn" and then discarded? That question appeals to a much larger debate about identification and spectator effect, but it is one that *explores* gender, race, and sexual mobility rather than one that fixes identity in spectator address.[29]

From the Arcades to the Cinema: The Mobilized Virtual Gaze

In the nineteenth century, a wide variety of devices turned the pleasures of flânerie into commodity form and negotiated new illusions of spatial and temporal mobility. The panorama and diorama, for example, relied on physical immobility as well as the painterly illusion of virtual presence.[30] Those protocinematic illusions introduced a virtual mobility that was both spatial—bringing the country to the town dweller—and temporal—transporting the past to the present.

The panorama—a cylindrical painting, viewed by an observer in the center—was patented by an Irishman, Robert Barker, in 1787.[31] The illusion presented by the panorama was created by a combination of realist techniques of perspective and scale and a mode of viewing that placed the spectator in the center of a darkened room surround by a scene lit from above. "The spectator," as Gernsheim and Gernsheim note, "lost all judgement of distance and space. . . . in the absence of any means of comparison with real objects, a perfect illusion was given."[32] Benjamin saw a direct relation between the panoramic observer and the flâneur: "The city-dweller . . . attempts to introduce countryside into the town. In the panoramas the city dilates to become landscape, as it does in a subtler way for the flâneur."[33] Before the advent of illustrated print journalism in the 1840s, the panorama supplied a visual illustration of places and events that one could only read about, in print. The panorama appealed not only to public interest in battles and historical illustration but also to a fascination with landscape art, travel literature, and travel itself. As Altick argues, the panorama was the "bourgeois public's substitute for the Grand Tour."[34]

Louis Jacques Mandé Daguerre, later famed for his 1839 patent on a photographic technique he named the daguerrotype, began his career as an assistant to the celebrated panorama painter Pierre Prévost. In 1822, Daguerre debuted a viewing device that expanded on the panorama's ability to transport the viewer—an apparatus he called the diorama. The diorama differed significantly from the panorama: the diorama spectator was immobile, at the center of the building, and the views were mobilized as the entire diorama building with its pulleys, cords, and rollers became a machine for changing the spectator's view. Daguerre's visitors looked through a proscenium at a scene composed of object arranged in front of a backdrop; after a few minutes, the auditorium platform rotated, exposing another dioramic opening.[35] Like the diaphanorama—in which translucent watercolors were illuminated from behind—the diorama relied on the manipulation of light through transparent painting. The exhibit was thus designed to construct and restructure the viewer's relation to the spatial and temporal present.[36] As a local newspaper account indicated, the diorama made it possible for "Parisians who like pleasure without fatigue to make the journey to Switzerland and to England without leaving the capital."[37] Gernsheim and Gernsheim extend this description of the diorama as a substitute for travel: "The many foreign views . . . no doubt had a special appeal to the general public who, before the days of Cook's Tours, had little chance of travelling abroad."[38] There were variations on the diorama. The Pleorama, which opened in Berlin in 1832, had the audience seated in a ship and taken for an hour's "voyage" as the illusion of movement was created by a backdrop moving slowly across the stage.[39]

Both the panorama and its successor, the diorama, offered new forms of virtual mobility to their viewers. But a paradox here must be emphasized: as the mobility of the gaze became more virtual—as techniques were developed to paint (and then to photograph) realistic images and as mobility was implied by changes in lighting (and then cinematography)—observers became more immobile, passive, and ready to receive the constructions of a virtual reality placed in front of their unmoving bodies.

The virtual tours that these new devices presented were, in a sense, apparatical extensions of the spatial flânerie through the arcades. Not all of these distractions were located in or near an arcade, but many of them were. In Paris, the Passage des Panoramas was lit by the same skylight that illuminated the panorama itself. The Galerie Vivienne (constructed in 1823) contained the cosmorama, an 1832 invention by Abbé Gazzara that used magnifying mirrors to reproduce landscapes with illusory depth.[40] The Théâtre Séraphin—site of marionette theatre, shadow plays, and phantasmagorias—moved in 1858 from an arcade in the Palais Royal to the Passage Jouffroy—an extension of Passage des Panoramas. In 1882, the Musée Grevin, a wax-figure museum modeled after Madame Tussaud's London exhibition, opened in the Passage Jouffroy.[41] The Musée Grevin was the site of the first Paris performances of legerdemain by another soon-to-be-famed illusionist: Georges Méliès. These architectural passages, as much sites of departure as destinations, became depots for the temporal slippage of a mobilized gaze. The mobilized gaze of shopping and tourism combined with the virtual gaze of photography to produce a new form: the mobilized and virtual gaze of the cinema.[42]

In October 1895, months after reading H. G. Wells's utopian novel, *The Time Machine,* the British inventor R. W. Paul applied for a patent for a "novel form of exhibition" in which "spectators have presented to their view scenes which are supposed to occur in the future or past, while they are given the sensation of voyaging upon a machine through time."[43] *The Time Machine* fictionalized an intricately crafted mechanism that could transport its passenger into the future or the past at the rate of a year a minute; pull of the lever in one direction would "gain yesterdays," and in the other, one could "accumulate tomorrows." Wells's science fantasy of time travel found literal embodiment in the recently perfected machine of illusion—the cinematic apparatus.

In 1926, film historian Terry Ramsaye drew the direct relation between Wells's conception of a time machine and the behavior of a motion picture film. Ramsaye wrote to Wells to inquire about the "motion-picture root" for his time machine, but Wells was "unable to remember the details."[44] The close coincidence between Wells's novel (published in 1895) and Paul's patent application (October 24, 1895), causes Ramsaye to enthuse over the "Wells-Paul idea": "It sought to liberate the spectator from the instant of Now. . . . It was a plan to give the spectator possession, on equal terms, of Was and To Be along with Is."[45] Like the cinéorama and other devices that combined projection lanterns, scenic settings, and platform devices to simulate motion, the mechanism in the Paul patent was a platform that positioned spectators to face an opening onto a screen. The platform was to be suspended by cranks, which provided a "general rocking motion." A current of air blown over the spectators was "intended to represent to spectators the means of propulsion." Paul's patent application described a mechanism that was arranged like the diorama, with spectators seated on a platform that would "create the impression of travelling":

> After the starting of the mechanism, and a suitable period having elapsed, representing, say a certain number of centuries, during which the platforms may be in darkness, or in alternations of darkness and dim light, the mechanism may be slowed and a pause made at a given epoch, on which the scene upon the screen will come gradually into view of the spectators, increasing in size and distinctness from a small vista.

But unlike the diorama, with its painted vistas, the views presented were cinematic. The "realistic effect" in this mechanism was composed of:

1. A hypothetical landscape, containing also the representations of the inanimate objects in the scene.
2. A slide, or slides, which may be traversed horizontally or vertically and contain representations of objects such as navigable balloons, etc. which is required to traverse the scene.

3. *Slides or films, representing in successive instantaneous photographs, after the manner of the Kinetoscope, the living persons or creatures in their natural motions. The films or slides are prepared with the aid of the kinetograph or special camera,* from made-up characters performing on the stage[46] (emphasis added).

On March 22 of the same year that Paul requested his patent, the French brothers Louis and Auguste Lumière gave a private showing of a film recorded and projected with their patented device, the *Cinématographe*. And on December 28, 1895, the first public projection of Lumière *actualités* took place in a *petite salle* in the basement of the Grand Café on the Boulevard des Capucines. The *Cinématographe* had brought time travel to the boulevard café.

The Shopping Mall

Let us now shift from origins to exponents, from causes to effects, from the first fissures in modernity to its present-day debris. Nineteenth-century artificial city environments such as parks, passageways, department stores, and exhibition halls seem to have culminated in today's urban center: the shopping mall. If, for Benjamin, the arcade instantiated all of modernity, the shopping mall is an equally pivotal site—the key topos—of postmodern urban space.

The nineteenth-century *passage* was readable to Benjamin while in its decline. Perhaps, equally, the contemporary shopping mall now emerges as a comprehensible cultural space as it becomes threatened with its own obsolescence. (Electronic technologies now bring information, entertainment, products, and services into the home, and therefore the privatized public space of the shopping mall may soon be replaced by the electronic mall and the home shopping network.[47]) But whether or not life in the public realm diminishes, electronic *flânerie* further turns spaces into their virtual replacements—"conduits" that supplant the need for physical mobility.[48] Just as the shift to a credit economy has relied on the virtual buying power of plastic, so the virtual realities, electronic villages, and invisible data highways have become the new frontier. *Virtual* has entered the vernacular as the present predictive.[49]

The shopping mall developed as a site for combining the speculative activity of shopping with the mobilities of tourism; the shopping mall multiplex cinema epitomizes both in a virtual form.

The mall is not a completely public place. Like the arcade, it keeps the street at a safe distance. The mall engulfs a passive subject within an illusory realm. Like the theme park, the mall is "imagineered" with maintenance and management techniques that conceal its delivery bays and support systems and with the security guards and bouncers who control its entrances. It defers urban realities and blocks such urban blights as the homeless, beggars, crime, traffic, and even weather. While it is a temperature-controlled refuge from hostile environments, the presence of trees and large plants gives the illusion of the outdoors. Visitors can walk from store to store without encountering wind or rain and without taking off or putting on garments at each entrance and exit. The mall creates the nostalgic image of a clean, safe, legible town center.

The mall is open to anyone regardless of race, class, and gender, and no purchase is required. If shopping activates the power of the consumer gaze, then purchasing asserts power over the objects beheld.[50] But the shopper who buys nothing pays a psychic penalty: the unpleasure of unsated consumer desire. As a form of incorporation, shopping can be likened to identification: "I shop; therefore I am" but also "I am what I buy." The flâneuse may have found a space for an empowered mobilized gaze—women constitute 85 percent of all mall shoppers[51]—yet analysis of the images she is encouraged to consume makes this empowerment seem questionable.

The mall encourages the perceptual mode of flânerie while instrumentalizing it for consumer objectives. Jerde, architect of a paradigmatic Los Angeles shopping mall—the Westside Pavilion—describes his concept of the American variation on flânerie.

> Urban and suburban Americans seldom stroll aimlessly, as Europeans do, to parade and rub shoulders in a crowd. We need a *destination, a sense of arrival* at a definite location. My aim, in developments such as Horton Plaza and the Westside Pavilion, *is to provide a destination that is also a public parade and a communal center*[52] (emphasis added).

For Jerde, the speculative gaze of the shopper provides the motor for such flânerie.

Like the nineteenth-century train station, the shopping mall provides the "sense of arrival" and of departure; the shopper strolls distractedly past an assortment of stores that promise consumerist digression. Shopping mall planners utilize a mechanist rhetoric to describe the circulation of consumers: magnet stores, generators, flow, pull. Escalators provide an illusion of travel, a mechanized mobility to the shopper's gaze in a serene glide through an entirely consumerist space.

In *The Malling of America*, William Kowinski provides a detailed descriptive account of malling as the "chief cultural activity in America."[53] He asserts, "There are more shopping centers in the United States than movie theaters (and most movie theaters are now in shopping centers)."[54] Yet, in this piece of syllogistic accounting, Kowinski has not calculated the exact relation between the movie theater and the shopping center. He approaches an equation between them in the following epiphanic passage:

> I saw the white pools of light, the areas of relative darkness, the symmetrical aisles and gleaming escalator, the bracketed store facades, the sudden strangeness of live trees and plants indoors. It was as if I were standing on a balcony, looking down on a stage, waiting for the show to begin. . . .
> That was it. This theatrical space. The mall is a theater.[55]

But it is not a movie theater:

> this sense of a special world—permits a kind of unity of experience within an effortless enclosure that is something like the classic theater's unities of time, place and action. It's all here, now. The mall concentrates drama, suspends disbelief.[56]

While the grand equation "mall as theater" is suggestive, Kowinski leaves it undeveloped. Unlike the theater, which still retains an aura of performance and the real, the cinema offers a less aura-endowed, more uniformly repeatable experience. The shopping mall has not replaced the movie theater: it has become its logical extension. The mall itself is a machine of timelessness, a spatial and architectural manifestation of the cinematic and televisual apparatuses, but it is a selling machine.[57] Shopping mall cinemas demand an expenditure. They offer the pleasure of purchase, but instead of delivering a tangible product, they supply an experience—a time tourism similar to that of the panorama or diorama. Like tourism, which is prepared by mass publicity and cliché, the film industry prepares the contemporary spectator with auxiliary discourses of publicity. Licensed movie tie-ins are reinforced in displays in mall stores.[58] The shopping mall—and its apparatical extension, the shopping mall multiplex—offer safe transit into other spaces, other times, other imaginaries. These elsewheres are available to the consumer in a theatrical space where psychic transubstantiation is possible through purchase. Thought of in this way, the spectator-shopper tries on different identities—with limited risk and a policy of easy return. The cinema spectator engages in a kind of identity bulimia. Leaving the theater, one abandons the garment, taking away only the memory of having worn it for a few hours—or having been worn by it.[59]

The Cinema and Postmodernity

In his two key essays on postmodernity, Fredric Jameson establishes an analogy between borderline schizophrenia (a language disorder in which a break in the relations of signifiers plunges the subject into a perpetual present, marked by uncertainty, paradox, and contradiction) and postmodern subjectivity (which Jameson characterizes by the collapse of temporality, the failure of the ability to locate or fix events historically, and the *mise-en-abîme* of referents lost in the labyrinthine chain of signifiers).[60] Jameson's discussion of the cinema and the postmodern focuses on nostalgia films. This genre—or, perhaps, a period style—includes films that not only address the past but also somehow evoke a past, even when they are set in the future. Jameson cites films that take place in some "indefinable nostalgic past"[61] or, like *Chinatown* and *The Conformist*, films that take place in "some eternal Thirties; beyond historical time."[62] His discussion of the cinema, therefore, is quite literal: it assumes that the stylistic or diegetic world of a film, rather than its effect on the spectator, is sufficient to illustrate his models of schizophrenia or pastiche.

Although Jameson does not make the following taxonomy explicit, his descriptions divide nostalgia films into three categories: (1) those that are about the past and set in the past (*Chinatown, American Graffiti*; we could add *The Last Emperor, Harlem Nights, Diner*), (2) those that reinvent the past (*Star Wars, Raiders of the Lost Ark*; we could add *Batman, Blade Runner, Robocop, The Terminator*), and (3) those that are set in the present but invoke the past (*Body Heat*; we could add *Blue Velvet, Trouble in Mind, The Fabulous Baker Boys*). The narrative or art direction of a nostalgia film may confuse its sense of temporality. But film viewing itself confirms the illusion of a perpetual present interminably recycled. One of the essential properties of cinema spectatorship is its temporal displacement: The time of a film's production, the time of its fiction, and the time of its projection are all conflated into the same

"Timeshift Video," New York, 1988. Photograph © Anne Friedberg.

moment in viewing. The reality effect, created by cinematic conventions of narrative and by illusionistic construction, works to conceal that conflation and to produce representations that are taken for perceptions, or—as Metz would have it—a *discours* that is taken for *histoire.*[63]

Taken to its apparatical extreme, what Jameson describes only in the nostalgia genre is true of every film's relation to its historical referent. Beyond a mere marking of contemporary style, such fluidity of time and space is a condition of the mobilized virtual gaze of spectatorship itself. And if as I have argued, postmodernity is marked by the increasing centralization of features implicit in the mobilized virtual gaze of spectatorship, then the emergence of the cinema in the nineteenth century can be seen as a protopostmodern cultural symptom.

Virtual Flânerie

Cinema spectatorship in the 1990s has been transformed by the time-shifting changes in spectatorship produced by the multiplex cinema and the VCR. Multiplex cinemas metonymize the cinema screen into a chain of adjacent shop windows. To get to these screens in a shopping mall cinema, one must pass through a cornucopia of framed images: shop windows designed to perform a muted and static form of consumer address. The screens in a shopping mall cinema transform the stillness of the shop mannequin into the live action of film performance, as if the itinerary through the mall to reach the cinema theater reenacts the historical impulse from photography to film. The VCR metonymizes the same bounty of images temporally. Films are packaged and boxed as uniform commodities regardless of date of production. The multiplex cinema and the VCR have taken the flânerie of the mobilized gaze and recast it into a more accessible and repeatable exponent.[64]

In this way, the VCR has become a privatized museum of past moments—of different genres, times, and commodities—all reduced to uniform, interchangeable, equally accessible units. A remote control magic wand governs that time tourism; each spectator has become the Docteur Crase of René Clair's 1924 film *Paris Qui Dort*, that is, possessor of a machine to stop, accelerate, and reverse time. The videocassette turns film experience into a book-size, readily available commodity. Videotapes market an exponent of the spatial loss (the loss of aura that, as Benjamin describes, accompanies mechanical reproduction) and offer a loss of aura of the second order—the temporal loss (which the opportunities for replay produce). One can literally rent another space and time when one borrows a videotape to watch on a VCR.[65] Or, as Virilio describes the temporal consequences of the VCR: "The machine, the VCR, allows man to organize a time which is not his own, a *deferred time*, a time which is somewhere else—and to capture it. . . . The VCR . . . creates two days: a reserve day which can replace the ordinary day, the lived day"[66] (emphasis added). Time shifting removes the ontology of live television and aligns televisual reception with the elsewhere and elsewhen that have always characterized cinematic spectatorship.[67]

The shopping mall multiplex cinema extends the spectatorial flânerie of the VCR along both the spatial and the temporal axes. The multiplex positions its cinema screens in the spatial metonymy of a chain of adjacent shop windows; the temporal metonymy of show times is arrayed as if the multiplex is a set of contiguous VCRs. Multiplex multiple-screen cinemas become spatially contiguous VCRs, presenting a ready panoply of other temporal moments, the *not-now* in the guise of the *now*.

The cinema spectator and the armchair equivalent—the home-video viewer, who commands fast forward, fast reverse, and many speeds of slow motion; who can easily switch between channels and tape; who

Shop window, New York, 1988. Photograph © Anne Friedberg.

is always able to repeat, replay, and return—is a spectator *lost in* but also *in control of* time. The cultural apparatuses of television and the cinema have gradually become causes for what is now so blithely described as the postmodern condition.

As I've begun to indicate, both cinema's and television's capacity for endless replay and repetition—the remarketing of the past—consists in more than the textual or thematic use of nostalgia, but becomes a commodity form itself. To assess the politics of contemporary representation, we must continue to theorize these aspects of the everyday and their effect on the unconscious—our relation to time and to the real. In short, our prior theorizations of the cinema have been burst asunder.

NOTES

1. Walter Benjamin, "The Work of Art in the Age of Mechanical Reproduction," in *Illuminations*, trans. Harry Zorn (New York: Schocken, 1969), p. 236. The essay "The Work of Art," perhaps the most celebrated of Benjamin's posthumous career, contains his most sustained discussion of film. Situated in the larger context of Benjamin's work (the essay was drafted in January-February 1935), "The Work of Art" was written while he was "in the midst of" his ambitious and never-to-be-completed utopian project to analyze the "far-flung ruins and debris" of the nineteenth century: the *Passagen-Werk*, a study of the Paris arcades. For a discussion of "The Work of Art" in relation to the *Passagen-Werk*, see Susan Buck-Morss, "Benjamin's *Passagen-Werk*: Redeeming Mass Culture for Revolution," *New German Critique* 29 (Spring/Summer 1983), 211–41.

2. Ibid.

3. Benjamin's phrase "neue Strukturbildungen der Materie," translated as "entirely new formations of the subject," refers to the material representation of the close-up and not to a subject with subjectivity. Nevertheless, my sentence performs an avowed sleight of hand by sliding ambiguously into a consideration of the postmodern subject, a rhetorical twist that translation allows. See Walter Benjamin, *Das Kunstwerk im Zeitalter seiner technischen Reproduzierbarkeit* (Frankfurt: Suhrkamp Verlag, 1966), p. 41.

4. Miriam Hansen has provided an excellent critical history of the emergence of cinema spectatorship and its consequent transformation of the public sphere. Hansen's work draws on the German debates about the public sphere in the writings of Jürgen Habermas, Oskar Negt, and Alexander Kluge. Hansen relies on Kluge's and Negt's conception of the "counter public sphere," an "oppositional" potential not present in much of the other post–Frankfurt School writings on the public sphere. Hansen argues that the category of spectator did not coincide with the invention of the cinema in the 1890s. Rather, she links the historical construction of the spectator to a shift (roughly between 1907 and 1917) in early cinematic style and modes of narration. See Miriam Hansen, *Babel and Babylon* (Cambridge, Mass.: Harvard University Press, 1991).

5. Unfortunately, packaged tourism cannot be discussed at any length in this essay. Thomas Cook, British entrepreneur of tourism, began organizing tours in 1841. A collaborator with the temperance movement, he posed the tour as a substitute for alcohol. The tourist industry successfully commoditized a combination of voyeurism (*sight*-seeing) and narrative. The tourist, like the cinema spectator, is simultaneously present and absent, positioned both here and elsewhere.

Work on travel and tourism has suggested productive analogies between shopping, tourism, and film viewing. Wolfgang Schivelbusch describes connections between a railway journey and other forms of panoramic travel: walking through city streets and shopping in department stores. See Wolfgang Schivelbusch, *The Railway Journey* (Berkeley and Los Angeles: University of California Press, 1986), and Dean MacCannell, *The Tourist: A New Theory of the Leisure Class* (New York: Schocken, 1976).

6. While these technological changes are products of multinational capitalism in the First World, the global cultural imperialism of American culture is evident in the double-edged way that the Third World is both simultaneously a tourist haven and a consumer market for American culture. In the global schema, First World culture works in centripetal and centrifugal ways: Centripetal imperialism is introjective, incorporating the other: a Banana-Republic-anization (bringing the Third World to the first by mail order—the exotic made safe for tourism)—whereas centrifugal imperialism is projective, projecting onto the other: a Coca-Colonization (bringing the taste of the First World into the Third).

In his book *Video Night in Katmandu and Other Reports from the Not-so-Far-East* (New York: Knopf, 1988), Pico Iyer has documented the impact of both an implied centripetal imperialism:

> In Asia alone, Bali, Tahiti, Sri Lanka and Nepal have already been so taken over by Paradise stores, Paradise Hotels and Paradise cafes that they sometimes seem less like utopias than packaged imitations of utopias. . . . No Man, they say, is an island, in the age of international travel, not even an island can remain an island for long. (p. 14)

And a centrifugal imperialism:

> Yet in the Third World, a hunger for American culture is almost taken for granted, and making it often means nothing more than making it in the Land of the Free. Communist guerrillas in the Philippines fight captialism while wearing UCLA T shirts. The Sandinista leaders in Nicaragua wage war against "U.S. Imperialism" while watching prime-time American TV on private satellite dishes. And many whites in South Africa cling to apartheid, yet cannot get enough of Bill Cosby, Eddy Murphy and Mr. T. (p. 12)

Recent statistics indicate that there is even a higher VCR penetration in "less diversified media environments." See Douglas A. Boyd, Joseph D. Straubhaar, and John A. Lent, *Videocassette Recorders in the Third World* (New York: Longman, 1989), and Gladys D. Glanley and Oswald H. Ganley, *Global Political Fallout: The VCR's First Decade* (Cambridge, Mass.: Program on Information Resources Policy, Harvard University, 1987).

7. The term *postmodernism* has been used in literature since the early 1960s, since the middle 1970s in architecture, and since the late 1970s in dance and performance, but it has been applied to film and television only since the late 1980s. In film studies, the term usually describes a style, not the social dimension of postmodernity. To clarify the debate about the postmodern, I use *modernism* and *postmodernism* to denote cultural movements, and *modernity* and *postmodernity* to refer to their social and philosophical dimensions. (See Jochen Schulte-Sasse, "Modernity and Modernism, Postmodernity and Postmodernism: Framing the Issue," *Cultural Critique* 5 [1986–1987], 5–22.) Film theorists have not fully related the postmodern to modernism or modernity. To characterize cinematic and televisual apparatuses in postmodernity, one has to go beyond a stylistic description of diegetic properties and consider the apparatus of reproduction and distribution.

Anne Friedberg

Jameson, one of the key monographers of postmodernity, catalogs its symptoms as "*the disappearance of history*, the way in which our entire contemporary social system has little by little begun to lose its capacity to retain its own past, has begun to live in *a perpetual present* and in a perpetual change that obliterates traditions." (Emphasis added.) See Fredric Jameson, "Postmodernism and Consumer Society," *The Anti-Aesthetic*, ed. Hal Foster [Port Townsend, Wash.: Bay Press, 1983], p. 125].

Although television differs greatly from the cinema in its perceptual transmission and reception, it has, in the age of the VCR, produced many of the same subjective manipulations of space and time.

8. *Das Passagen-Werk* (the Arcades Project) occupied Benjamin from 1927 until his death in 1940; it was not published in his lifetime. The fragments of Benjamin's *Das Passagen-Werk*, edited by Rolf Tiedemann, were published in two volumes in 1983 (Frankfurt am Main: Suhrkamp, 1983); the German edition was translated into French and published 1989 as *Paris, Capitale du XIXe siècle: le livre des passages*, trans. Jean Lacoste (Paris: Editions du Cerf, 1989). Only a few shards of the work have appeared in English. See *Charles Baudelaire: A Lyric Poet in the Era of High Capitalism*, trans. Quintin Hoare and Harry Zohn (London: Verso, 1983); "N [Theoretics of Knowledge; Theory of Progress]," *The Philosophical Forum*, trans. Leigh Hafrey and Richard Sieburth, XV:1-2 (1983–1984), 1–40. Susan Buck Morss's *Dialectics of Seeing* (Cambridge, Mass.: Massachusetts Institute of Technology Press, 1989) provides an excellent concordance to the massive Arcades Project.

9. Walter Benjamin, "The Paris of the Second Empire in Baudelaire," in *Charles Baudelaire: A Lyric Poet in the Era of High Capitalism*, trans. Harry Zohn (London: Verso, 1983), p. 36.

10. For Siegfried Kracauer, this form of distracted observation reached its epitome in the "mass ornament" of the cinema. See "Kult der Zerstreuung," trans. Tom Levin, *New German Critique* 40 (Winter 1987). See also Heide Schlupmann, "Kracauer's Phenomenology of Film," in the same issue.

11. Walter Benjamin, "Paris, Capital of the Nineteenth Century," in *Charles Baudelaire: A Lyric Poet in the Era of High Capitalism*, trans. Quintin Hoare (London: Verso, 1983), p. 170.

12. Susan Buck-Morss, "The Flaneur, the Sandwichman and the Whore: The Politics of Loitering," *New German Critique* 39 (Fall 1986), 99–140.

13. "A une passante," is the poem that Benjamin discusses in the *Flâneur* section of "The Paris of the Second Empire in Baudelaire." See also William Chapman Sharpe, "Poet as *Passant*: Baudelaire's 'Holy Prostitution,'" in *Unreal Cities: Urban Figuration in Wordsworth, Baudelaire, Whitman, Eliot, and Williams* (Baltimore: Johns Hopkins University Press, 1990).

14. See Rachel Bowlby, *Just Looking: Consumer Culture in Dreiser, Gissing and Zola* (New York: Metheun, 1985), p. 6.

15. See Susan Porter-Benson, *Counter Cultures: Saleswomen, Managers, and Customers in American Department Stores, 1890–1940* (Urbana: University of Illinois Press, 1986); Michael B. Miller, *The Bon Marché: Bourgeois Culture and the Department Store 1869–1920* (Princeton, N.J.: Princeton University Press, 1981); William R. Leach, "Transformations in a Culture of Consumption: Women and Department Stores, 1890–1925," *Journal of American History* 71:2 (1984); and Elizabeth Wilson, *Adorned in Dreams: Fashion and Modernity* (London: Virago Press, 1985).

16. Walter Benjamin, "Capital," p. 171.

17. Charles Baudelaire, *Les Fleurs du Mal*, poem 26, trans. Richard Howard (Boston: David R. Godine, 1983).

18. The impossibility of a *flâneuse* has been forcefully argued by Janet Wolff. Wolff contends that modernity was identified predominantly with the public sphere of work,

politics, and urban life—realms that were exclusively male. In her account, the literature of modernity accepts the confinement of women to the private sphere and hence fails to delineate women's experience. Certainly the literature Wolff surveys—that of Simmel, Baudelaire, and Benjamin—describes the experience of men in the public sphere, from which women are invisible. Even though Wolff wants to produce a feminist sociology that would supply the experiences of women, it would seem important to also turn to some literary texts by female "modernists." Or, as Griselda Pollack has shown with Berthe Morisot and Mary Cassatt, paintings by nineteenth-century women provide vivid illustration of women in urban spaces. And, although Wolff does mention that consumerism is a central aspect of modernity and that establishment of the department store in the 1850s and 1860s created an new arena for the public appearance of women, she does not consider the female consumer as an important figure. Yet it is precisely here that I find the origins of the new social character, the *flâneuse*. See Janet Wolff, "The Invisible Flâneuse: Women and the Literature of Modernity," *Theory, Culture and Society* 2:7 (1985), and Griselda Pollock, "Modernity and Spaces of Femininity," in *Vision and Difference: Femininity, Feminism and the Histories of Art* (London: Routledge, 1988), pp. 50–90.

19. Benjamin, "Capital," p. 170.

20. Bowlby describes shopping as a "new feminine leisure activity" (*Just Looking*, p. 19); see also T. J. Jackson Lears, "From Salvation to Self-Regulation: Advertising and the Therapeutic Roots of the Consumer Culture, 1880–1930," in Richard Wightman Fox and T. J. Jackson Lears, ed., *The Culture of Consumption: Critical Essays in American History 1880–1980* (New York: Pantheon, 1983), pp. 1–39.

21. Émile Zola, *The Ladies Paradise (Au Bonheur des Dames)* (Berkeley and Los Angeles: University of California Press, 1991), p. 8.

22. Ibid., pp. 16–17.

23. Ibid., p. 208.

24. Ibid.

25. L. Frank Baum, *The Art of Decorating Dry Goods Windows and Interiors* (Chicago: Show Window, 1900). From 1897 to 1902, Baum edited the trade journal *The Show Window: A Monthly Journal of Practical Window Trimming*. Stuart Culver relates Baum's work on window display to the representation of advertising and consumerism in *The Wonderful Wizard of Oz*. See Stuart Culver, "What Manikins Want: *The Wonderful World of Oz* and *The Art of Decorating Dry Goods Windows*," *Representations* 21 (1988), 97–116.

26. Baum, *The Art of Decorating Dry Goods Windows*, p. 146.

27. Ibid., p. 82.

28. See Charles Eckert, "The Carole Lombard in Macy's Window," *Quarterly Review of Film Studies* 3:1 (Winter 1978); Mary Ann Doane, *The Desire to Desire* (Bloomington: University of Indiana Press, 1987); and Jane Gaines, "The Queen Christina Tie-Ups: Convergence of Show Window and Screen," in the special issue "Female Representation and Consumer Culture," ed. Michael Renov and Jane Gaines, *Quarterly Review of Film and Video* 11:1 (Winter 1989).

29. Rhona J. Berenstein elaborated on the fluidity of gender and sexual orientation in cinema spectatorship in her discussion of viewing as transvestism and spectatorship as drag, in her chapter "Spectatorship as Drag: The Act of Viewing and Classic Horror Cinema," in this volume.

30. Phantasmagorias, panoramas, and dioramas—devices that concealed their machinery—were dependent on the relative immobility of their spectators, who enjoyed the illusion of the presence of virtual figures. Other optical entertainments requiring viewing devices—the stereoscope, the phenakistoscope—were dependent on quite different optical principles and hence produced quite different subjective effects. For example, both the stereoscope and the phenakistoscope rely on similar perceptual principles—based on the

reconciliation of differences (à la Helmholtz's "differential hypothesis")—but the two apparatuses produce different effects. The stereoscopic spectator is concerned with overcoming binocular disparity, a spatial disjunction. The phenakistoscope viewer is perceptually overcoming a temporal disjunction.

31. In 1787 in Edinburgh, Barker took out a patent for panoramic painting and opened the first completely circular panorama in Leicester Square in London in 1792.

In 1800, the Passage des Panoramas in Paris was built to connect the Palais Royal to the panorama building on boulevard Montmartre. Visitors entered the cylindrical panorama building through the arcade; the same glass-and-iron skylight illuminated both structures. In the two interior rotundas were two paintings—one that displayed a view of Paris from the Tuileries and another that showed the British evacuation during the Battle of Toulon in 1793. The immediate city—the Paris of only blocks away—was presented to itself, but so were a distant city (Toulon) and a distant time (six years before).

32. Helmut Gernsheim and Alison Gernsheim, *L. J. M. Daguerre: The History of the Diorama and the Daguerrotype* (New York: Dover, 1968), p. 6.

33. "Paris—Capital of the Nineteenth Century," trans. Edmund Jephcott, in *Reflections* (New York: Harcourt Brace Jovanovich, 1979), p. 150.

34. Richard D. Altick, *The Shows of London* (Cambridge, Mass.: Harvard University Press, 1978), p. 180. The London Coliseum had a show called A Trip Around the World, in 1785.

35. Gernsheim and Gernsheim, *L. J. M. Daguerre*, pp. 19–20.

36. When the diorama opened in Paris in 1822, it displayed two distant tableaux: "The Valley of Sarnen" (a scene from Switzerland) and "Interior of Trinity Church—Canterbury Cathedral" (a scene from England). Of the thirty-two scenes exhibited during the diorama's seventeen years of existence, ten of the paintings were interiors of distant chapels or cathedrals. See Gernsheim and Gernsheim, *L. J. M. Daguerre*, pp. 182–84.

37. Gernsheim and Gernsheim, *L. J. M. Daguerre*, p. 18.

38. Ibid., p. 43.

39. The concept of spectatorship in the *Pleorama* is much like that of the later "Hale's Tours," introduced by George C. Hale of Kansas City in 1903, in which the spectator sat in a simulated railway car and viewed a film taken from the front of a railway engine.

40. Johann Friedrich Geist, *Arcades: History of a Building Type*, trans. Jane O. Newman and John Smith (Cambridge, Mass.: Massachusetts Institute of Technology Press, 1985), p. 490.

41. Though the Musée Grevin is still in the Passage Jouffroy today, it has opened a branch in the underground shopping mall of Les Halles. This expansion proves that the museum's spectacles—like those of the multiplex cinemas in the mall and of the Vidéothèque, also located there—are extensions of the mobilized gaze that travels past shop windows.

42. Photography supplanted, in Roland Barthes's terms, the "here-now" with the "having-been-there." For Barthes, who distinguished between the photograph's essential *pastness* and the film's essential *presentness*, the film fused the spatial immediacy of a virtual gaze with temporal *presentness* (a "being-there"). See Roland Barthes, "Rhetoric of the Image," in *Image, Music, Text*, trans. Stephen Heath (New York: Hill & Wang, 1977), pp. 44–45.

> The type of consciousness the photograph involves is indeed truly unprecedented, since it establishes not a consciousness of the *being-there* of the thing (which any copy would provoke) but an awareness of its *having-been-there*. What we have is a new space-time category: Spatial immediacy and temporal anteriority, the photograph being an illogical conjunction between the *here-now*

and the *there-then* . . . . Film can no longer be seen as animated photographs: the *having-been-there* gives way to a *being-there* of the thing.

43. Quoted in chapter 12, "Paul and 'The Time Machine,'" of Terry Ramsaye's *A Million and One Nights* (New York: Simon & Schuster, 1926), pp. 152–61. This was reprinted in *Focus on the Science Fiction Film*, ed. William Johnson (Englewood Cliffs, N.J.: Prentice-Hall, 1972), pp. 18–26. The following references are contained in the Johnson edition.

44. Ramsaye, "Paul and 'The Time Machine,'" p. 18.

45. Ibid., p. 23. The Paul patent application included features of forward and backward movement through time. Ramsaye writes, "The photoplay of today moves backward and forward through Time with facile miracle from the Present into the Past and Future by the cutback, flashback, and vision scenes (p. 22).

46. Ibid., pp. 20–21.

47. For a history and analysis of the Home Shopping Network, see Mimi White, "Watching the Girls Go Buy: Shop-at-Home Television," in *Tele-Advising: Therapeutic Discourse in American Television* (Chapel Hill & London: University of North Carolina Press, 1992).

48. In a chilling document of market calculation entitled "The Miniaturization of Communications," Don Pepper, executive vice president of a Madison Avenue business development research group, has assessed the change from production economies to consumer information economies. Pepper predicts the future of communications in the format change from *package* to *conduit*.

> Conduits are on-line, on-stream, continuously broadcast or con-tinuously transmitted. Packages are discrete, tangible things you can take with you . . . a video cassette is a package. . . . In fifty years or so, you'll have almost no packages at all. . . . *You'll no longer be able to go down to the store and buy a video cassette or rent one, because there won't be any such store. Instead you'll pick up your phone and dial a toll free number. You'll hook up your modem on your laser compact disc recorder, and the film you want will be encoded on the disc.*

The cable television Viewer's Choice channel already delivers a pay-per-view movie to any cable subscriber who calls a toll-free number to request it.

49. A spate of recent publications have attempted to assess the vices, virtues, and possibilities of virtual technology: see Myron W. Krueger, *Artificial Reality I* (Reading, Mass.: Addison-Wesley, 1990), and *Artificial Reality II* (Reading, Mass.: Addison-Wesley, 1990); Sandra K. Helsel and Judith Paris Roth, ed., *Virtual Reality: Theory, Practice, and Promise* (Westport, Conn.: Meckler, 1991); Howard Rheingold, *Virtual Reality* (New York: Simon & Schuster, 1991); Gareth Branwyn, "Salon Virtual," *Utne Reader* (March/April 1991); Benjamin Wooley, *Virtual Worlds: A Journey in Hype and Hyperreality* (Cambridge, Mass.: Blackwell, 1992); Steve Aukstakalnis and David Blatner, *Silicon Mirage: The Art and Science of Virtual Reality* (Berkeley: Peachpit Press, 1992); Rudy Rucker, R. U. Sirius and Queen Mu, ed., *Mondo 2000: A User's Guide to the New Edge* (New York: Harper Perennial, 1992); and Ken Pimentel and Kevin Teixeira, *Virtual Reality: Through the Looking Glass* (New York: Intel/Windcrest/McGraw-Hill, 1993).

50. Meaghan Morris argues, "Like effective shopping, feminist criticism also allows the possibility of rejecting what we see, and refusing to take it as 'given.'" See Meaghan Morris, "Things to Do with Shopping Centres," *Center for Twentieth Century Studies*, Working Paper 1 (1988), p. 5.

51. Ernest Hahn, "The Shopping Center Industry," in *Shopping Centers & Malls*, ed. Robert Davis Rathbun (New York: Retail Reporting Corporation, 1986), p. 7.

52. Quoted in Leon Whiteson, "'This Is Our Time': And Architect Jon Jerde Is Trying to Write a 'Different Urban Script' for L.A.," *Los Angeles Times,* January 20, 1988, 5:1–2.

53. William Kowinski, *The Malling of America* (New York: William Morrow, 1985), p. 24.

54. Ibid., p. 20.

55. Ibid., p. 22.

56. Ibid., p. 23.

57. Kowinski catches some of these apparatical similarities, but does not develop them: "Watching TV, we can be everywhere without being anywhere in particular . . . the mall is like three dimensional television." Ibid., p. 74.

58. Following the historical precedents of department store tie-ins, in display windows and merchandising (see Jane Gaines, "The Queen Christina Tie-Ups"; Miriam Hansen, "Adventures of Goldilocks: Spectatorship, Consumerism and Public Life," *Camera Obscura* 22 [1990], 51–71), Warner Bros. has recently opened Studio Stores in malls in Beverly Hills, California; Chicago; Fairfax, Virginia; and Danbury, Connecticut, which sell videotapes, stuffed animals, and clothing all licensed from Warner's cartoon characters. Disney has more than 120 stores in malls worldwide. At this writing, Disney promises to have another hundred or so stores in Japan alone to follow the opening of Tokyo Disneyland.

59. Mary Ann Doane appeals to Joan Riviere's concept of a gender-mobile "masquerade" to describe the imaginary activity of the female spectator. See Mary Ann Doane, "Film and the Masquerade: Theorising the Female Spectator," *Screen* 23:3-4 (1982), 74–87.

60. See Fredric Jameson, "Postmodernism and Consumer Society," in *The Anti-Aesthetic,* ed. Hal Foster (Port Townsend, Wash.: Bay Press, 1983), pp. 11–125, and "Postmodernism, or the Cultural Logic of Late Capitalism," *New Left Review* 146 (1984), 53–92.

61. Jameson, "Consumer Society," p. 117.

62. Jameson, "Cultural Logic," 68.

63. Christian Metz, "Story/Discourse (A Note on Two Kinds of Voyeurism)," trans. Celia Britton and Annwyl Williams, in *The Imaginary Signifier* (Bloomington: Indiana University Press, 1982), pp. 91–97.

64. If Benjamin compared flânerie to the distracted style of newspaper journalism in the *feuilleton,* it does not take much to see the television spectator's use of a remote control device—the present-day equivalent of the radio listener's channel switching, which Theodor Adorno calls *aural flânerie* (See Buck-Morss, "Flaneur," p. 105).

65. Michel DeCerteau uses the metaphor of apartment rental—space borrowed by a transient—to illustrate the elsewhere produced by reading: "The procedures of contemporary consumption appear to constitute a subtle art of 'renters' who know how to insinuate their countless differences into the dominant text" (*The Practice of Everyday Life,* p. xxii).

While deCerteau details the spatial displacement of reading, he says little about temporal displacement. These displacements become less figurative when we view movies and videotapes. We not only "rent" fictional spaces, but we "rent" other times. Michel DeCerteau, *The Practice of Everyday Life,* trans. Steven Rendall (Berkeley and Los Angeles: University of California Press, 1984).

66. "The Third Window: An Interview with Paul Virilio," trans. Yvonne Shafir, in *Global Television,* ed. Cynthia Schneider and Brian Wallis (Cambridge, Mass.: Massachusetts Institute of Technology Press, 1988), pp. 185–97.

67. Television's ideology of presence—what Raymond Williams calls flow or what Stephen Heath and Gillian Skirrow (1977) refer to as absolute presence—has traditionally distinguished televisual spectatorship from its cinematic counterparts. Raymond Williams's study, *Television: Technology and Cultural Form,* described the ways in which

television altered social relationships, basic perceptions of reality, the scale and form of society, and the central processes of family, cultural, and social life. Separating television and cinema technologies from earlier public technology such as the railroad and city lighting, Williams described television as a technology that "served an at once mobile and home-centered way of living: a form of *mobile privatization*" (p. 26). Television developed in a sociohistorical context, Williams argues, wherein the social need for mobility occurred at the same time as a trend toward self-sufficiency. Williams's term, *mobile privatization*, takes the same virtual mobility that I have been emphasizing and places it in the privatized space of the home (*tele*[far]-*vision:* vision from elsewhere). The commodity-experience of early television spectatorship relied on the presence of the television set and the potential of live broadcasts in the living room.

In Williams's categories, the differences between the televisual and the cinematic become more distinct. To Williams, the technology of the televisual broadcast meant a centralized origin and an individual receiver. Cinematic technology offered a more diverse (Williams says "specific and discrete") set of origins and a collective system of reception. Whereas the telephone developed as a privatized system of individual-to-individual communication, the radio developed as a means to deliver words and music to a large audience at once. Williams emphasizes the radio as a model for television broadcasting.

Precinema, Early Cinema and Late Cinema: Historians View Spectators

Vanessa R. Schwartz

Cinematic Spectatorship
before the Apparatus:
The Public Taste for Reality
in Fin-de-Siècle Paris

"No people in the world are so fond of amusements—or *distractions* as they term them—as Parisians. Morning, noon and night, summer and winter, there is always something to be seen and a large portion of the population seems absorbed in the pursuit of pleasure."[1] Cassell's Paris guidebook confirmed that many visitors to France's capital expected to find a good time. Paris, by the last third of the nineteenth century, had become the European center of the burgeoning entertainment industry. But more important than pleasure, perhaps, the guidebook promised that "There is always something to be seen." Life in Paris, I would like to suggest, became powerfully identified with spectacle. Yet, real life was experienced as a show at the same time as shows became increasingly lifelike.

By examining a field of novel cultural forms and practices in late nineteenth-century Paris, I hope to situate early cinema as a part of the public taste for reality. Rather than understand cinematic spectatorship through a universal and timeless theory of psychic spectatorship constructed in direct relation to the cinematic apparatus or as an idealized vision produced through discourses about perception and embodied in technological innovations, I frame spectatorship within a particular cultural moment. As Guiliana Bruno has suggested, spectatorship is most aptly conceived of as a "kinetic affair"—a practice whose history, I would further suggest, can be understood by examining both the relation between the content and the form of technologies that produce possibilities for observation and the discourse produced by the experiences of those technologies in a specific context.[2] By looking at practices that were coterminous with cinema in its initial moments, I suggest that cinema ended up as more than just one in a series of novel gadgets, because it incorporated many elements that already could be found in diverse aspects of so-called modern life.

In three sites of popular pleasure in late nineteenth-century France—the unexpected location of the Paris Morgue, wax museums and panoramas, I situate *flânerie*, which has begun to be used as a shorthand for describing the new, mobilized gaze of the precinematic spectator—in its proper context as a cultural activity for those who participated in Parisian life—claiming that the late-nineteenth century offered a sort of flânerie for the masses.[3] But I also connect this flânerie to the new mass press, which served as a printed digest of the *flâneur*'s roving eye. Spectacle and narrative were integrally linked in Paris's burgeoning mass culture: the realism of spectacle was in fact often contingent on the familiarity of real-life newspaper narratives.

The Paris Morgue

"There are few people having visited Paris who do not know the Morgue," wrote Parisian social commentator Hughes Leroux in 1888.[4] Listed in practically every guidebook to the city, a fixture of Thomas Cook's tours to Paris, and a "part of every conscientious provincial's first visit to the capital,"[5] the Morgue had both regulars and large crowds of as many as 40,000 on its big days, when the story of a crime circulated through the popular press and curious visitors lined the sidewalk waiting to file through the *salle d'exposition* to see the victim.

A large and socially diverse audience went to the Morgue. The crowd was composed of "men, women and children," of "workers . . . *petits rentiers* . . . *flâneurs* . . . women workers . . . and ladies."[6] In fact, the location was so well frequented that vendors lined the sidewalk outside hawking oranges, cookies, and coconut slices.[7]

The morgue in question was built in 1864 in the center of Paris, behind the cathedral of Nôtre-Dame on the Quai de l'Archevêché (where the Memorial to the Deportation stands today) and was open to the public seven days a week from dawn to dusk. The institution began in the eighteenth century as the *basse-geôle* of the prison, the Châtelet, in a dark and dank room where "visitors could only present themselves one after another; they were forced to press their faces against a narrow opening"[8] in order to identify corpses that had been found in the public domain. By the late-nineteenth century, the Morgue, whose name comes from an archaic verb meaning to stare, featured a *salle d'exposition*, wherein two rows of corpses, each on its own marble slab, were displayed behind a large glass window, which had green curtains hanging at each side. In contrast to the situation at the *basse-geôle*, large crowds could gather and gaze at this almost theatrical display. Of the three large doors at the front, the middle one remained shut and visitors filed through, entering at the left and exiting at the right, prompting the Morgue's registrar to comment that it was nothing more than an *entresort* (a carnival attraction one paid to see by walking through a barrack and gaping at the sight within).[9]

The *salle d'exposition* was comparable to other displays that dotted the Parisian landscape in the second half of the nineteenth century. Ernest Cherbuliez, in an article in *La Revue des deux mondes*, highlighted this quality by recounting an anecdote in which a man walked down the Boulevard Sébastopol, stopped in front of a store window, and asked the window dressers for work. They suggested he ask at the Morgue.[10]

Most often, however, the Morgue was celebrated as public theater. Emile Zola remarked in *Thérèse Raquin* that it was a "show that was affordable to all. . . The door is open, enter those who will."[11] A poem in a popular edition called *Les Chansons de la Morgue* described the scene in the *salle d'exposition:* "The crowd, gay and without remorse, comes to the theater to take its place."[12] Upon the closing of the Morgue to the general public in March 1907, one journalist protested:

> The Morgue has been the first this year among theaters to announce its closing. . . . As for the spectators, they have no right to say anything because they didn't pay. There were no subscribers, only regulars, because the show was always free. It was the first free theater for the people. And they tell us it's being canceled. People, the hour of social justice has not yet arrived.[13]

In a time of increasingly private and commercial entertainment, the Morgue was open and free, and the display of dead bodies existed for the public to come and see. As a municipal institution, however, the Morgue's principal goal was to serve as a depository for the anonymous dead, whose public display administrators hoped might aid in establishing their identity. Yet the Paris Morgue was like no other municipal institution. Despite its location in the shadows of Nôtre-Dame, its deliberately undramatic facade, and its seemingly somber subject matter, the Morgue was "one of the most popular sights in Paris."[14] The identification of dead bodies was turned into a show.

Why did this show attract so many visitors? The historical record does not offer many direct answers. Looking at descriptions of the Morgue in the popular press and in administrative literature, however, offers a means through which one may attempt to reconstruct the Morgue's allure. The vast majority of visitors probably did not go to the Morgue thinking they actually might recognize a corpse. They went to look at real dead bodies under the pretense of acting out of civic duty. This was public voyeurism—flânerie in the service of the state.

Many commentators suggested that the Morgue satisfied and reinforced the desire to look, which permeated much of Parisian culture in the late nineteenth century. Clovis Pierre, the Morgue's registrar and a sometime poet, wrote that visitors came "to exercise their retinas at the window."[15] Why, however, go to the Morgue when there was so much to see in the city most often associated with the "spectacle of modern life?"[16]

The Morgue served as a visual auxiliary to the newspaper, staging the recently dead who had been sensationally detailed by the printed word. The late nineteenth century in France has been called the "golden age of the press"[17] and it is critical to understand the central role it played in the development of Parisian spectacle. Current events became the daily fare of the popular Parisian dailies, whose overall circulation increased 250 percent between 1880 and 1914.[18] Newspapers replaced opinion with so-called truth as the world "entered the age of information."[19] In the Parisian press, political life took a backseat to theater openings, horse races, and charity events, but it was the *faits divers*—reports of horrible accidents and sensational crimes—that filled the columns and the coffers above all else.

The *fait diver* was a popular newspaper rubric that reproduced in extraordinary detail, both written and visual, representations of a sensational reality. In addition to the sensationalism of the *fait diver*, newspapers offered serial novels. Clearly demarcated from the rest of the newspaper by a bar across the bottom of the page, these popular narratives were often based on actual newspaper stories, especially the *fait diver*.

Because of its featured role in so many *faits divers*, the Morgue appeared regularly in the newspaper. As Alphonse Devergie, medical inspector of the Morgue, explained, "Once the newspapers announce a crime, one sees a great number of the curious arrive at the Morgue."[20] And, of course, when a large crowd gathered at the Morgue, *it* then became the subject of further news reports, which in turn kept the corpse, the unsolved crime, and the Morgue in the public eye, guaranteeing a flow of people to the Quai de l'Archevêché.

Press coverage heightened public awareness and interest. Guillot argued that the newspaper constituted a source that stimulated public interest for what "in newspaper jargon is called the *plat du jour.*"[21] He believed that all the reporting turned the Morgue into a "glass house" and that if the Morgue could be considered a theater of crime, then the newspaper was its program.[22] One of the Morgue registrars argued that newspaper reading prompted visits by women workers to the Morgue because the women's spirits had been haunted by the newspapers' serial novels.[23] Other comments suggest that the Morgue was a version of the newspaper's *feuilleton*. *L'Éclair*, for example, described the Morgue as "this living illustration of a serial-novel mystery."[24]

Some people believed that the popularity of public visits to the Morgue, like interest in the newspaper itself, stemmed from the public interest in so-called reality. "What if rather than your stories, your most frightening paintings, they prefer reality and what a reality," Firimin Maillard, one of the Morgue's earliest historians, suggested.[25] An article in *Le Paris* boasted that the Morgue was worth a visit because what one saw "are not imitations, not *trompe l'oeil.*"[26] Yet, while the newspapers may have encouraged many visits, a look at one of the many *causes célèbres* of the Morgue reveals that the show in the window was far more spectacular than the ordinary placement of corpses on slabs facing the public.

In August 1886, the cover of *Le Journal Illustré* featured a doyenne of the Morgue, the "Enfant de la Rue du Vert-Bois"—a four-year-old girl found on July 29, 1886, in a stairwell at 47 Rue du Vert-Bois, near the Conservatoire des Arts et Métiers. The corpse, which was transferred to the Morgue, showed no apparent signs of injury except a slight bruise on the right hand. The newspapers reported that the display attracted "a considerable crowd," which by August 3 was estimated at about 50,000.[27] The body, clothed in a dress, was mounted in the *salle d'exposition*, "on a chair covered in a red cloth that brought out the paleness of the little dead one even more."[28] *Le Matin* reported that despite the "service d'ordre" that had been established, the size of the crowd forced

PARIS. — LE MYSTERE DE LA RUE DU VERT-BOIS : EXPOSITION DU PETIT CADAVRE A LA MORGUE. (Dessin d'après nature de M. Paul Destez.)

Display of corpse of the "Child of Vert-Bois Street." Le Monde Illustré, *August 15, 1886.*

traffic to a halt and vendors hawked coconut, gingerbread, and toys, turning the Quai de l'Archevêché into "a genuine fairgrounds."[29] On August 5, the papers reported severe disorder: "The mob rushes the doors with savage cries; fallen hats are tromped on, parasols and umbrellas are broken, and yesterday, women fell sick, having been half suffocated."[30]

By then, *Le Matin* estimated that 150,000 people had filed past the body (in groups of no more than fifty at a time, in rows of five, who were forbidden to stand in front of the glass). Each night the corpse was put in a refrigerated case to preserve it. In order to avoid altering it in any way, Morgue attendants simply strapped the corpse to the red velvet chair and deposited the complete display in the refrigerator.

Because of the state of decomposition, Morgue doctors decided to perform an autopsy on August 6.[31] *Le Petit Journal* reported the sentiments of the crowds that had gathered that day only to "have had the disappointment not to have caught sight of the child displayed on its little chair."[32] After the autopsy, doctors concluded that the child had died a natural death, having suffocated by choking on an earthworm.

Images of both the child and the crowd at the Morgue appeared in the popular press throughout the period of display. *Le Journal Illustré* featured an illustrated narration—a sort of illustrated serial novel and a genre that often accompanied a cause célèbre at the Morgue. The illustrated journal showed the building on the Rue du Vert-Bois, two men discovering the corpse, a crowd outside the morgue, and the display of the corpse in the salle d'exposition. When the illustrations appeared on August 15, part of the case had already been resolved, but the child's civil status and why she had been abandoned remained a mystery. She was buried on August 17, and although the photograph remained on display at the entrance, the child went unidentified.[33]

The Morgue's visitors came neither to identify corpses nor simply to see them laid out on slabs. No doubt the Morgue was a morbid attraction.[34] More significant, however, it was "part of the catalogued curiosities, of things to see, under the same heading as the Eiffel Tower, Yvette Guilbert, and the catacombs."[35] In other words, this public service was experienced as a Parisian attraction. Newspapers featured stories about the crowds at the Morgue, and like newspapers, the Morgue re-presented a spectacularized Parisian life. The *salle d'exposition*, its curtain, the lines outside, corpses dressed and seated on chairs, and newspaper illustrations guaranteed that the Morgue's reality was re-presented, mediated, orchestrated, and spectacularized.

In part a visual digest of the printed word, the Morgue transformed real life into spectacle. It is worth noting that the Morgue was finally closed to the public in 1907—a year often considered a watershed among cinema historians and which in France was marked, in particular, by a proliferation of institutions devoted exclusively to cinema.[36] The audience, it seems, moved from the *salle d'exposition* to the *salle du cinéma*.

In trying to explain the Morgue's popularity, its administrative director remarked, "The Morgue is considered in Paris like a museum that is much more fascinating than even a wax museum because the people displayed are real flesh and blood."[37] He was not alone, however, in drawing a connection between these two institutions of Parisian spectacle.

The Musée Grévin

When the Musée Grévin opened in 1882 on the boulevard Montmarte, in the heart of "modern" Paris, a newspaper cartoon linked the wax museum to the already-popular Morgue. In it two working-class men gape at a wax figure laid out on a slab. One says, "Geez, you'd think it was a real stiff." His friend replies, "This is almost as much fun as the real Morgue."[38] An immediate success, the museum attracted a half a million visitors yearly and remains open to this day. An emblem of the burgeoning entertainment industry, one reviewer noted its fundamental tie to the public: "It is not from the Institute that Grévin will seek approval, it's from the public."[39] Why did the wax museum capture the public imagination in fin-de-siècle Paris?

The Musée Grévin was modeled, in part, after London's very popular Madame Tussaud's, itself a direct descendant of the well-known wax cabinet of Philippe Curtius, popular in Paris during the revolutionary era. Unlike Madame Tussaud's, the Musée Grévin was founded by a well-known boulevard journalist Arthur Meyer and the newspaper caricaturist Alfred Grévin. Both men envisaged the museum as an improvement upon newspapers, as a more realistic way to satisfy the public interest in *les actualités* (current events). The museum's founders promised their display would "represent the principal current events with scrupulous fidelity and striking precision . . . [It will be] a living newspaper."[40]

The two also believed that written reporting did not entirely satisfy the public. As the preface to the museum's first catalog, written by *Le Figaro*'s Albert Wolff, explained,

> By adding an image to the text, illustrated newspapers . . . have made a decisive advance in modern communication. The museum's founders appraised, with reason, that one could go even further and create a *journal plastique*, where the public would find those people that occupied their attention, reproduced with a scrupulous respect for nature.[41]

Critics constantly remarked on the museum's verisimilitude, calling it a chronicle in action and an animated newspaper despite the fact that the tableaux did not move.

The realism of the displays relied on many devices other than the lifelike quality of the wax figures themselves. Accessories, ornaments, and the framing device of the tableau worked together to effect the real. For example, the museum used authentic accessories. The figure of Victor Hugo held his real pen, and a tableau of the death of Marat featured the actual tub in which he had been murdered (and for which the museum paid a hefty 5,000 francs), a genuine soldier's pike from the revolutionary era, and a 1791 edition of *l'Ami du Peuple*—the newspaper edited by the murdered revolutionary. The figure of Zola wore a suit donated by the author.

A tableau's realism might also be derived from its status as an authentic copy. For example, the president's library was a replica of the room at the Elysée, and a tableau of a scene from the new opera *Françoise de Rimini* was the "exact and absolute facsimile of the National Academy of Music," from the costumes to the furniture and the sets.[42]

The tableaux created recognizable, taxonomical, and appropriate settings for the figures—mini-narratives in the form of peepholes into Parisian life. As the museum catalog explained,

> It was necessary to make the museum interesting not only because of the exact likeness of the characters, but also by the composition of groups, in showing individuals in their milieu.[43]

Left unsaid, however, was the necessity of the tableaux for public recognition of the figures. Visitors, for the most part, had probably never seen either in a newspaper or in person most of the subjects represented at the museum because the only mass-produced visual images available were at best color engravings. Photographs were not to be easily reproduced for newspapers until the twentieth century. The tableaux and their abundant details—whether genuine objects or copies—were essential in effecting verisimilitude simply because of the crowd's inability to actually assess the likeness of the various personalities represented, for they had either no visual basis for comparison or one that was hardly itself an exact copy.

Aside from the vivacity of the wax sculpture and taxonomic groupings of the dioramas, the museum formed a pantheon that relied on the public's recognition of and familiarity with its characters; its success dwelled ultimately in the eye of the beholder. Rather than a definitive collection decided on from above like at most museums, the Musée Grévin held a rapidly changing collection whose content was contingent on the public's interest and visual recognition. Whereas traditional pantheons may be characterized by their selectivity, the Musée Grévin boasted of its range and inclusiveness. The novelist Paul Bourget celebrated the museum: "In three or four rooms is it not the abridged version of the modern city?"[44]

As a broad-ranging pantheon, the museum mimicked the newspaper's form: tableaux most often stood side by side in no particular relation to one another, as did newspaper columns filled with seemingly unconnected stories.[45] The juxtaposition of political leaders, actors, and artists attested to the prominence of the modern social order: one dominated by celebrity and based on popularity. With what seemed like "intrepid whimsy," celebrities filled this "Parisian Pantheon."[46] That the café-concert singer Yvette Guilbert and the president of the republic might stand side by side suggested that the wax museum also echoed the basis of political legitimacy in Third Republic France, in which politicians—like performers and artists—rose and fell seemingly by virtue of the crowd's fancy. The wax museum materialized that new social order based on the whims of the crowd.

While representing a social order created in and by the public eye, the museum also offered its visitors visual privilege through seeming proximity to the celebrities. One newspaper review explained, "The likenesses of our great men, of our famous artists or society people pleases us . . . and it is to see them up close that the public crowds to the Musée Grévin."[47]

Beyond representing celebrities, the tableaux also afforded museum-goers something special: an up-close-and-personal view of dignitaries who might otherwise be seen only at official functions, if seen at all. For example, a tableau featuring Napoleon seeking shelter from the snow upon his retreat from Russia represented the emperor huddling in the cold. The catalog explained, "Napoleon's look is poignantly filled with anxiety: you can already see foreshadowed there the Empire's destiny."[48] One found the country's fate in its leader's emotional physiognomy as opposed to on the battlefields. Visitors also saw the famous explorer Savorgnan de Brazza relaxing in his tent and Bismarck meeting with the Marshall Von Moltke in a "private visit" at Varzin, where he "often rested from the fatigues of politics."[49] These tableaux personalized politics, transforming the scale of history and contemporary politics into something with which visitors might identify.

But privilege did not stop at the relation between the viewer and the subjects represented. The three-dimensional tableaux created a particular perspective between the spectator and the display, which func-

View from the Eiffel Tower. Musée Grévin, 1889. (Musée Grévin Archives, hereafter MGA.)

tioned as one of the museum's lasting attractions. At the Musée Grévin, visitors could inhabit multiple perspectives—panoramic views—at the same time as the displays often offered privileged access: peepholes into Paris.[50]

In 1889, the museum opened a tableau of the Eiffel Tower. Rather than reconstruct the sight that could be seen on the Champ de Mars, the museum offered a view, in midconstruction, of a visit by Eiffel and Exposition and Parisian officials Lockroy, Alphand, and Berger. The scene included workers who had been interrupted by the visit and who were represented as watching the visiting dignitaries. The museum visitor, therefore, saw what most people had never seen: the tower under construction—in a sort of dress rehearsal. At the same time, the scene depicted a panoramic view of Paris as it would have been seen from the second level of the Eiffel Tower. The catalog boasted that "Everything is rendered with a fidelity that can be appreciated by only the rare privileged who have already made this marvelous ascent."[51] The display represented a privileged view of a privileged view of Paris. Visitors enjoyed not

Vanessa R. Schwartz

Workers looking at dignitaries on the Eiffel Tower. Musée Grévin , 1889. (MGA.)

only a panoramic view of the city but also the peephole view of workers being interrupted by a visit of dignitaries. Not one, but three, sights confronted the museum visitor: the panoramic view of Paris, the view of the visitors Eiffel et al., and the view of the workers watching the visit.

Over the years, the Musée Grévin's tableaux featured several *coulisses*—representations of a perspective not usually accessible to most spectators and the domain most often reserved for the allegedly privileged *flâneur*. Here *their* voyeurism was extended to every visitor who could pay the museum's small admission price. The museum spectator's privilege resided in the tableau's offer of more than one view at a time: that of both a spectator of the show and a spectator of other spectators.[52] In 1885, for example, the museum represented "A Dancer's Loge" at intermission. The scene showed a dancer being visited in the dressing room by an elegant man. In 1890, that tableau was replaced by "Les Coulisses de l'Opéra: Le Foyer de la Danse." Here, the visitor simultaneously saw both onstage and offstage. The catalog underscored the tableau's privileged perspective: "all [here] works to give the spectator the illusion of a visit to so curious a corner of the grand Parisian stage, a visit only permitted an elect few."[53]

While the themes may not have been unfamiliar to at least those visitors who had attended various Impressionist salons, the display's three-dimensionality and verisimilitude were touted as effecting the illusion of presence or reality in a way that paintings simply could not. An 1887 diorama of the Comédie-Française further reveals what the wax museum offered. "A Rehearsal at the Comédie-Française" represented the director's loge during a dress rehearsal. There the museum's visitors observed Juliette Adam, editor of *La Nouvelle Revue;* Ambroise Thomas, director of the Opéra; Jules Clarétie, director of the Comédie; and Edouard Pailleron, author of *La Souris,* watching a scene from that play. The tableau was structured around its three-dimensionality and the visitor's mobility. It was assumed that the spectator would approach the tableau from the left, where the figures in the box appeared to be watching something. As spectators walked to the right, they could then see the inset of the dress rehearsal being watched, which was represented as though through the eyes of those seated in the box and which because of its angle could not really be seen by museum visitors until they aligned themselves with the visual perspective of the wax figures. The tableau's designers intended that people walk through and thus offered them movement through sequential points of view. This not only vested spectators with the power of making the scene happen through their own motion but also offered a primitive way of introducing motion into the display—an effect that the museum actively pursued in another way. In 1892, the Musée Grévin became the first institution to offer pro-jected moving images in the form of Émile Reynaud's "Pantomimes Lumineuses."[54]

If spectators' movement might have been incorporated into the museum's display, narrativity also built motion into the displays. The response to "l'Histoire d'un Crime"—the museum's serial novel—clar-ifies the imbrication of serial narrative to motion at the Musée Grévin. A series of seven tableaux, the display portrayed the vicissitudes of a crime from start to finish: the murder, the arrest, the confrontation of the murderer and his victim at the Morgue, the trial, the cell of the condemned, preparation for execution, and the execution. An early review noted that its "thrilling realism made it the display that most interested the crowd; it was difficult even to approach, the crowd was so enormous."[55] Reviewers explained, "It is a *fait divers* in seven tableaux, of an extraordinarily realistic execution which creates an intensity of

A rehearsal at the Comédie Française. Musée Grévin, 1887. (MGA.)

effect that is stunning."[56] Another simply called it a "living [live] fait divers."[57]

The enhanced realism of the series of tableaux was embedded in its familiar narrativity, while its seriality presented a sequence of freeze-frames set into motion by the spectator's walk through the display.

The Story of a Crime, 1882. Musée Grévin. The Murder. (MGA.)

The Arrest.

Confrontation with the Victim's Corpse at the Morgue.

The Trial.

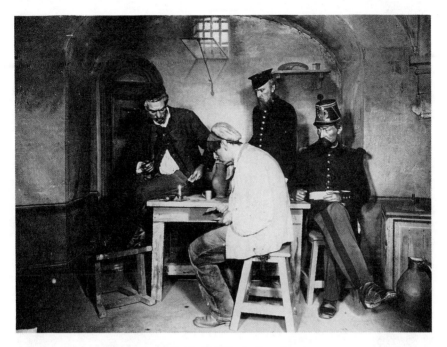

Waiting in the Cell at La Roquette.

Preparing for Execution.

The Convicted Being Led to the Guillotine.

"L'Histoire d'un Crime" also offered a familiar form of narrative in its conceptualization as a serial novel—a standard feature of almost all newspapers by the late nineteenth century. "L'Histoire d'un Crime" announced itself as a serial novel, yet was reviewed as though it were a *fait divers.* Not only does this echo the blurring between reality and fiction that characterized each genre, but it also suggests that what was so strikingly real about "l'Histoire d'un Crime" was neither its props nor its wax figures but rather its serial narrativity. The seven wax tableaux seemed more realistic than even a serial novel. The spectator's motion infused the display with its seemingly lifelike quality; such serial motion linked "l'Histoire d'un Crime" to real life. It should come as no surprise that Ferdinand Zecca, an early filmmaker at Pathé, established his fame with a 1901 film titled *l'Histoire d'un Crime,* based on the Musée Grévin display.[58]

The content of the tableaux and the way they situated spectators helped turn museum visitors into *flâneurs.* It offered the public, at the very least, views of the places and perspectives that seemed to belong only to the hounds of modern life. But visitors to the Musée Grévin also entered a plastic newspaper—a world dominated by events (the making of the sight bite, if you will) and a Pantheon of the present—where the will of the crowd might determine the content of the collection and in which the powerful were rendered familiar and personable. The technology of the tableaux offered museum visitors a world of visual mastery and access to privilege, giving them both panoptic and peephole visual fields. The Musée Grévin's dedication to the public taste for reality, its use of wax sculpture to reproduce that so-called reality, its focus on current events and rapid change, its link between both spectacle and narrative, and the scopic organization of its tableaux are all elements associated with early cinema and yet found at the Musée Grévin well before the alleged invention of film.

Panoramas

While crowds gathered at the Musée Grévin, Parisians and tourists sought out other realist entertainments. Cassell's 1884 *Guide to Paris* remarked, "with the last few years there has been a perfect eruption of panoramas in every quarter of Paris."[59] "We are entering Panoramania," declared an article in *Le Voltaire* in response to the opening of the third panorama in a year's time.[60] Indeed, that late eighteenth-century entertainment, which had virtually disappeared by midcentury, witnessed a renaissance in the 1880s and 1890s.

Panoramas and dioramas have often been discussed as technological inventions of the early nineteenth century that can be understood as antecedents to film. In particular, scholars have drawn attention to the way panoramas and dioramas marshaled vision to transport spectators in time and place through the illusion of realistic representation.[61] Rather than simply limit a discussion of panoramas and similar entertainments to the moment of their invention in the early nineteenth century, I want to show how, like wax museums, panoramas flourished in the 1880s and 1890s because they attempted to capture and re-present an already familiar version of reality—a reality in which life was captured through motion. The panoramas' realism hinged on the notion that to capture life, a display had to reproduce it as bodily and not merely visual experience.

The 1880s and 1890s witnessed a proliferation of realistic details in the panoramas. Photography helped. Some panorama painters painted from photographs; others projected enlarged slides onto the canvas and then traced the projected images. Even before photography, panoramas mixed three-dimensional objects with the painted canvas to improve the display's realism. Langlois incorporated a real set in the 1830s in his "Battle of Navarino," in which spectators found themselves on an actual battleship. In his 1881 panorama "Les Cuirassiers de Reichshoffen," depicting a defeat by French troops in the Franco-Prussian war, Poilpot used tinsel for the weapons and for the buttons on the military costumes on his canvas. The catalog of "Les Cuirassiers de Reichshoffen" acknowledged sculptor Jules Talrich for providing the wax figures that "represent the bodies strewn out on the natural setting in such an astonishing and true manner."[62]

The caricaturist Robida mocked the increasing verisimilitude of panoramas in a cartoon featuring the Panorama of the Battle of Champigny during the siege of Paris. One of the captions explained that to truly evoke the siege, visitors were forced to stay for three days and were each given only one smoked herring to eat. Another caption noted that the attraction was freezing cold and visitors could be drenched by a simulated rainstorm. With shells exploding and military music in the background, Robida concluded that "One deserved a military medal upon exiting." Although no panorama actually went so far as Robida's parody, his point was clear: people delighted in the realistic re-creation of this terrible event.

Whereas panoramas of the early nineteenth century may have provided news in a world prior to the mass press, in the 1880s panoramas served as visual corollaries of the popular press in much the same way that the wax museum did.[63] Panoramas began to represent particular moments of the daily events reported in newspapers, such as the "Tsar's Coronation" or the "Visit by the President to the Russian Fleet." A definition of panoramas and dioramas from the 1890s described their realism as generated by the subjects they represented rather than as a product of their technologies:

> Scenes of current events have the knack of attracting the crowd that is still struck with emotion about a recent event, a catastrophe, an execution or a famous assassination. They reexamine the accident or the crime in a tableau that creates the illusion of reality.[64]

Late nineteenth-century panoramas broke with traditional, landscape-oriented panoramic representations despite the fact that illustrating individuals was not as effective as landscape in the creation of the realistic panorama effect. Realism was no longer simply an effect of visual representation. For example, the success of Charles Castellani's panorama "Le Tout Paris" resided in cultural fascination with representations of celebrities in the familiar sights of modern Paris. The tableau grouped Paris's celebrities at and around one of the symbols at the center of modern Paris: the Opéra. Spectators were positioned as though standing in front of the Opéra; around them were the adjacent boulevard des Capucines, the Grand Hôtel, the rue du Quatre Septembre, the Café de la Paix, and the Louvre at the end of the long Avenue de l'Opéra. A review celebrated the choice of the Place de l'Opéra: "No better place could have been chosen in this shining and noisy Paris to represent Parisian life in all its ardor, vigor and feverishness."[65] "Le Tout Paris" was intended to satisfy public interest and curiosity—one that was clearly tied to press culture. One review explained that the panorama would attract many of the people who "always wanted to know and see the poets, writers, painters, sculptors, actors, and politicians whose names they read in the newspaper every day."[66] The gallery served as a sort summa of the popular press.

The panorama contained none of the foreground objects that had been added to other attractions, but only by virtue of circumstance. Located within the actual Exposition grounds on the Esplanade des Invalides, its site was nonetheless considered a dead area of the Exposition.[67] This poor location worried the panorama's financiers, who insisted on keeping expenses down. As a result, as Castellani complained about the attraction, "We had neither accessories, nor false terrains, nor any of the things that are absolutely indispensable for producing what the public likes: trompe l'oeil and illusion."[68] The reviews suggested, however, that the illusion of life might be otherwise generated.

Popular despite the poor location that had worried its financial backers, the panorama remained open for the entire Exposition, during which time over 300,000 people visited.[69] Aside from celebrating the range and sheer number of celebrities represented, reviews noted the panorama's lifelike qualities. A simple circular painting, without props and sets, one would imagine that it could not compete with other panoramas in terms of its verisimilitude. Yet critics celebrated "the astonishing expression of activity and life that animates the entire composition."[70] It was as though its subject matter somehow animated the composition itself. Another review described the panorama as though it were a freeze-frame—an instant captured:

... seized while passing by in a carriage, on horseback, in groups, with even more truth than an instant photograph can give the idea of. What's more, aren't there the charm of color, the representation of gestures and looks, the entire Parisian spirit spread among the brilliant, animated crowd that is so lively that we have the perfect illusion of its movement and its reality?[71]

Although the painting did not portray an actual moment, it depicted an idealized and possible moment in Parisian life that most readers of the daily press could have imagined based on their familiarity with the location and the people populating it. In other words, the painting seemed lifelike because it visually materialized a world that formed a familiar popular narrative: the real world that one found represented in the Parisian press. Like the wax museum, the panorama's success was in the eye and the mind of the beholder; realism was not merely a technological evocation.

Of course, public interest in reality also drove many other panoramas toward ever-increasing realism in the form of simulation. The panoramas of the late nineteenth century relied less on an imagined transport and instead offered simulations of voyages and literally moving landscapes.

The first moving panorama was the "Panorama of the Fleet of the Compagnie Générale Transatlantique," where visitors boarded a re-creation of the company's newest steamer *La Touraine*.[72] Opened in May 1889, on the Quai D'Orsay, within the Exposition grounds, the attraction received more than 1.3 million visitors.[73] The painter Poilpot served as the artistic director of the display, which incorporated a view of the entire port of Le Havre, including a view of the company's eighty other ships harbored. The attraction also featured eleven other canvases and a coastal landscape that moved as the ship allegedly went by. Passengers climbed aboard this life-sized reproduction of the ship through an elegant vestibule and walked up a set of stairs and then out onto the captain's deck into the supposed open air. Wax figures of crew members in lookout positions and of the captain describing the port to a female passenger mingled with live sailors and officers dressed in the uniforms of the Transatlantic Company. Reviewers noted that "He [Poilpot] has succeeded in reconstituting scenes from life on board in its most minor details with surprising fidelity. . . . The artist has completely achieved his goal; he has mixed reality and fiction in such a way that we are practically fooled."[74]

With as many visitors as the attraction had, each paying the small sum of one franc, it should come as no surprise that reviewers remarked on the diversity of the crowd, which included peasants, workers (who had never seen the sea, the reviewer noted), bourgeois men and women, shopkeepers, and diplomats.[75] Visitors of different classes must have had divergent experiences on *La Touraine*. Those bourgeois visitors who had actually taken a cruise could judge the quality of the simulation. For others, it might be the only time that they set foot on a ship, and one imagines that the Compagnie Transatlantique hoped it would not be their last time.

Poilpot continued in his attempts to achieve a more realistic effect by simulating motion. His 1892 panorama, which represented the sinking of the French Ship *Le Vengeur* during the Revolutionary War against the British in 1794, provided a technological watershed. Spectators stood on the deck of the battleship *Le Hussard* surrounded by enemy ships and across from the sinking *Vengeur*. The deck of *Le Hussard* pitched back and forth, literally giving spectators the feeling that they were on a ship.[76] Reviewers celebrated what they considered an advance toward greater illusion in this panorama, opened on May 25, 1892. In July, Poilpot added to his spectacle the feature of sound in the form of gunfire, cannons, a chorus singing *the Marseillaise*, and two actors reciting a lyric poem about the accomplishments of the sinking ship. Despite its critical acclaim, "Le Vengeur" did not stay open for more than a year; its enormous costs simply did not allow the two-franc panorama to make a sufficient profit.[77]

Between 1892 and the next Exposition in 1900, many attractions successfully simulated motion. For example, Parisians could see the "Pantomimes Lumineuses" at the Musée Grévin starting in October 1892. In 1894, they could see moving photographs in Edison's Kinetoscope, and as of December 1895, the Lumière Brothers' films could be seen at the Grand Café.

Entrepreneurs sought to incorporate the new moving pictures into already existing amusements. Moving pictures were initially considered simply a novel technique for representing motion, and it was not clear that they might suffice as an entertainment in their own right. Moving pictures did, however, blend well with the cultural agenda of the panoramas. So, for example, in 1898, Louis Régnault opened "Maerorama" on the boulevard across from the Porte Saint-Martin. A simulated boat ride, it incorporated the moving platform used in "Le Vengeur," adding compressed air to make wind and waves. The exhibitor, dressed in a captain's uniform, warned, "We announced that those susceptible to falling seasick should abstain."[78] The lights then dimmed, and instead of a painted canvas rolling by, visitors watched "movies" of coastal views photographed from boats: the Corsican coast, Africa, the Italian lakes, and finally a view of Marseille, where, after two toots of the ship's horn, passengers were asked to descend and allow other tourists, "Eager to experience the wonders of 'Maerorama,'" to be given their chance.[79] Régnault presented a similar attraction at the 1900 Exposition; there passengers were seated in a funicular instead of on a boat. The advent of film did not replace mechanical panoramas: film was not, at least in its early years, perceived as the answer to the public's taste for reality.

Panoramas and similar entertainments reproduced reality in a variety of ways: by relying on spectator-generated optical illusions, by echoing other realist genres such as the press, and by simulating reality. One can find no technological telos toward ever more perfectly realistic reproduction culminating in the invention of cinema. Rather, as this focus on panoramas during the 1880s and 1890s has tried to suggest, these spectacles technologically generated "reality" and its concomitant animation in a variety of ways during the same period. Further, the various representations of "real-life" experiences offered sensationalized versions of reality—a sensationalism that ranged from narrative suspense to physical simulations.

To many fin-de-siècle observers, Parisians demonstrated a new and marked taste for reality. Stretching beyond the bounds of realism and illusionism, I have tried to argue that their taste for the real was posited on the blurring of life and art—on the way that reality was spectacularized (as at the Morgue) at the same time that spectacles were obsessively realistic. Reality, however, was complexly constituted and defined. Looking at contemporaneous observations suggests that, as in any technological apparatus, the reality effect resides as much in spectators' abilities to make connections between the spectacles they saw and the familiar press narratives that they already knew.

To understand cinematic spectatorship as a historical practice, it is essential to locate cinema in the field of cultural forms and practices associated with the burgeoning mass culture of the late nineteenth century. It is not mere coincidence that apart from people's interest in reality, the activities described here transpired among large groups of people in whose mobility some of the spectacles' realistic effects resided. Those practices suggest that flânerie was not simply the privilege of the bourgeois male but a cultural activity for all who participated in Parisian life. Thus, rather than identify the seeds of cinematic spectatorship, this sort of flânerie for the masses instead points to the birth of the audience. For it is necessarily in a crowd that one finds the cinematic spectator.

NOTES

1. *Guide to Paris* (London: Cassell's, 1884), p. 111.

2. Giuliana Bruno, *Streetwalking on a Ruined Map* (Princeton, N.J.: Princeton University Press, 1993), p. 38.

3. See Anne Friedberg, *Window Shopping* (Berkeley and Los Angeles: University of California Press, 1993), on the relationship between *flânerie* as modern spectatorship.

4. Hughes Leroux, *L'Enfer parisien* (Paris: 1888), p. 353.

5. *Le Temps*, September 25, 1882.

6. Ernest Cherbuliez, "La Morgue," in *La Revue des deux mondes* January 1891, p. 368, and Émile Zola, *Thérèse Raquin* (Paris: Flammarion, 1970), p. 131, and Adolphe Guillot, *Paris qui souffre: le basse-geôle du Grand-Châtelet et les morgues modernes*, 2nd ed. (Paris: Chez Rouquette, 1888), p. 177.

7. Leroux, p. 353, and Guillot, p. 177.

8. Guillot, p. 43.

9. Clovis Pierre, *Les Gaietés de la Morgue* (Paris: Gallimard, 1895).

10. Cherbuliez, p. 360.

11. Zola, p. 131.

12. Angelin Ruelle, *Les Chansons de la Morgue* (Paris: Léon Varnier, 1890).

13. Pierre Véron, "La Morgue," in *Le Magasin Pittoresque* (March 1907), pp. 171–72.

14. E. A. Reynolds-Ball, *Paris in Its Splendours*, 2 vols., vol. 2 (London: 1901), p. 312.

15. Clovis Pierre, *Les Gaietés de la Morgue* (Paris: Flammarion, 1895).

16. Georg Simmel, as cited in Walter Benjamin, "Some Motifs in Baudelaire," in *Charles Baudelaire*, tr. Quintin Hoare (London: New Left, 1973), p. 151.

17. Jacques Wolgensinger, *L'Histoire à la une: la grande aventure de la presse* (Paris: Decouvertes Gallimard, 1989).

18. Anne-Marie Thiesse, *Le Roman du quotidien* (Paris: Le Chemin Vert, 1984), p. 17.

19. Émile Zola in Wolgensinger, *L'Histoire*, p. 67.

20. Alphonse Devergie, *Notions générales sur la Morgue de Paris* (Paris: Félix Malteste, 1877), p. 11.

21. Guillot, *Paris qui souffre*, p. 182.

22. Ibid., pp. 199, 258.

23. *La Presse*, March 22, 1907.

24. *L'Éclair*, March 21, 1907.

25. Firmin Maillard, *Recherches historiques et critiques sur la Morgue* (Paris: Delahays, 1860), pp. 94–95.

26. *Le Paris*, August 31, 1892.

27. *Le Petit Journal*, August 3, 1886.

28. *Le Matin*, August 2, 1886.

29. *Le Matin*, August 4, 1886.

30. *La Liberté*, August 5, 1886.

31. Archives of the Police Prefect, Morgue register, 1886.

32. *Le Petit Journal*, August 6, 1886.

33. Archives of the Police Prefect, Paris; Morgue registers.

34. See Anne, Margaret, and Patrice Higonnet, "Façades: Walter Benjamin's Paris," *Critical Inquiry* 10:3 (March 1984), 391–419, in which the Morgue is discussed as part of the nineteenth-century bourgeois obsession with death.

35. *Le Voltaire*, July 22, 1892. Yvette Guilbert was a well-known singer in the café-concerts.

36. For more on the closing of the Morgue, see my dissertation, "The Public Taste for Reality: Early Mass Culture in Fin-de-Siècle Paris" (University of California at Berkeley, 1993).

37. *La Presse*, 22 March 1907.

38. Cartoon from Musée Grévin Archives (hereafter "MGA").

39. *Le Monde Illustré*, May 22, 1882.

40. Stock prospectus, Bibliothèque Historique de la Ville de Paris, Actualités Anciennes, 102.

41. *Catalogue-Almanach du Musée Grévin*, MGA (1882).

42. Ibid.

43. Ibid.

44. *Le Parlement*, June 8, 1882.

45. See Richard Terdiman, *Discourse/Counter-Discourse* (Ithaca, N.Y.: Cornell University Press, 1985), p. 122, for a discussion of newspapers.

46. Jules Lemaître, *Impressions de Théâtre*, 2nd series (Paris: Société Française de l'Imprimerie, 1897) 8th ed., originally 1887, p. 325.

47. *L'Indépendance Belge*, June 12, 1882.

48. *Catalogue du Musée Grévin*, MGA, 54th ed.

49. *Catalogue-Almanach du Musée Grévin*, MGA, 32nd ed.

50. For an important discussion of spectator position at wax museums, see Mark Sandberg, "Missing Persons: Spectacle and Narrative in Late Nineteenth Century Scandinavia." Dissertation (University of California at Berkeley, 1991).

51. *Catalogue du Musée Grévin*, MGA, 57th ed.

52. As Robert Herbert has noted, this theme could be found represented in many Impressionist paintings and in other more popular images as well. Herbert, *Impressionism* (New Haven, Conn.: Yale University Press, 1988), p. 104.

53. *Catalogue du Musée Grévin*, MGA, 82 ed.

54. For more on the cinema at Musée Grévin, see my article coauthored with Jean-Jacques Meusy "Le Musée Grévin et le cinématographe: l'histoire d'une recontre," in *1895* 11 (December 1991), 19–48.

55. *Le Temps*, June 7, 1882.

56. *L'Express*, June 7, 1882.

57. *Le Parlement*, June 6, 1882.

58. This 140-meter film, lasting between five and six minutes, was based on the tableaux that could still be found at Musée Grévin, with one exception: whereas the wax scene of the convict in his cell shows him playing cards, the film version shows him in an activity that would later become the primary metaphor of the filmic experience—he is dreaming.

59. Cassell's *Guide to Paris* (Paris, 1884), p. 117.

60. *Le Voltaire*, January 3, 1881, as cited in François Robichon, "Les Panoramas en France au XIXe siècle" (University of Paris, Nanterre, 1982), p. 216.

61. Friedberg, *Window Shopping*, pp. 20–22. Jonathan Crary has made a distinction between the two; in the panorama, one is compelled to turn one's head and look around, while the diorama actually turns its spectators, transforming the observer, he argues, into a component of the machine. Crary, *Techniques of the Observer* (Cambridge, Mass.: Massachusetts Institute of Technology Press, 1990), p. 113.

62. *Les Cuirassiers de Reichshoffen* (Paris: Société des Grands Panoramas, 1881), BHVP, Actualités Anciennes, ser. 103.

63. See Richard Altick, *The Shows of London* (Cambridge, Mass.: Harvard University Press, 1978). Altick argues that panoramas provided news for those who could not get it. The problem here is that the audience for panoramas and newspapers was one and the same: only the bourgeoisie read newspapers or could afford panoramas.

64. *Encyclopédie enfantine recommandée pour les écoles*, BHVP, Actualités Anciennes, ser. 103.

65. *Le Figaro*, February 23, 1889.

66. *Le Petit Moniteur*, May 16, 1889.

67. See Charles Castellani, *Confidences d'un panoramiste* (Paris: Maurice Dreyfous, n.d.), p. 281.

68. Ibid., p. 281.

69. Charles Rearick, *Pleasures of the Belle Epoque* (New Haven, Conn.: Yale University Press, 1985), p. 173.

70. *Le Rappel*, March 12, 1889.

71. *Le Courier des Expositions*, March 1889.

72. Readers will note that many of the attractions were sponsored by companies that actually offered the real trips on their modes of transport. That fact should serve as an important corrective for those who associate such corporate entertainment with twentieth-century America in general and, say, the Disney theme parks in particular.

73. Robichon, "Les Panoramas en France," p. 504.

74. P. Bluysen, *Paris en 1889* (Paris: P. Arnould, 1890), p. 19.

75. *La Nature* (June 15, 1889), 34, in Robichon, "Les Panoramas en France," p. 507.

76. A two-horsepower gas-generated machine activated two pistons of a hydraulic press that moved the platform. See Robichon, "Les Panoramas en France," p. 520.

77. Ibid., p. 516.

78. R. M. Arlaud, *Cinéma-Bouffe* (Paris: Jacques Melot, n.d.), p. 66. I thank Jean-Jacques Meusy for this reference.

79. Ibid., p. 67. It should be clear that this well predates Hale's Tours. See Raymond Fielding, "Hale's Tours: Ultra-Realism in the Pre-1910 Motion Picture," in John Fell, ed. *Film before Griffith* (Berkeley and Los Angeles: University of California Press, 1983).

Tom Gunning

An Aesthetic of Astonishment: Early Film and the (In)Credulous Spectator

Terror in the Aisles

*The damming of the stream of real life, the moment
when its flow comes to a standstill, makes itself felt as
reflux: this reflux is astonishment.*
— Walter Benjamin, "What Is Epic Theatre?"
(first version)

In traditional accounts of the cinema's first audiences, one image stands out: the terrified reaction of spectators to Lumiere's *Arrival of a Train at the Station*. According to a variety of historians, spectators reared back in their seats, or screamed, or got up and ran from the auditorium (or all three in succession). As with most myths of origin, the source for these accounts remains elusive. It does not figure in any report of the first screening at the Salon Indien of the Grand Café that I have located.[1] And as with such myths, its ideological uses demand probing as much as its veracity. This panicked and hysterical audience has provided the basis for further myths about the nature of film history and the power of the film image.

The first audiences, according to this myth, were naive, encountering this threatening and rampant image with no defenses, with no tradition by which to understand it. The absolute novelty of the moving

From *Art and Text* 34 (Spring 1989). Reprinted by permission of the author and *Art and Text*. The original article was dedicated to Miriam Hansen.

image therefore reduced them to a state usually attributed to savages in their primal encounter with the advanced technology of Western colonialists, howling and fleeing in impotent terror before the power of the machine. This audience of the first exhibitions exists outside of the willing suspension of disbelief, the immediacy of their terror short-circuiting even disavowal's detour of "I know very well . . . but all the same." Credulity overwhelms all else, the physical reflex signaling a visual trauma. Thus conceived, the myth of initial terror defines film's power as its unprecedented realism, its ability to convince spectators that the moving image was, in fact, palpable and dangerous, bearing towards them with physical impact. The image had taken life, swallowing, in its relentless force, any consideration of representation—the imaginary perceived as real.

Furthermore, this primal scene at the cinema underpins certain contemporary theorisations of spectatorship. The terrorised spectator of the Grand Café still stalks the imagination of film theorists who envision audiences submitting passively to an all-dominating apparatus, hypnotised and transfixed by its illusionist power. Contemporary film theorists have made careers out of underestimating the basic intelligence and reality-testing abilities of the average film viewer and have no trouble treating previous audiences with similar disdain. The most subtle reading of this initial terror comes from Metz. But Metz's admirable subtlety renders his analysis all the more deficient from a historical point of view. Metz describes this panicked reaction on the part of the Grand Café audience as a displacement of the contemporary viewer's credulity onto a mythical childhood of the medium. Like the childhood when one still believed in Santa Claus, like the dawn of time when myths were still believed literally, belief in this legendary audience, Metz claims, allows us to disavow our own belief in the face of the cinema. *We* don't believe in the screen image in the manner that *they* did. Our credulity is displaced onto an audience from the infancy of cinema.[2]

Metz's penetrating analysis of the mythical role of this first audience does not lead to demythologisation. He instead introjects this primal audience, removing it from historical analysis by internalising it as an aspect of a presumably timeless cinema viewer. No longer a historical spectator in the Grand Café in 1895, the naive spectator "is still seated *beneath* the incredulous one, or in his heart."[3] Thus removed from place and time, this inner credulous viewer supplies the motive power for Metz's understanding of the fetishistic viewer, wavering between the credulous position of believing the image and the repressed, anxiety-causing, knowledge of its illusion. The historical panic at the Grand Café would be, according to Metz, simply a projection of an inner deception onto the mythical site of cinema's "once upon a time."

Although I have my doubts whether actual panic took place in the Grand Café's Salon Indien, there is no question that a reaction of astonishment and even a type of terror accompanied many early projections. I therefore don't intend to simply deny this founding myth of the cinema's spectator, but rather to approach it historically. We cannot simply swallow whole the image of the naive spectator, whose reaction to the image is one of simple belief and panic; it needs digesting. The impact of the first film projections cannot be explained by a mechanistic model of a naive spectator who, in a temporary psychotic state, confuses the image for its reality. But what context does account for the well-attested fact that the first projections caused shock and astonishment, an excitement pushed to the point of terror, if we exclude childlike credulity? And, equally important, how could this agitating experience be understood as part of the *attraction* of the new invention, rather than a disturbing element that needed to be removed? And what role does an illusion of reality play in this terrified reception?

Only a careful consideration of the historical context of these earliest images can restore an understanding of the uncanny and agitating power they exerted on audiences. This context includes the first modes of exhibition, the tradition of turn-of-the-century visual entertainments, and a basic aesthetic of early cinema I have called the cinema of attractions, which envisioned cinema as a series of visual shocks. Restored to its proper historical context, the projection of the first moving images stands at the climax of a period of intense development in visual entertainments, a tradition in which realism was valued largely for its uncanny effects. We need to recognise this tradition and speculate on its role at the turn of the century.

As I have shown elsewhere, many early spectators recognised the first projection of films as a crowning achievement in the extremely sophisticated developments in the magic theatre, as practiced by Méliès at the Théâtre Robert Houdin and his English mentor Maskleyne at London's Egyptian Hall.[4] At the turn of the century, this tradition used the latest technology (such as focused electric light and elaborate stage machinery) to produce apparent miracles. The seeming transcendence of the laws of the material universe by the magical theatre defines the dialectical nature of its illusions. The craft of late nineteenth-century stage illusions consisted of making visible something which could not exist, of managing the pay of appearances in order to confound the expectations of logic and experience. The audience this theatre addressed was not primarily gullible country bumpkins, but sophisticated urban pleasure seekers, well aware that they were seeing the most modern techniques in stage craft. Méliès's theatre is inconceivable without a widespread decline in belief in the marvellous, providing a fundamental rationalist context. The magic theatre laboured to make visual that which it was impossible to believe. Its visual power consisted of a trompe l'oeil play of give-and-take, an obsessive desire to test the limits of an intellectual disavowal—I know, but yet I see.

Trompe l'oeil as a genre of aesthetic illusion underscores the problematic role perfect illusion plays within traditional aesthetic reception. As Martin Battersby puts it, trompe l'oeil aims not simply at accuracy of representation, but at causing "a feeling of disgust in the mind of the beholder." This disquiet arises from "a conflict of messages": on the one hand, the knowledge that one is seeing a painting, and on the other, a visual experience sufficiently convincing as "to warrant a closer examination and even the involvement of the sense of touch."[5] The realism of the image is at the service of a dramatically unfolding spectator experience, vacillating between belief and incredulity. Although trompe l'oeil shares with *The Arrival of a Train* and the magic theatre a pleasurable vacillation between belief and doubt, it also displays important differences from them. The usually small scale of trompe l'oeil paintings and the desire to reach out and touch them contrast sharply with the "grandeur naturale"[6] of the Lumière train film and the viewer's impulse to rear back before it, as well as with the spectator's physical distance from the illusions of the magic theatre. But all three forms show that, rather than being a simple reality effect, the illusionistic arts of the nineteenth century cannily exploited their unbelievable nature, keeping a conscious focus on the fact that they were only illusions.

In fact, in the most detailed and articulate account we have of an early Lumière projection, Maxim Gorky (reporting on a showing at the Nizhny-Novgorod Fair in July of 1896) stresses the uncanny effect of the new attraction's mix of realistic and non-realistic qualities. For Gorky, the cinématographe presents a world whose vividness and vitality have been drained away: "before you a life is surging, a life deprived of words and shorn of the living spectrum of colours—the grey, the soundless, the bleak and dismal life." The cinématographe, Gorky explains, presents not life but its shadow, and he allows no possibility of mistaking this cinematic shade for substance. Describing *The Arrival of a Train*, Gorky senses its impending threat: "It speeds right at you—watch out! It seems as though it will plunge into the darkness in which you sit, turning you into a ripped sack full of lacerated flesh and splintered bones." But, he adds, "this too is but a train of shadows." Belief and terror are larded with an awareness of illusion and even, to Gorky's sophisticated palate, the ennui of the insubstantial, the bleak disappointment of the ungraspable phantom of life.[7]

One might dismiss Gorky's reaction as the sophisticated disdain of a cultured intellectual, deliberately counter to the more common reception of early film images. Gorky's negative assessment of the cinema *was* unusual in a period when new advances in the technology of entertainment were generally hailed with excitement and satisfaction. But his recognition that the film image combined realistic effects with a conscious awareness of artifice may correspond more closely to general audience reaction than the screaming dupes of traditional accounts. While contemporary accounts of audience responses, particularly unsophisticated viewers, are hard to come by, the very mode of presentation of the Lumière screenings (and of other early filmmakers as well) contains an important element which served to undermine a naive experience of realism. It is too infrequently pointed out that in the earliest Lumière exhibitions the films were initially presented as frozen unmoving images, projections of still photographs. Then, flaunting a mastery of visual showmanship, the projector began cranking and the image moved. Or as Gorky described it, "suddenly a strange flicker passes through the screen and the picture stirs to life."[8]

While such a presentation would seem to forbid any reading of the image as reality—a real physical train—it strongly heightened the impact of the moment of movement. Rather than mistaking the image for reality, the spectator is astonished by its transformation through the new illusion of projected motion. Far from credulity, it is the incredible nature of the illusion itself that renders the viewer speechless. What is displayed before the audience is less the impending speed of the train than the force of the cinematic apparatus. Or to put it better, the one demonstrates the other. The astonishment derives from a magical metamorphosis rather than a seamless reproduction of reality. The initial impact of this transformation at the Lumière premiere is described by an expert in such effects, Georges Méliès:

> a *still* photograph showing the place Bellecour in Lyon was projected. A little surprised. I just had time to say to my neighbor:

"They got us all stirred up for projections like this! I've been doing them for over ten years."

I had hardly finished speaking when a horse pulling a wagon began to walk towards us, followed by other vehicles and then pedestrians, in short all the animation of the street. Before this spectacle we sat with gaping mouths, struck with amazement, astonished beyond all expression."[9]

This coup de théâtre, the sudden transformation from still image to moving illusion, startled audiences and displayed the novelty and fascination of the cinématographe. Far from being placed outside a suspension of disbelief, the presentation acts out the contradictory stages of involvement with the image, unfolding, like other nineteenth-century visual entertainments, a vacillation between belief and incredulity. The moving image reverses and complicates the trajectory of experience solicited by a trompe l'oeil still life. The film first presents itself as merely an image, rather than appearing to be the actual butterflies, postcards, or cameos which the initial apperception of a trompe l'oeil canvas seems to reveal. Instead of a gradual disquiet arising from the divergence of what we know and what we see, the shock of the film image comes from a sudden transformation while the hardly novel projected photograph (Gorky also stressed his initial disappointment at this "all too familiar scene"[10]) gives way to the astonishing moment of movement. The audience's sense of shock comes less from a naive belief that they are threatened by an actual locomotive than from an unbelievable visual transformation occurring before their eyes, parallel to the greatest wonders of the magic theatre.

As in the magic theatre the apparent realism of the image makes it a successful illusion, but one understood as an illusion nonetheless. While such a transformation would be quite capable of causing a physical or verbal reflex in the viewer, one remains aware that the film is merely a projection. The initial still image demonstrated that irrefutably. But this still projection takes on motion, becomes endowed with animation, and it is this unbelievable moving image that so astounds. The initial projection of a still image, withholding briefly the illusion of motion which is the apparatus's raison d'être, brought an effect of suspense to the first film shows. The audience knew that motion was precisely what the cinématographe promised (hence Méliès's restlessness). By delaying its appearance, the Lumière exhibitor not only highlights the device but signals his allegiance to an aesthetic of astonishment which goes beyond a scientific interest in the reproduction of motion.

Another account of early projections, this time from the other side of the Atlantic, further demonstrates the theatricality of this device and clearly aligns the terror of early spectators with a conscious delectation of shocks and thrills. The memoirs of Albert E. Smith, one of the founders of the Vitagraph company, describe his early years as a travelling exhibitor with Vitagraph cofounder J. Stuart Blackton. Smith had toured earlier with quick-sketch artist Blackton as an illusionist combining "sleight of hand and invisible mechanical appliances of his own invention."[11] But like a large number of stage illusionists, they had turned to the exhibition of moving pictures as the most technologically advanced form of visual entertainments. Smith contributed a mechanical improvement to the Edison projecting kinetoscope—a water cell between the film and the light source that absorbed heat and allowed the film to be projected as a still image a bit longer without danger of the celluloid bursting into flames.

The most popular item on Smith and Blackton's exhibition tours was *The Black Diamond Express,* a one-shot film of a locomotive rushing towards the camera. As in most early film shows, a patter spoken by Blackton accompanied the projection, preparing the audience for the film and providing dramatic atmosphere. Smith describes Blackton's role in presenting *The Black Diamond Express* as that of a "terrorist mood setter." As he recalled it, Blackton's lecture (delivered over the frozen image of the locomotive) went like this:

> Ladies and gentlemen you are now gazing upon a photograph of the famous Black Diamond Express. In just a moment, a cataclysmic moment, my friends, a moment without equal in the history of our times, you will see this train take life in a marvellous and most astounding manner. It will rush towards you, belching smoke and fire from its monstrous iron throat.

Although Smith's memory of Blackton's oration decades later may not be entirely reliable, it captures the address of the first film shows and places the audience's terror in a new light. Blackton directly addresses the audience, mediating between it and the film and stressing the actual act of display. Like a fairground barker, he builds an atmosphere of expectation, a pronounced curiosity leavened with anxiety as he stresses the novelty and astonishing properties which the attraction about to be revealed will possess. This sense of expectation, sharpened to an intense focus on a single instant of transformation, heightened the startling impact of the first projections. Far from being a simple reality effect, the impact derives from a moment of crisis, prepared for and delayed, then bursting upon the audience. This suspenseful presentation of an impossible transformation, Smith reports, caused women to scream and men to sit aghast.[12]

The Aesthetic of Attractions

There came a day when a new and urgent need for stimuli was met by the film. In a film, perception in the form of shocks was established as a formal principle.
—Walter Benjamin,
"Some Motifs in Baudelaire"

While these early films of on-coming locomotives present the shock of cinema in an exaggerated form, they also express an essential element of early cinema as a whole. I have called the cinema that precedes the dominance of narrative (and this period lasts for nearly a decade, until 1903 or 1904) The cinema of attractions.[13] The aesthetic of attraction addresses the audience directly, sometimes, as in these early train films, exaggerating this confrontation in an experience of assault. Rather than being an involvement with narrative action or empathy with character psychology, the cinema of attractions solicits a highly conscious awareness of the film image engaging the viewer's curiosity. The spectator does not get lost in a fictional world and its drama, but remains aware of the act of looking, the excitement of curiosity and its fulfilment. Through a variety of formal means, the images of the cinema of attractions rush forward to meet their viewers. These devices range from the implied collision of the early railroad films to the performance style of the same period, when actors nodded and gestured at the camera (e.g., Méliès on screen directing attention to the transformations he causes) or when a showman lecturer presented the views to the audience. This cinema addresses and holds the spectator, emphasising the act of display. In fulfilling this curiosity, it delivers a generally brief dose of scopic pleasure.

And pleasure is the issue here, even if pleasure of a particularly complicated sort. When a Montpellier journalist in 1896 described the Lumière projections as provoking "an excitement bordering on terror," he was praising the new spectacle and explaining its success.[14] If the first spectators screamed, it was to acknowledge the power of the apparatus to sweep away a prior and firmly entrenched sense of reality. This vertiginous experience of the frailty of our knowledge of the world before the power of visual illusion produced that mixture of pleasure and anxiety which the purveyors of popular art had labelled sensations and thrills and on which they founded a new aesthetic of attractions. The on-rushing train did not simply produce the negative experience of fear but the particularly modern entertainment form of the thrill, embodied elsewhere in the recently appearing attractions of the amusement parks (such as the roller coaster), which combined sensations of acceleration and falling with a security guaranteed by modern industrial technology. One Coney Island attraction, the Leap Frog Railway, literalised the thrill of *The Arrival of a Train.* Two electric cars containing as many as forty people were set towards each other at great speed on a collision course. Just before impact one car was lifted up on curved rails and skimmed over the top of the other. Lynne Kirby has also noted the popularity of staged collisions between railroad locomotives at the turn of the century, both at county fairs and in such films as Edison's 1904 *The Railroad Smash-Up.*[15]

Confrontation rules the cinema of attractions in both the form of its films and their mode of exhibition. The directness of this act of display allows an emphasis on the thrill itself—the immediate reaction of the viewer. The film lecturer focuses attention on the attraction, sharpening viewer curiosity. The film then performs its act of display and fades away. Unlike psychological narrative, the cinema of attractions does not allow for elaborate development; only a limited amount of delay is really possible. But such a film program consists of a series of attractions, a concatenation of short films all of which offer the viewer a moment of revelation. The succession of thrills is potentially limited only by viewer exhaustion. This concatenation may have some thematic structuring and builds toward a climactic moment, a final *clou* (such as Smith and Blackton's *Black Diamond Express*). The showman rather than the films themselves gives the program an overarching structure, and the key role of exhibitor showman underscores the act of monstration that founds the cinema of attractions.[16]

A film like Edison's *Electrocuting an Elephant* from 1903 shows the temporal logic of this scenography of display. The elephant is led onto an electrified plate, and secured. Smoke rises from its feet and after a moment the elephant falls on its side. The moment of technologically advanced death is neither further explained nor dramatised. Likewise a fictional film produced by the Biograph Company in 1904, *Photographing a Female Crook,* presents a single shot of a woman held between two uniformed policemen who try to steady her for a mug shot. The camera tracks in on this group, ending by framing the woman in medium close-up. Attempting to sabotage the photographing of her face for identification purposes, the female crook mugs outrageously, contorting her face. The inward movement by the movie camera and the progressive enlargement of the woman's face emphasise the act of display which underlies the film. While both these films show considerable formal differences from *The Arrival of a Train,* they all three demonstrate the solicitation of viewer curiosity and its fulfilment by the brief moment of revelation typical of the cinema of attractions. This is a cinema of instants, rather than developing situations.

As I have stated elsewhere,[17] the scenography of the cinema of attractions is an exhibitionist one, opposed to the cinema of the unacknowledged voyeur that later narrative cinema ushers in. This display of unique views belongs most obviously to the period before the dominance of editing, when films consisting of a single shot—both actualities and fictions—made up the bulk of film production. However, even with the introduction of editing and more complex narratives, the aesthetic of attraction can still be sensed in periodic doses of non-narrative spectacle given to audiences (musicals and slapstick comedy provide clear examples). The cinema of attractions persists in later cinema, even if it rarely dominates the form of a feature film as a whole. It provides an underground current flowing beneath narrative logic and diegetic realism, producing those moments of cinematic *dépaysement* beloved by the surrealists.[18]

This aesthetic so contrasts with prevailing turn-of-the-century norms of artistic reception—the ideals of detached contemplation—that it nearly constitutes an anti-aesthetic. The cinema of attractions stands at the antipode to the experience Michael Fried, in his discussion of eighteenth-century painting, calls absorption.[19] For Fried, the painting of Greuze and others created a new relation to the viewer through a self-contained hermetic world which makes no acknowledgement of the beholder's presence. Early cinema totally ignores this construction of the beholder. These early films explicitly acknowledge their spectator, seeming to reach outwards and confront. Contemplative absorption is impossible here. The viewer's curiosity is aroused and fulfilled through a marked encounter, a direct stimulus, a succession of shocks.

By tapping into a visual curiosity and desire for novelty, attractions draw upon what Augustine, at the beginning of the fifth century, called *curiositas* in his catalogue of "the lust of the eyes." In contrast to visual *voluptas* (pleasure), *curiositas* avoids the beautiful and goes after its exact opposite "simply because of the lust to find out and to know." *Curiositas* draws the viewer towards unbeautiful sights, such as a mangled corpse, and "because of this disease of curiosity monsters and anything out of the ordinary are put on show in our theatres." For Augustine, *curiositas* led not only to a fascination with seeing, but a desire for knowledge for its own sake, ending in the perversions of magic and science.[20] While beauty in Augustine's Platonic schema may form the first rung of an ascent to the ideal, *curiositas* possesses only the power to lead astray. Attractions imply the danger of distraction, a cardinal sin in Augustine's contemplative and vigilant model of Christian life.

The aesthetic of attractions developed in fairly conscious opposition to an orthodox identification of viewing pleasure with the contemplation of beauty. A nineteenth-century satirical engraving shows London's Egyptian Hall (which existed as a home for natural curiosities—freaks and artifacts of natural history—before it became the home of Maskelyne's magic theatre) proclaiming itself "the Hall of Ugliness" and advertising the "Ne Plus Ultra of Hideousness."[21] This attraction to the repulsive was frequently rationalised by appealing to that impulse which Augustine found equally dubious, intellectual curiosity. Like the early film exhibitions, freak shows and other displays of curiosities were described as instructive and informing. Similarly, a popular and longlasting genre of the cinema of attractions consisted of educational actualities (such as Charles Urban's *Unseen World* series beginning in 1903), which presented magnified images of cheese mites, spiders and water fleas.[22] As late as 1914 a proponent of the reform movement in cinema objected to the vulgarity of films displaying such "slimy and unbeautiful abominations," which he claimed repulsed spectators with more refined sensibilities.[23] But showmen were well aware that a thrill needed an element of repulsion or a controlled threat of danger. Louise Lumière understood that his films, which directed physical action out at the audience, added a vital energy alongside the scientific curiosity addressed by his reproduction of motion and daily life.

Distraction and the Ambivalence of Shock

The film corresponds to profound changes in the apperceptive apparatus—changes that are experienced on an individual scale by the man in the street in big city traffic, on a historical scale by every present day individual.
—Walter Benjamin, "The Work of Art in
the Age of Mechanical Reproduction"

While the impulse to *curiositas* may be as old as Augustine, there is no question that the nineteenth century sharpened this form of "lust of the eyes" and its commercial exploitation. Expanding urbanisation with its kaleidoscopic succession of city sights, the growth of consumer society with its new emphasis on stimulating spending through visual display, and the escalating horizons of colonial exploration with new peoples and territories to be categorised and exploited all provoked the desire for images and attractions. It is not surprising that city street scenes, advertising films, and foreign views all formed important genres of early cinema. The enormous popularity of foreign views (already developed and exploited by the stereoscope and magic lantern) expresses an almost unquenchable desire to consume the world through images. The cinema was, as the slogan of one early film company put it, an invention which put the world within your grasp. Early cinema categorised the visible world as a series of discreet attractions, and the catalogues of the first production companies present a nearly encyclopoedic survey of this new hyper-visible topology, from landscape panoramas to microphotography, from domestic scenes to the beheading of prisoners and the electrocution of elephants.

If not all the attractions of early cinema express the violence of an on-rushing train, some sense of wonder or surprise nonetheless underlies all these films, if only wonder at the illusion of motion. Even a filmed landscape panorama does not lend itself to pure aesthetic contemplation. One is fully aware of the machine which mediates the view, the camera pivoting on its tripod. The most common form of landscape panorama—films shot from the front or back of trains—doubled this effect, invoking not only the motion picture machine but the locomotive which pulls the seated viewer through space. These train films provide an even more technologically mediated example of what Wolfgang Schivelbusch, in his description of the transformation of perception occasioned by the railway journey, calls panoramic perception.

In contrast to the traditional traveller's experience of a landscape, the train passenger "no longer belongs to the same space as the perceived objects; the traveller sees the objects, landscapes, etc., *through* the apparatus which moves him through the world."[24] A film taken from the front of a train, an "unseen energy swallowing space" (as one journalist described the experience of such a train panorama[25]), doubled this effect imposed by industrial apparatuses, intensifying the alienation *and* the dynamic sensation of train travel. Such train films might turn the on-rushing Black Diamond Express inside out, but still provoked viewer amazement through a technologically mediated experience of space and movement.

Ultimately the encyclopedic ambition of this impulse of early cinema, transforming all of reality into cinematographical views, recalls Gorky's vague discomfort and depression before the cinématographe. While the cinema of attractions fulfills the curiosity it excites, it is in the nature of curiosity, as the lust of the eye, never to be satisfied completely. Thus the obsessional nature of early film production and the early film show the potentially endless succession of separate attractions. But beyond the unlimited metonymy of curiosity, Gorky's unease derived from the abstraction and alienation of this new pursuit of thrills.

Gorky also found a pervasive ennui in the dreamworld home of attractions, Coney Island (which he visited in 1906), calling it "a slavery to a varied boredom." For Gorky, Coney Island purveyed "an amazement in which there is neither transport nor joy."[26] While the tone of a European intellectual's distaste for the mass pleasures of a capitalist society is unmistakable, Gorky also provides insight into the need for thrills in an industrialised and consumer-oriented society. The peculiar pleasure of screaming before the suddenly animated image of a locomotive indicates less an audience willing to take the image for reality than a spectator whose daily experience has lost the coherence and immediacy traditionally attributed to reality. This loss of experience creates a consumer hungry for thrills.

The cinema of attractions not only exemplifies a particularly modern form of aesthetics but also responds to the specifics of modern and especially urban life, what Benjamin and Kracauer understood as the drying up of experience and its replacement by a culture of distraction. While Benjamin's writing provides the most brilliantly dialectical (and ambivalent) description of the modern transformation of perception and experience,[27] Kracauer's essay "The Cult of Distraction: On Berlin's Picture Palaces" provides a specific focus on the role of cinema and particularly that element foregrounded by the cinema of attractions—exhibition.[28]

Lost sight of now after decades of text-obsessed film analysis, the exhibition situation transforms and structures a film's mode of address to an audience. In early cinema, the act of presentation was stressed by both exhibition context and the direct address of the films themselves. By the 1920s, when Kracauer wrote, the architecture of the picture palace and the variety format of the evening's program played a major role in defining movie-going as a succession of attractions, what Kracauer describes as the "fragmented sequence of splendid sense impressions."[29] The opulence and design of the Berlin movie theatres served to offset the coherence that classical narrative cinema had brought to film. As Kracauer described it:

> The interior design of the movie theatres served one sole purpose: to rivet the audience's attention to the peripheral so that they will not sink into the abyss. The stimulations of the senses succeed each other with such rapidity that there is no room left for even the slightest contemplation to squeeze in between them.[30]

The spectacular design of the theatre itself (accented and temporalised by elaborate manipulations of light) interacted with the growing tendency to embed the film in a larger program, a revue which included music and live performance. The film in a larger program, a revue which included music and live performance. The film was only one element in an experience that Kracauer describes as a "total artwork of effects" which "assaults every one of the senses using every possible means."[31] For Kracauer, the discontinuity and variety of this form of cinema program (juxtaposing a two-dimensional film with three-dimensional live performances) strongly undermined film's illusionistic power. The projected film "recedes into the flat surface and the deception is exposed."[32] As in the first projections, the very aesthetic of attraction runs counter to an illusionistic absorption, the variety format of the picture palace program continually reminding the spectator of the act of watching by a succession of sensual assaults. As if in defiance of the increased length and the voyeuristic fictional address of the featured films, the effect of a discontinuous suite of attractions still dominates the evening.

But in spite of (or rather motivating) this smorgasbord of sensual thrills, Kracauer discerns an experience of lack not unrelated (even if differently interpreted) to Gorky's malaise. The unifying element of the cult of distraction lies in what Kracauer calls pure externality. And this celebration of the external responds to a central lack in the life of its audience, particularly that of the working masses:

> an essentially formal tension which fills their day without making it fulfilling. Such a lack demands to be compensated, but this need can only be articulated in terms of the same surface which imposed the lack in the first place. The form of entertainment necessarily corresponds to that of enterprise.[33]

The sudden, intense, and external satisfaction supplied by the succession of attractions was recognised by Kracauer as revealing the fragmentation of modern experience. The taste for thrills and spectacle, the particularly modern form of *curiositas* that defines the aesthetic of attractions, is moulded by a modern loss of fulfilling experience. Once again, Wolfgang Schivelbusch's understanding of the changes in modern perception brought about by railway travel provides a theoretical tool. Crossbreeding Freud's metapsychological formulations with the urban sociology of Simmel (and thus following a trajectory traced by Benjamin), Schivelbusch describes a stimulus shield, which inhabitants of the overstimulated environments of the modern world develop in order to ward off its constant assaults.[34] But one could also point out that this stimulus shield dulls the edge of experience, and more intense aesthetic energies are required to penetrate it. As Miriam Hansen points out in her reading of Benjamin, the modern experience of shock corresponds to "[t]he adaptation of human perception of industrial modes of production and transportation, especially the radical restructuration of spatial and temporal relations."[35] Shock becomes not only a mode of modern experience, but a strategy of a modern aesthetics of astonishment. Hence the exploitation of new technological thrills that flirt with disaster.

Attractions are a response to an experience of alienation, and for Kracauer (as for Benjamin) cinema's value lay in exposing a fundamental loss of coherence and authenticity. Cinema's deadly temptation lay in trying to attain the aesthetic coherence of traditional art and culture. The radical aspiration of film must lie along the path of consciously heightening its use of discontinuous shocks, or as Kracauer puts it, "must aim radically towards a kind of distraction which exposes disintegration rather than masking it."[37] As Hansen has indicated, Benjamin's analysis of shock has a fundamental ambivalence, moulded certainly by the impoverishment of experience in modern life, but also capable of assuming "a strategic significance—as an artificial means of propelling the human body into moments of recognition."[38]

The panic before the image on the screen exceeds a simple physical reflex, similar to those one experiences in a daily encounter with urban traffic or industrial production. In its double nature, its transformation of still image into moving illusion, it expresses an attitude in which astonishment and knowledge perform a vertiginous dance, and pleasure derives from the energy released by the play between the shock caused by this illusion of danger and delight in its pure illusion. The jolt experienced becomes a shock of recognition. Far from fulfilling a dream of total replication of reality—the *apophantis* of the myth of total cinema—the experience of the first projections exposes the hollow centre of the cinematic illusion. The thrill of transformation into motion depended on its presentation as a contrived illusion under the control of the projectionist showman. The movement from still to moving image accented the unbelievable and extraordinary nature of the apparatus itself. But in doing so, it also undid any naive belief in the reality of the image.

Cinema's first audiences can no longer serve as a founding myth for the theoreticalisation of the enthralled spectator. History reveals fissures along with continuities, and we must recognise that the experience of these audiences was profoundly different from the classical spectator's absorption into an empathetic narrative. Placed within a historical context and tradition, the first spectators' experience reveals not a childlike belief, but an undisguised awareness (and delight in) film's illusionistic capabilities. I have attempted to reverse the traditional understanding of this first onslaught of moving images. Like a demystifying showman, I have frozen the image of crowds scattered before the projection of an on-rushing train and read it allegorically rather than mythically. This arrest should astonish us with the realisation that these screams of terror and delight were well prepared for by both showmen and audience. The audience's reaction was the antipode to the primitive one: it was an encounter with modernity. From the start, the terror of that image uncovered a lack, and promised only a phantom embrace. The train collided with no one. It was, as Gorky said, a train of shadows, and the threat that it bore was freighted with emptiness.

NOTES

1. Accounts of the first exhibitions can be read in most standard film histories. Georges Sadoul, in *Histoire générale du cinéma*, t. I. *L'Invention du cinéma 1832–1897* (Paris: Denoël, 1948), p. 288, describes the panic of the crowds before *The Arrival of a*

Train, but, curiously, the testimony he cites refers to a Lumière street scene, rather than the train film. Other testimonies sometimes cited, such as Maxim Gorky's article discussed below, or the article Lynne Kirby quotes from *L'Illustration* (30 May 1896), describe the threat inscribed in the image itself, but do not indicate actual panic in the audience (see Lynne Kirby, "Male Hysteria and Early Cinema," *Camera Obscura* 17 (May 1988), 130. Recent histories are content to cite Sadoul, or simply repeat the legend. However, Charles Musser tells me that his research on early travelling exhibitor Lyman H. Howe has uncovered a number of references to spectators screaming during early projections of train films, although not at the first Lumière screenings.

I would like to indicate here the inspiration provided by Kirby's article and her ongoing work on early cinema and trains. I feel few writers have so well grasped the importance of shock in early cinema, even if I view its implications for early spectatorship somewhat differently than she does. I would also like to acknowledge the conversations with NYU graduate student Richard Decroix, which stimulated my thinking about this essay.

2. Christian Metz, *The Imaginary Signifier: Psychoanalysis and the Cinema,* tr. Celia Britton, Annwyl Williams, Ben Brewster, and Alfred Guzzetti (Bloomington: Indiana University Press, 1982), pp. 72–73. Ben Singer has pointed out the limitations of Metz's application of Freud's concept of the fetish to cinema in his article "Film, Photography and Fetish: The Analyses of Christian Metz," *Cinema Journal* 27/4 (Summer 1988). However, my main problem with Metz's always stimulating discussion lies in its ahistorical nature, which leads to an oversimplified view of cinema spectatorship. At the same time, I find that the lack Metz finds at the centre of the cinematic image is a profound insight, worthy of more than a metapsychological treatment.

Charles Musser (in his forthcoming volume in the History of American Film Series, vol. I, *The Emergence of Cinema in America*) points out that in *Ars magna lucis et umbrae* of 1671—the first full treatment of the catoptric lamp, a forerunner of the magic lantern—Athanasius Kircher declared that demystifying illusion is essential to any display of the apparatus, absolutely forbidding any understanding of the spectacle as magic. The religious and social motivations (Kircher was a Jesuit) for such a demystification are obvious. Musser makes the provocative claim that this moment "suggests a decisive turning point for screen practice when the observer of projected/reflected images became the historically constituted subject we now call the spectator" (p. 31). In other words, Musser would see demystification as essential to the existence of the spectator, and points out that a tradition of screen spectatorship preceded Lumière by centuries.

3. Metz, op. cit., p. 72.

4. See my article "Primitive Cinema: A Frame Up? or The Trick's On Us," in *Cinema Journal* 29/2 (Winter 1988–89). Accounts of Méliès's theatrical illusions can be found in Madeliene Maltete-Méliès, ed., *Méliès et la naissance du spectacle cinéma-tographique* (Paris: Klincksieck, 1984), esp. pp. 53–58, and in Pierre Jenn, *Méliès, Cinéaste* (Paris: Albatros, 1984), pp. 139–68. Paul Hammond's *Marvellous Méliès* (London: Gordon Fraser, 1974, pp. 15–26) also includes a discussion of Méliès's stage work and an indication of his debt to Maskelyne.

5. Martin Battersby, *Trompe l'Oeil: The Eye Deceived* (London: Academy Editions, 1974), p. 19. I must signal here that my essay has been both inspired and provoked by Mary Ann Doane's fascinating essay "When the Direction of the Force Acting on the Body Is Changed: The Moving Image," *Wide Angle* 7/2-3. There is a great deal of convergence in the topics covered by my essay and hers, as well as a great deal of divergence in method and conclusion.

6. The importance of the large scale of the original Lumière projections, particularly in competition with the Edison kinetoscope, has been pointed out by Jacques and Marie

André in their volume *Une Saison Lumière à Montpellier* (Perpignan, France: Institut Jean Vigo, 1987), pp. 64–65.

7. Gorky's account is included as an appendix in Jay Leyda, *Kino: A History of the Russian and Soviet Film* (London: Allen & Unwin, 1960), pp. 407–9. The translation is by "Leda Swan."

8. Ibid., p. 407. I must add that it was Annette Michelson who first pointed out this fact to me when I was a graduate student years ago. Her discussion of the *frisson* of this instance of motion was a generative point for this essay. One might point out that a possibly equally rich projection trope can be found in Lumière's *Destruction of a Wall*, which was projected first forwards and then in reverse, creating the magical effect of the wall reassembling and rising to its original height. A Montpellier journalist noted that this film "has always drawn applause from its admirers" (André, *Une Sasion Lumière*, p. 84, my translation).

9. Quoted in Georges Sadoul, *Histoire Général du Cinéma*, p. 271 (my translation).

10. Erik Barnouw, *The Magician and the Cinema* (New York: Oxford University Press, 1981), p. 75. The phrase is quoted from an 1899 article in the magical trade periodical *Mahatma*.

11. Albert E. Smith, in collaboration with Phil A. Koury, *Two Reels and a Crank* (Garden City, N.Y.: Doubleday, 1952), p. 39. Smith's book is notoriously inaccurate, as Charles Musser has shown. However, most of these errors seem to be misleading claims of fanciful achievements (e.g., filming in Cuba during the Spanish American War) and don't necessarily lessen the value of the description of his film shows.

12. Ibid., pp. 39–40.

13. See Tom Gunning, "The Cinema of Attraction: Early Film, Its Spectator and the Avant-Garde," Wide Angle 8/3-4. This term was first introduced by myself and André Gaudreault in a paper delivered to the colloquium Nouvelles approches de l'histoire du cinéma at Cerisy in 1985, called "Cinéma des premiers temps: un défi à l'histoire du cinéma?" Conversations with Adam Simon, a teaching assistant at the Carpenter Center of Visual and Environmental Studies of Harvard University, 1984–85, were also influential in developing these ideas. The term *attractions* refers backwards to a popular tradition and forwards to an avant-garde subversion. The tradition is that of the fairground and carnival, and particularly its development during the turn of the century in such modern amusement parks as Coney Island. The avant-garde radicalisation of this term comes in the theoretical and practical work in theatre and film of Sergei Eisenstein, whose theory of the montage of attractions intensified this popular energy into an aesthetic subversion, through a radical theoreticisation of the power of attractions to undermine the conventions of bourgeois realism. For a clear account of this theory and a discussion of its roots in popular culture, see Jacques Aumont's *Montage Eisenstein*, tr. Lee Hildreth, Constance Penley, and Andrew Ross (Bloomington: Indiana University Press, 1987), pp. 41–48), as well as Eisenstein's own essays "The Montage of Attractions" and "The Montage of Film Attractions,"" in Eisenstein, Writings, Vol. I 1922–1934, ed. and tr. Richard Taylor (Bloomington, University of Indiana Press, 1988).

14. Quoted in Jacques and Marie André, *Une Saison Lumière*, p. 66.

15. John F. Kasson, *Amusing the Millions: Coney Island at the Turn of the Century* (New York: Hill & Wang, 1978), pp. 77–78. Lynne Kirby, (from *L'Illustration*), pp. 119–120.

16. The role of the exhibitor showman in early American cinema has been brilliantly demonstrated in the work of Charles Musser, particularly in his article "The Nickelodeon Era Begins, Establishing the Framework for Hollywood's Mode of Representation" (*Framework*, Autumn 1983), as well as his forthcoming volumes on Edwin S. Porter and Lyman Howe.

17. Gunning, "Cinema of Attraction," p. 64. This issue is also discussed in my book *D.W. Griffith and the Origins of American Narrative Cinema* (Urbana: University of Illinois Press, 1991).

18. On the surrealist love of disorienting images in the cinema, see Paul Hammond, ed., *The Shadow and Its Shadow: Surrealist Writings on the Cinema* (London: British Film Institute, 1978), particularly Breton's essay "As in a Wood" (p. 14).

19. Michael Fried, *Absorption and Theatricality: Painting and Beholder in the Age of Diderot* (Berkeley and Los Angeles: University of California Press, 1980). See, for example, pp. 64, 104. A similar exclusion of the spectator is evident in the scenography and style of the nineteenth-century naturalist theatre, embodied in the idea of the fourth wall.

20. St. Augustine, *The Confessions*, tr. Rex Warner (New York: New American Library, 1963), pp. 245–47.

21. This satirical drawing is reproduced in Richard D. Altick, *The Shows of London* (Cambridge, Mass.: Harvard University Press, 1978), p. 254. As Miriam Hansen has pointed out to me, Michael Fried's discussion of Thomas Eakins' painting "Gross Clinic" raises issues relevant to the aesthetic of attractions and its relation to repulsion. Although Fried convincingly places the painting within a tradition of absorption, the foci of Gross' bloodstained fingers and scalpel and the patient's open wound seem to provide another experience, which "mixes pain and pleasure, violence and voluptuousness, repulsion and fascination" (Fried, "Realism, Writing and Disfiguration in Thomas Eakins' Gross Clinic," *Representations*, 9, Winter 1985, 71). As Fried says, "It is above all the conflictedness of that situation that grips and excruciates and in the end stupefies us before the picture" (p. 73). This seems to me to describe the essential experience of the aesthetic of attractions; however, it is somewhat unclear to me how Fried sees this in relation to the experience of absorption. Fried does not relate this conflict to the tradition of the sublime, which clearly represents the acceptable form of the aesthetic of attractions (recall that Burke defines astonishment as the effect of the sublime in the highest degree). The relation of popular entertainment to the sublime is a basically unexplored and potentially fascinating topic, beyond the confines of this essay. But it is not irrelevant to point out that Fried follows Thomas Weiskel in associating the effect of the sublime with a Freudian understanding of the terror of castration. Although I am not inclined at the moment to pursue it, speculation in this direction about the trauma produced by the first projections could provide a new way of approaching the issue of fetishism in early cinema, locating the trauma that Metz did little to isolate. The interest of this speculation could be considerable if approached from a historical point of view, as in Benjamin's and Schivelbusch's understanding (which I will discuss later in this essay) of the Freudian concept of the stimulus shield as a response to modern experience, rather than a biological principle.

22. Urban's series of films is described in Rachel Low and Roger Manvell, *The History of the British Film, Vol. I 1896–1906*, (London: Allen & Unwin, 1948), p. 60.

23. Harry Furniss, *Our Lady Cinema*, reprint of 1914 ed. (New York: Garland Publishing, 1978), p. 41.

24. Wolfgang Schivelbusch, *The Railway Journey* (New York: Urizen Press, 1979), p. 66.

25. From the *New York Mail and Express* (25 September 1897), reprinted in Kemp R. Niver, *The Biograph Bulletins 1896–1908* (Los Angeles: Locare Research Group, 1971), p. 27. The journalist was commenting on a Biograph film shot from a locomotive going through the Haverstraw Tunnel.

26. Maxim Gorky, "Boredom," The Independent (8 August 1907), 311–12.

27. The key essays are, of course, "The Work of Art in the Age of Mechanical Reproduction" (in *Illuminations*, ed. Hanna Arendt, tr. Harry Zohn: New York: Schocken Books, 1969) and the two drafts of the essay on Baudelaire (in *Charles Baudelaire: A Lyric*

Poet in the Era of High Capitalism, tr. Harry Zohn: London: NLB, 1973). My understanding of Benjamin's work has been shaped by Miriam Hansen's masterful essay "Benjamin, Cinema and Experience: The Blue Flower in the Land of Technology," *New German Critique* 40 (Winter 1987). This essay and Hansen's forthcoming work on the spectator of American silent film, *Babel and Babylon*, provide an essential background to my own essay. Her influence has been pervasive, and I see my ideas as developing out of a dialogue with her, without in any way implicating her in their final formulation. I also wish to thank her for her comments on a draft of this essay.

28. Siegfried Kracauer, "The Cult of Distraction," *New German Critique* 40 (Winter 1987). I would also like to indicate my debt to Heide Schlüpmann's penetrating essay on Kracauer's early film theory, "Phenomenology of Film: On Seigfried Kracauer's Writings of the 1920s" (in the same issue), as well as the valuable discussions of Kracauer contained in the essays by Thomas Elsaesser, Patrice Petro, and Sabine Hake in this extraordinary issue on Weimar Film Theory.

29. Kracauer, ibid., p. 94.

30. Ibid.

31. Ibid., p. 92.

32. Ibid., p. 96.

33. Ibid., p. 93.

34. Schivelbusch, *The Railway Journey*, pp. 156–7.

35. Miriam Hansen, *Benjamin, Cinema*, p. 184. Lynne Kirby observes about the popularity of staged railroad smash-ups: "As a spectacularisation of technological destruction based on an equation of pleasure with terror, the 'imagination of disaster' says volumes about the kinds of violent spectacle demanded by a modern public, and the transformation of 'shock' into eagerly expected, digestible spectacle" (Kirby, from *L'Illustration*, p. 120).

36. Kracauer, "Cult of Distraction," p. 96.

37. Hansen, *Benjamin, Cinema*, pp. 210–211.

Miriam Hansen

Early Cinema, Late Cinema: Transformations of the Public Sphere

There tends to be a moment, in the development of cultural practices, when discourses of the recent past become history; they are no longer merely outdated but, like bell-bottom jeans, miniskirts, and platform shoes, acquire historicity. This is what seems to have happened with film theory of the 1970s and early 1980s, in particular as it revolved around the notion of the spectator. I am thinking here of psychoanalytic-semiotic approaches, often inflected with Marxist and feminist politics, associated with the names of Jean-Louis Baudry, the later Christian Metz, Raymond Bellour, Stephen Heath, and Laura Mulvey, to mention only a few. As has been pointed out widely, the paradigmatic distinction of 1970s film theory—its break with earlier film theory—consisted in a shift of focus from textual structures or ontologies of the medium to processes of reception and spectatorship. Whether concerned with the cinematic apparatus or with textual operations of enunciation and address, these approaches converged in the question of how the cinema works to construct, interpellate, and reproduce its viewer as subject and how it solicits actual moviegoers to identify with and through ideologically marked positions of subjectivity. In either case, the inquiry hinged on the hypothetical term of an *ideal* spectator, a unified and unifying position offered by the text or apparatus even though, as feminist and, more recently, subaltern critics have pointed out, this position for some

This is a slightly expanded version of an essay that originally appeared in *Screen* 34:3 (Autumn 1993), 197–210. Reprinted by permission of the author and *Screen*.

viewers turns out to be a "locus of impossibility,"[1] of self-denial or masochism.

I will not reiterate the by now ritual critique of that type of film theory, whether concerning its epistemological and methodological short-cuts, its monolithic notion of classical cinema, or its abstract, passive conception of the spectator and processes of reception; these were important issues when the theory was still current. What I find more interesting is that the very category of *the* spectator developed by psychoanalytic-semiotic film theory seems to have become obsolete—not only because new scholarship has displaced it with historically and culturally more specific models but because the mode of reception this spectator was supposed to epitomize is itself becoming a matter of the past. The historical significance of 1970s theories of spectatorship may well be that they emerged at the threshold of a paradigmatic transformation of the ways films are disseminated and consumed. In other words, even as those theories set out to unmask the ideological effects of the classical Hollywood cinema, they might effectively, and perhaps unwittingly, have mummified the spectator-subject of classical cinema.

We are only now beginning to understand the massive changes that have assailed the institution of cinema over the past two decades. Those changes are the result of a combination of technological and economic developments that have displaced the cinema as the only and primary site of film consumption. New electronic technologies propped onto television, in particular video playback, satellite, and cable systems, have shifted the venues for film viewing in the direction of domestic space and have profoundly changed the terms on which viewers can interact with films. The spatioperceptual configuration of television within the domestic environment has broken the spell of the classical diegesis; the compulsive temporality of public projection has given way to ostensibly more self-regulated yet privatized, distracted, and fragmented acts of consumption. As critics have observed, an aesthetics of the glance is replacing the aesthetics of the gaze—the illusionist absorption of the viewer that is considered one of the hallmarks of classical cinema.[2]

These changes have in turn affected the cinema in the old sense: as the public, commercial projection of films on theatrical premises. For one thing, there have never—not since the days of the nickelodeon—been as many complaints about people talking during the shows as in the American press of recent months, with pundits charging that the vulgarians simply can't tell the difference between watching a movie in the theater and watching a video in their living room. What such complaints signal is that the classical principle by which reception is controlled by the film as an integral product and commodity is weakened by the social proliferation of film consumption in institutionally less regulated viewing situations. For another, the increased dependence of film production on the video market has exacerbated the crisis of the audience that Hollywood has confronted in various forms at least since the popularization of television in the 1950s. Blockbuster films, for instance, are catering to as many diverse constituencies as possible, confronting the problem of, as Timothy Corrigan puts it, "an audience fragmented beyond any controllable identity."[3] Such films—from *Gremlins* through the *Terminator* films to *Bram Stoker's Dracula*—no longer attempt to homogenize empirically diverse viewers by way of unifying strategies of spectator positioning (as 1970s film theorists claimed with regard to classical films). Rather, the blockbuster gamble consists of offering something to everyone, of appealing to diverse interests with a diversity of attractions and multiple levels of textuality. All this is not to say that the classical mode of spectatorship has vanished without a trace; on the contrary, it makes powerful returns in the nostalgia mode. But it has become one of a number of options, often contextualized and ironized, and it no longer functions as the totalitarian norm it is supposed to have been during the 1930s and 1940s.[4]

On a geopolitical level, the shift in film-spectator relations corresponds to the emergence of new, transnational corporate networks that circulate movies and videos along with music, foods, fashions, advertising, information, and communication technologies. While systems of distribution and exchange are interconnected and unified on a global scale, the process is characterized by a burgeoning diversification of products and, at the same time, increased privatization of the modes and venues of consumption.[5] New forms and genres of diasporic and indigenized mass culture have emerged, at once syncretistic and original, and imported products are transformed and appropriated through highly specific forms of reception.[6] Thus, parallel with the demise of classical cinema, we have been witnessing the end of so-called modern mass culture—the kind of mass culture that prevailed, roughly, from the 1920s through the 1960s and is commonly associated with a Fordist economy, with standardized production and social homogenization, and with critical keywords like secondary exploitation, Americanization, and cultural imperialism. Today's postmodern, globalized culture of consumption has developed new, and ever more elusive, technologies of power and commodification, to be sure, operating through diversification rather than homogenization: the worldwide manufacture of diversity does anything but automatically translate into a "new culture politics of difference."[7] But it has also multiplied the junctures at which such a politics could— and, in many places has—come into existence, in particular with alternative practices in film and video.[8] At any rate, whatever political score one may assign to these developments, it is obvious that they require different theories of reception and identification from those predicated on classical Hollywood cinema and the American model of mass culture.

As classical forms of film consumption seem to be unraveling on a worldwide scale, the situation has a certain *déja-vu* effect. In more than one way, contemporary forms of media culture evoke the parallel of early cinema. As recent scholarship has stressed, the paradigmatic distinction of early cinema from classical cinema involved not only different conceptions of space, time, narrative, and genre but, above all, a different conception of the relations between film and viewer. That difference has been traced both at the stylistic level—in textual modes of representation and address—and at the level of exhibition practices—the performance of films in commercial settings.

Aiming at the specificity of early film-viewer relations, Tom Gunning has coined the by now familiar phrase *cinema of attractions*, which plays on the Eisensteinian sense of *attraction* as well as its more colloquial usage in the context of fairgrounds, circuses, variety shows, dime museums, and other commercial entertainment venues that had also inspired Eisenstein's use of the term.[9] Early cinema inherited from those venues a diversity of genres and topics such as boxing matches, scenes from the wild west and passion plays, travelogues in the manner of the stereopticon lectures, trick films in the tradition of magic shows, sight gags and comic skits from the burlesque or vaudeville stage, pornographic flicks in the peep-show vein, and highlights from popular plays and operas. With this tradition, early films adopted a particular aesthetics of display, of showmanship, defined by the goal of assaulting viewers with sensational, supernatural, scientific, sentimental, or otherwise stimulating sights, as opposed to enveloping them into the illusion of a fictional narrative. The style of early films was presentational rather than representational; that is, they tended to address the viewer directly—as in frequent asides to the camera and the predominantly frontal organization of space—rather than indirectly—as classical films do through perceptual absorption into a closed diegetic space.[10]

True to their variety lineage, early films lured patrons with a diversity, if not an excess of appeals, as opposed to the later subordination and integration of polymorphous spectatorial pleasures under the regime of classical narrative. Such appeals included physical jolts, shocks, and sensations—whether of a kinetic, pornographic, or abjective sort—from the many films shot from moving vehicles (e.g., *Interior N. Y. Subway, 14th Street to 42nd Street*) to actualities or reenactments of disasters and executions (e.g., *The Electrocution of an Elephant*). Even though such physiological responses were soon denigrated or marginalized in favor of the classical ideal of disembodied, specularized spectatorship, they have resurfaced in various guises, from such interludes as Cinerama and 3-D to the latest versions (influenced by MTV) of cult, horror, and action films.[11]

Moreover, early films relied more overtly on cultural intertexts, such as the popular stories, songs, or political cartoons on which many of them were based, whether illustrating or spoofing them. Indeed, as Charles Musser has shown, the major distinction between early narrative films and protoclassical ones was the extent to which narrative comprehension of the former depended on the audience's familiarity with the story or event depicted.[12] Porter's film *Waiting at the Church* (1906), for instance, makes little sense if we don't know the popular hit by the same title sung by Vesta Victoria, and *The "Teddy" Bears* (1907) requires foreknowledge not only of the Goldilocks story but also of political satire surrounding Theodore Roosevelt's hunting exploits. Such overt forms of intertextuality placed a much greater emphasis on the enactment of the film by the audience and on the audience's interaction with the film, but it also meant that reception was at the mercy of factors that could be neither controlled nor standardized by means of strategies of production. Key to the shift toward classical cinema was, consequently, the more systematic effort, from about 1907 on, to develop a mode of narration that made films self-explanatory and self-contained and that allowed films to be understood by a mass audience regardless of individual cultural and ethnic background and of site and mode of exhibition.

It is a mark of early cinema's specificity that its effects on the viewer were determined less by the film as complete product and inter/nationally circulated commodity than by the particular context of exhibition—the particular show. The format of presentation typical of early cinema was shaped by the commercial entertainments in whose context films were first shown, in particular vaudeville and traveling shows. From those entertainment forms, the cinema borrowed two major principles: (1) a disjunctive style of programming—the variety format—by which short films alternated with live performances (vaudeville turns; animal, acrobat, and magic acts; song slides) and (2) the mediation of the individual film by personnel present in the theater, such as lecturers, sound effects specialists, and, invariably, musicians. Both principles preserved a perceptual continuum between the space/time of the theater and the illusionist world on screen, as opposed to the classical segregation of screen and theater space with its regime of absence and presence and its discipline of silence, spellbound passivity, and perceptual isolation. What is more, early cinema's dispersal of meaning across filmic and nonfilmic sources, such as the alternation of films and numbers, lent the exhibition the character of a live event, that is, a performance that varied from place to place and time to time depending on theater type and location, audience composition, and musical accompaniment. Some of these practices, such as the variety format and the priority of the theater experience over the film experience—persisted well into the nickelodeon period and throughout the silent period, even as the films themselves were increasingly patterned on classical principles.[13]

Yet this attempt to delineate early cinema's paradigmatic difference by pinpointing consistent traits and traditions may be essentializing and misleading. The diversity that characterizes early cinema's offerings and appeals was far from institutionalized: it was more likely an effect of experimental instability. As Gunning suggests, "It is perhaps early cinema's very mutability and fragmented nature (into many practices with unstable hierarchies of importance) that contrasts most sharply with what has become the model of classical Hollywood cinema."[14] However stable and functional *classical* cinema may have appeared by contrast (and that stability is as much the product of a particular historiographic optics as of the dominant industrial mode), *contemporary* film and media culture seems to be reverting to a state in which transitory, ephemeral practices are mushrooming, the institution of cinema is increasingly fragmented and dispersed, and long-standing hierarchies of production, distribution, and exhibition have lost their force.

The comparison between preclassical and contemporary modes of film consumption has occasionally been floated in recent years, charged with more or less polemical valences. In an essay published in 1982, Noël Burch observes that "United States network television constitutes a return to the days of the nickelodeon" and argues, with considerable alarm, that the disengaged, disjunctive format of U.S. television might represent "a veritable turning back of the clock," a regresoion that is nothing less than "innocent." That observation leads him to defend, as essential to a politically progressive form of media practice, the otherwise much maligned "strong diegetic effect" of classical cinema, the "Institutional Mode of Representation."[15] A decade later, parallels between preclassical and postclassical forms of spectatorship, between early modern and postmodern forms of distraction and diversity, are even more pronounced, though no less in need of discussion. What is the point of such a comparison? How can we make it productive beyond formalist analogy, beyond nostalgia or cultural pessimism? How can we align those two moments without obliterating their historical difference?

I suggest that drawing a trajectory from postclassical to preclassical cinema makes sense not only because of formal similarities in the relations of representation and reception. More important, these formal similarities warrant closer scrutiny because both moments mark a major transition in the development of the public sphere. I am using the term *public* here in the most general sense, denoting a discursive matrix or process through which social experience is articulated, interpreted, negotiated, and contested in an intersubjective, potentially collective, and oppositional form. My understanding of the term is indebted to debates in the tradition of the Frankfurt School, associated with the work of Jürgen Habermas, Oskar Negt, and Alexander Kluge. Indeed, I would argue that the question of the public is probably the Frankfurt School's most fruitful legacy for film and mass culture theory today.

I see the debates on the public in the tradition of the Frankfurt School as the continuation of a critical project that registered, early on, the key role of cinema and mass culture in the profound restructuration of subjectivity. At the same time it saw the modern media's liberatory, democratic potential evaporate in media's alienating, conformist, and manipulative use in Fordist-liberal capitalism, to say nothing of fascism. Kluge may well have shared Adorno's analysis of the culture industry (and its administrative, postwar West German counterpart). But he drew different aesthetic and political conclusions from that analysis: he became a filmmaker and activist promoting an alternative film and media culture. Drawing on Adorno's own philosophy, in particular *Negative Dialectics* and the concept of nonidentity, Kluge set out to mobilize the aporias of the culture industry thesis—by switching the frame from the logics of commodity and identity to the dynamics of the public sphere.[16]

In English-language contexts, the category of the public has become increasingly important to a wide variety of fields and debates: philosophy; anthropology; history; South Asian, East Asian, and African studies; postcolonial and subaltern studies; the postmodern art scene; and feminist, gay/lesbian, and queer politics. If public sphere theory has so far had little impact on cinema and media studies, it has been for a good or, rather, not so good reason. Many of these debates take as their point of departure the framework developed by Habermas in his 1962 study *The Structural Transformation of the Public Sphere*, which only recently appeared in English translation.[17] The advantage of Habermas's approach, that he historicizes the concept of the public sphere by tracing its emergence in the eighteenth century, turns into a disadvantage when it comes to the mass-mediated publics of later centuries. Positing the Enlightenment idea of the public sphere as a critical norm (even as historically it has degenerated into an ideology), Habermas can view subsequent formations of public life only in terms of disintegration and decline. With the shift from cultural *räsonnement* to cultural consumption, says Habermas, the dialectics of public and private unravels into individuated acts of reception, even in the context of mass events. The problem with this approach is not only that it remains squarely within the paradigm of the culture industry but that the underlying notion of the public is predicated on face-to-face communication, hence insufficient for conceptualizing mass-mediated forms of public life.[18]

It is in view of this paradox—the problem of how to conceptualize the dimension of the public in a technologically and industrially mediated public sphere that has eroded the very conditions of discursive interaction, participation, and self-representation—that Negt's and Kluge's study *The Public Sphere and Experience* (1972) offers a useful intervention.[19] Like a number of Habermas's recent American critics, Negt and Kluge argue that the ideal of the eighteenth-century public sphere was ideological in its very conception, masking the de facto exclusion of substantial social groups (workers, women, servants) and of vital social issues such as the material conditions of production and reproduction (sexuality, child rearing). Negt and Kluge insist on the need to understand postliberal and postliterary formations of the public sphere—crucially defined by the photographic and electronic media—in terms other than those of disintegration and decline.

Negt's and Kluge's argument rests on two major moves; One is to call into question the very concept of the public as it is traditionally understood. The authors survey the various institutions and activities that *claim* the term *public* (public opinion, public force, public relations), and they then contrast these rather limited and ossified, professionalized practices with another sense of the term, that of a "general *horizon of experience* in which what is really or supposedly relevant for all members of society is summarized."[20] This expansion of the category of the public involves a shift from the formal conditions of communication (free association, free speech, equal participation, polite argument) to the more comprehensive notion of a "social horizon of experience," grounded in what Negt and Kluge call "the context of living" (*Lebenszusammenhang*), in material, psychic and social re/production.[21] This horizon includes, emphatically, what the dominant public sphere either leaves out, privatizes, or acknowledges only in an abstract and fragmented form. Predicated on inclusion and interconnection (*Zusammenhang*), the horizon involves the dialectical imbrication of three distinct layers: (1) the experience of re/production under capitalist, alienated conditions; (2) the systematic blockage of that experience as a horizon in its own right, that is, the separation of the experiencing subjects from the networks of public expression and representation; and (3) as a response to that blockage— imaginative and resistant modes of realigning the sundered chunks of experience and of reality and fantasy, time, and history and memory.[22]

Negt's and Kluge's second move is that they do not construct this horizon in analogy to the bourgeois-liberal model—as a presumably autonomous sphere above the marketplace and particular interests—but rather trace its contours in the new industrial-commercial publics that no longer pretend to such a separate, independent status. These "public spheres of production" include a variety of contexts, such as factory communities, spaces of commerce and consumption (restaurants, shopping malls), and, of course, the cinema and other privately owned media of the "consciousness industry."[23] Lacking legitimation of their own, the industrial-commercial publics enter into alliances with the disintegrating, bourgeois public sphere, from opera and masterpiece theater to political parties and institutions of parliamentary democracy; the latter in turn increasingly depends on industrial-commercial publicity for its continued operation and power. (The idea of an "electronic townhall," whose populist veneer is part and parcel of its syncretistic and contradictory public character, marks a further step in that direction.) But even as the public spheres of production reproduce the ideological, exclusionary mechanisms of the bourgeois prototype, they also aim, for economic reasons, at a maximum of inclusion. Lacking substance of their own, they voraciously absorb, as their fodder, or raw material, contexts of living that are hitherto bracketed from representation—if only to appropriate, assimilate, abstract, and commodify vital areas of social experience and if only to render them obsolete once exhausted and thus again insignificant. It is in their potentially indiscriminating, inclusive grasp, Negt and Kluge argue, that the public spheres of production make visible, at certain junctures, a different function of the public, namely that of a social horizon of experience.

In *The Public Sphere and Experience*, Negt and Kluge refer to this emphatically inclusive horizon by the self-consciously anachronistic term *proletarian public sphere*, which they see prefigured in alternative and oppositional publics or counterpublics. True to the Marxian sense of the term, the *proletarian public sphere* is not an empirical category (and certainly has little to do with traditional labor organizations) but a category of negation in both a critical and a utopian sense, referring to the fragmentation of human labor, existence and experience, and its dialectical opposite: the practical negation of existing conditions in their totality. In their subsequent collaboration, *History and Obstinacy* (1981), Negt and Kluge locate that utopian possibility in the very process of (alienated) production, in the "historical organization of labor power."[24] For, while constituted in the process of separation (e.g., primitive accumulation and division of labor), labor power contains and reproduces capacities and energies that exceed its realization in/as a commodity: resistance to separation, *Eigensinn* (stubbornness, self-will), self-regulation, fantasy, memory, curiosity, cooperation, feelings, and skills in excess of capitalist valorization. Whether and how those energies can become effective depends on the organization of the public sphere.

Methodologically, this translates into a principled oscillation between an empirical approach—analyzing the organization of public life in a given situation—and an emphatic sense of publicness that traces the dynamics of that situation in terms of its forgotten or unrealized possibilities. The critical measure in each case will be the extent to which experience is dis/organized from above—by the exclusionary standards of high culture or in the interest of profit—or from below—by the experiencing subjects themselves, on the basis of their context of living. The political task is to create "relationality" (Jameson's translation of *Zusammenhang*); to make connections between isolated chunks of experience across segregated domains of work and leisure, fiction and fact, and past and present; and to identify points of contiguity among diverse and/or competing partial publics and counterpublics. This politics of relationality is up against the hegemonic form of *Zusammenhang*—the violent pseudosynthesis of the dominant public sphere, which is maintained by the alliance of industrial-commercial and bourgeois publicity and which masquerades as *the* public sphere (the subject of the evening news, the "nation").

But this is not an either/or argument. Negt and Kluge insist that it is impossible to define or describe *Offentlichkeit, or publicness,* in the singular, as if it had any homogeneous substance. Rather, it can be understood always and only as an aggregation or mixture of different types of public life, corresponding to uneven stages of economic, technical, and social organization ranging from local to global parameters. If Negt and Kluge, for heuristic purposes, distinguish among bourgeois, industrial-commercial, and proletarian prototypes, they argue that none of these can be grasped in purity or isolation from each other but only in their mutual imbrication and in specific overlaps, parasitic cohabitations, and structural contradictions.

Conceptualizing the public as a mixture of competing forms of organizing social experience means thinking of it as a potentially volatile *process,* defined by different speeds and temporal markers. Such syncretistic dynamics harbors a potential for instability, for accidental collisions and opportunities, and for unpredictable conjunctures and aleatory developments. It is in the seams and fissures between uneven formations of public life that alternative alignments and alliances can emerge.[25] And it is in the degree to which a public sphere affords these windows of improvisation and reconfiguration that, I think, Gunning's observation about early cinema's relative instability has its larger reference point. And this particular dynamic of the public is also what realigns early cinema, not with its classical successor but with the current phase of film and media culture.

What is the point of thinking about cinema in terms of the public? Kluge himself, in his writings, films, and video practice, has been putting the politics of the public sphere into practice on several levels. Central to his film aesthetics is a concept of montage predicated on relationality—he refers to montage as the morphology of relations (*Formenwelt des Zusammenhangs*)[26]—a textual climbing wall designed to encourage viewers to draw their own connections across generic divisions of fiction and documentary and of disparate realms and registers of experience. A film is successful in that regard if it manages to activate (rather than merely usurp) what Kluge calls "the film in the spectator's head"—the horizon of experience as instantiated in the subject. The specific connections encouraged by the film respond to the structural blockages of experience perpetuated by the dominant public sphere, in particular, in the case of (West) Germany, the divisions imposed by the ossified programming structures of state-sponsored television.[27] But since the monopoly of the latter has been breaking up over the past decade, with a proliferation of private channels (close to forty) approximating the diversification level of television in the United States, Kluge has reoriented his project in view of the complex and dramatic changes in the German—and European—media landscape. Producing a weekly program for commercial television, he has been trying to reinvent alternative forms of cinema—a contemporary cinema of attractions—in the politically compromising, potentially neutralizing environment of advanced electronic publicity.[28]

Beyond Kluge's own, still to some extent modernist, film aesthetics, the concept of the public can be mobilized to address a number of key concerns of film and media studies in recent years and to take them a step further. In particular, thinking of the cinema in terms of the public involves an approach that cuts across theoretical and historical as well as textual and contextual modes of inquiry, for the cinema functions both as a public sphere of its own—defined by specific relations of representation and reception—and as part of a larger social horizon—defined by other media and by the overlapping local, national and global, face-to-face and deterritorialized structures of public life. This dual focus allows us to salvage some of the insights of formalist and psychoanalytic film theory—insights into the workings of cinematic texts and the psychic mechanisms of reception—while changing their paradigmatic status. For even if we situate reception within a specific historical and social framework, and even as the category of *the* spectator has become problematic, we still need a theoretical understanding of the possible relations between films and viewers, between representation and subjectivity. The questions raised in the name of alternative appropriations of late-capitalist mass culture cannot be answered by empirical reception studies. These questions need to be discussed in terms of experience (in the emphatic Frankfurt School sense, which includes memory and the unconscious) and the conditions of its possibility—the structures that simultaneously restrict and enable agency, interpretation, and self-organization.

The turn to (or, to some extent, revival of) more empirically oriented reception studies—and with it the methodological conflation of the actual social viewer and the spectator-subject—has been flanked, especially in Europe, by a nostalgic revival of the cinema as a good object. In a recently published anthology of cinephile reminiscences, *Seeing in the Dark*, the editors complain that methods of empirical audience research fail to

> fully capture the individual, subjective experience of filmgoing, since they miss out idiosyncratic detail and the personal dreamworld. Mea-

suring applause does not reveal that the movie was memorable for the woman in the third row because the building on screen reminded her of where she went to school and all those childhood memories came flooding back intercut with the film while the auditorium gently shook as an underground train passed beneath and a cigarette ash fluttered down from the balcony in the projector beam.[29]

To be sure, empirical audience research misses all these marvelous, and essential, dimensions of moviegoing (as would, for that matter, a Lacanian-Althusserian analysis of spectatorial positioning). But to reduce these dimensions, in a subjectivist vein, to the merely personal and idiosyncratic will mean missing out on the more systematic parameters of subjectivity that structure, enable, and refract our personal engagement with the film. These include, for instance, the particular cinematic style that set off the viewer's memory; the contrast between the nostalgically evoked local theater setting (e.g., cigarette smoke, high-modern urban technology) and the context of electronic and global postmodernity (e.g., the likelihood that the viewer in the third row, like the one behind her, may usually watch soap operas); and the fact that the viewer belongs to the social group of women—differentiated according to class, race, ethnicity, sexual orientation, and generation—which renders her relation to the film shown, probably one version or another of classical cinema, problematic in particular ways. These and other factors structure the horizon of experience that we carry around with us, whether we watch a film alone or collectively. At the same time, that horizon enables and allows us to reflect upon individual experience; indeed, the ability of a film and a viewing situation to trigger personal and collective memory is a measure of its quality as a public sphere.

Thinking of the cinema in terms of the public means reconstructing a horizon of reception not only in terms of sociological determinants, whether pertaining to statistically definable demographic groups or traditional communities, but also in terms of multiple and conflicting identities and constituencies. Indeed, the cinema can, at certain junctures, function as a matrix for challenging social positions of identity and otherness and as a catalyst for new forms of community and solidarity. That this may happen on the terrain of late-capitalist consumption, however, does not mean that we should resign ourselves to the range of existing products and modes of production. On the contrary, the category of the public retains a critical, utopian edge, predicated on the ideal of collective self-determination. (This perspective mandates not only main-

taining critical distinctions with regard to the commercially disseminated fare but also envisioning alternative media products and the alternative organization of the relations of representation and reception. In
that sense, the concept of the public forestalls the idealization of consumption that has become habitual in some quarters of cultural studies.)

To conclude, I return to the significance of early cinema, in
particular for assessing contemporary developments. I have argued elsewhere that early cinema, and the persistence of early exhibition practices
through and even beyond the nickelodeon period, provided the conditions for an alternative public sphere.[30] Specifically, it did so as an
industrial-commercial public sphere that during a crucial phase depended on peripheral social groups (immigrants, members of the recently
urbanized working class, women) and thus, willingly or not, catered to
people with specific needs, anxieties, and fantasies—people whose experience was shaped by more or less traumatic forms of territorial and
cultural displacement. The problems posed by the cinema's availability
to ethnically diverse, socially unruly, and sexually mixed audiences in
turn prompted the elaboration of classical modes of narration and spectator positioning. Rather than taking the industrial promotion of classical
cinema (and with it the gentrification of theaters and the streamlining of
exhibition practices) as the prime determining factor, however, I see
silent cinema as the site of overlapping, uneven, and competing types of
publicity. These include the more local spheres of late-nineteenth-century popular amusements, new commercial entertainments such as
vaudeville and amusement parks, and the emerging sphere of mass-
cultural production and distribution. As a composite public sphere, the
nickelodeon combined traditions of live performance with an industrially produced commodity circulated on both national and international
scales; that is, technologically mediated forms of publicity coexisted
with forms of public life predicated on face-to-face relations.

Above all, the conception of film exhibition as a live performance
(the incompleteness of the film as circulated commodity) created a
margin of improvisation, interpretation, and unpredictability that made
it a public event in the emphatic sense and a collective horizon in which
industrially processed experience could be reappropriated by the experiencing subjects. This means that films were viewed differently and were
likely to have a wide range of meanings depending on the neighborhood
and status of the theater, on the ethnic and racial background of the
habitual audience, on the mixture of gender and generation, and on the
ambition and skills of the exhibitor and the performing personnel. In

Chicago movie theaters catering to African-Americans during the 1910s and 1920s, for instance, the nonfilmic program drew heavily on Southern black performance traditions, and live musical accompaniment was more likely inspired by jazz and blues than by Wagner and Waldteufel.[31] Although the films shown in such theaters were largely white main-stream productions, their meaning was bound to be fractured and iron-ized in the context of black performance and audience response. I am not saying that such reappropriation actually happened in every single screening or every theater, nor do I think that empirical methods of research could determine whether it did or not. But the syncretistic makeup of cinematic publicity furnished the structural conditions under which that margin could be actualized, under which alternative forms of reception and meaning could gain a momentum of their own.

This dynamic was not limited to the local level, but could, because of its mass-cultural distribution, spread across traditional cul-tural and territorial boundaries. A case in point is the star system, in particular the rise of stars whose marketable persona conflicted with Hollywood's traditional racial and sexual orientations. As studies on individual stars such as Greta Garbo, Rudolph Valentino, Paul Robeson, and Mae West suggest, there is never a seamless among between studio publicity, fan magazines, and actual audiences, and the push and pull among these forces have again and again given rise to subcultural formations of reception.[32]

Today, the lines of the frontiers of transgression are drawn differently, and transgressiveness itself has become infinitely more part of the game than it was during the 1920s. Valentino has been vindicated by a long line of androgynous performers, from Elvis through Mick Jagger to Prince and Michael Jackson, and Madonna makes us nostalgic for the aesthetic implantation of perversions afforded by the Production Code. But racism and homophobia persist, and the gains made by the women's movement are inseparable from masculinist backlash, the antiabortion campaign, and heterosexual violence. Now as then, these issues are negotiated through the most advanced forms of industrial-commercial publicity—then a cinema and fan culture increasingly submerged into the hegemonic homogeneity of classic mass culture, today a global electronic media culture that reproduces itself through ceaseless diversification.

To return to my earlier question: how can we compare post-classical and preclassical modes of spectatorship or early modern and postmodern forms of mass and consumer culture? Obviously, we are dealing with substantially different stages of historical development, not only on the social and cultural level but, fundamentally, in terms of the organization of capital and the media industries. Nonetheless, from the perspective of the public sphere, a number of affinities suggest themselves. Both periods are characterized by a profound transformation of the relations of cultural representation and reception and by a measure of instability that makes the intervening decades look relatively stable by contrast, for they are anchored in and centered by the classical system. Both stages of media culture vary from the classical norm of controlling reception through a strong diegetic effect, ensured by particular textual strategies and a suppression of the exhibition context. By contrast, preclassical and postclassical forms of spectatorship give the viewer a greater leeway, for better or for worse, in interacting with the film—a greater awareness of exhibition and cultural intertexts. Both early modern and postmodern media publics draw on the *periphery*—then, on socially marginalized and diverse constituencies within American national culture, and today, on massive movements of migration on a global scale that, along with the globalization of media consumption, have irrevocably changed the terms of local and national identity.

Early cinema could have developed in a number of ways, inasmuch as it contained "a number of roads not taken."[33] Postmodern media culture seems to be characterized by a similar opening up of new directions and possibilities combined, however, with vastly enhanced powers of seduction, manipulation, and destruction. Putting early modern and postmodern forms of media consumption in a constellation may take away some of the inevitability the classical paradigm has acquired both in Hollywood self-promotion and in functionalist film histories.[34] Drawing a trajectory between these two moments in the history of public life may make classical cinema and the classical mass culture of the New Deal and Cold War eras look more like a historical interlude, a deep-freeze perhaps, than the teleological norm that it has become and that has shaped our approaches to reception. And once we have shifted the frame, classical cinema itself may no longer look quite as classical as study of its dominant mode suggests.

NOTES

1. Mary Ann Doane, "Misrecognition and Identity," *Cine-Tracts* 3:3 (Fall 1980), 29.

2. See John Ellis, *Visible Fictions: Cinema, Television, Video* (London: Routledge, 1982), pp. 24, 50, 128, 137ff.; also see Charles Eidsvik, "Machines of the Invisible: Changes in Film Technology in the Age of Video," *Film Quarterly* 42:2 (Winter 1988–89), 21.

3. Timothy Corrigan, *A Cinema without Walls: Movies and Culture after Vietnam* (New Brunswick, N.J.: Rutgers University Press, 1991), p. 23.

4. Ironically, the European art film has become one of the more likely places for contemporary viewers to expect a relatively high degree of classical absorption. This may partially explain the U.S. success of *The Crying Game* (Neil Jordan, 1992), a film that, despite its self-conscious politics of reading, still very much depends on a classical diegetic effect (without which its trick would not work).

5. Among the growing literature on these developments see, for instance, Arjun Appadurai, "Disjuncture and Difference in the Global Cultural Economy," *Public Culture* 2 (Spring 1990), 1–24; Mike Featherstone, ed., *Theory, Culture & Society (SAGE)* 7: 1-2 (Beverly Hills, London: 1990) (special issue on global culture); Kevin Robins, "Tradition and Translation: National Culture in Its Global Context," in John Corner and Sylvia Harvey, eds., *Enterprise and Heritage: Crosscurrents of National Culture* (London: Routledge, 1991), pp. 21–44; Armand Mattelart, *La Communication-monde: histoire des idées et des strategies* (Paris: La Découverte, 1992). See also Cynthia Schneider and Brian Wallis, eds., *Global Television* (New York: Wedge Press; Cambridge, Mass., Massachusetts Institute of Technology Press, 1988).

6. See, for instance, Hamid Naficy, "Autobiography, Film Spectatorship, and Cultural Negotiation," *Emergences* 1 (Fall 1989), 29–54, and "The Poetics and Practice of Iranian Nostalgia in Exile," *Diaspora* 1:3 (1991), 285–302; Kobena Mercer, "Diaspora Culture and the Dialogic Imagination: The Aesthetics of Black Independent Film in Britain," in Manuel Alvarado and John O. Thompson, eds., *The Media Reader* (London: British Film Institute, 1990), pp. 24–35.

7. Cornel West, "The New Cultural Politics of Difference," in Russell Ferguson, Martha Gever, Trinh T. Minh-ha, and Cornel West, eds., *Out There: Marginalization and Contemporary Cultures* (New York: New Museum of Contemporary Art; Cambridge, Mass., and London: Massachusetts Institute of Technology Press, 1990), p. 29.

8. Examples in the United States include Guerrilla TV, Edge, Paper Tiger, and Deep Dish Television. On some of the theoretical issues involved in such efforts, see Patricia Mellencamp, "Prologue," *Logics of Television* (London: British Film Institute; Bloomington: Indiana University Press, 1990), pp. 1–13. Also pertinent in this regard is the ongoing debate over indigenous uses of film and video in ethnography; see, for instance, Terence Turner, "Defiant Images: The Kayapo Appropriation of Video," *Anthropology Today* 8:6 (December 1992), 5–16.

9. Tom Gunning, "The Cinema of Attraction[s]," *Wide Angle* 8:3-4 (1986), 63–70; rpt. in Thomas Elsaesser and Adam Barker, eds., *Early Cinema: Space, Frame, Narrative* (London: British Film Institute, 1990), pp. 56–62.

10. See essays in pt. I of Thomas Elsaesser and Adam Barker, *Early Cinema;* Noël Burch, "Porter, or Ambivalence," *Screen* 19:4 (Winter 1978/79), 91–105, and *Life to Those Shadows*, ed. and tr. Ben Brewster (Berkeley and Los Angeles: University of California Press, 1990); Kristin Thompson, pt. 3 of David Bordwell, Janet Staiger, and Kristin Thompson, *The Classical Hollywood Cinema: Film Style and Mode of Production to 1960* (New York: Columbia University Press, 1985); Charles Musser, *The Emergence of Cinema: The American Screen to 1907* (New York: Scribner's, 1990); *Before the Nickelodeon: Edwin S. Porter and the Edison Manufacturing Company* (Berkeley and Los Angeles: University of California Press, 1991). The question of early film-viewer relations is elaborated in greater detail in my book *Babel and Babylon: Spectatorship in American Silent Film* (Cambridge, Mass.: Harvard University Press, 1991), chs. 1–3.

11. Cf. Linda Williams, "Film Bodies: Gender, Genre, and Excess," *Film Quarterly* 44 (Summer 1991), 2–13, and *Hard Core: Power, Pleasure, and the "Frenzy of the Visible"* (Berkeley and Los Angeles: University of California Press, 1989); also see Tom Gunning,

"An Aesthetic of Astonishment: Early Film and the (In)Credulous Spectator," *Art & Text* 34 (Fall 1989), 31–45.

12. Charles Musser, "The Nickelodeon Era Begins: Establishing the Framework for Hollywood's Mode of Representation" (1983), rpt. in Elsaesser and Barker, *Early Cinema,* 256–73.

13. See Richard Koszarski, *An Evening's Entertainment: The Age of the Silent Feature Picture, 1915–1928* (New York: Scribener's, 1990), ch. 2, and Douglas Gomery, *Shared Pleasures: A History of Movie Presentation in the United States* (Madison: University of Wisconsin Press, 1992), ch. 3.

14. Tom Gunning, "Enigmas, Understanding, and Further Questions: Early Cinema Research in Its Second Decade since Brighton," *Persistence of Vision* 9 (1991), 6.

15. Noël Burch, "Narrative/Diegesis—Thresholds, Limits," *Screen* 23:3 (July-August 1982), 33 (rev. in *Life to Those Shadows* 263). Also see Thomas Elsaesser, "TV through the Looking Glass," *Quarterly Review of Film & Video* 14:1-2 (1992), 5.

16. On Kluge's relationship to Adorno, see Stuart Liebman's interview "On New German Cinema, Art, Enlightenment," *October* 46 (Fall 1988), 23–59, especially pp. 36ff. For Kluge's influence in turn on Adorno, see the latter's 1966 essay "Transparencies on Film," tr. Thomas Y. Levin, *New German Critique* 24-25 (1981–82), 199–205, as well as my "Introduction," Ibid. 186–98.

17. Jürgen Habermas, *Strukturwandel der Offentlichkeit* (Darmstadt and Neuwied, West Germany: Luchterhand, 1962), tr. Thomas Burger, *The Structural Transformation of the Public Sphere* (Cambridge, Mass.: Massachusetts Institute of Technology Press, 1989). See Craig Calhoun, ed., *Habermas and the Public Sphere* (Cambridge, Mass., and London: Massachusetts Institute of Technology Press, 1992); also see Bruce Robbins, ed., *The Phantom Public Sphere* (Minneapolis: University of Minnesota Press, 1993).

18. See Nicholas Garnham, "The Media and the Public Sphere," in Calhoun, *Habermas and the Public Sphere*, pp. 359–76; also see Michael Warner, "The Mass Public and the Mass Subject," ibid., pp. 377–401, and Benjamin Lee, "Textuality, Mediation, and Public Discourse," ibid., pp. 402–18.

19. Oskar Negt and Alexander Kluge, *Offentlichkeit und Erfahrung* (Frankfurt: Suhrkamp, 1972); *The Public Sphere and Experience,* tr. Peter Labanyi, Jamie Daniel, and Assenka Oksiloff (Minneapolis: University of Minnesota Press, 1993). For a more detailed discussion of that book, see my Foreword to the American edition, also published in *Public Culture* 5:2 (Winter 1993), 179–212.

20. Negt and Kluge, *Offentlichkeit und Erfahrung*, pp. 17–18.

21. There are interesting contiguities between Negt's and Kluge's notion of the context of living and Michel de Certeau's reflections on *The Practice of Everyday Life*, tr. Steven Randall (Berkeley and Los Angeles: University of California Press, 1984).

22. The concept of experience (*Erfahrung*) assumed here is a highly specific one, elaborated—in different ways—by Benjamin, Bloch, Kracauer, and Adorno. See Hansen, "Foreword," *Public Sphere and Experience,* pp. xvi–xix; "Benjamin, Cinema and Experience: 'The Blue Flower in the Land of Technology,'" *New German Critique* 40 (Winter 1987), 179–224; "Of Mice and Ducks: Benjamin and Adorno on Disney," *South Atlantic Quarterly* 92:1 (Winter 1993), 40–41.

23. Negt and Kluge adopt this term from Hans Magnus Enzensberger, "Constituents of a Theory of the Media" (1970), tr. Stuart Hood, in Reinhold Grimm and Bruce Armstrong, eds., *Critical Essays* (New York: Continuum, 1982), pp. 46–76.

24. "We are interested in what, in a world where it is so obvious that catastrophes occur, performs the labor that brings about material change." Preface, *Geschichte und Eigensinn* (Frankfurt: Zweitausendeins, 1981), p. 5. Also see Fredric Jameson, "On Negt and Kluge," *October* 46 (1988), 151–77, and Christopher Pavsek, "Alexander Kluge and Postmodernism or Realism and the Public Sphere," unpublished manuscript.

25. See Meaghan Morris's "television anecdote" (about the 1988 Sydney birthday cake scandal), which offers a graphic example of the conjunctural quality of public life, involving a fleeting appropriation or tactical intervention on the part of Australian Aborigines, in "Banality in Cultural Studies," *Logics of Television*, ed. Patricia Mellencamp, (Bloomington: Indiana University Press, 1990), 28f. Morris emphasizes the aspect of "*timing*, a seizing of propitious moments," which tallies with Kluge's concept of public intervention; see in particular his 1974 film on the Frankfurt housing struggle, *In Danger and Dire Distress the Middle of the Road Leads to Death*. The name of his film production company is *kairos*, Greek for *propitious moment*.

26. Alexander Kluge, "On Film and the Public Sphere," tr. Thomas Y. Levin and Miriam Hansen, *New German Critique* 24-25 (Fall/Winter 1981–82), 206.

27. See Negt and Kluge, *Offentlichkeit und Erfahrung*, chs 3–5.

28. On Kluge's television work, see Margaret Morse, "Ten to Eleven: Television by Alexander Kluge," *1989 American Film Institute Video Festival* (Los Angeles: American Film Institute, 1989), pp. 50–53; Miriam Hansen, "Reinventing the Nickelodeon: Notes on Kluge and Early Cinema," *October* 46 (Fall 1988), 178–98; Stuart Liebman, "On New German Cinema, Art, Enlightenment, and the Public Sphere: An Interview with Alexander Kluge," ibid., 23–59, especially pp. 30ff.; Yvonne Rainer and Ernest Larsen, "'We Are Demolition Artists': An Interview with Alexander Kluge," *The Independent* (June 1989), Vol. 12, 5:18–25; Gertrud Koch, "Alexander Kluge's Phantom of the Opera," *New German Critique* 49 (Winter 1990), 79–88.

29. Ian Breakwell and Paul Hammond, eds., *Seeing in the Dark: A Compendium of Cinemagoing* (London: Serpent's Tail, 1990), p. 8.

30. Hansen, *Babel and Babylon*, ch. 3.

31. See Mary Carbine, "'The Finest Outside the Loop': Motion Picture Exhibition in Chicago's Black Metropolis, 1905–1928," *Camera Obscura* 23 (May 1990), 9–41; Gomery, *Shared Pleasures*, ch. 8.

32. See, for instance, Jane Gaines, "The Queen Christina Tie-Ups: The Convergence of Show Window and Screen," *Quarterly Review of Film and Video* 11:1 (1989), 35–60; Gaylyn Studlar, "The Perils of Pleasure? Fan Magazine Discourse as Women's Commodified Culture in the 1920s," *Wide Angle* 13:1 (1991), 6–33; Hansen, *Babel and Babylon*, chs. 11 and 12; Richard Dyer, *Heavenly Bodies: Film Stars and Society* (New York: St. Martin's Press, 1986), ch. 2; and Pamela Robertson, "'The Kinda Comedy That Imitates Me': Mae West's Identification with the Feminist Camp," *Cinema Journal* 32:2 (Winter 1993), 57–72.

33. Tom Gunning, "An Unseen Energy Swallows Space: The Space in Early Film and Its Relation to American Avant-Garde Film," in John L. Fell, ed., *Film before Griffith* (Berkeley and Los Angeles: University of California Press, 1983), p. 366.

34. See, for instance, David Bordwell, Janet Staiger, and Kristin Thompson, *The Classical Hollywood Cinema* (n. 10, above).

Viewing Antitheses

Judith Mayne

Paradoxes of Spectatorship

No matter how controversial and contested theories of the cinematic institution have been, few would argue with their basic premise that the capacity of the cinema to seduce, entertain, or otherwise appeal to its audiences needs to be understood in ideological and psychic terms. The trick, however, is not only in understanding the relationship between the two realms of psychic and social life—a rather large undertaking in any case—but in defining with precision the ways in which the cinema is describable in terms of ideological and psychoanalytic theory, and the extent to which different types of cinema and varied contexts articulate spectatorship in different ways. Even the cognitive approach, which departs most sharply from the assumptions of 1970s film theory, is concerned with conditions of coherence and intelligibility which relate to the kind of ideological analysis central to 1970s film theory.

Does the analysis of the cinematic institution as a staging and restaging of the crises of male Oedipal desire, as a regressive plenitude, apply only to a specific historical mode of the cinema—i.e., the classical, narrative Hollywood film? Or, rather, given that the emergence of the cinema is so closely linked to the fictions of Western patriarchal culture, is the cinematic apparatus as theorized in film theory bound to be the condition of *all* cinematic representation? Even within the classical Hollywood cinema, are female spectators thus bound by the Scylla of male spectatorial desire and the Charybdis of exclusion from cinematic fantasies? Given the extent to which analysis of spectatorship has focussed on sexual difference (whether foregrounded or so blatantly ignored as to function as a symptom, as in Baudry's case), are other forms of

From *Cinema and Spectatorship* (London and New York: Routledge, 1993). Reprinted by permission of the author and Routledge.

spectator identity—race, class, sexual identity other than gendered identity, age, and so on—always built upon the model of sexual difference, or are they potentially formative in their own right? And to what extent is identity a misleading route toward understanding spectatorship, particularly if it is limited by literalist assumptions, i.e., that black audiences can identify only with black characters, female audiences with female ones, and so forth? If apparatus theory displaced character identification as the central dynamic in understanding spectatorship, this does not mean that questions of identity have been in any way resolved. For the displacement of identification, however necessary and valuable to the project of 1970s film theory, was nonetheless accomplished at a price—a too easy equation between the subject and the attributes of dominance.

Perhaps one of the greatest ironies of contemporary film studies is that the obsessive attention devoted to the cinematic institution occurred at a time when there has perhaps existed more diversity than ever before insofar as modes of cinematic representation and address are concerned. In the United States alone, independent film and video, specifically addressed to a variety of markets—gay and lesbian, feminist, black, Hispanic—continues to grow. One of the largest problems confronting spectatorship studies is the simultaneous affirmation of diversity and the recognition that diversity can easily function as a ploy, a way of perpetuating the illusions of mainstream cinema rather than challenging them. Put another way, there is no simple division between the cinema that functions as an instrument of dominant ideology, and the cinema that facilitates the challenges to it. Now if you assume, as some theorists of the 1970s did, that there is nothing about cinema that is not saturated with ideology, then the radical or contestatory powers of the cinema were limited to those films which functioned to demonstrate the ideological complicity of film.

The most promising and influential work on spectatorship assumes the necessity for understanding cinema as ideologically influenced, but not necessarily monolithically so. Linda Gordon speaks of the necessity to hold competing claims of domination and resistance in unwavering tension, refusing to collapse one into the other.[1] In spectatorship studies, several concepts have emerged to engage with the tension between cinema as monolithic institution and cinema as heterogeneous diversity. The competing claims of homogeneity (of the cinematic apparatus) and heterogeneity (of the spectator and therefore of the different ways in which an apparatus can be understood) frame this chapter.

If the cinematic apparatus is as fully saturated with the ideology of idealism and Oedipal desire as 1970s film theory would suggest, then there can be no real history of the cinema except as variations on a common theme. Or rather, there can be no history within the cinema if all cinema is ideological in the same way. We have already encountered criticisms of models of the cinematic apparatus for establishing a mono-lithic role for the spectator and for literalizing whatever analogy was articulated, from Plato's cave to the Lacanian imaginary. An opposition between homogeneity and heterogeneity underscores these criticisms, since most alternatives to 1970s film theory take the spectator, not as the effect of the cinema institution, but as a point of departure, and not the ideal spectator as theorized by the cinematic apparatus, but the socially defined spectator, who is necessarily heterogeneous—i.e., ad-dressed through a variety of discourses. In other words, responses to apparatus theory are founded on a gap between the ideal subject postu-lated by the apparatus and the spectator, who is always in an imperfect relation to that ideal.

In this chapter, I will examine three terms which have emerged in spectatorship studies to conceptualize the competing claims of the homogeneous cinematic institution and heterogeneous responses to it: the gap between *address* and *reception; fantasy;* and *negotiation.* Linda Gordon speaks of the need to find a method in between the claims of domination and resistance, and the terms I will examine in this chapter are precisely that: concepts meant to convey the contradictory ways in which spectatorship functions. First, the relationship between cinematic address and cinematic reception opens up a space between the ideal viewer and the real viewer. Address refers to the ways in which a text assumes certain responses, which may or may not be operative in different reception conditions. Central to this apparent paradox is the role of the cinematic text, whether defined as the individual film or as a set of operations which situate the spectator in certain ways. If spectators can and do respond to films in ways that contradict, reject, or otherwise problematize the presumably ideal spectator structured into the text, then the value of textual analysis—arguably the most significant meth-odological direction undertaken by 1970s film theory—needs to be seri-ously rethought or reevaluated.

I have previously noted that the version of psychoanalysis pro-moted within theories of the cinematic subject tends toward a uniform and totalizing version of the unconscious, almost always understood as the resurgence of various crises of (male) Oedipal identity. The advantage of such a view, of course, is that the psychic foundations of the cultural order are open to investigation, but the disadvantages far outnumber such advantages. For the unconscious thus defined becomes one more totalizing system, and the work of the psychoanalytically inspired critic becomes just as framed by a master code as any other application of a method. In the context of these problems with psychoanalytic theory and criticism, the notion of fantasy has received increasing attention and is the second concept to be discussed in this chapter. An exploration of fantasy allows a far more radical exploration of psychic investment in the cinema and suggests, as well, intersections between the psychic and the political. Yet it is not altogether clear whether the implications of fantasy for the cinema allow for an understanding of the social in terms that exceed the family romance so central to any psychoanalytic understanding of culture.

It is one thing to compare the claims that can be made for cinema as a homogeneous and homogenizing, versus a heterogeneous, institution, and another thing to valorize heterogeneity as necessarily contestatory. The third concept I will discuss is the term *negotiation*, which is used frequently to suggest that different texts can be used, interpreted, or appropriated in a variety of ways. Sometimes the diversity thus postulated by negotiated readings or viewings is assumed to challenge the power of the institution. The sheer fact that a spectator or group of spectators makes unauthorized uses of the cinema is no guarantee that such uses are contestatory. Here, the central question has less to do with the status of the text than with the value one assigns to differing modes of response: how those responses are assessed and how film-going is read in relationship to other social, cultural, and psychic formations. Indeed, the emphasis on negotiation deemphasizes the primacy of the cinematic text, focussing rather on how different responses can be read, whether critically, symptomatically, or otherwise.

Address and Reception

A common characteristic of textual theories of the spectator was the assumption that the cinematic apparatus *situates, positions,* or otherwise assigns a position of coherence to the implied spectator. Now, however much this implied spectator position functioned as something of a phantom, and not a person to be confused with real viewers, it nonetheless managed to marginalize any consideration of how real viewers might view films in ways considerably more various than any monolithic conception of the cinematic apparatus could imply. It is one thing to assume that cinema is determined in ideological ways, to assume that cinema is a discourse (or a variety of discourses), and to assume, that is, that the various institutions of the cinema *do* project an ideal viewer, and another thing to assume that those projections *work*. One of the most significant directions in spectatorship studies has investigated the gap opened up between the ways in which texts construct viewers and how those texts may be read or used in ways that depart from what the institution valorizes.

The operative assumption here is that apparatus theories are not completely wrong, but rather incomplete. The issue is one of flexibility, of recognizing that an apparatus can have unexpected effects and that no apparatus can function quite so smoothly and efficiently as most film theory of the 1970s would suggest. That theory was most obviously lacking and problematic in the kinds of hypotheses it led to concerning any kind of alternative cinematic practice, particularly insofar as a deconstruction of so-called dominant modes and a presumable repositioning of the spectator are concerned. Both assume a fairly stable, fixed, one-way, top-down model of agent and object, with a spectator still locked into a programme of representation defined romantically and mechanistically according to the agenda of the filmmaker or the institution: an active viewer is still one positioned to be so by textual constructs.

Yet to go to the other extreme, and to define texts as offering only the positions that viewers create for them and thereby to mediate *any* notion of the cinematic institution out of existence, substitutes one monolithic political notion for another. The challenge, then, is to understand the complicated ways in which meanings are both assigned and created. If apparatus theorists were overly zealous in defining all meanings as assigned ones, there has been considerable zeal at the other end of the spectrum as well, by virtually disavowing any power of institutions and conceptualizing readers/viewers as completely free and autonomous agents—a tendency that has been particularly marked, for instance, in some versions of reader-response theory and cultural studies (especially in the United States).[2] Since dominant ideology is neither a person nor a one-dimensional set of concepts, it is virtually impossible to say with certainty that a particular effect is complicit with or resistant to the force of an institution. But one can assess the different effects of cinema in relationship to other discourses in order to assess the complicated ways in which the cinema functions, for instance.

One of the great difficulties here is a fairly obvious one. Individual films lend themselves to far neater and easier hypotheses about structure and excess than individual viewers or groups of viewers do. A mistrust of sociological surveys has been one of the most ingrained features of contemporary theoretical work, and so it is perhaps something of a surprise to see the analysis of real viewers return in recent years, as a theoretically credible exercise. The influence of cultural studies—as defined specifically through the work of Stuart Hall and the Centre for Contemporary Cultural Studies at the University of Birmingham and more generally by analyses of the ways different specific audiences respond to instances of mass culture—has been enormous.

In a series of interviews with teenage girls, for instance, Angela McRobbie concluded that their passion for a film like *Flashdance* had far more to do with their own desire for physical autonomy than with any simple notion of acculturation to a patriarchal definition of feminine desirability.[3] Now it seems to me that one can be stunned by these tentative conclusions only if the model of the cinematic institution one had in the first place corresponded to the conspiracy theory view of capitalism popular in some New Left circles in the 1960s. While I find McRobbie's study intriguing, and will turn to it in more detail later in this chapter, I am not convinced that her hypotheses lead necessarily to a dismissal of the power of the cinematic institution. Unfortunately, this type of work has led to a peculiar reading of the reception of mass culture, whereby any and all responses are critical ones. Some sort of understanding of the noncoincidence of address and reception is required in which power is analyzed rather than taken for granted.

One of the most influential studies along these lines is Janice Radway's *Reading the Romance,* an analysis of romance novels as they are read by a group of devoted women fans.[4] Because many of the issues that Radway raises have equal relevance to film studies, and in particular because her book has been cited many times as a model of how film researchers might rethink many of the theoretical assumptions that have been seen increasingly as limitations, her book merits examination for the questions it raises for film spectatorship.[5] While Radway examines the structural and ideological features of the romance novel as a genre, she situates that analysis alongside what is perhaps the most noteworthy achievement of the book: a complex profile of a group of eager and committed romance readers. The advantage of Radway's analysis is that she acknowledges the persuasive power of the romance novel as a genre at the same time as she refuses to reduce the genre to a series of ideological complicities. Put another way, one senses throughout *Reading the Romance* that the textual evidence is put to the test of Radway's sample audience, and vice versa.

Radway's study focuses on a group of women fictitiously referred to as the Smithton women, all of whom bought the majority of their romance-reading material from a salesclerk named Dorothy Evans (Dot), an expert on romance fiction. Radway's study of this group of women took the form of group and individual interviews (with sixteen women), as well as a lengthy questionnaire distributed to forty-two women. Radway describes her sample as consisting for the most part of "married, middle-class mothers," and she notes that while "not representative of all women who read romances, the group appears to be demographically similar to a sizable segment of that audience as it has been mapped by several very secretive publishing houses."[6] Much of the force of Radway's analysis comes from a variety of juxtapositions of differing notions of the ideal—from the ideal reader as posited in much narrative analysis, to the ideal romance as postulated by the Smithton women, to a feminist ideal which seems to characterize much of how Radway approaches the women's responses to romance fiction.

Radway echoes much feminist analysis of mass cultural forms when she argues that romance novels function as "compensatory fiction," that is, "the act of reading them fulfills certain basic psychological needs for women that have been induced by the culture and its social structures but that often remain unmet in day-to-day existence as the result of concomitant restrictions on female activity."[7] Like Vladimir Propp in his famous analysis of the Russian folktale, Radway notes that romance fiction is composed of certain unchanging elements—notably patriarchy, heterosexuality, and male personality.[8] But within those unchanging rules, romances offer the possibility of fantasizing solutions that are otherwise unavailable. Throughout *Reading the Romance*, the reading of romance fiction is portrayed as emblematic of the ambivalence which these particular women feel about themselves not just in relationship to patriarchy but in relationship to feminism as well. Indeed, the emphasis on female autonomy within a passionate relationship and the simultaneity of dependence and independence suggest that—to reiterate a phrase that appears frequently in Radway's analysis—romance readers want to have it both ways.

That Radway herself is ambivalent about how to read the results of her analysis is evident, especially in her conclusion. She says, "the question of whether the activity of romance reading does, in reality, deflect such change [i.e., the restructuring of sexual relations] by successfully defusing or recontaining this protest must remain unanswered for the moment."[9] I find it curious that such a dualistic political framework should be erected in this book, but in some ways this either/or—the either/or, that is, of a conservative status quo versus radical change, of celebration versus critique—remains as a stubborn reminder that the theoretical problem raised by the apparatus (cinematic or otherwise) has not been wished away, for the very notion of a cinematic apparatus suggests a rigid distinction between what is contaminated by dominant ideology and what is not, suggests the possibility of knowing with certainty whether an activity is contestatory or conservative. What always seems to happen with such dualisms is the hardening of one abstraction or another—only a deconstruction of the apparatus is genuinely revolutionary! Readers and viewers are always active producers of meaning—before it has been possible to consider in more depth the complexity of the issues at hand.

The major problem in Radway's analysis is that for all of the criticism offered of theoretical modes which ignore real readers in favor of the critic's own projections, there is a fair share of projection and idealization going on here as well. For the white, heterosexual, middle-class women that Radway discusses may well be complex agents who live the contradictions of middle-class patriarchal culture in equally complex ways, but they are also projections of American, middle-class, academic feminism. This is not meant in any way as a condemnation—far from it. But the desire to name real readers is neither transparent nor innocent, for the women readers who appear in Radway's analysis are mediated by her questions, her analyses, and her narrative. It is inevitable that such projections exist in this kind of analysis, and unless those projections are analyzed, we are left with an ideal reader who seems more real because she is quoted and referred to, but who is every bit as problematic as the ideal reader constructed by abstract theories of an apparatus positioning passive vessels.

It would, of course, be presumptuous of me to hypothesize what function the Smithton women have in Radway's imagination, but I can say what her analysis suggests quite strongly to me: a desire, on the part of feminists like myself, to see my mother and by extension members of my mother's generation as not so invested in patriarchy, as prefeminist or protofeminist, as a figure who nurtured feminism even while she argued otherwise, as someone who was really a feminist but didn't know it yet. Lest a particularly literal-minded soul wants to remind me that not all mothers of middle-class feminists fit this bill, I would say that this is precisely the point. For regardless of whether we are talking about literal mothers (as I am here), or about mothers in the sense of a generation of women from whom the contemporary feminist movement developed and against whom it reacted, or about a group of women who function as a horizon against which much feminist activity operates, we are talking about a construction. I doubt seriously, for instance, if the Smithton women would agree with the necessity of understanding the reading of romance fiction in the categorical terms of critique or celebration.

If analyses such as Radway's are to be based on taking other readers seriously, then they must also mean taking ourselves seriously as readers—and by *seriously* here, I mean putting our own constructions to the test. Tania Modleski has argued that with the turn to ethnography as a revitalized strategy for the analysis of mass culture, a curious assumption has been made that critics and researchers are not valid readers or viewers of mass culture, but rather detached observers.[10] I think Modleski is correct in assuming that the analysis of spectatorship is an analysis of one's own fascination and passion. Unless this is acknowledged, we are left with a series of fuzzily defined ideal readers in whom it is difficult to know how much of their responses are displaced representations of the critic's own.

From another perspective, it could be argued that the ideal reader has not been challenged so much as displaced from one realm—that of the textual properties of address—to another—that of the empirically observable woman. One of the most important strategies of Radway's analysis is, as I've indicated, the juxtaposition of the ideal reader assumed by the romance-fiction industry with women who *do* fit that profile, who are therefore the desired audience for romance novels, but who are also at the same time irreducible to structure, formula, or cliché. Unfortunately, however, this challenge to the presumed homogeneity of the ideal reader does not go quite far enough. One of Radway's most important sources is Nancy Chodorow's *Reproduction of Mothering*, a study of the asymmetrical gender patterns whereby men learn to be mothered and nurtured and women learn to provide mothering and nurturing.[11] Whereas Chodorow argues that women are socialized into mothering precisely through the (often unfulfilled) promise that the pre-Oedipal patterns so central to their own development will be recreated, Radway argues that romance fiction provides precisely the kind of nurturance otherwise absent or largely missing from these women's lives.

In the appeal to Chodorow's analysis I sense most strongly the need to specify the particular nature of the needs being fulfilled. To what extent are we talking about white women whose lives are missing the kind of community network and patterns often characteristic of the lives of black women, for instance? What kind of middle-class identity is at stake: the kind of precarious middle-class life characteristic of many white-collar workers? Or rather an economic identity defined largely by lifestyle? Is the heterosexual identity of the women as stable as they, and Radway as well, seem to take great pains to stress? I am aware that these questions will strike some readers as the kind of checklist of account-ability that characterizes some holier-than-thou political criticism. But my goal here is not some kind of standard of inclusivity. Rather, it is the notion of an ideal reader—no matter who defines it as ideal—that I think is severely limiting.

Radway's study remains the most influential example of an analysis that attempts to account, simultaneously, for the power of institutions (what she calls an institutional matrix) and the complex ways in which real women accomplish the "construction of texts."[12] The positive critical reception that Radway's book has received suggests at the very least enormous dissatisfaction with just those limitations of exclusive textually based theories of readership. I am wary, however, of some of this positive critical reception, since I am not convinced that the notion of the *ideal reader* has been problematized or undone so much as it has been displaced. What this suggests to me is the need to be careful of the appeals that are made in the name of empirical audiences or ethnography as the truth that will set us free from the overly abstract theorization of the past. I suspect that it may be impossible to do away entirely with the notion of an ideal reader, since we all live this culture's fictions and institutions and participate in them to some extent. I do not say this in order to imply cynically that no alternative positions of spectatorship are possible, but rather to suggest that one of the most persistent myths of spectatorship (and of theory) that has perturbed and in many ways hindered the analysis of spectatorship is the belief that it is not only possible, but necessary, to separate the truly radical spectator from the merely complicitous one. The recognition that we are all complicitous to some extent (and the *some* is clearly what needs to be investigated) does not mean that alternative positions are impossible. Rather, that recognition would make it possible to speak of readership or spectatorship not as the knowledge the elite academic brings to the people, nor as a coded language that can be deciphered only by experts, but as a mode of encounter between, say, Radway and the women whose responses she collected and studied.

Fantasy

While I share many of the criticisms of psychoanalytic theory that have been made in film studies in the past twenty years, the failure to take psychoanalytic investigation seriously can only lead to spectatorship studies that posit one limited definition of the subject in place of another. It is mistaken to assume, however, that all psychoanalytic film theorists subscribe to all aspects of apparatus theory or that psychoanalytic investigations have remained unchanged in orientation since the early to mid-1970s. Indeed, one of the most significant rethinkings of psychoanalytic film theory has been in the area of fantasy, which Constance Penley specifically claims as an alternative to the bachelor machines characteristic of Metz's and Baudry's approaches to the cinema. "The formulation of fantasy," she writes, "which provides a complex and exhaustive account of *the staging and imaging of the subject and its desire*, is a model that very closely approximates the primary aims of the apparatus theory: to describe not only the subject's desire for the film image and its reproduction, but also the structure of the fantasmatic relation to that image, including the subject's belief in its reality."[13]

Two essays in particular have been extremely influential in the development of a model of spectatorship which draws upon the psychoanalytic definition of fantasy. Freud's "A Child Is Being Beaten"[14] has been read as offering a theory of multiple masculine and feminine positions, thereby lending itself to a definition of spectatorship as oscillation rather than identification in a univocal sense.[15] The specific definition of fantasy upon which Penley draws is located in an extremely influential essay by Jean Laplanche and Jean-Bertrand Pontalis, "Fantasy and the Origins of Sexuality."[16] Elaborating upon their claim that "fantasy is the fundamental object of psychoanalysis,"[17] in this essay the authors explore a variety of components of fantasy which suggest, even more forcefully than the dream analogy so often claimed as the basis for psychoanalytic exploration of the cinema, a situation which is embodied in the cinema.

Laplanche and Pontalis distinguish three *original* fantasies— original in the sense that they are bound up with the individual's history and origins: "Like myths, they claim to provide a representation of, and a solution to, the major enigmas which confront the child. Whatever appears to the subject as something needing an explanation or theory, is dramatized as a moment of emergence, the beginning of a history." Hence, Laplanche and Pontalis define three such fantasies of origins: "the primal scene pictures the origin of the individual; fantasies of seduction, the origin and upsurge of sexuality; fantasies of castration, the origin of the difference between the sexes."[18] These fantasies are original not in the sense that they always produce or cause a given scenario, but in the sense that they form the structure of fantasy which is activated in a variety of ways.

Three characteristics of fantasy as read by Laplanche and Pontalis are particularly crucial for an understanding of the cinema as fantasy, and toward a revision of theories of the apparatus whereby the subject of the cinematic fantasy can be only and always male. First, the distinction between what is conscious and what is unconscious is less important in fantasy than the distinction between those original fantasies described above, and secondary fantasies. Laplanche and Pontalis stress what they describe as the "profound continuity between the various fantasy scenarios—the stage-setting of desire—ranging from the daydream to the fantasies recovered or reconstructed by the analytic investigation."[19] As we have seen, one of the problems with much apparatus theory is a mechanistic notion of the unconscious, due largely to the fact that the desire for regression is always postulated as the repetition of the same Oedipal scenario. The three original fantasies of which Laplanche and Pontalis speak are not so regimented. And given that fantasy occupies such a distinct place in psychoanalysis insofar as it extends across the boundaries of conscious and unconscious desires, then the analysis of the cinema as a form of fantasy does not require what almost inevitably amounts to a decoding approach, a rigid distinction between manifest and latent content. The area of fantasy is one where the notion of homology operates quite differently from the case with the cinematic apparatus, since here the homology is between different types of fantasy, of which cinematic spectatorship is one example.[20] Put another way, fantasy is more useful for its implications than for its possible status as equivalent to or anticipatory of the cinema.

Second, it is the very nature of fantasy to exist for the subject across many possible positions. Noting that "'A father seduces a daughter'" is the skeletal version of the seduction fantasy, Laplanche and Pontalis describe this function as follows: "The indication here of the primary process is not the absence of organization, as it sometimes suggested, but the peculiar character of the structure, in that it is a scenario with multiple entries, in which nothing shows whether the subject will be immediately located as *daughter;* it can as well be fixed as *father,* or even in the term *seduces.*"[21] Despite the claims to anti-essentialism of many apparatus theorists, there is a consistent tendency to conflate literal gender and address—to assume, that is, that if the film addresses its subject as male, then it is the male viewer who is thus addressed. The reading of cinematic fantasy allows no such reduction. Indeed, the notion of fantasy gives psychoanalytic grounding not only to the possibility but to the inevitability and necessity of the cinema as a form of fantasy wherein the boundaries of biological sex or cultural gender, as well as sexual preference, are not fixed.

Finally, emphasis is placed throughout Laplanche and Pontalis's discussion on fantasy as the staging of desire, fantasy as a form of mise-en-scène. "Fantasy . . . is not the object of desire, but its setting. In fantasy the subject does not pursue the object or its sign: he appears caught up himself in the sequence of images."[22] Cowie has noted that the importance of the emphasis on fantasy as a scene "cannot be overestimated, for it enables the consideration of film as fantasy in the most fundamental sense of this term in psychoanalysis."[23] While I am somewhat suspicious of any mimetic analogy, the understanding of film as fantasy does open the door to some questions and issues about spectatorship which apparatus theory tended to shut out. In any case, I think the value of fantasy for psychoanalytic readings of the cinema needs to be seen less in terms of a better analogy than dreams, the mirror stage, or the imaginary, and more in terms of the series of questions it can engender.

In Cowie's reading of fantasy in film which relies extensively on the Laplanche and Pontalis essay, two such questions are raised: "If fantasy is the mise-en-scène of desire, whose desire is figured in the film, who is the subject for and of the scenario? No longer just, if ever, the so-called 'author.' But how does the spectator come into place as desiring subject of the film? Secondly, what is the relation of the contingent, everyday material drawn from real life, i.e. from the *social,* to the primal or original fantasies?"[24] Cowie notes how, in *Now, Voyager,* there is an Oedipal fantasy, "but where the subject positions are not fixed or completed, Charlotte is both mother and daughter, Mrs. Vale and Tina." In partial response to her first question, then, Cowie says that it is not enough to define the fantasy as Charlotte Vale's; rather, it must be defined as the spectator's:

This is not Charlotte's fantasy, but the "film's" fantasy. It is an effect of its narration (of its *énonciation*). If we identify simply with Charlotte's desires, that series of social and erotic successes, then the final object, the child Tina, will be unsatisfactory. But if our identification is with the playing out of desiring, in relation to the opposition (phallic) mother/child, the ending is very much more satisfying, I would suggest. A series of "daydream" fantasies enfold an Oedipal, original fantasy. The subject of this fantasy is then the spectator; inasmuch as we have been captured by the film's narration, its *énonciation*, we are the only place in which all the terms of the fantasy come to rest.[25]

Cowie's response to her second question—concerning the relationship between the psychic and the social which the analysis of fantasy can comprehend—focuses on the illicit desires which the subject's pleasure in the fantasy fulfills. In *Now, Voyager*, this concerns the evacuation of the father; in another film discussed by Cowie, *The Reckless Moment*, what she describes as an "unstoppable sliding of positions" results in pairings and oppositions whereby a set of equivalences is set up, and an inference is made "which is an attack on the family as imprisoning."[26] These claims are reminiscent of the kinds of implications in "reading against the grain" arguments about the classical cinema—i.e., that what appears to be a smooth ideological surface is marred, rather, by rebellion, critique, or even implicit rejection of those norms. What the reading of fantasy brings to such claims, however, is the insistence that investment and pleasure in film watching involve a range of subject positions. Apparatus theory tends to pose a spectator so aligned with one subject position that anything departing from that position would have to seem radical or contestatory by definition. The exploration of the classical cinema in terms of fantasy enlarges considerably what possibilities are contained within the fantasy structures engaged by film viewing and in so doing inflects differently the notion of a "reading against the grain." For from the vantage point of fantasy, the distinction between with and against the grain of the film becomes somewhat moot.

Constance Penley assesses the importance of Cowie's approach to fantasy in terms of its assumption that positions of sexual identification are not fixed: "Cowie's model of identification involves a continual construction of looks, ceaselessly varied through the organization of the narrative and the work of narration. The value of such a model is that it leaves open the question of the production of sexual difference in the film rather than assuming in advance the sexuality of the character or the spectator."[27] However, while it may be a matter of indifference in psychoanalytic terms whether the spectator encouraged or enabled to adopt a variety of positions is male or female, it is a matter of crucial importance within the context of spectatorship, to the extent that spectatorship involves a spectator who always brings with her or him a history, and whose experience of spectatorship is determined in part by the ways in which spectatorship is defined outside the movie theater.

Cowie emphasizes that whatever shifting of positions occurs in the fantasies of the cinema, they "do so always in terms of sexual difference."[28] It is one thing to assume sexual difference to refer to the way in which any definition of "femininity" is inevitably bound to accompanying definitions of masculinity, and another thing to assume that the only possible relationship between the two is in some version of heterosexuality. Put another way, the insistence upon sexual difference has had a curious history in film studies, by collapsing the shifting terms of masculinity and femininity into a heterosexual master code. Interestingly, the model of fantasy elaborated by Laplanche and Pontalis has the potential to challenge film theory's own compulsory heterosexuality. In a study of Sheila McLaughlin's film *She Must Be Seeing Things*, for instance, Teresa de Lauretis argues that the film articulates a *lesbian* version of the primal scene, where the positions of onlooker and participant are occupied by women.[29]

Barbara Creed has observed that despite the fact that the castration scenario is but one of three originary fantasies in Laplanche and Pontalis's account, it has been the near-exclusive focus of 1970s film theory. Creed suggests that perhaps "the fantasy of castration *marks* all three primal fantasies to some degree."[30] The same could be said of any of the three fantasies. What might rather be the case is that the classical Hollywood cinema is made to the measure of the fantasy of sexual difference, which is of course what 1970s film theory claimed. It is unclear, in other words, just how much of a critical advantage the fantasy model offers, if it emerges as just another way of affirming the primacy of one particular configuration of desire. Alternatively, it could be argued that this is precisely where fantasy offers an understanding of the tension between the demands for regulation and homogeneity on the one hand, and the mobility of spectatorial investment on the other. The positions offered the spectator may be multiple, but the multiplicity finds its most cohesive articulation in the fantasy of sexual difference.

Jacqueline Rose has made a more pointed observation about the current interest in fantasy, particularly insofar as it functions as a "saving device" against the "depressing implications" of the psychoanalytic position that the classical cinema offers the female spectator only an impossible relation to its fictions.[32]

> Unconscious fantasy can . . . be read in terms of a multiplicity of available positions for women (and men), but the way these positions work against and defensively exclude each other gets lost . . . while we undoubtedly need to recognize the instability of unconscious fantasy and the range of identifications offered by any one spectator of film, this can easily lead to an idealization of psychic processes and cinema at one and the same time (something for everyone both in the unconscious and on the screen).[33]

Rose's warning echoes an earlier debate in film studies concerning the monolithic quality of film narrative, with psychoanalysis functioning as a nagging reminder that the resistance of the unconscious cannot in any easy or simple way be equated with resistance understood in political terms.

Fantasy does offer the possibility of engaging different desires, contradictory effects, and multiple stagings. A certain version of the scenario of sexual difference emerges again and again in film theory as obsessive structure and point of return, and it is not always clear when the obsession and return are an effect of the cinema or of the theorist. In any case, it appears as though the homogeneous effects of the cinematic apparatus are understood in limited terms in the fantasy model: limited to the extent that they have only one point of reference—a notion of sexual difference which assumes the kind of essentialist quality otherwise so disavowed by psychoanalytic critics. I have no intention of reviving the political fantasy of integrating Marxism and/or feminism and/or psychoanalysis; rather, it is psychoanalysis on its own terms that requires investigation, not rescue by some other discourse, for it is questionable whether fantasy can engage with the complex effects of spectatorship without some understanding of how its own categories—of sexual difference, the couple, and desire—are themselves historically determined and culturally variable.

Negotiation

To put this problem a bit differently, as well as to make the transition to the next tension I want to address, the institutional models of spectatorship have been read as so rigid that there has been a real temptation to see any response that differs slightly from what is assumed to be the norm or the ideal as necessarily radical and contestatory. Such claims to alternatives require that the theory of the institution that gave rise to it be challenged simultaneously. What remains nonetheless peculiar about many theories of the cinematic institution is that they give particular and sometimes exclusive signifying possibilities to the individual film. That is to say, the individual film is taken to be a well-functioning instance of the larger effects of the cinematic institution. When other practices are taken into account, like advertising or consumer tie-ins, they are assumed to create a narrative flow every bit as seamless as that of the classical scenario itself.

Once the cinematic institution is defined and analyzed as consisting of a number of different forms of address, however, it should be possible to unpack and question the excessive monolithic quality of the apparatus. But as I suggest above, I think it is crucial to resist the temptation to see difference or multiplicity as liberatory or contestatory qualities in themselves. This attention to difference (and simultaneous inquiry into the difference that difference makes) can be understood in a variety of ways, both in terms of a single film within which a variety of not necessarily harmonious discourses collide and in terms of the various components that define film-going in a cultural and psychic sense.

One of the key terms that has emerged in this context is *negotiation*. In an influential essay associated with cultural studies, Hall's "Encoding/Decoding," three decoding strategies—that is, practices of reading and making sense of cultural texts—are proposed. The dominant reading is one fully of a piece with the ideology of the text, while the negotiated reading is more ambivalent; that is, the ideological stance of a product is adjusted to specific social conditions of the viewers. The oppositional reading is, then, one totally opposed to the ideology in question.[34]

As influential as this model has been, particularly in the foregrounding of reception contexts, it raises some problems of its own, particularly insofar as the dominant and oppositional readings are concerned. What is the relationship between activity and passivity in the reader/viewer, whether the reading is dominant or oppositional? If a reader/viewer occupies an oppositional stance, how does this square with the process of interpellation necessary for any response to a text? Dominant and oppositional readings may be more usefully understood, perhaps, as horizons of possibility, as tendencies rather than actual practices of reading. However, in order to foreground the activity of reading, viewing, and consuming mass culture, what Hall's model leaves relatively intact is the notion of a text's dominant ideology. This is peculiar insofar as the activity/passivity of the apparatus model appears to be reversed in favor of an active reader/viewer and a relatively stable, if not completely passive, text.

It may well be more useful to designate all readings as negotiated ones, to the extent that it is highly unlikely that one will find any pure instances of dominant or oppositional readings. In other words, a purely dominant reading would presume no active intervention at all on the part of the decoder, while a purely oppositional reading would assume no identification at all with the structures of interpellation of the text. In that case, some notion of textual determination must still be necessary in order for the negotiation model to be useful.

I stress this because there is a tendency to assume that because the model of negotiation posits both the activity of the reader/viewer and the heterogeneity of the different elements of social formations, it conceives of a variety of readings, and that very heterogeneity, that very activity, is then taken to be indicative of a resistance to dominant ideology. Since I do not think that individual texts can be any more easily categorized as purely dominant than spectators or readers can, I find it difficult to be quite so enthused about different or unauthorized readings as necessarily contestatory. As I suggested earlier in this chapter, one of the problems in spectatorship studies is the desire to categorize texts *and* readings/responses as either conservative or radical, as celebratory of the dominant order or critical of it. This duality forecloses the far more difficult tasks of questioning what is served by the continued insistence upon this either/or and, more radically, of examining what it is in conceptions of spectators' responses and film texts that produces this ambiguity in the first place.

One of the severe limitations of much apparatus theory is the assumption that certain textual strategies will necessarily produce desired reassignations of dominant subject/object relationships and subject positions. A textual strategy does not necessarily produce anything. But if, consequently, there is no such thing as an inherently radical technique, then there is no such thing either as an inherently conservative one. While I think most contemporary film scholars would agree with the former—would agree, that is, that this particular aspect of 1970s film theory is in need of severe revision—I am not sure that the latter will meet with such agreement, since the notion of a dominant narrative structure still appears with great regularity.

I am alluding to two extreme positions which can be sketched as follows. For many textual theorists of the 1970s, Raymond Bellour and the editors of *Camera Obscura* in particular, the value of textual analysis was to demonstrate that classical narrative produces a variety of ruptures, deviations, and crises only to recuperate them in the name of a hierarchial closure or resolution. From this point of view, any validation of those ruptures is at best naive voluntarism and at worst a refusal to acknowledge what one does not want to know: that the cinematic apparatus works with great efficiency to channel all desire into male, Oedipal desire. The apparatus works; closure and resolution are achieved. Inspired in many cases by the work of Hall and cultural studies, others, like John Fiske, insist upon the social formations of audiences as the only ultimately determining factors.[35] Both positions ascribe an unqualified power to the text on the one hand, and socially defined readers/viewers on the other. The problem in each case is that the activity of making meaning is assumed to reside in one single source: either the cinematic apparatus or the socially contextualized viewer. To be sure, variations are allowed in either case, but they are never significant enough to challenge the basic determinism of the model in question.

While there are advantages to both of these positions, I do not want to suggest that one can take what is most appealing about two different sets of assumptions and put them together in a happy integration. Unfortunately, while the notion of negotiation is potentially quite useful, it can inspire precisely a kind of Pollyanna dialectics—the institution remains monolithic, but never so monolithic that readers cannot be actively oppositional. Now, I do think that spectatorship studies are most useful when local, that is, when examined—as I suggest in the critique of Radway's book—insofar as they problematize the ideal reader or viewer. But there still needs to be some recognition of the theoretical questions at stake. There is no necessary discontinuity between theory and local analysis. Indeed, theory becomes much more challenging when contradiction and tension, for instance, exist not as textual abstractions but as complex entities which do not always lend themselves easily to one reading or another. Film theory of the 1970s erred in attempting to account for a cinematic subject in categories that are absolute. (Even when labeled Western, this usually amounts to the same thing; e.g., some will confess that they speak only of the Western [white, male, etc.] subject and then proceed as if *Western* and *universal* were still fully commensurate terms.) But surely the conclusion is not that all theorizing is doomed to such levels of abstraction.

One particularly influential invocation of negotiation is instructive in this context, since it sets out the issues that the concept is meant to address. Indeed, in Angela McRobbie's essay "Dance and Social Fantasy," a study of how teenage girls respond to dance and how those responses read in relationship to the films *Flashdance* and *Fame*, negotiation seems to describe not only the teenage girls by McRobbie herself as a researcher. Noting that the significance of extratextual codes and knowledge in the reception of mass culture leads to the necessity for the researcher to "limit strictly the range of his or her analysis," McRobbie continues:

> It also means working with a consciously loose rather than tight relation in mind, one where an inter-discursive notion of meaning structures and textual experience leads to a different working practice or methodology. Instead of seeking direct causal links or chains, the emphasis is placed on establishing loose sets of relations, capillary actions and movement, spilling out among and between different fields: work and leisure, fact and fiction, fantasy and reality, individual and social experience.[36]

Several negotiations form the core of McRobbie's analysis, not least of which is the juxtaposition of the responses of teenage girls to dancing as both a social and an individual activity and the textual forms that seem to encourage such fantasies in two dance films, *Flashdance* and *Fame*. Within the two films, there are several processes of negotiation at work. In *Flashdance*, McRobbie notes, while the dance scenes are very much directed at that ubiquitous entity, the male spectator within the film, other narrative elements of the film are drawn so clearly from the woman's film that it is impossible to say with certainty that the address of the film is directed toward the woman defined unambiguously as the object of the male gaze.[37] The process of negotiation here concerns, then, two different genres—the musical and the woman's film—the conventions of which may rub against each other rather than function compatibly. McRobbie also notes that in both films, there is a sometimes peculiar juxtaposition of old and new elements; the films "place together images and moments of overwhelming conformity with those which seem to indicate a break with Hollywood's usual treatment of women."[38] In other words, the classical formulae of both films could be said to acknowledge and retreat from their own limitations insofar as representations of women are concerned.

McRobbie also insists upon the importance of understanding films like these in an intertextual network, and in the case of these two films, the expectations of dance culture can inflect the readings of the films, and vice versa. Thus the process of negotiation refers to how the films are structured as cinematic texts, as well as to how the meanings of these films are negotiated in relationship to one's knowledge of the dance scene outside the movie theater. Noting that the dancehall or disco shares some similarities with the movie theater (a "darkened space" where the spectator/dancer "can retain some degree of anonymity or absorption"), McRobbie notes as well a significant difference: "Where the cinema offers a one-way fantasy which is directed solely through the gaze of the spectator toward the screen, the fantasy of dancing is more social, more reciprocated."[39] Such a mapping of one context onto the other may account for a reception of these films that departs sharply from the pronouncements of film theory about the inevitability of the colonization of the female body.

Two particular points of reference recur in McRobbie's essay, and they echo some of the questions I raised in relation to Radway's *Reading the Romance*. Richard Dyer has suggested that one of the basic appeals of the movie musical is the utopian dimension, a way of providing pleasures and satisfactions that are otherwise unavailable in the culture at hand and yet which are defined in such a way as to suggest that they can be satisfied only within capitalism.[40] Radway suggests that this utopianism—defined within the context of Chodorow's reading of women's desires for re-creation of their pre-Oedipal bond—is a function of the reading of romance novels, and McRobbie's reading of dance and dance films is equally suggestive of a utopian impulse.

I do not wish to evoke a traditional and moralistic Marxism whereby art provides us with a glimpse of the truly integrated human beings we will all become in the communist future. But I find that sometimes the utopian dimension becomes clouded by the understanding of desire as always in conflict with the dominant culture. McRobbie notes, for instance, that *Fame* presents a desire for community and family as necessarily intertwined,[41] and certainly an interesting area of research is the way in which films articulate definitions that both reflect dominant ideology (the family is the basis for all community) and challenge them (communities provide what families do not, or cannot, in our culture). What makes me somewhat suspicious is the way that the discussion of utopianism seems to fall into exactly the kind of large abstractions—having to do with the "human subject under capitalism and/or patriarchy"—that McRobbie sets out (specifically in the passage cited earlier) to challenge. In case I sound as if I am contradicting myself as far as the necessity of combining local analyses with theoretical reflection is concerned, let me say that I do not think that theory means falling back into large clichés about the human subject—or the female subject.

The second recurring point of reference in McRobbie's essay is an illustration of the first. Noting that dance "carries a range of often contradictory strands within it," she affirms the conformity of dance with conventional definitions of femininity, but says that at the same time the pleasures of dance "seem to suggest a displaced, shared and nebulous eroticism rather than a straightforwardly romantic, heavily heterosexual 'goal-oriented' drive."[42] In another context, McRobbie describes the dance scene and suggests that as it offers a "suspension of categories, there is not such a rigid demarcation along age, class, ethnic terms. Gender is blurred and sexual preference less homogeneously heterosexual."[43] Curiously, this "suspension of categories" is itself suspended when McRobbie reports that her sources on the pleasures of dance are "predominantly heterosexual"; hence "these fantasy scenarios make no claim to represent gay or lesbian experience."[44] While gay and lesbian experiences of dance may well be different, this disclaimer erects the categories of sexual preference just when the analysis of dance seems to put them into question.

I suspect that since the question of sexual preference is far more controversial than, say, the desire for a community (whether based on the family or not) and is perhaps threatening to those very viewers/participants whose desires one is attempting to take seriously, the temptation is to shelve a consideration of it for some future analysis or to open the question about the permeability of sexual boundaries without really pursuing it in any depth. But the deployment of gay and lesbian identities in popular culture, and the complicated responses that viewers bring to homosexuality as a moral, sexual, and political issue, seem to me just the kind of specific area of inquiry for investigation into the utopian impulse that desires for community avoid.

Film theory has been so bound by the heterosexual symmetry that supposedly governs Hollywood cinema that it has ignored the possibility, for instance, that one of the distinct pleasures of the cinema may well be a safe zone in which homosexual as well as heterosexual desires can be fantasized and acted out. I am not speaking here of an innate capacity to read against the grain, but rather of the way in which desire and pleasure in the cinema may well function to problematize the categories of heterosexual versus homosexual. To be sure, this safety zone can also be read as a displacement—insurance that the happy ending is a distinctly heterosexual one. But as has been noted many times, the buddy film, if it affirms any kind of sexual identity aside from a narcissistic one, is as drawn to a homosexual connection as it is repelled by it.

Taking into account the complexity of the range of responses to the stability of sexual identities and sexual categories would require an approach to negotiation that specifies the psychic stakes in such a process, rather than just stating that the psychic remains significant or important. I am not referring here to the kind of psychoanalytic theorizing typical of much 1970s film theory, where the unconscious usually meant a master plot repeated again and again, an inevitable source of meaning and comprehensibility. What has been surprisingly absent from much psychoanalytic film theory is an investigation of the ways in which the unconscious refuses the stability of any categorization. The example of heterosexuality and its various others seems to me a particularly crucial one to take into account, since so much of the ideology of the cinematic institution is built simultaneously on the heterosexual couple as the common denominator, on the promise of romantic fulfillment, at the same time that that couple seems constantly in crisis, constantly in need of reassurance. One would have thought this an area where the concept of negotiation would provide a useful corrective.

To take this in a somewhat different direction: The notion of negotiation is useful only if one is attentive to the problematic as well as utopian uses to which negotiation can be put by both the subjects one is investigating and the researchers themselves. While I have not seen this spelled out in any detail, negotiation seems to be a variation of the Marxist notion of mediation—the notion, that is, of a variety of instances that complicate or mediate in various ways the relationship between individuals and the economic structure of capitalism. Raymond Williams has noted that while the concept of mediation has the advantage of complicating significantly the cause-and-effect notion of reflection so typical of a traditional Marxism and of indicating an active process, it remains limited in its own way. Williams notes that "it is virtually impossible to sustain the metaphor of 'mediation' . . . without some sense of separate and pre-existent areas or orders of reality . . . Within the inheritance of idealist philosophy the process is usually, in practice, seen as a mediation between categories, which have been assumed to be distinct."[45]

Negotiation can replicate the problems that inhere in the notion of mediation by replacing the language of subjection and imposition with that of agency and contradiction but without significantly exploring how the notion of an active subject can be just as open to projections and subjections as a passive subject can. While the field of cultural studies, with its emphasis on negotiation as the way readers/viewers shape mass culture to their own needs, has had an enormous impact on film studies, another direction in literary studies also makes persistent use of negotiation in a rather different way. The so-called new historicism has had only a limited relationship with film studies, yet some of the ways in which the concept of negotiation has emerged in new historicist studies offer a useful counterpoint to the inflection offered by cultural studies.

New historicism is most immediately associated with English Renaissance studies. But the problems new-historicist work addresses are not so different from those central to film studies, particularly insofar as a reckoning with both the advances and the limitations of 1970s film theory are concerned. Louis A. Montrose, for instance, has said that "the terms in which the problem of ideology has been posed and is now circulating in Renaissance literary studies—namely as an opposition between 'containment' and 'subversion'—are so reductive, polarized, and undynamic as to be of little or no conceptual value."[46] That this assessment applies to film studies, particularly in relation to spectatorship, may have less to do with a striking coincidence between film studies and the new historicism and more to do with questions central to virtually all forms of cultural analysis in the 1980s and 1990s that attempt to develop new forms of criticism and theory at the same time as they engage with their own historical legacies, particularly insofar as the 1960s and 1970s are concerned in their status as simultaneous political turning points and mythological burden.

While it is not my purpose either to align myself with a new-historicist project or to provide an extended introduction to this field, it is noteworthy that the term *negotiation* in its new historicist usage tends more toward questioning those very possibilities of radical agency that the cultural-studies approach finds in its negotiations. Stephen Greenblatt notes that capitalism "has characteristically generated neither regimes in which all discourses seem coordinated, nor regimes in which they seem radically isolated or discontinuous, but regimes in which the drive toward differentiation and the drive toward monological organization operate simultaneously, or at least oscillate so rapidly as to create the impression of simultaneity."[47] From the vantage point of this simultaneity, then, the immediate assumption that all unauthorized uses of films, and therefore spectatorial positions that depart from the presumed ideal of capitalist ideology, are virtually or potentially radical is a reading of the nature of discourse and power in our culture as more dualistic than it is.

A large part of the problem here is that the analysis of spectatorship in film studies has as a significant part of its legacy a commitment to the creation of alternative cultures and political identities which refuse to comply with dominant ideology. Phrases like *alternative cultures* and *refusal to comply* can of course mean a variety of things, including contradictory things. The reactions of black male spectators to the filmed popularization of Alice Walker's novel *The Color Purple* cannot be squared in any easy or even complex way with the feminist critique of the "woman as object of the male look," yet both constitute claims to validation by marginalized groups.[48] Part of the 1960s/1970s legacy of film studies is a romanticized vision of the politicized past, based on the assumption (erroneous and inaccurate) that the common denominator *socialist* could account for any and all kinds of radical and progressive social change—a utopian definition of socialism which was quickly enough put to rest by feminism and gay and lesbian liberation movements. Curiously, what seems to have persisted is a vague discourse of subversion and alternative scenarios amidst conceptual confusion about just what is being subverted and for what.

Catherine Gallagher says—in what could easily function as a critique of the tendencies present in much writing about spectatorship—that new historicists have attempted to show "that under certain historical circumstances, the display of ideological contradictions is completely consonant with the maintenance of oppressive social relations."[49] It has been crucial to spectatorship studies to understand that visions of the cinema as the inflexible apparatus of the ideological subject are as much projections of theorists' own desires as they are hypothetically interesting and useful and also historically conditioned postulates about going to the cinema. But it is equally important for such an inquiry to take place in what amounts to a new stage of spectatorship studies, where the model is no longer the passive, manipulated (and inevitably white and heterosexual) spectator, but rather the contradictory, divided, and fragmented subject.

The new-historicist reminder that *negotiation* is a marketplace term tempers too quick an enthusiasm about what may ultimately be strategies of consumerism. But it is too easy to assume the cynical route (which is, after all, only the reverse of romanticism), that is, to assume in a kind of more-Foucauldian-than-thou posture that there are no alternative positions, only fictions of them. What remains vital, in the critical examination of spectatorship, is the recognition that no negotiation is inherently or purely oppositional, but that the desire for anything inherent or pure is itself a fiction that must be contested.

What I am suggesting, in this extremely schematic encounter between new historicism and cultural studies, is that a desire for unproblematized agency—whether that of the critic or of the imaginary or real spectator(s) under investigation—persists. Even though McRobbie does question the notion of the ideal viewer, which, as I suggest above, is one of the limitations of Radway's analysis, there remain some echoes of an idealized female subject in her account. In an extremely provocative essay on the status of negotiation as a critical concept in studies on female spectatorship, Christine Gledhill sees negotiation as providing a possible way out of the limitations of the implications of feminist/psychoanalytic film theory and the attendant split between text and reception, particularly insofar as texts were seen as capable of situating alternative subjective positions. "The value of 'negotiation' . . . as an analytical concept is that it allows space to the subjectivities, identities, and pleasures of audiences," writes Gledhill.[50] But *subjectivity, identity,* and *pleasure* are here defined in a way that acknowledges the critique of the fictions of bourgeois identity that has been central to Lacanian-inspired film theory. At the same time, those critiques are fictions, too, in supposing that any notion of identity may supposedly be done away with.

In a move somewhat reminiscent of Jane Gallop's claim that "identity must be continually assumed and immediately put into question,"[51] Gledhill says,

> the concept of negotiation stops short at the dissolution of identity suggested by avant-garde aesthetics. For if arguments about the non-identity of self and language, words and meaning, desire and its objects challenge bourgeois notions of the centrality and stability of the ego and the transparency of language, the political consequence is not to abandon the search for identity . . . The object of attack should not be identity as such but its dominant construction as total, non-contradictory and unchanging.[52]

I am suggesting, as is perhaps obvious by now, that this "dominant construction" enters into the ways in which researchers themselves construct their audiences. This should not, of course, come as startling news to anyone familiar with the dynamics of transference and counter-transference. But in order for studies of spectatorship to engage fully with the complex dynamics that define the process of negotiation, such constructions need to be accounted for.

As Gledhill's comments suggest, one of the key issues at stake here is the competing claims of "identity," which have been associated with some of the most fervent debates in film studies and related fields in the past two decades. Studies of reception and negotiation are often meant to challenge the ways in which post-structuralist theorists are seen to critique any notion of the self as an agent as an inevitable fiction of bourgeois/patriarchal/idealist culture. What becomes quite difficult in that process of challenge is acknowledging the necessity of the critique of the fictions of the self without resurrecting them yourself. Somewhat curiously, the challenges to apparatus theory described in this chapter return to the problem of identification, as if to suggest that however mobile and multiple subject positions may be, spectatorship still engages some notion of identity. But then theorists of the cinematic apparatus never banished identification from film theory, but rather redefined its terms beyond those of character or a one-to-one correspondence between viewer and screen. In any case, the current visibility of identity as a problem in film studies—whether as spectre, curse, or positive value—speaks to the continued friction between subjects and viewers.

NOTES

1. Linda Gordon, "What's New in Women's History," in *Feminist Studies/Critical Studies*, ed. Teresa de Lauretis (Bloomington: Indiana University Press, 1986), pp. 20–30.

2. Mike Budd, Robert M. Entman, and Clay Steinman, "The Affirmative Character of U.S. Cultural Studies." *Critical Studies in Mass Communication* 7:2 (June 1990), 169–84.

3. Angela McRobbie, "Dance and Social Fantasy," in Angela McRobbie and Mica Nava, eds., *Gender and Generation* (London: Macmillan, 1984), pp. 130–61.

4. Janice Radway, *Reading the Romance: Women, Patriarchy, and Popular Literature* (Chapel Hill and London: University of North Carolina Press, 1984).

5. Janet Bergstrom and Mary Ann Doane, eds., *Camera Obscura* 20-1 (1989): special issue on The Spectatrix.

6. Radway, p. 12.

7. Ibid., pp. 112–13.

8. Ibid., p. 143.

9. Ibid., p. 213.

10. Tania Modleski, "Some Functions of Feminist Criticism, or the Scandal of the Mute Body," *October* 49 (1989), 3–24.

11. Nancy Chodorow, *The Reproduction of Mothering: Psychoanalysis and the Sociology of Gender* (Berkeley and Los Angeles: University of California Press, 1978).

12. Radway, pp. 11–12.

13. Constance Penley, "Feminism, Film Theory and the Bachelor Machines," *m/f* 10 (1985), 39–59.

14. Sigmund Freud, "'A Child Is Being Beaten': A Contribution to the Origin of Sexual Perversions," in *Sexuality and the Psychology of Love* (New York: Collier, 1919, rpt. and tr. 1972), pp. 107–32.

15. See D. N. Rodowick, "The Difficulty of Difference," *Wide Angle* 5:1 (1982), 4–15, and *The Difficulty of Difference* (New York and London: Routledge, 1991); Mary Ann Doane, "'The Woman's Film': Possession and Address," in Mary Ann Doane, Patricia Mellencamp, and Linda Williams, eds., *Re-vision: Essays in Feminist Film Criticism* (Frederick, Md.: American Film Institute/University Publications of America, 1984), pp. 67–80; and Miriam Hansen, "Pleasure, Ambivalence, Identification: Valentino and Female Spectatorship," *Cinema Journal* 25:4 (1986), 6–32.

16. Jean Laplanche and Jean-Bertrand Pontalis, "Fantasy and the Origins of Sexuality," in Victor Burgin, James Donald, and Cora Kaplan, eds., *Formations of Fantasy* (London and New York: Methuen, 1964; tr. 1986), pp. 5–34.

17. Jean Laplanche and Jean-Bertrand Pontalis, *The Language of Psychoanalysis*, tr. D. Nicholson-Smith (London: Hogarth Press, 1967, tr. 1973), p. 317.

18. Laplanche and Pontalis, "Fantasy and the Origins of Sexuality," p. 19.

19. Ibid., p. 28.

20. Ibid., p. 21.

21. Ibid., p. 22–3.

22. Ibid., p. 26.

23. Elizabeth Cowie, "Fantasia," *m/f* 9 (1984), 77.

24. Ibid., p. 87.

25. Ibid., p. 91.

26. Ibid., p. 101.

27. Constance Penley, "Introduction: The Lady Doesn't Vanish: Feminism and Film Theory," in Constance Penley, ed., *Feminism and Film Theory* (New York and London: Routledge, 1988), p. 11.

28. Cowie, p. 102.

29. Teresa de Lauretis, "Film and the Visible," paper presented at the "How Do I Look?" conference, New York City, October 1989.

30. Barbara Creed, "Response," *Camera Obscura* 20:1 (1990), 135.

31. Ibid., p. 135.

32. Jacqueline Rose, "Response," *Camera Obscura* 20:1 (1990), 275.

33. Ibid., p. 275.

34. Stuart Hall, "Encoding/Decoding," in Stuart Hall, D. Hobson, A. Lowe, and P. Willis, eds., *Culture, Media, Language* (London: Hutchinson, 1980), pp. 128–38.

35. John Fiske, "British Cultural Studies and Television," in Robert C. Allen, ed., *Channels of Discourse: Television and Contemporary Criticism* (Chapel Hill: University of North Carolina Press, 1987), pp. 254–89.

36. McRobbie, "Dance and Social Fantasy," p. 142.

37. Ibid., p. 138.

38. Ibid., p. 150.

39. Ibid., p. 144.

40. Richard Dyer, "Entertainment and Utopia," *Movie* 24 (Spring 1977), 2–13.

41. McRobbie, "Dance and Social Fantasy," p. 158.

42. Ibid., p. 134.

43. Ibid., p. 146.

44. Ibid., p. 145.

45. Raymond Williams, *Marxism and Literature* (New York and Oxford: Oxford University Press, 1977), p. 99.

46. Louis A. Montrose, "Professing the Renaissance: The Poetics and Politics of Culture," in H. Aram Veeser, ed., *The New Historicism* (New York and London. Routledge, 1989), p. 22.

47. Stephen Greenblatt, "Towards a Poetics of Culture," in H. Aram Veeser, ed., *The New Historicism* (New York and London: Routledge, 1989), p. 6.

48. See Jacqueline Bobo, "*The Color Purple:* Black Women as Cultural Readers," in E. Deidre Pribram, ed., *Female Spectators* (London and New York: Verso, 1988), pp. 90–109.

49. Catherine Gallagher, "Marxism and the New Historicism," in H. Aram Veeser, ed., *The New Historicism* (New York and London: Routledge, 1989), p. 44.

50. Christine Gledhill, "Pleasurable Negotiations," in E. Deidre Pribram, ed., *Female Spectators* (New York and London: Verso, 1988), p. 72.

51. Jane Gallop, *The Daughter's Seduction: Feminism and Psychoanalysis* (London: Macmillan, 1982), p. xii.

52. Gledhill, p. 72.

Carol J. Clover

The Eye of Horror

> *We all understand that eyes are the most vulnerable of our sensory organs, the most vulnerable of our facial accessories, and they are (ick!) soft. Maybe that's the worst. . . .*
>
> Stephen King, *Danse Macabre*

Eyes are everywhere in horror cinema. In titles: *The Eyes of Laura Mars, Eyes of a Stranger, The Hills Have Eyes, The Eye Creatures, Terrorvision, Scanners, White of the Eye, Don't Look Now, Crawling Eye, Eyes of Hell, Headless Eyes,* and so forth. Or on posters, videocassette box covers, and other promotional materials, where wide-open eyes staring up in terror (for example) at a poised knife or a naked face or something off-box or off-poster are part of the standard iconography. Or the extreme close-up of an eye in the film's opening moments or credit sequence (e.g., *Vertigo, The Eyes of Laura Mars, White of the Eye, Black Widow, Dream Lover, Incubus, Repulsion*). Only after the credits have run their course does the camera draw back to let us see whose eye it is (often a dead person's) and what the sequence is about.

Insofar as it introduces a narrative that necessarily turns on problems of vision—seeing too little (to the point of blindness) or seeing too much (to the point of insanity)—and insofar as its scary project is to tease, confuse, block, and threaten the spectator's own vision, the opening eye of horror announces a concern "with the way we see ourselves and others and the consequences that often attend our usual manner of

This is an abridged version of the final chapter of *Men, Women, and Chain Saws: Gender in the Modern Horror Film* (Princeton, N.J. Princeton University Press, 1992). Substantive cuts are marked [. . .]. Reprinted by permission of the author and Princeton University Press.

perception."[1] Horror privileges eyes because, more crucially than any other kind of cinema, it is about eyes.

More particularly, it is about eyes watching horror. Certainly the act of watching horror films or horror television also looms large in horror films. Horror film characters are forever watching horror movies, either in theaters (e.g., *Demons*) or on television at home (e.g., *Halloween*), and not a few horror plots turn on the horrifying consequences of looking at horror (e.g., *Demons, Terrorvision, Videodrome*). Responses of horror movie characters—shuddering, nausea, shrinking, paralysis, screaming, and revulsion—serve as a kind of instructive mirror to horror movie audiences, and that mirroring effect is one of the defining features of the genre. [. . .].

Modern horror repeatedly aligns us not just with victims facing monsters but with audiences of horror movies in which victims face monsters, or with audiences of horror movies who are watching horror movies in which victims face monsters, and so on. It is not only the look-at-the-monster that is at issue here but the look-at-the-movie. [. . .].

Bull's-Eye: *Peeping Tom*

I take as my point of departure Michael Powell's *Peeping Tom*—a film that sets out with astonishing candor and clarity a psychosexual theory of cinematic spectatorship. [. . .].

Peeping Tom tells the story of a professional cinematographer, Mark, who moonlights as a photographer for pornographic magazines. Mark, it turns out, is also given to killing the (female) objects of his gaze. Precisely how he does so is not immediately clear, for our vision is limited to what we can see through his movie-camera's eye as we move in for a close-up of the woman's face registering first bewilderment as light flashes into her eyes and then terror at something, unseen by us, in the vicinity of the camera—at which point the narrative cuts. Why the sudden expression of fear, and what the blinding light, are questions fully answered only in the film's final moments, when Mark demonstrates his cinematographic method to Helen, the young woman neighbor toward whom he feels his first stirrings of nonmurderous friendship. The tripod is equipped with a hidden, extendable spike and the movie camera with a mirror, neither of which appears in the visual frame of the murder scenes; when Mark moves in for a close-up, the spike pierces the victim's throat and she sees her own terrified face in the mirror. "Do you know what the most frightening thing in the world is? It's fear," Mark tells Helen. "So I did something very simple. *Very* simple. When they felt this spike touching their throats, and knew I was going to kill them, I made them watch their own deaths. I made them see their own terror as the spike went in. And if death has a face, they saw that, too."

But if the revelation of the "killer camera" explains the past murders of the prostitute and the actress, it simultaneously explains the film's other past: Mark's own childhood, filmed in excruciating detail by his scientist father. We are shown passages of those childhood films, grainy black-and-white home movies, in which Mark as a child is filmed asleep, at play, viewing his mother's corpse, stealing a look at a couple embracing on a park bench, and, above all, in situations of fear—fear induced by the tortures the father inflicts on him. The magic camera, as it comes to be called in the film, has passed from father to son, and indeed, the son has made it his life's work to carry on his father's life's work—not only by extending it to other subjects (the prostitute and the actress) but by continuing his own story where his father left it off. The film *"Peeping Tom"* is about the making of another film: the documentary record of Mark's life, begun by his father and continued by Mark himself (through the filming of his murders and of the public reaction that attends them) and finally completed by him as well, as he films his own suicide with and by the same "magic camera."

"I hope to be a director, very soon," Mark declares to Helen—an ambition also visible on the director's chair bearing his name, Mark Lewis, in his upstairs workroom. Lest we suppose that directors are less sadistic than cinematographers, we are shown a long sequence on the movie set in which a director requires an actress to do fifty-odd takes of a fainting scene on grounds that she is unconvincing. The episode is played for comedy, and we are invited to laugh when the vain and incompetent actress finally pleases the director by fainting in fact, out of sheer exhaustion from her earlier efforts. There is an edge to the joke, however. The actress's tumble into unconsciousness recalls the film's earlier photographic session, in which one of Mark's pornographic models asks him to obscure the bruises that mar her body, and the other to obscure her grotesquely scarred lip ("He said you needn't get my face"). Where the bruises and the damaged face come from we do not know, but the point is clear: to be on the object side of the camera is to be hurt. The only difference between Mark and the director he aspires to be is that the latter has, in the terms of the film, internalized the magic camera. It is the cinematic apparatus itself, not just its mechanical representative the camera, that is in question. Just because the sadism of that apparatus is less overt on the movie set than it is in Mark's individual photographic sessions does not mean that it is less brutal. For Powell, clearly, the difference between Mark's direct sadisms and the institutionalized sadisms of the movie set is merely one of degree. The point is driven home by the fact that the role of Mark's sadistic father, in the childhood footage, is played by director Powell himself, and the boy Mark by his son.

One day a psychoanalyst appears on the movie set. When Mark approaches, the psychoanalyst asks him what his job on the set is. "Focus puller," Mark replies. "So am I, in a way," the analyst replies. Mark introduces himself as the son of the famous Dr. Lewis and, after listening to the expected encomia, moves to his real concern: does the psychoanalyst know of his father's final, unpublished research? "What was the subject?" the analyst asks. "I don't remember what he called it," Mark responds, "but it has something to do with what causes people to be Peeping Toms." "Scoptophilia!" the analyst pronounces emphatically, "the morbid urge to gaze!"—the cure for which, Mark is crestfallen to learn, is a couple of years in analysis.

The exchange is a heavily coded one, of course, not only because of the conventional understanding, in films of that era, that psychiatrists and their ilk speak the truth but also because of the utterance of the term *Peeping Tom* and the equation between focus pulling (reversing the relationship of foreground and background in an image, or, more generally, cinematography) and psychoanalysis. It has all the earmarks, in short, of a classic narrative-film explanation. Still, there is reason to wonder whether this particular psychoanalytic pronunciamento is as sterling as it seems. The fact that the analyst is after all an admiring colleague of Mark's father would seem to compromise his judgment on the face of it. The film's strong implication is that the field of psychiatric research is itself built on sadistic inquiry, and if that is so, then the psychoanalyst stands as morally condemned as the father. Too, there is under the circumstances something unsettling about the "focus-pulling" joke. When Mark, in response to the psychoanalyst's question, identifies himself as a focus-puller, we understand the term in both its workaday sense (cinematographer) and in our privileged sense (camera murderer), and when the psychoanalyst then replies, "So am I, in a way," he plays to that double possibility, again inviting us to link the practice of psychoanalysis with violence. (Mark's father, after all, was a focus puller in both senses.) It is in any case clear from his persistent questioning that the psychoanalyst is far more interested in getting his hands on Dr. Lewis's unpublished papers on scoptophilia than he is in Mark. And, of course, there is the simple fact that the psychoanalyst is apparently in the employ of the studio and hence part of a cinematic apparatus that the film defines as assaultive.

Finally, there is the obvious inadequacy, relative to the film's own workings, of the psychoanalyst's snap label "scoptophilia" and its definition as "the morbid urge to gaze." It is no small part of the brilliance of *Peeping Tom* that it splits this unitary formulation into two gazes and two varieties of morbidity—gazes and morbidities that coexist in one and the same person (here Mark) and gazes that, by extension, are claimed to coexist in the cinematic spectator. The two gazes are neatly formulated—share double billing, as it were—in the opening doubled sequence. The sequence presents us with two viewings of the same event (the assault on the prostitute) by the same person (Mark) from precisely the same perspective. The present half of the sequence is preceded by a shot of a whirring camera (held close to the chest between jacket lapels), which we then move behind and look through. Our vision from this point on is through the viewfinder, which, like a rifle-sight, is marked by cross hairs. We approach and tacitly solicit a prostitute, follow her upstairs, watch her begin to undress, then bear down on her as light flashes on her face and she reacts in terror—all this through the cross hairs. This is the narrative's present and causal gaze, its "doing" gaze. It is also, of course, a predatory, assaultive gaze—in the story's own terms, a phallic gaze. Mark has his movie camera with him always, slung over his shoulder. "You have it *in* you, boy," Vivian says of it; according to Helen, it is "growing into an extra limb." When in the wake of his second murder he hands it over to a police officer for inspection, he is visibly nervous and keeps half-reaching to get it back.

The second, or past, half of the sequence simply duplicates the first half—but without the hairline cross, for, as the opening shot of a whirring projector announces, we are now watching, through Mark's eyes, a screening of the earlier film. It is over this replay that the screen credits roll. At the climactic moment, Mark at last (and for the first time) enters our vision as he half-rises in a state of agitation and faces his screen. If the present or doing gaze was predatory, penetrating, murderous, at once brutalizing the woman and recording that brutalization, *causing* the event to happen, the second or past gaze is after the fact, at some contemplative distance—a distance underwritten by the relocation of the image further back in our screen (in such a way as to show us a screen in a screen) and by the superimposition of screen credits. What was action is now speculation. What was present is now pluperfect. What was real life is now movie—now *our* movie, too. What was active cinematographer is now passive spectator. We never saw the cinematographer of the opening sequence; but at the end of the screening, we see the spectator as he interposes himself between the screen and the images he earlier created, now projected on his own body.

But what does this gesture of Mark's—rising to face the screen—*mean*? Contrary to Elliott Stein, who states matter-of-factly that it denotes sexual climax,[2] I would suggest that it is deliberately ambiguous—a tease, an invitation to stay tuned for the explanation. It is actually the second tease of the film, the first being the light and expression of fear in the prostitute's face. That is, each of the two gazes that open *Peeping Tom* poses a distinct question—one having to do with Mark's stake as a photographer (what is he *doing* to that woman?) and one having to do with his stake as a spectator (why is he rising toward the screen?). I emphasize the twiceness of the opening sequence—the doubled representation of the prostitute's murder and the "tease" embedded in each—because it is so frequently ignored in discussions of the film, with the result that the binary it proposes, and that underwrites the film proper, has not been done critical justice.[3]

Mark, we come to understand, has survived in adulthood the spectatorial cruelties of his childhood by splitting and reenacting them—on one hand through the assumption of his father's role, using the camera to "kill and fuck" (as Stein puts it)[4] and on the other through the obsessive re-viewing of his own boyhood experience of having been on the *receiving* end of his father's cinematic "killing and fucking." If the emotional project of the first gaze is to assault, the emotional project of the second is to be oneself assaulted—vicariously, through the process of projection in both senses. In that re-view of unpleasure there lies perverse pleasure, for the sight of pain inflicted on others is "enjoyed masochistically by the subject through his identification of himself with the suffering object."[5] This second gaze—the horrified gaze of the victim, or more complexly, one's gaze at surrogates for one's own past victimized self—I shall for want of a better term call "reactive."

The two gazes of *Peeping Tom* divide straightforwardly along sexual lines. Those who photograph are males (Mark as an adult; his father, Dr. Lewis; the film director), and the act of photographing is plainly figured as an act of phallic cruelty.[6] Those who are photographed are, with the sole exception of Mark as a child, females (prostitute, actress, models), and the experience of being photographed—of gazing reactively—is figured as an experience of being bruised, scarred, terrified, made to faint, and stabbed to death. Mark thus occupies both categories: as an adult on the side of the masculine and as a child on the side of the feminine. Preadolescent boys are frequently figured as premasculine in traditional cultures (and in our own popular culture), but Mark's is a more complicated case, for he has carried his femininity with him into adulthood, and it is a living part of his psyche. He is the bearer of both gazes, and it is the relation and distinction between them that Powell's film is all about.

Assaultive and reactive gazing are, in the case of Mark, housed in one and the same person, and they are, at least in the initial sequence, structurally identical: the "present" half of the prostitute sequence (the assaultive view) is in all phenomenal aspects (with the exception of the cross hairs) identical to the "past" half (the reactive view). The same footage does for both. The point of this homology is not, however, to demonstrate the one-and-the-sameness of the two gazes. They are marked as experientially different by a whole range of signs: pace, present/past, camera/projector, and, above all, Mark's dialogue lines and acting (facial gestures in particular, but also tone of voice). Rather, the homology points up the causal relationship between the two. In the same way that child abusers in the present were abused children in the past, assaultive gazing, for Powell, proceeds from and is predicated on the reactive gazing (in my meaning of that term). Inside every Peeping Tom is a peeped-at child, trying incessantly to master his own pain by re-viewing it in the person of another. Mark's "feminine" look is not at odds with his "masculine" one, but constitutive of it, its necessary condition.

The reactive gaze of *Peeping Tom* is doubly marked as masochistic: in its drive to pleasure-in-pain and in its characteristic need to revisit, over and over again, an originary story in hopes of getting it right so as to put it to rest. "Every night you turn on this film machine," Helen's mother complains, and Mark himself observes that although he plans for every murder to be his last, none quite satisfies: the light is somehow always wrong. So the circle: the compulsion to repeat "what is unpleasant or even painful" inherent in the "reactive" gaze needs a steady supply of projected images that only the direct application of an "assaultive" camera can satisfy.[7] With the exception of the (significantly) blind Mrs. Lewis, virtually every character in *Peeping Tom* is implicated in some such circle. To suppose that *Peeping Tom* is about one psychopath is very much to miss the point; in one way or another, the traffic in pictures involves us all. [. . .].

As a *horror* spectator, Mark is more than a failed voyeur; he is a positively successful masochist. If, in his capacity as horror filmmaker, Mark is fighting for voyeuristic distance from the victim, he is in his capacity as horror spectator not only failing to resist her embrace but hurling himself into it. Uniting with the victim position seems to be the point of his spectatorial enterprise, the shameful fantasy his home studio has been constructed to fulfill. When Mrs. Stephens accuses Mark of running his projector so incessantly, it is not clear which footage is in question—the childhood footage figuring himself as victim or the adult footage figuring women as victims. Nor does it matter; as projections, they are, functionally speaking, one and the same movie.

Peeping Tom, in short, should also be taken at face value as a commentary not only on the symbiotic interplay of sadistic and masochistic impulses in the individual viewer but equally as a commentary, within the context of horror film making, on the symbiotic interplay of the sadistic work of the filmmaker and the masochistic stake of the spectator—an arrangement on which horror cinema insists.[8] There may be no such thing as purely masochistic spectatorship (or even, perhaps, purely sadistic moviemaking), but the job of horror—the job of movies people see *in order to be scared*—is to give the viewer as pure a dose as possible. [. . .].

Actually, what I, like others before me, have referred to as the opening sequence of *Peeping Tom*, the prostitute sequence, is not the film's first moment. The prostitute sequence is preceded by two close-up images. The first is a brief and startling close-up image of an archery target, which, after a static second or two, is suddenly punctured at the center—in the bull's-eye—by an arrow hurtling from some source off-frame. The moment has no story—no archer, no setting, no context—and immediately upon the penetration of the bull's-eye, the film cuts abruptly to the second prenarrative image: the super close-up of a human eye, first closed, then opening as if in alarm. The fact that this eye doublet bears no narrative relation to the remainder of the film—and is the *only* narratively disembodied moment in the entire film—fairly shouts out its supertextual status. In case we doubted which of the eye's two operations *Peeping Tom* wishes to privilege in its analysis of horror cinema, this opening minute spells it out: not the eye that kills, but the eye that is killed.

Looking in and at Horror

The question is whether *Peeping Tom*'s analysis of horror is borne out by horror itself—whether horror movies too draw a distinction between the assaultive gaze, figured as masculine, of the camera (or some stand-in) and the reactive gaze, figured as feminine, of the spectator, and at which pole they locate the horror experience. It is to other horror, mostly of recent vintage, that I now turn.

The Assaultive Gaze

For obvious reasons, it is on the assaultive gaze of modern horror that critical attention has by and large been trained. To judge from the commentaries, assaultive gazing, more or less phallically figured, is the sine qua non of the modern horror movie: its cause, its effect, its point. To argue (as I mean to) that this judgment is defective—that it fails to take account of the larger system of looking to which assaultive gazing is inevitably subordinated—is not to deny the existence and at least temporary power of the male gaze in modern horror. On the contrary, as the following examples suggest, horror movies are obsessively interested in the thought that the simple act of staring can terrify, maim, or kill its object—that a hard look and a hard penis (chain saw, knife, power drill) amount to one and the same thing.

The most phallic camera on record is undoubtedly the one that imprisons, rapes and impregnates Susan in *Demon Seed* (1977). Susan's home security system is invaded by an advanced intelligence system named Proteus, who, once installed, proceeds to lock her in, train his lens on her, and force her, by a variety of household tortures (including electrical shock) to do his will—all of which she watches on video monitors. Although we never see Proteus (as pure intelligence, he has no being), we assume his masculinity from his name, low (digitalized) voice, and telescopic metal penis. "What do you want?" Susan finally screams in desperation. "A child," answers the camera and after some preliminaries extrudes a lenslike appendage with which he rapes and impregnates her—the only rape I know of that is filmed from the ostensible point of view of the penis. [9] Although *Demon Seed*'s manifest concern is with technology gone wild, its constellation of lenses, monitors, and camera-penis is only an update of *Peeping Tom*'s mirror and spike. The difference is that Mark's camera fucked symbolically and killed literally, whereas *Demon Seed's* reverses the priority.

In *From Beyond*, the phallic gaze is materially (and presumably ironically) realized in the representation of an externalized pineal gland as a third, sexual eye or seeing genital. In his mad and (what in horror amounts to the same thing) impotent desire to stimulate the pineal, Dr. Pretorius invents a "resonator," to which he himself, his assistant Crawford, and Dr. Katherine McMichaels are all serially subjected. In the first phase, the resonator effect entails a heightening of sexual appetite in its more sadomasochistic forms. In the second phase, the pineal bursts through the forehead, dangling and waving in the air like a small penis-camera, seeking on one hand to see and on the other to attack and penetrate others' brains—mind-fucking in the most literal sense. "She will go into my mind, and I will go into hers," declares Pretorious at his pineal, and sadomasochistic, mightiest. "It's the greatest sensual pleasure there is." For this genital eye, rape and vision are one and the same thing. Only when his dangling pineal is bitten off by Katherine can Crawford resume his normal life.[10]

Predatory gazing through the agency of the first-person camera is part of the stock-in-trade of horror. The mechanics are laboriously spelled out by Laura Mars in her effort to explain the nature of her proleptic visions of women being stalked and stabbed in the eyes (*The Eyes of Laura Mars*, 1978).[11] "Look through that," she tells the investigating officer, handing him a camera. "Now if you think of that camera as the eyes of the killer, what you're seeing through that lens is what the killer sees. It's on the monitor, there. When it happens to me [that is, when she has a vision that allows her to see what the unknown killer sees when he stalks a victim], I can't see what's in front of me. What I see is that [the scene on the monitor]. Do you understand?" Like Mark in *Peeping Tom*, Laura Mars is not only a photographer but a photographer of women—of beautiful women surrounded and threatened by violence—and on the set we see her as we saw Mark, camera poised.[12] At first glance, *The Eyes of Laura Mars* seems something of a gender-bender in its positioning of a female behind an assaultive camera that bears down on women only (and one gay man). But it turns out that she is not, in fact, the subject of the assaultive gaze as much as the unwitting conduit or medium of the *real* assaultive gazer—the killer-cop whose vision she has tapped into—and in the end, she becomes his object as well. As a photographer who objectifies women, Laura aids and abets phallic gazing, but the act itself remains emphatically male.[13]

One of the most popular assaultive gazing stories of the past two decades is the telekinesis or telepathy film. David Cronenberg's *Scanners* (1980) features certain gifted individuals able, by looking, to link themselves into the nervous system of others, thus causing headaches or nosebleeds or, in the extreme case, exploded brains or incinerated bodies.[14] What is striking about the telekinesis film is that it is the one subset of horror which regularly features females as assaultive gazers.[15] Merely by casting a concentrated glance, the girl-heroes of *Carrie, Firestarter, The Fury,* and *Friday the 13th VII* can respectively demolish an entire high school, spark a firestorm, bloody the noses of bystanders, and move heavy objects.[16] It is worth noting that the damaging power of these girls' looks stems not from their natural selves—not even their natural selves equipped with cameras or chain saws—but rather from the supernatural apparatus of telekinesis.

That apparatus does not sit easily on the female, however. The plots of these films turn on the girls' ambivalent relationship to their power (they alternate between abuse and renunciation) and, more to the point, on institutional efforts to contain or correct it. The prepubescent Charlie (Charlotte) McGee (girl-hero of *Firestarter*) comes by her blaze-starting glance in the same way that Mark came by his camera and Leatherface his chain saw: her father, to whom she is unusually close (her mother, like the mothers of Mark and Leatherface, being dead), gave it to her. When her father dies and Charlie flees to safety—to the home of a kindly farm couple, who will now stand in for the proper parents she never had—she renounces the gaze that has brought her so much grief. It is at this moment, at the very end of the film, that we hear her for the first time referred to by her real name—Charlotte. To this extent the story is a virtual calque, one suspects intentional, on Freud's account of the young girl's march toward femininity, which entails a renunciation of her own phallic strivings (in this case her powerful gaze). But the film's dramatic conflict—what it is *about*—complicates and undermines a strictly internal reading. For when government agents become aware of Charlie's psychic powers, they capture her and in a controlled environment try to harness her gift for good (anti-Soviet) purposes. Failing that, they decide simply to annihilate her. "My God," says the agent in charge of the mission, "one of these days she'll grow up to be a beautiful woman. Can you imagine what kind of destruction she'll be able to cause then? She must be stopped!" But she escapes, pursued by men armed with flamethrowers and grenades, and flees to the couple who greet her as Charlotte and who promise, by virtue of their own sturdy normality, to make a regular girl of her. The march toward femininity is indeed inevitable in this account, not because it is in the psychosexual scheme of things but because society—indeed, the very survival of the state—rests on disempowering half its citizens. If Charlie's gaze is phallic, in other words, then the message of the film, is simply, better castrated than dead.

But far and away the most conspicuous sort of assaultive gazing follows the 1978 lead of John Carpenter's *Halloween*, in which we adopt the vision of an entity that stalks a house, peers in windows, enters and goes to the kitchen for a carving knife, then proceeds upstairs, opens a door, and stabs a young woman to death—all without knowing who "we" are, and all without direct reference to the mediation of a camera.[17] There is a camera, of course, and presumably in the interests of realism, it is in Carpenter's use unmounted, yielding an image that wavers and trembles much the way a mad killer might. But no camera, no photographer, is shown. If *Peeping Tom* clearly established the camera as the machine between us and it, *Halloween* seeks to efface the intervention of the photographer, to try for the direct connection: we are invited to look not through a murderous camera, but with our own murderous eyes, listening to the beat of our heart and the breathing of our lungs. The device is probably the most widely imitated—and widely parodied—cliché of modern horror.[18] That this first-person, assaultive gaze is a gendered gaze, figured explicitly or inexplicitly in phallic terms, is also clear. Slasher films draw the equation repeatedly and unequivocally: when men cannot perform sexually, they stare and kill instead. The first-person sequence that opens the standard slasher duplicates, without the cross-hairs, the opening sequence of *Peeping Tom:* the I-camera stalks and stabs an attractive woman. The woman we see through the I-camera is thus, according to the code, scheduled for death. And the reason she must be killed, rather than fucked, is that slasher killers are by generic definition sexually inadequate—men who kill precisely because they *cannot* fuck.[19]

––––––––––

Mick Martin and Marsha Porter echo the common response to such first-person camera horror movies of the *Halloween* or *Friday the Thirteenth* sort when they write that the director "uses a subjective camera in the stabbing scenes, which, essentially, makes the viewer the killer. The camera moves in on the screaming, pleading victim, 'looks down' at the knife, and then plunges it into chest, ear, or eyeball. Now that's sick."[20] What Martin and Porter and others like them fail to note, however, are the shortcomings and ultimate failure of that gaze. For one thing, it does not see well—at least not since 1978, when John Carpenter popularized the use of the unmounted first-person camera to represent the killer's point of view.[21] Although critics tend to assign a kind of binding power to marked first-person cinematography, the fact is that the view of the first-person killer is typically cloudy, unsteady, and punctuated by dizzying swishpans. Insofar as an unstable gaze suggests an unstable gazer, the credibility of the first-person killer-camera's omnipotence is undermined from the outset. One could go further and say that the assignment of real vision to normal characters draws attention, in the handheld or Steadicam sequences, to the very item the filmmaker ostensibly seeks to efface: the camera. Moreover, inasmuch as the vision of the subjective camera calls attention to what it cannot see—to dark corners and recesses of its vision and above all to the space and what might be in it, just off-frame—it gives rise to the sense not of mastery but of vulnerability.

More to the point, assaultive gazing never prevails, and mean lookers do not survive as such (if at all). A remarkably durable theme of horror involves turning the assaultive gaze back on itself. *The Incredibly Strange Creatures Who Stopped Living and Became Crazy Mixed-Up Zombies,* a cult-horror classic from 1964, offers a paradigmatic example. A group of three teenagers go to the carnival. After sampling the rides, Jerry proposes to his companions, a boy and a girl, that they go to the girlie show. Offended by Jerry's leering attitude, the girl refuses, and the other boy takes her home. Jerry enters the tent and joins a crowd of hundreds of men whistling and shouting at the exotic dancers. He becomes visibly entranced by the stripper Carmelita. When a note is passed to him inviting him to a back room to meet her, he goes eagerly. At the appointed place sits a gypsy woman, ostensibly the go-between, but as he waits, she induces him to look into a whirligig, which pulls his gaze hypnotically into its eye.[22] If the assaultive gaze here could hardly be more phallic, its object could hardly be more vaginal. The swaggering male imagines his gaze potent until faced with the "insatiable organ hole" of the feminine; in that war of "visions," he cannot but lose.[23]

We may also consider the scene in *Gothic* in which Claire realizes a long-standing fantasy of Shelley's by baring her breast and entreating him to look into her eyes—at which point her nipples become lids that slowly open to reveal monstrous eyes, causing him to look away. This relocation of the eyes to the nipples reconfigures the torso as a face of sorts, with the mouth now occupying the position of "insatiable organ hole." The idea takes its most elaborate form in *Poltergeist*, a film structured around the sucking of first the gaze and then the gazer into a series of vacuums: the vacuum tube of the television that Carol Anne watches with such emotional intensity, the vacuum of the storm that nearly pulls Robbie out the window, and the vacuum of the red and fleshy sucking hole that opens and tries to pull the whole family in. The vaginal nature of this series of vortices becomes more or less explicit when Diane, with the help of Dr. Lesh and the medium (spiritual midwives, as it were), finally lets herself be drawn into the last hole (the red cavern) in order to extract her daughter from the first hole (the television) and allow themselves to be reborn, complete with blood and amniotic slime, into the world.

Life Force, a science fiction horror version of the femme fatale story, is also an extended reverie on just how the assaultive gaze can backfire. On a strange planet, space travelers from earth find a sleeping beauty in a glass capsule and, after looking at her at lustful length, decide to bring her back to Earth. On Earth, however, those perfect looks prove vampiric; the girl attracts the desiring gaze of males only to destroy them by draining them of their life force. *Life Force* is at one level a standard femme fatale story, but on another, like others of its kind, it is an object lesson along Medusan lines on the danger of would-be-phallic looking. It is striking how many femme fatale stories begin with overzealous male gazing. At best, it seems, assaultive gazing is risky business.

At worst, it is fatal. If the jerky vision of the first-person murderer is a cliché of horror, it is an inexorable law of horror that this vision must be extinguished, that its bearer be punished and incapacitated—typically blinded or killed or both. If jerky vision signals a force ready to be unleashed, it also signals its own imminent demolition; the gaze is unstable because its bearer is doomed. [. . .].

The Reactive Gaze

As *Peeping Tom* insists, the eye of horror works both ways. It may penetrate, but it is also penetrated: so the plethora of images of eyeballs gouged out or pierced with knives, ice picks, and hypodermic needles, and so the scenes of persons suddenly blinded by hot coffee, acid, insect spray, or simply—and significantly—bright light.[24] The opening eye of horror is far more often an eye on the defense than an eye on the offense. The eyes on promotional posters and videocassette boxes are in the great majority of cases threatened, frightened eyes—commonly a woman's eyes reacting in horror at a poised, bloody knife, an advancing shape, or something off-poster or off-box. A standard moment in horror is one when a person is caught by surprise—her vision assaulted—by the sight of things she does not want to see: Laurie, in *Halloween,* for example, who looks into a closet only to see the dead body of her friend staring her in the face. Over and over, horror presents us with scenarios in which assaultive gazing is not just thwarted and punished but actually reversed in such a way that those who thought to penetrate end up themselves penetrated. The multieyed aliens of *The Eye Creatures* (1965) threaten, by virtue of their superior vision, to take over the world—until the army turns spotlights on them and, piercing them with light, causes them to explode. And when the two chief scanners in Cronenberg's *Scanners* face off, the loser ends up incinerated, and the winner, Daryl Revok, completely inhabited by the persona of his opponent. Scanning, it seems, gets as good as it gives—a point clarified by Revok himself, whose head is populated by all the people who have gotten in during his scanning career.

Looking at screens is particularly perilous and perilous in particular ways. As a film manifestly *about* the perils of horror spectatorship, Lamberto Bava's *Demons* (1986) is worth considering in some detail. A number of people are lured to a new movie theater to see a free mystery movie as part of the opening celebrations. A character hopes aloud that it won't be horror, but it of course turns out to be just that. As suspense mounts, members of the audience become sexually aroused, especially at the sight of a woman being stabbed repeatedly in close-up by an off-frame killer. One audience member, a black prostitute, senses something on her cheek and reaches up to feel a strange boil emerging from a lesion—a development that precisely mirrors what is happening to the cheek of one of the film-within-the-film characters. The hooker goes off to the lavatory to investigate her face, but she is within minutes transformed into a crazed zombie and begins to roam the back corridors of the theater building. Meanwhile, in the auditorium, the audience is raptly watching a second woman, the film-within-a-film's heroine, about to fall to the killer's knife. She is pleading and screaming, and the knife is on the verge of sinking in, when the screen onto which those images are projected is suddenly slashed and ripped from behind, and the zombie lunges through it out onto the proscenium and down into the frantic audience.[25] That zombie attacks and transforms others, who in turn attack and transform still others. As more audience members are infected and those trying to escape discover that all exits are locked, mayhem reigns.[26] "The movie is to blame for this!" someone shouts. In an effort to halt the unfolding horror, other members of the audience break into the projection room, and once they register the fact that there is no projectionist (the system is automatic), they smash the projector itself to bits. "Now the movie is not going to hurt us any more," says one of the attackers. "It's not the movie, it's the theater," someone answers. Bava's point seems to be that the foul impulses of horror lie not in the movie but in the spectator. But in either case, his scenario admits the power and the aim of the movie to excite such foul impulses, and in this sense, his movie-within-the-movie is indeed invasive and does indeed hurt.

Likewise television: *Demons II* tells of a woman, Sally, who watches a television horror film in which a vicious zombie is raised from the dead. As Sally stares at the tube, the vicious zombie, in close-up, seems to stare back for a moment before pouring itself, the tube reformed around it, through the screen, and lunging out after Sally. In *Terrorvision*, space invaders step into a human living room from a television screen, into which they have been conveyed via a satellite dish, and kill the American viewing family one at a time. A special broadcast warns that "its appetite is insatiable, its curiosity is boundless, its strength knows no limits—it will continue to absorb all life forms." Similarly *Looker*, which turns on an advertising scheme to "use computer animation to put an electronic light impulse in the eyes of the commercial"—an impulse that is beamed out into the receptive eyes of the home viewer. The hero, Larry, is literally slugged in the eyes from the screen—until he dons protective glasses that enable him to go around slugging others in *their* eyes. And *Max Headroom's* "blipvert" program causes certain television spectators—over-weight and inactive ones—to become neurally overheated and explode. Even telekinetic vision can work the other way. In *The Fury* (1978), a nurse at the Paragon Institute explains to her telekinesis students that, in effect, the power of invading rests on being invadable: "Try to remember that Alpha is another word for passive. . . . Visualize sitting in an empty theater in front of a blank screen—and let that screen fill your mind."

In *Poltergeist*, the "fatal-television" story enters the main-stream. Carol Anne perceives people in a blank, static-filled television screen and is eventually drawn in to join them. What distinguishes *Poltergeist's* television set from others in the tradition is that it does not strike out and penetrate its viewers but instead sucks them in and swallows them up—in images and language that could hardly be more vaginal.[27]

The most elaborate expression of "snuff television" is undoubtedly David Cronenberg's *Videodrome* (1982)—a film whose message William Beard sums up as: "Look not too deeply into the television screen, lest it begin to look into you."[28] "The battle for the mind of North America will be fought in the video arena—the videodrome," Professor Brian O'Blivion declares. "The television screen is the retina of the mind's eye. Therefore the television screen is part of the physical structure of the brain. Therefore whatever appears on the television screen emerges as pure experience for those who watch it. Therefore television is reality and reality is—less than television." The front organization for O'Blivion's videodrome is an optical company whose new line of eyeglasses is being promoted by the slogans "Love comes in at the eye" and "The eye is the window of the soul." The eyes/Screens in question here are those of Max Renn, a producer of hard-core pornography whose fascination with the outlaw video signal leads to his eventual fusion with it. One evening, while Max is watching a videodrome-produced tape that includes footage of his girlfriend Nicki, the television itself begins to swell and writhe, and the screen (displaying an extreme-close-up image of Nicki's lips) comes bulging out toward him. He kneels and buries his face in it. Shortly thereafter his abdomen develops a huge gash—into which a videodrome goon will later shove a videocassette tape. "What do you want with me?" the invaginated Max asks. "I want you to open up, Max. Open up to me," comes the answer. And Max does open up, is implanted, and is doomed. Notes one critic, "TV is lethal because it quite literally penetrates your brain and fucks with it."[29]

To the extent that Michael Powell meant *Peeping Tom* to be a commentary on the production and consumption of horror cinema, it is brilliantly on point. Mark's alternation between assaultive and reactive gazing is commonly taken to suggest the interdependence of sadistic and masochistic impulses. But a survey of modern horror confirms that it is equally a function of the fact that Mark happens, in a way that most folks do not, to be both producer and consumer of his own movies; separate those functions the way they are separated in the real world and you have an arrangement whereby—at least in its horror film codification—assaultive gazing is associated with those who hold the camera, and reactive gazing with those who stare at the screen after the fact.

Over and over, and in a remarkable variety of ways, modern horror plays out the same adversarial scenario. The implication, of course, is that the audience in question is meant to represent *us* in relation to the screen *we* are watching, and now and then the equation is drawn directly. I refer to Hitchcock's marginal note in the shooting instructions for the shower scene of *Psycho:* "The slashing. An impression of a knife slashing, as if tearing at the very screen, ripping the film." We could hardly ask for a clearer set of equivalents: as Norman is to Marion, Hitchcock is to the audience of *Psycho,* or, more generally, as slasher is to slashed, horror filmmakers are to horror audiences.[30] Hitchcock's "impression" becomes Bava's diegetic reality when, in *Demons,* the screen of the movie-within-the-movie is suddenly slashed and ripped from behind by raging zombies, who flood through it into the theater. The equation is overt: as the diegetic audience is to the diegetic movie, so we are to Bava's *Demons;* as the screen of the diegetic horror movie "attacked" its audience, so the screen of *Demons* means to attack *us.*[31]

Certainly horror plays repeatedly and overtly on the equation between the plight of the victim and the plight of the audience. Whatever else it may be, the ploy of showing us an about-to-be-attacked woman watching a horror film depicting an about-to-be-attacked woman is also a clear metacinematic declaration of our common spectatorial plight. But the screen-within-the-screen arrangement only makes explicit what is perhaps universally implicit in horror: the alignment of the audience with screen victims in general, regardless of how directly or indirectly they are figured as themselves spectators. [. . .].

No one who has attended a matinee or midnight showing of a horror film with a youth audience can doubt the essentially adversarial nature of the enterprise. The performance has the quality of a cat-and-mouse game: a "good" moment (or film) is one that "beats" the audience, and a bad moment (or film) is one in which, in effect, the audience wins. Judged by plot alone, the patterns of cheering and booing seem indiscriminate or unmotivated or both. It is when they are judged by the success or failure of the film to catch the audience by surprise (or gross it out) that the patterns of cheering and booing fall into place. At such moments, the diegesis is all but short-circuited, and the horror filmmaker and the competent horror viewer come remarkably close to addressing one another directly: the viewer by shouting out his approval or disapproval not to the on-screen characters but to the people who put them there, and the people who put them there, in their turn, by marking the moment with either a tongue-in-cheek gesture or an actual pause to accommodate the reaction—both amounting to a silent form of second-person address.

And, of course, horror films *do* attack their audiences. The attack is palpable; we take it in the eye. For just as the audience eye can be invited by the camera to assault, so it can be physically assaulted by the projected image—by sudden flashes of light, violent movement (of images plunging outward, for example), or fast-cut or exploded images. These are the stock-in-trade of horror. Film after film blinds us with a flash of lightning or spotlight, or points a gun or camera at us and shoots, or has a snakelike alien or rat burst toward us. It is no surprise that 3-D should at more or less the moment of its invention seize on such moments and include at least one in every film as a matter of course.[32] It is also no surprise that the narrative flow of images should burst into fragments at the most gruesome or shocking moments. The locus classicus, of course, is the shower scene of *Psycho,* which lasts for forty seconds and is composed of as many shots: a rapid-fire concatenation of images of the knife-wielding hand, parts of Marion, parts of the shower, and finally the bloody water as it swirls down the drain. [33] It is a breathtaking piece of cinematic violence—and as much at the editorial as at the diegetic level. The extinction of the protagonist midway through the story is an act of violence at the narrative level.[34] The fact that such sudden visual attacks are typically preceded by a protracted sequence of calm underscores their violent intent. Much of the art of horror lies in catching the spectatorial eye unawares—penetrating it before it has a chance to close its lid. Only when the house curtain drops can our own "curtains" relax.[35] And indeed, horror cinema repeatedly equates the film screen and the dream screen, guarded by the eye, as sites for invasion.[36]

(We also take it in the ear, of course. Although my interest here and throughout is with the ocular, I would be remiss not to mention sound in connection with horror's directly assaultive effects. The shower sequence of *Psycho* shocks at the auditory as well as the visual level; preceded by an ominous silence [the unadorned natural sounds of Marion's preparations], the attack triggers the sound of shrieking violins, whose hammering thrusts duplicate both the stabbing action of the diegesis and the editorial shattering of the image.[37] Some viewers claim that they are more disturbed by the "music" of horror movies than the images and that they cover not their eyes but their ears in the "scary parts." Sound in cinema in general has been undertheorized, and horror sound scarcely theorized at all.)

Horror movies themselves, in short, bear out in both letter and spirit the double gaze of *Peeping Tom.* On one side is the killer's (or monster's) predatory or assaultive gaze, with which, as in *Peeping Tom,* the audience is directly invited to collude—at least formally and at least temporarily. Such gazing is repeatedly associated with the camera (as either theme or device), and it is resolutely figured as male. What is striking about this male gaze, however, is how often it remains at the level of wish or threat—how seldom it carries through with its depredations and, even when it does succeed, how emphatically it is then brought to ruin. It has, in horror, the status of a fiction straining to be a fact, and not a few plots precisely turn on exposing its posturings for what they are. On the other side is the reactive gaze. It too is associated with the cinematic or televisual apparatus—but as its object, not its subject. The frequency, in horror, of images of victim-eyes under attack underlines the interest of horror in hurtable vision, vision on the defense. The reactive gaze too invites our collusion through the steady accumulation of "normal" first-person shots and, on the narrative level, through a marshaling of all the usual empathic devices. And the reactive gaze too is resolutely gendered—but as feminine, not masculine. In *Peeping Tom*, to be on the receiving end of the camera is to be feminine by definition. In a representational system in which cinematic or televisual apparatuses "kill and fuck," in other words, *Videodrome*'s Max is as inevitably invaginated and implanted as *Demon Seed*'s Susan is raped and impregnated. When the reactive gazer is male, he is either too young to count—like Robbie in *Poltergeist*,[38] or—like Max in *Videodrome*—literally regendered by the experience. It is the reactive gaze that has pride of place in the scopic regime of horror: both within the diegesis—as the look that sees the truth—and outside it, in the theater—as the look that is assaulted from the screen.[39]

Cruel Cinema

Let me turn now to the tendency, in both criticism and theory, to regard camera and spectator in a collusive relation intended to generate a sense of mastery, more or less sadistic, over the object of their common vision. At the theoretical level, the idea that cinematic pleasure is funded by the desire for voyeuristic command derives chiefly from the work of Laura Mulvey and Christian Metz.

Mulvey identifies two ways cinema looks at women, both of which presuppose a male (or masculine) gazer: a sadistic-voyeuristic look, whereby the gazer salves his unpleasure at female lack by seeing the woman punished, and a fetishistic-scopophilic look, whereby the gazer salves his unpleasure by fetishizing the female body in whole or part. Mulvey's work has been rightly appreciated, but in recent years it has also come in for criticism, including Mulvey's own.[40] The chief complaint has to do with the place (no place) of the female spectator in the model, but the question I would like to raise here is a rather different one—namely, whether cinematic looking always and inevitably implies mastery over its object, even when the looker is male and his object female. Rodowick has suggested that Mulvey's concern to construct a sadistic male subject led her to overlook the masochistic potential of fetishistic scopophilia. Given her assumption that active voyeurism is sadistic, her failure to consider the possibility that passive fetishistic scopophilia may point to masochism constitutes a blind spot. Mulvey, Rodowick writes, "defines fetishistic scopophilia as an overvaluation of the object, a point which Freud would support. But he would also add that this phenomenon is one of the fundamental sources of *authority* defined as passive submission to the object: in sum, *masochism*."[41]

For Metz, too, the viewer necessarily identifies with the camera in an operation that is essentially assaultive. In the often-cited passage from *The Imaginary Signifier* entitled "The Passion for Perceiving," Metz argues that because cinema is predicated on a distance between the spectator and the object of vision (a distance in time as well as space), the cinematic spectator is necessarily a voyeur, and voyeurism, with its drive to mastery, is by nature sadistic.[42] That construction has been queried by Silverman, who, following Jean Laplanche, argues that in the scenario of the primal scene (for Metz and others the Ur-movie),[43] the seeing child is, at the level of identification, not master but victim of the situation. "Far from controlling the sounds and images of parental sexuality, the child held captive within the crib is controlled—indeed, overwhelmed—by them. Adult sexuality invades him or her through the eyes and ears, puncturing, as it were, those vital organs. The mastering, sadistic variety of voyeurism discussed by Metz can perhaps best be understood as a psychic formation calculated to reverse the power relations of the primal scene—as a compensatory drama whereby passivity yields to activity through an instinctual 'turning around' and reversal."[44]

Metz himself, in fact, gestures in the direction of reactive or "punctured" vision in an earlier passage ("Identification, Mirror") from the same essay. Because the passage in question has been underappreciated by critics, I quote it here in toto:

> All vision consists of a double movement: projective (the "sweeping" searchlight) and introjective: consciousness as a sensitive recording

surface (as a screen). I have the impression at once that, to use a common expression, I am "casting" my eyes on things, and that the latter, thus illuminated, come to be deposited within me (we then declare that it is these things that have been "projected," on to my retina, say). A sort of stream called the look, and explaining all the myths of magnetism, must be sent out over the world, so that objects can come back up this stream in the opposite direction (but using it to find their way), arriving at last at our perception, which is now soft wax and no longer an emitting source.

The technology of photography carefully conforms to this (banal) phantasy accompanying perception. . . . During the performance the spectator is the searchlight I have described, duplicating the projector, which itself duplicates the camera, and he is also the sensitive surface duplicating the screen, which itself duplicates the filmstrip. There are two cones in the auditorium: one ending on the screen and starting both in the projection box and in the spectator's vision insofar as it is projective, and one starting from the screen and "deposited" in the spectator's perception insofar as it is introjective (on the retina, a second screen).[45]

The oscillation between these two gazes, Metz adds, is crucial to the apparatus: "In the cinema, as elsewhere, the constitution of the symbolic is only achieved through and above the play of the imaginary: projection-introjection, presence-absence, phantasies accompanying perception, etc."[46]

It is hardly surprising that Metz's introjective gaze has been shunned by subsequent commentaries, for after putting it forward, Metz himself quickly subordinates it to the figure of the camera,[47] which in turn quickly resumes its status as the quintessential tool of projective and voyeuristic gazing. As it is formulated above, however, the distinction between projective and introjective looking, the latter described as a "receiving, recording, sensitive surface" onto which "things are deposited" or "projected" onto the "retina," corresponds more or less exactly to the distinction that I have argued horror itself draws between assaultive and reactive gazing. (I cannot help noting how close Metz's characterization of the retina as a "second screen" comes to Professor O'Blivion's definition, in *Videodrome*, of the television screen as the "retina of the mind's eye.") At first glance, horror's tendency to locate the reactive gaze outside and "against" the camera, not inside and "with" it, would seem to stand in direct contradiction to Metz's model of two gazes internal to the camera. A psychoanalytic perspective explains horror's scenario as a secondary formation of fiction, one that hypostasizes the gazes as both mechanical and imaginary opposites. A narrative form that materializes a split psyche as Jekyll and Hyde, in other words, will also materialize a split "viewer" as filmmaker and film spectator.

Where is masochism in all of this? Its absence in Metz's text screams for attention, for while he emphatically identifies projective looking as sadistic, he does not, for reasons on which we can only speculate, proffer an equivalent analysis of introjective looking. His blind spot thus corresponds exactly to Mulvey's. His language is suggestive enough (the receiving spectator is a "sensitive surface," "our perception . . . is now soft wax," "things . . . come to be deposited within me," and so on), but there the matter drops. It is in horror, I suggest, that Metz's (and Mulvey's) blank is filled in. For even more variously than it imagines ways that projective looking (to use Metz's terms) can be sadistic, horror imagines ways that our "sensitive surface" can be intruded upon, that "things" can come to be deposited within us—that our eyes are "soft."

Before I turn to the matter of masochism per se, however, let me revert to an aspect of horror gazing that stands as a corollary to the opposition between assaultive/reactive or projective/introjective gazing: I am referring to the extraordinarily popular theme of assaultive gazing that is foiled—thwarted, swallowed up, turned back on itself—and of assaultive gazers who end up blinded or dead or both. Within the classical psychoanalytic paradigm, needless to say, the notion of fallible phallic gazing is something of an oxymoron, and the question is how to make sense of its ubiquity in horror. A solution is suggested in a distinction proposed by Lacan between the gaze and the "eye" (look)—the former, in Silverman's elaboration, occupying much the same position in relation to the latter as the phallus does to the penis. The gaze, in other words, is the transcendental ideal—omniscient, omnipotent—which the look can never achieve but to which it ceaselessly aspires. The best the look can hope for is to pose and pass itself off as the gaze, and to judge from film theory's concern with the "male gaze," Silverman argues, it sometimes succeeds.[48]

It is just this distinction, I suggest, that horror repeatedly elaborates. Of the many examples enumerated above of wanna-be gazers who are blown out of the water, one stands out as particularly apt: the passage in *The Incredibly Strange Creatures Who Stopped Living and Became Crazy Mixed-Up Zombies* in which Jerry, having leered possessively at a stripper-dancer named Carmelita and having imagined that the power of his gaze earned him an invitation to a rendezvous after the show, ends up having his "look," and his consciousness, sucked right out of him into the gypsy woman's whirligig (he awakes to find himself not only not in possession of Carmelita but incarcerated). What is striking about this example is not just the fact that the male looker fails to "fix" the female object, but the fact that she ends up fixing him, and in a way that is as vaginal in its figuration as his would-be gaze is phallic.[49] So common is the theme of failed gazing in horror that I would venture as a rule of the genre that *whenever* a man imagines himself as a controlling voyeur—imagines, in Lacanian terms, that his "look" at women constitutes a gaze—some sort of humiliation is soon to follow, typically in the form of his being overwhelmed, in one form or another, by the sexuality of the very female he meant to master. In *Scanners*, theme assumes the proportions of theory when Revok explains that his gazing eye is in fact a front designed and installed to mask the invadable hole leading to his brain (he "put an eye on the door so they won't know it's a door, and they can't get back in because they see the eye").[50] Again, like Mark's murderous gaze in *Peeping Tom*, Revok's monstrous look in *Scanners* is not a primary or natural feature but a secondary and counterdefective one, a construction "born in this act [the act of covering over his vulnerability] of his younger self."[51]

The question is whether this pattern of "looks" in horror's diegesis represents or misrepresents the terms of its extradiegetic scopic regime. As I suggested earlier, there is some variation on this point. There are horror passages that would seem to position the spectator at least temporarily as an assaultive gazer. But the most decried of these passages, the first-person killer-camera of slasher films, is also the one that calls the most blatant attention to its own insufficiency and instability. And although many horror films provide other, more "normal" opportunities for assaultive gazing (looking, that is, that more or less successfully passes itself off as the gaze), I would argue that it is generally speaking the case that such passages are fewer, more attenuated, and more pro forma in horror than they are in the most mainstream Hollywood cinema. (Few horror films approach *The Unbearable Lightness of Being* in the unembarrassed empowerment of male looking.) Assaultive gazing in horror is by and large the minority position, and the real investment of the genre is in the reactive or introjective position, figured as both painful and feminine.

Masochism has only belatedly been taken up in connection with the study of film.[52] One reason for the delay must have to do with the long-standing emphasis on voyeurism's presumed sadism, which has the virtue of rhyming with the aggressive sexuality attributed to conventional heterosexual masculinity—a virtue that has put feminist film theorists from Mulvey on (who view it as deplorable) in an unholy alliance with most male critics (who view it as inevitable).[53] Another reason must have to do with the complexities of the topic. Freud's changes of mind on the subject, as well as Theodor Reik's views and Gilles Deleuze's revision, have been usefully read by Silverman, who also pursues the political implications of exposing the masochistic dimension of particularly those texts produced by and addressed primarily to men.[54]

Horror is probably the most convention bound of all popular genres, its conventions are organized around the experience of fear, and this conjunction—scary stories endlessly repeated—stands as a narrative manifestation of the syndrome of repetition compulsion (*Wiederholungszwang*). Defined as an "ungovernable process originating in the unconscious" whereby a person "deliberately places himself in distressing situations, thereby repeating an old [but unremembered] experience," repetition compulsion thus has its roots in unpleasure.[55] The function and effects of repetition compulsion are not clear. (It is conspicuously driven, however, by the wish to "get it right," one of the oft-noted dynamics of horror films.)[56] What *is* clear is that where there is *Wiederholungszwang* there is historical suffering—suffering that has been more or less sexualized as "erotogenic masochism."[57] At the risk of circularity, I would argue that the very repetitiousness of fear-inducing scenarios in horror cinema is prima facie evidence of horror's central investment in pain.

It is in the nature of repetition compulsion that the repeater "does not recall [the] prototype" of the repetition scenario which need not be a traumatic event. It may in Freud's formulation inhere in any and all of the developmental phases:

> Erotogenic masochism accompanies the libido through all its developmental phases and derives from them its changing psychical coatings. The fear of being eaten up by the totem animal (the father) originates from the primitive oral organization; the wish to be beaten by the father comes from the sadistic-anal phase which follows it; castration, although it is later disavowed, enters into the content of masochistic phantasies as a precipitate of the phallic stage of organization; and from the final genital organization there arise, of course, the situations of being copulated with and of giving birth, which are characteristic of femaleness.[58]

[. . .]. Although Freud was to undergo a radical change of mind between 1919 and 1924 (between the essays "'A Child Is Being Beaten'" and "The Economic Problem of Masochism") as to the place of masochism in the psychic economy (in particular its role vis-ú-vis the pleasure principle and the death instinct,) he retained his observation that the perversion took as its programmatic form the assumption of the feminine position. In "The Economic Problem of Masochism," he spoke of male masturbatory fantasies of which

> the manifest content is of being gagged, bound, painfully beaten, whipped, in some way maltreated, forced into unconditional obedience, dirtied, and debased. . . . if one has an opportunity of studying cases in which the masochistic phantasies have been especially richly elaborated, one quickly discovers that they place the subject in a characteristically female situation; they signify, that is, being castrated, or copulated with, or giving birth to a baby. For this reason I have called this form of masochism, *a potiori* as it were [i.e., on the basis of its extreme examples], the feminine form, although so many of its features point to infantile life.[59]

It is frequently noted that although the condition of being bound, painfully beaten, and so on, is regarded by Freud as essentially feminine, all of the cases he lists in this essay are male, the implication being that, although masochism "is a centrally structuring element in both male and female subjectivity," it is only in the female that it is accepted as natural and thus only in the male that it is considered perverse or pathological.[60] One stumbles over the asymmetry, but it makes sense if one accepts the argument Freud sets forth (on the basis of mainly female cases) in "'A Child Is Being Beaten'" to the effect that all children, male and female, are subject to the unconscious fantasy that they are being beaten—that is, "loved"—by the *father*. Whereas the girl's fantasy is "straight" (at least in Freud's reading),[61] the boy's involves a gender complication: to be beaten/loved by his father requires the adoption of a position coded as feminine or receptively homosexual. Thus *"feminine masochism"* refers not to masochism in women but to the essence of masochistic perversion in *men*,[62] and it is in this sense that I use the term here. Although Freud's designation of such fantasies as "feminine" has been assailed, it has the advantage of highlighting Freud's abiding interest in a kind of bedrock bisexuality. If bisexuality, in his account, seems to rest on and naturalize a masculine/feminine binary in ways modern critics find uncomfortable, it is a notion that opened the gate to more current formulations, including the idea that one's sex/gender/sexuality has no existence outside the acts or performances that constitute it.[63] Another advantage of the designation *feminine masochism* is simply that it may tell the truth about the way men who have such fantasies might understand them. And if that understanding is on one hand mixed up with a sense of degradation, it on the other contemplates the female body—a *specifically* female body—as a site of intense sexual feeling.[64] It is worth remembering in this connection Freud's declaration, in "Analysis Terminable and Interminable," that the most deeply embedded male anxiety has to do not with castration in any blanket or straightforward sense but with the fear of standing in a passive or "feminine" relation to another man and the particular sort of "castration" that might proceed from that.[65]

The relevance of feminine masochism in this technical sense to a body of cinema addressed to male viewers and featuring female characters in some form of distress, more or less sexual, is self-evident. Indeed, *"feminine masochism"* as it is articulated by Freud suggests a distinctive psychosexual profile or experience base for each of the genres in question: the possession film seems organized around the thought of being "copulated with" and impregnated; the slasher around thoughts of being beaten, castrated, and penetrated (the proportions varying with the film); and the rape-revenge film, obviously, around thoughts of being or having been humiliatingly and violently penetrated (this plot more fully than the others allowing for the process of sadistic reversal). *Feminine masochism* also makes remarkably good sense of the figuring, for a predominantly male audience, of horror spectatorship itself as a feminine or feminizing experience.[66] [. . .].

Finally there is the issue of suspense.[67] Masochism (in both its sexualized and desexualized forms) is unusually generative of vivid fantasies—fantasies, according to Reik, characterized by "the demonstrative factor" (whereby the masochist imagines himself on display) and "the suspense factor" (whereby the masochist imagines himself facing a pain-pleasure fate that is inevitable but also, up to a point, delayable). Consider, for example, the following fantasy, reported to Reik by a male patient:

> The cruel and nymphomaniac queen of a legendary realm uses explorers who are lost in her domain for her sexual satisfaction. When she loses interest in them the queen has the prisoners impaled, flayed or castrated. The patient now imagines a young man as the next aspirant to the

queen's cruel favor. He witnesses the horrible execution of one of his predecessors and feels the terror of him whom a similar destiny awaits in the near future. He identifies himself with this victim—a brother-figure—and experiences with him the fettering, torture, and death.[68]

Here—either as is or with sexes switched—is an embryonic horror movie if ever there was one. What interests me in it are not the actual cinematic analogues, of which dozens come to mind, but its anticipatory and seriatim structure: the way, person by person, the terrorizer approaches the fantast's surrogate, whose mounting anxiety is the scenario's organizing experience. That, of course, is the standard structure of multiple-victim horror, of which the slasher film is only the most obvious example. Moreover, in both the "execution" fantasy described above and multiple-victim horror cinema, the protagonist *sees* his or her fate in advance as it is visited on the person or persons ahead in line. Single-victim horror is equally suspenseful, the difference being that the advancing terror is not directly theatricalized but left to the mind's eye. In either case, the protagonist is poised between the absolute desire to escape his turn and the equally absolute knowledge that it is inevitable, and as the threat draws nearer, the tension achieves explosive proportions.

Note the lines of identification here. Reik's patient is not himself "in" the story in the first person. Rather, he operates through a third-person surrogate. As Silverman notes of another of Reik's cases, the fantast is "bound to the scenario through a complex imaginary network. His immediate point of insertion occurs via the young man who will be next to fall victim . . . but that figure himself identifies closely with the victim presently suffering that mutilation."[69] The fantasy's imaginary protagonist, in other words, stands in the same relation to the person ahead of him in line that the fantast stands to his imaginary protagonist. Likewise, the Final Girl of slasher films stands in the same relation to her teen friends who are ahead of her in line as the viewer of slasher films stands to the Final Girl.[70] "It is certain that the daydreamer identifies with one of the victims," Reik writes of such a fantasy, "usually not the one who is just being castrated but with the next, who is compelled to look on at the execution of his companion. The patient shares every intensive affect of this victim, feels his terror and anxiety with all the physical sensations since he imagines that he will himself experience the same fate in a few moments."[71] I repeat here John Ellis's observation that the crucial dynamic of the war or male action film is the "notion of survival through a series of threats of physical mutilation, to which many characters succumb. It is a phantasy that is characteristic of the male."[72]

The staging here squares with the staging identified in laboratory experiments as requisite to the sensation of suspense: "The more convinced audience members are that the protagonist is in genuine peril and is about to succumb to the opposing forces with which he/she is in conflict, up to the point of total subjective certainty of defeat, the more suspenseful is the presentation," write Paul Comisky and Jennings Bryant. Moreover, "it is clear that the characteristics of the protagonist matter a great deal. The audience evidently 'gets involved with' and anxious about a hero whom it can like."[73] Beyond "goodness," what makes a figure likable are vulnerability, helplessness, and a situation of powerlessness[74]—characteristics, one cannot help noting (though Comisky and Bryant make no mention of gender), traditionally coded as feminine and, in horror, conventionally embodied in female characters. [. . .].

Horror in any case bears a startling resemblance to the masochistic fantasies recounted by both Freud and Reik. It tells the same sort of stories (over and over), creates the same sort of protagonists who stand in the same sort of relation to the "viewer," represents those protagonists as "feminine" (in the sense outlined by Freud), is predicated on a peculiar kind of turn-taking suspense, privileges vision in the creation of that suspense, and openly trades in fear and pain.[75] The similarities, I have suggested, are more than casual. I suspect that the masochistic aesthetic is and has always been the dominant one in horror cinema and is in fact one of that genre's defining characteristics; that the experience horror moviegoers seek is likewise rooted in a pain/pleasure sensibility; that the fantasies in which horror cinema trades are particularly (though not exclusively) tailored to male forms of masochistic experience (accounting for the disproportionate maleness of the audience); and that the willingness of horror moviegoers to return for sequel on sequel, imitation on imitation, and remake on remake bespeaks a degree of *Wiederholungszwang* that in turn stands as proof of the pudding. Although the odd horror movie does follow a masochistic scenario to its annihilatory end point (e.g., *The Incredible Shrinking Man*), most undo the dream or fantasy through an eleventh-hour reversal—longer or shorter and more or less sadistic—and thus deliver the spectator back into the status quo. If one focuses (as critics tend to) on the endings of horror films, one sees sadism. But if one takes it as a point of fact that endings (as well as beginnings) are generically overdetermined and that it is in narrative middles that crucial matters are contested and if one accordingly focuses on those parts of horror films—their middles, especially their late middles—in which the tension is greatest and the audience body most engaged, one sees masochism, and in remarkably blatant forms.[76]

I do not mean to propose that horror movies have nothing to offer but a s/m bang. Nor am I claiming that horror is alone among cinematic genres in its exploitation of the pleasure/pain response; action movies and thrillers are obvious candidates, and the suggestion has been made of sentimental genres, and even early train-wreck movies, as well.[77] (If vision is always both projective and introjective, then *all* visual forms are presumably amenable to a "two-way" analysis, though they may differ in their proportions and intensity.) Nor, finally, do I doubt that female spectators too may engage at some level with the masochistic scenarios are by the lights of psychoanalysis typically male, the general masochistic fantasy of passivity or imprisonment ("pleasure without responsibility") knows no sex, and women, practiced as they are at wresting their own pleasure from forms made by and addressed to men, can presumable translate from horror, too. It is also possible that the surface stories of certain horror subgenres—slashers and rape-revenge films, for example—may offer satisfactions of their own to women viewers, including, perhaps, satisfactions of a more sadistic nature.[78] What I *am* saying is that feminine masochism as it has been outlined in psychoanalysis finally offers the best answer to the question that modern horror repeatedly raises: Just why is it that male viewers would choose to "feel" fear and pain through the figure of a female—a female, in fact, whose very bodily femaleness is at center stage?[79]

My interest at this point, however, is not so much in what this construction makes of the female body (which has been richly noted elsewhere) as in what it makes of the male one. It has been argued, most cogently by Silverman and Bersani, that insofar as masochism swerves away from or shatters the male subject's relation to the phallic order, it is subversive of that order and of what Bersani sarcastically calls the "proud subjectivity" that props it up.[80] The psychoanalytic validity of these claims I leave to others. Nor am I prepared to comment on cultural practices over the broad range. My concern is with film theory and horror film criticism and practice—and with the extent to which those discourses may denaturalize, for some people, the received categories of sexual difference.

At the critical/theoretical level the strongest argument for the possibility that there is something subversive about the masochistic experience base of cinematic spectatorship may be an argument *e silentio*. I am referring to the repeated denial or avoidance of that possibility in both critical and theoretical writings—in contrast to the wealth of attention lavished on male sadism.[81] Mulvey's blind spot (her designation of voyeurism as active and scopophilia as passive—but the both of them as phallic and sadistic) has been argued by Rodowick to be politically motivated (to acknowledge that the masochistic potential in scopophilic gazing would undo her feminist project), but to my knowledge Metz's even more glaring blind spot (his designation of projective gazing as phallic/sadistic and his failure to provide an equivalent experiential base for introjective gazing—a lacuna all the more glaring in light of the fact that the distinction between projective and introjective is his own) has not been equivalently explained. And *that* failure—the failure of gender-interested critics/theorists to come to grips with Metz's blind spot—constitutes yet *another* blind spot. Such lapses might seem accidental were they not so consonant with the larger prejudice that the lower cinematic forms play by definition to male sadistic tastes. [. . .].

Identifying male sadism—especially toward women—and holding men at least theoretically culpable for such acts as rape, wife beating, and child abuse are major achievements of modern feminism. Texts like Susan Brownmiller's *Against Our Will*, which accumulates case on case of male brutality until the evidence seems crushing, have been instrumental in those achievements. Recent years have seen the production of similar texts by men (texts like Klaus Theweleit's *Male Fantasies* and Anthony Wilden's *Man and Woman, War and Peace*), and Tania Modleski has wondered about the politics that underlie such extended iterations of male sadism.[82] On the basis of my own reading of horror film criticism, which speaks volumes on sadism and only the occasional sentence on masochism, I second Modleski's nervousness (about any such text, regardless of the author's sex), for although the practice of remarking male sadism in a film (like the practice of *showing* male sadism in a film) may be intended to align the remarker with feminism, it also works to naturalize sadistic violence as a fixture of masculinity— one of the few fixtures of masculinity remaining in a world that has seen the steady erosion of such. It is a gesture, in other words, that ends up confirming what it deplores. Appalling though it may be (the unstated logic goes), the capacity for sadistic violence is what finally distinguishes male from female. (I take this to be one reason for the current popularity of "war" movies, whether set in Vietnam, Latin America, or American city ghettos: *this* turf men own.[83] The reason, then, for the critical eloquence on the subject of male sadism is that it holds the gender bottom line. And the reason for the virtual silence in horror film criticism and for the blank spot in film theory on the possibility of male masochism is that to broach it is not only to bring homosexuality into the picture but also to unsettle what is apparently our ultimate gender story.

The argument *e silentio* goes another step. As I have noted with respect to both slasher and rape-revenge films, the striking tendency of modern horror to collapse the figure of the savior-hero (formerly male) into the figure of the victim (eternally female) leaves us with an arrangement whereby a largely male audience is in the hands of a female protagonist—an arrangement that self-evidently exposes the ability of male viewers to identify across sexual lines. It is probably safe to assume that the male viewers of horror are in this respect not fundamentally different from male viewers in general, past and present; although horror may exploit the mechanism of cross-gender identification more intensely than other sorts of cinema, the mechanism itself surely knows no genre. Again, however, it is a mechanism that has scarcely been mentioned in film theory and criticism. The silence on male-with-female identification (in contrast to the common assumption of female-with-male identification) thus matches the silence on male masochism (in contrast to the lavish acknowledgment of male sadism), and it seems reasonable to suppose that the coincidence is not accidental.[84]

I take this double silence—silence about masochism and silence about identification with the female—as evidence that something crucial to the system of cultural representation is at stake.[85] That something must be the operation whereby female figures are made to stand for, and act out, a psychosexual posture that in fact knows no sex but that, for a variety of reasons that add up to male dominance, is routinely dissociated from the male.[86] It is, in short, an operation which ensures that men can eat their psychosexual cake and have it too: experience the pain/pleasure of (say) a rape fantasy by identifying with the victim, and then disavow their personal stake on grounds that the visible victim was, after all, a woman, and that they as spectators are "naturally" represented by the visible male figures: male saviors or sadistic rapists, but *manly* men however you cut it.[87]

The critical reaction to *I Spit on Your Grave* is a superbly crude case in point. A film that employs every narrative and cinematic device to position us with the victim during both her violation and her acts of revenge and a film whose second half is precisely predicated on our feeling horribly violated (the ghastliness of the revenge standing in direct relation to the ghastliness of our violation), *I Spit on Your Grave* provides, for many long stretches of its hour-and-a-half narration, as pure a feminine-masochistic jolt as the movies have to offer. No such possibility is even hinted at in the reviews that led to its condemnation and censorship, however. On the contrary, the film was characterized, in tones of outrage and in the name of feminism, as the ultimate incitement to male sadism, a "vile film for vicarious sex criminals," a "sleazy exploitation movie" that "makes rapists of us all." But there is something off here: something too shrill and too totalizing in the claim of misogyny, something dishonest in the critical rewritings and outright misrepresentations of the plot required to sustain that claim, something suspicious about the refusal to entertain even in passing the possibility of involvement with the victim's part, something perverse about the unwillingness to engage with the manifestly feminist dimensions of the script, and something dubious in the refusal to note its debt to *Deliverance* and the critical implications of that debt. *I Spit on Your Grave* is a problematic case for feminism, but the Siskel-Ebert position (if the protest may be summed up as such) should not be allowed the last word. Whatever else the Siskel-Ebert position may be, it is also the critical equivalent of Revok's eye: its insistence that *I Spit on Your Grave* makes rapists of us all works, in fact, to deflect attention from the possibility that it just as well makes Jennifers of us all and that the powerful feelings the film evokes may have less to do with a sense of mastery than with the sense that one has just been shafted.

It is no surprise that this feint is reenacted endlessly in movies themselves; that must be one main thing movies are *for*. What is rather more surprising is the extent to which film criticism and theory have fallen for it—indeed, in the name of feminism, embraced it. And what is most surprising of all (at least to those who believe paradigms can be subverted only from above) is the fact that it is in modern horror that the feint is most obviously exposed for what it is, and that the dominant fiction which generates it is most clearly laid bare. The disappearance of male heroes (often males of any kind) from genres like the rape-revenge and slasher, a disappearance that leaves us alone in the company of a first victimized and then heroic woman, is a remarkable cultural admission.[88] It admits the pleasure/pain nature of the core experience of certain kinds of narrative (certain parts of all kinds of narrative, perhaps), and it admits the ways that literal representations—"images"—are conventionally deployed to cover over the male investment in that experience in such a way as to make it seem specific to the female. Horror, in short, "tells on" the movies to an unprecedented and revelatory degree.

Let me draw this together. The ethnic evidence suggests that the first and central aim of horror cinema is to play to masochistic fears and desires in its audiences—fears and desires that are repeatedly figured as feminine. It may play on other fears and desires too, but dealing out pain is its defining characteristic; sadism, by definition, plays at best a supporting role. To the extent that a movie succeeds in hurting its viewers in this way, it is good horror; to the extent that it fails, it is bad horror; to the extend that it does not try, it is not horror, but something else.[89] This self-portrait of horror is not disguised; it is right on the surface, in a variety of concrete forms, plain for all to see. Its very plainness makes all the more puzzling the insistence of critical commentaries on the primacy of the sadistic dimension. The failure of those commentaries to see beyond sadism, I have suggested, has everything to do with their stake in the dominant fiction.

It may be objected that horror is qualitatively different from other genres (it is certainly one of the most insistently marked and segregated categories) and that its sensibility is sui generis. I would argue, however, both on the basis of the "two-way" eye/camera implicit in the accounts of Mulvey and Metz (despite their attempts to keep it "one way") and on the basis of the psychoanalytic theory of two-way aggression (sadism/ masochism) that underpins it, that horror merely takes to an overt extreme an operation that is surely as endemic to the act of cinematic spectatorship as aggressive voyeurism is, even if it is less exploited, and/or less admitted, in higher forms. To exaggerate somewhat for purposes of clarity: I am suggesting that, rather than exposing the cultural lie on which higher forms of cinema are based, film theory has wittingly or unwittingly colluded with it, and that it has done so because it is itself deduced from higher forms, in which the dimension of introjective or masochistic gazing is either less important or more muted or both.[90] It is true that when Mulvey and Metz were theorizing sadistic spectatorship in the early seventies, horror was considerably less brazen and less sustained in its exploitation of "feminine masochism" than it has been in the last decade. It is also true, however, that themes and images of painful looking and pierced eyes have long been a staple of the tradition and that it is not possible to look at many horror movies from any era without confronting the idea; and there was *Peeping Tom*, a film that from its first image (the pierced bull's-eye) to its last (the darkened screen, as Mark's own vision is extinguished by suicide, and the voice-over of a frightened boy saying "Good night, Daddy—hold my hand") insists that the pleasure of looking at others in fear and pain has its origins in one's own past-but-not-finished fear and pain.

Carol J. Clover

NOTES

1. J. P. Telotte, "Through a Pumpkin's Eye: The Reflexive Nature of Horror," in Gregory A. Waller, ed., *American Horrors: Essays on the Modern American Film* (Urbana: University of Illinois Press, 1987), p. 16. See also his "Faith and Idolatry in the Horror Film," *Literature/Film Quarterly* 8 (1980), 143–55, and rpt. in Barry Keith Grant, ed., *Planks of Reason* (Metuchen, N.J.: Scarecrow Press, 1984); Bruce F. Kawin's "*The Funhouse* and *The Howling*," in Waller, ed., *American Horrors*; and Dennis Giles's "Conditions of Pleasure in Horror Cinema," in Grant, ed., *Planks of Reason*.

2. Elliott Stein, "A Very Tender Film, a Very Nice One," *Film Comment* 15 (1979), 57–59.

3. One of the few critics to distinguish between the gaze of Mark the cinematographer and that of Mark the spectator is Peary. "In Mark's peculiar case," he writes, "the murder of a woman does not by itself give him sexual satisfaction. The insertion of the blade into her is a necessary step, but his onanistic 'climax' takes place in the back room when he projects her dying expression on his wall. And only when his camera has captured in her face the absolute expression of fear (he is always disappointed/frustrated) can he truly be sexually satisfied." Immediately upon suggesting that there are two "pleasures" involved here, however, Peary backs off and proposes that it is really a question of two perspectives, two distances—on one and the same pleasure—a voyeuristic, sadistic pleasure. "By having Mark's 'sexual act' take place in two stages—the murder and the screening of the murder—Powell makes the distinction between participation (count us out) and voyeurism (count us in). Both have their own erotic appeal: for instance, one can enjoy active sex and still derive a different pleasure from watching sexual acts at a distance" (Danny Peary, *Cult Movies: The Classic, the Sleepers, the Weird, and the Wonderful* (New York: Dell, 1981), p. 254).

4. Stein, "A Very Tender Film," p. 59.

5. Jean Laplanche and J.-B. Pontalis (quoting Freud) in *The Language of Psycho-Analysis*, tr. Donald Nicholson-Smith (New York: Norton, 1973), s.v., "Sadism/Masochism," p. 402.

6. Just before Mark murders her, the actress Vivian steps behind Mark's camera and attempts to see through it. Helen, who is notably uninterested in Mark's camera, survives it.

7. Laplanche and Pontalis, *The Language of Psycho-Analysis*, s.v., "Compulsion to Repeat," p. 79.

8. Williams appreciates the distinction: "In making his films (the *mise-en-scene* of which is murder), Mark assumes the role of his sadistic father, mastering his own terror by becoming the victimizer himself. Then in watching his films he can relive his original experience of terror at a safe distance, identify with his own victims and repossess his own look of terror from a safer aesthetic distance." She does not, however, take her logic to its end point—that the second look is driven by masochism, that Mark is at that moment in the position the film otherwise assigns to the feminine, and that even when the *man* looks, he "recognizes" himself. On the contrary, she reverts to the male-sadistic model: "*Peeping Tom* thus lays bare the voyeuristic structure of cinema and that structure's dependence on the woman's acceptance of her role as narcissist" (Linda Williams, "When the Woman Looks," in Mary Ann Doane, Patricia Mellencamp, and Linda Williams, eds., *Re-Vision: Essays in Feminist Film Criticism*, American Film Institute Monograph Series 3 [Frederick, Md.: University Publications of America, 1984], especially p. 92).

9. The fact that realistic photography gives way, at the moment of penetration, to a sequence of startling psychedelics speaks volumes on the issue of representation and female sexuality.

10. The pineal eye of *From Beyond* is remarkably like the one adumbrated by Georges Bataille, *Visions of Excess: Selected Writings, 1927–1939* (Minneapolis: University of Minnesota Press, 1985), especially p. 82.

11. Though directed by Irvin Kershner, *The Eyes of Laura Mars* was scripted by John Carpenter and David Zelag Goodman based on a story written by John Carpenter (and Jon Peters, uncredited) before *Halloween*. Despite directorial changes, the Carpenterian concern with vision remains intact.

12. For an exploration of specularity in *The Eyes of Laura Mars*, see Lucy Fischer and Marcia Landy, "*Eyes of Laura Mars:* A Binocular Critique," in Waller, ed., *American Horrors*.

13. "Thus Laura Mars has what we might term 'male vision'—a way of seeing that reflects the dominant sexist ideology," write Fischer and Landy. "What is intriguing about this narrative configuration is not Laura's status as a psychic, which seems a mere narrative ploy. Rather, what stands out is the connection implied between Laura's work as a photographer and the act of homicide, her artistic vision and the murderer's point of view (ibid., p. 65). It is worth noting that the character whose eyes are punctured when the binoculars "backfire" in *Horrors of the Black Museum* is a woman, and recalling that the only time the image of *Peeping Tom* grows fuzzy is when a woman is at the cinematographic helm (when Mark's stepmother attempts to film Mark and his father).

14. Scientist Ruth's explanation of scanning has a particularly meta-horror-cinematic ring: "Telepathy is not mind reading. It is the direct linking of two nervous systems separated by space. I want you to make a link from your brain to his heart. I want your brain to make his heart beat faster."

15. The theme owes much of its popularity to the imagination of Stephen King. His novel *Carrie* (brought out as a film in 1976) expressed the idea tentatively, Brian De Palma exploited it more fully in *The Fury* (1978), and King's *Firestarter* (brought out as a film in 1984) is the story full-blown.

16. The appearance of the telekinesis theme in *Friday the 13th VII* is yet another indication that the slasher formula pure and simple was exhausted by the late eighties. That film's rewriting of the Final Girl as a telekinetic heroine in the Carrie mode bespeaks not only the conceptual affinity between the two character types but also the way in which subgenres (and genres) are constantly cannibalizing one another.

17. Even the infamous *Halloween*, however, complicates the gaze. See the suggestive analysis by Steve Neale, who concludes, on the basis of a close analysis of that film, that "the identifications of the spectator are thus split between the polarities of a sadistic, aggressive and controlling position and a masochistic, suffering, and controlled position" (Steve Neale, "*Halloween*": Suspense, Aggression, and the Look," *Framework* 14 [1981], 25–29; rpt. in Grant, ed., *Planks of Reason*, pp. 341–42).

18. See, for example, the opening sequence of Brian De Palma's *Blow-Out*, in which a panting, heart-beating, lurching first-person camera approaches a house and peers in the window.

19. The idea is neatly formulated in the notorious "crotch episode" of *Texas Chain Saw Massacre II*, in which the female victim-hero Stretch is cornered by Leatherface—chief of the deadly gazers in a series famous for its deadly gazing. Power fails Leatherface's chain saw at just the moment he is about to do her in, however, and in a state of apparent confusion, he instead slides the now-quiet saw up her leg to her crotch, where he moves it back and forth. Despite her terror, Stretch immediately senses the issue: "You're really good, you really are good, you're the best," she murmurs—at which point Leatherface achieves his first orgasm. Although a chain saw is not a camera in the normal scheme of things, Leatherface's particular chain saw and Mark's particular camera have a great deal in common. Both are specifically figured not as simply phallic but as ersatz substitutes for the real thing. Both are used to bear down on and do violence to female victims—though

both also lose their power in the presence of a special woman. Both are the products of phallic transmission—gifts from punishing, all-powerful fathers. Although we do not see the action through Leatherface's chain saw in the way we see it through Mark's camera, we do see it mainly through Leatherface's eyes—in a way that suggests a classic displacement upwards.

20. Mick Martin and Marsha Porter, *Video Movie Guide: 1987*, (New York: Ballantine, 1986), p. 690.

21. Carpenter and others draw a distinction between the handheld camera and the Panaglide or Steadicam, which produces an effect midway between handheld and dolly-mounted. Says Carpenter of the Panaglide: "So it doesn't have the rock-steadiness of a dolly, but it also doesn't have the human jerky movements of a hand-held—it's somewhere in between" (as quoted by Robert C. Cumbow, *Order in the Universe: The Films of John Carpenter* [Metuchen, N.J.: Scarecrow Press, 1990], p. 51). My own sense is that insofar as any shot is marked as different from normal, it is marked as deviant and untrustworthy.

22. The moment is quoted in *Hairspray* in a scene in which John Waters appears as the whirligig-equipped hypnotist charged with keeping Tracy immured in her bedroom. *Bringing Up Baby* offers a comic turn on the idea when David says to Susan, "The only way you'll get me to do what you want is to hold a bright object in front of my eyes and twirl it."

23. Michele Montrelay, "Inquiry into Femininity," *m/f* 1 (1978), 83–101, tr. from "Recherches sur la fémininité," in *L'Ombre et le nom* (Paris: Minuit, 1977), p. 91. Creed also speaks of the "voracious maw, the mysterious black hole which signifies female genitalia as the monstrous sign which threatens to give birth to equally horrific offspring as well as threatening to incorporate everything in its path. This is the generative archaic mother, constructed within patriarchal ideology as the primeval 'black hole.'" Although that "black hole" can be the sign of castration, it is not so in the horror texts she studies. There, emphasis is on the "gestating, all-devouring womb of the archaic mother," which, unlike the female genitalia, "cannot be constructed as a 'lack' in relation to the penis. The womb is not the site of castration anxiety. Rather, the womb signifies 'fullness' or 'emptiness' but always is its own point of reference" (Barbara Creed, "Horror and the Monstrous Feminine: An Imaginary Abjection," *Screen* 27 [1986], 44–70; rpt. in James Donald, ed., *Fantasy and the Cinema* [London: British Film Institute, 1989], p. 63.

24. The eye in *Un Chien andalou*, slit in close-up by a razor, is perhaps the grandfather of the tradition, and the Salvador Dali eye in *Spellbound*, cut by scissors, the father. Both point up the relation between surrealist notions of shock and the larger project of horror. Consider too Bataille's "pineal eye": "The eye, at the summit of the skull, opening on the incandescent sun in order to contemplate it in a sinister solitude, is not a product of the understanding but is instead an immediate existence; it opens and blinds itself like a conflagration, or like a fever that eats the being, or more exactly, the head . . . the head has received the *electric power of points*" (Bataille, *Visions of Excess*, p. 82). Prawer too notes the special emphasis on the eye in horror: "Within the face it is of course the eye which leads most directly to where we live—and the human eye has, indeed, played an especially important part in the terror-film. The photographed eye may be that of a sinister watcher, as in some frightening close-ups of Robert Siodmak's *The Spiral Staircase* (1946), which also shows the distorted way in which the watcher's mind interprets what his eye sees; or it may be the eye of a sad victim, the mirror of a tortured soul, as at the opening and close of Polanski's *Repulsion*. It hardly needs saying that the vulnerability of the eye is also played on by sequences enlisting our fear of physical injury, in films that range from *An Andalusian Dog* to *The Flesh and the Fiends* (1959)" (S. S. Prawer, *Caligari's Children: The Film as Tale of Terror* [Oxford: Oxford University Press, 1980], pp. 75–76).

25. The setup is reminiscent of the scene in *The Blob* (1958) in which "goo came dripping down from the projection booth and onto our surrogate selves watching a horror

movie at the downtown theater" (as Twitchell puts it in James B. Twitchell, *Dreadful Pleasures, An Anatomy of Modern Horror* [New York and Oxford: Oxford University Press, 1985], p. 15).

26. The scene recalls the passage in *King Kong* (1933) in which an audience is similarly invited to a mystery spectacle. They expect a movie only to be confronted with reality: Kong himself. And Kong too breaks out of the spectacle position, rampaging into the viewing audience and causing pandemonium.

27. For all its garishness, the female body imagery of *Poltergeist* has been little mentioned in the commentaries, which focus for the most part on the role of the father and the haunted house.

28. William Beard, "The Visceral Mind: The Major Films of David Cronenberg," in Canada Council, ed., *The Shape of Rage* (Don Mills, Ontario, Canada: Academy of Canadian Cinema; New York: New York Zoetrope, 1983), p. 70.

29. Geoff Pevere, "Cronenberg Tackles Dominant Videology," in Canada Council, ed., *The Shape of Rage*, p. 142. In an interview, Cronenberg himself responded to a question about "interchangeability happening between the sexes" in his films as follows: "Yes. You realize how important sexuality is to the human race, in terms of art, culture, society, psychology, everything. My instinct tells me that an enormous amount of sexuality, and everything that springs from that in our society, is a very physical thing. Human beings could swap sexual organs, or do without sexual organs as sexual organs per se, for procreation. We're free to develop different kinds of organs that would give pleasure, and that would have nothing to do with sex. The distinction between male and female would diminish, and perhaps we would become less polarized and more integrated creatures to the extent that there is, generally speaking, a male sensibility and a female sensibility. . . . I'm not talking about transsexual operations [in *Crimes of the Future* in particular]. I'm talking about the possibility that human beings would be able to physically mutate at will, even if it took five years to finish that mutation. Sheer force of will would allow you to change your physical self. I think that there would be a diminishing of sexual polarity, and there would be a reintegration of human beings in a very different way" ("The Interview," in Canada Council, ed., *The Shape of Rage*, pp. 190–91).

30. William Rothman argues that Hitchcock in this sequence "divides our identification. We identify with Marion, who must now confront the vision that was ours. But we are also implicated in this visitation and cannot separate ourselves from the being whose sudden intrusion frightens Marion. We view Marion through this creature's eyes, as she turns to possess it in her gaze" (William Rothman, *Hitchcock: The Murderous Gaze* [Cambridge, Mass.: Harvard University Press, 1982], p. 301). Rothman elsewhere (p. 296) admonishes that "our pleasure in viewing Marion [shortly before the attack] cannot be separated from our fantasy that we are about to possess her sexually. (If this is a male fantasy, it is not one that only the men in Hitchcock's audience may indulge. For men and women among the film's viewers, the act of viewing possesses both active and passive aspects, call them 'masculine' and 'feminine'.)" I note that Rothman invokes "active and passive" and the possibility of cross-gender identification only to secure the possibility that women participate in aggressive male fantasies. The case could further be made that even when Rothman claims to be in Marion's position, he constructs it as a function of male desire (especially p. 296). One of the aims of my own chapter is to hold critics like Rothman to the lip service they pay to cross-gender identification.

31. The trope crops up in the "woman's film" as well. "The image and voice in these films act as the 'third persons' of the paranoid delusion (the agents of persecution), and ultimately it is the cinema itself, through its organization of image and sound, which attacks the woman, becoming the machine of her torment. This operation is literalized in a significant number of films which explicitly activate the materials of the cinematic signifier, or even the cinema itself, in an assault on the female protagonist" (Mary Ann

Doane, *The Desire To Desire: The Woman's Film of the 1940s* [Bloomington: Indiana University Press, 1987], pp. 152–53).

32. Maxim Gorky has written of the shock he experienced at the moment, in the Lumière film *L'Asseur arrosé (Teasing the Gardener)*, that the gardener squirted the hose: "You think the spray is going to hit you too, and shrink back." As quoted by Siegfried Kracauer, *Theory of Film: Redemption of Physical Reality* (New York: Oxford University Press, 1960), p. 31.

33. Rothman, *Hitchcock*, pp. 296–309.

34. As Greenberg notes, "it is incomprehensible that Janet Leigh should simply cease to be. Never before had a star of such magnitude, a female sex goddess, been so utterly expunged in midstream. Thus Hitchcock drives home the incontrovertibility, the awesome finality of death. Our yen for sanctioned sex and sadism has been dreadfully surfeited by Marion's crucifixion. With Leigh gone, the comfortable conventions of the Hollywood suspense vehicle have been totally violated" (Harvey R. Greenberg, *The Movies on Your Mind* [New York: Dutton, 1975], p. 126).

35. It is remarkable how resilient a feature of movie theaters the curtain is and how many of even the most functional "plexes," stripped of nearly all the other traditional accoutrements, retain it.

36. For a more general consideration of film screen and mind or eye screen, see Bruce F. Kawin, *Mindscreen: Bergman, Godard, and First-Person Film* (Princeton, N.J.: Princeton University Press, 1978), especially chapter 1, "The Mind's Eye."

37. Rothman, *Hitchcock*, p. 100. Further: "Much of the shattering impact of this moment derives from Bernard Herrmann's score. Hitchcock's original intention was to release the shower-murder sequence with no musical accompaniment at all, but Herrmann prevailed on him to try it out with music. . . . It is above all the sudden high-pitched shriek of violins, so compellingly suggestive of an attacking birdlike creature, that creates the shock that constitutes *Psycho*'s best-known effect" (p. 298). See also Stephen Heath, "Body, Voice" in *Questions of Cinema*, (Bloomington: Indiana University Press, 1981), pp. 176–93).

38. Again, young boys, like women and old men, are regarded as "unsubjects." See chapter 2, especially n. 20.

39. In an interview with Derry, director William Friedkin makes much of the "expectancy set" that operates among horror audiences. "The cinema takes advantage of this factor. Alfred Hitchcock takes advantage of the fact that an audience comes into the theatre expecting to be scared. When they are standing in line they are afraid. So he takes them for about an hour and dangles them and lets them do it for themselves until he hits them with something. . . . The same is true for *The Exorcist*. People are afraid while they're standing in line. And for the first hour of the film, while there is little more than exposition and some of that very hard to follow unless you've read the book, people are working themselves into an emotional state that is inducive to becoming terrified" (Charles Perry, *Dark Dreams: A Psychological History of the Modern Horror Film* [London: Thomas Yoseloff, 1977], pp. 123–24).

40. As has often been noted, Mulvey's model, in its original formulation, allows for female spectatorial pleasure only as a male-identified or "transvestite" activity. In her later "Afterthoughts on 'Visual Pleasure,'" she suggests a psychosexual model for the cross-gender "visual pleasure" of the female spectator (Laura Mulvey, "Afterthoughts on 'Visual Pleasure and Narrative Cinema' Inspired by King Vidor's *Duel in the Sun* [1946]," *Framework* 15-17 [1981], 12–15; rpt. in Mulvey, *Visual and Other Pleasures* [Bloomington: Indiana University Press, 1981]. See also the issue of *Camera Obscura* devoted to "The Spectatrix" ([1989], 20–21).

41. D. N. Rodowick, "The Difficulty of Difference," Wide Angle 15 (1982), p. 7. Gaylyn Studlar (*In the Realm of Pleasure: Von Sternberg, Dietrich, and the Masochistic*

Aesthetic [Urbana: University of Illinois Press, 1988], especially chapters 2 and 8) suggests that the relocation of fetishism to the pre-Oedipal period (relating it to the loss of the mother rather than phallic loss) provides a model for a masochistic relation to the screen. Although it is my impression that horror scenarios bear out Freud's view that masochistic fears can stem from any period of development, I would argue emphatically that Oedipal conflicts occupy pride of place.

42. Christian Metz, *The Imaginary Signifier: Psychoanalysis and the Cinema* (Bloomington: Indiana University Press, 1982), especially pp. 58–65.

43. "For the spectator," Metz writes, "the film unfolds in that simultaneously very close and definitively inaccessible 'elsewhere' in which the child sees the amorous play of the parental couple, who are similarly ignorant of it and leave it alone, a pure onlooker whose participation is inconceivable. In this respect the cinematic signifier is not only 'psychoanalytic'; it is more precisely Oedipal in type. . . . The cinema retains something of the prohibited character peculiar to the vision of the primal scene . . . but also, in a kind of inverse movement which is simply the 'reprise' of the imaginary by the symbolic, the cinema is based on the legislation and generalisation of the prohibited practice" (*The Imaginary Signifier*, pp. 64–65). See also Patrick Brantlinger, "What Is 'Sensational' about the 'Sensation Novel'?" *Nineteenth-Century Fiction* 37 (1982), especially pp. 25–26.

44. Kaja Silverman, "Too Early/Too Late: Subjectivity and the Primal Scream in Henry James," *Novel* 21 (1988), pp. 156–57. See also her "Masochism and Male Subjectivity," *Camera Obscura* 17 (1988), p. 50, and Jean Laplanche, *Life and Death in Psychoanalysis,* tr. Jeffrey Mehlman (Baltimore: John Hopkins University Press, 1976), especially p. 102.

45. Metz, *The Imaginary Signifier,* pp. 50–51. The passage is noted by Kaja Silverman in *The Acoustic Mirror: The Female Voice in Psychoanalysis and Cinema* (Bloomington: Indiana University Press, 1988), p. 23.

46. Metz, The Imaginary Signifier, p. 51. Studlar also stresses the double movement of the apparatus, and she too wants to correct the usual bias by stressing the passive and receptive side of the equation; see especially her "Masochism and the Perverse Pleasures of the Cinematic Apparatus" (chapter 8 of *In the Realm of Pleasure*). For a provocative discussion of two-way vision in relation to transvestite pornography, see Berkeley Kaite, "The Pornographic Body Double: Transgression Is the Law," in Arthur and Marielouise Kroker, eds., *Body Invaders: Panic Sex in America* (New York: St. Martin's Press, 1987),

47. "When I say that I 'see' the film, I mean thereby a unique mixture of two contrary currents: the film is what I receive, and it is also what I release, since it does not preexist my entering the auditorium and I only need close my eyes to suppress it. Releasing it, I am the projector, receiving it, I am the screen; in both these figures together, I am the camera, which points and yet records" (Metz, *The Imaginary Signifier,* p. 51).

48. "Although the gaze might be said to be 'the presence of others as such,' it is by no means coterminous with any individual viewer, or group of viewers. It issues 'from all sides,' whereas the eye '[sees] only from one point.' The gaze, moreover, is 'unapprehensible,' i.e., impossible to seize or get hold of. The relationship between eye and gaze is thus analogous in certain ways to that which links penis and phallus; the former can stand in for the latter, but can never approximate it. Lacan makes this point with particular force when he situates the gaze outside the voyeuristic transaction, a transaction within which the eye would seem most to aspire to a transcendental status, and which has consequently provided the basis, within feminist film theory, for an equation of the male voyeur with the gaze" (Kaja Silverman, "Fassbinder and Lacan: A Reconsideration of Gaze, Look, and Image," *Camera Obscura* 19 [1989], pp. 71–73).

49. See Karen Horney's remarks on the male fear of the vagina not as a signifier of mutilation, but as a distinct, and for some men uniquely frightening, genital ("The Dread

of Woman," in Karen Horney, ed., *Feminine Psychology* [New York: Norton, 1976], pp. 133–46).

50. Revok's formulation is remarkably like the formulation of the woman analysand who worried, in terms that her analyst regarded as genitally based, as follows: "I used to feel I had never learned how *not* to be open all the time. I always felt open and couldn't ever shut myself off. But actually what I do is *look like* I'm open on the outside so I take people in, they think I'm really open. But sometimes I'm so frightened I can't really let them in at all, in fact I don't even want to. I stay shut off inside so people can't invade my space. If people can't see where my space is, they can't invade it. I hide it. Like having a hole in a wall and I scurry around patching the whole wall so no one knows where it is and they can't get in" (Elizabeth B. Mayer, "Everybody Must Be Just like Me: Observations on Female Castration Anxiety," *International Journal of Psychoanalysis* 66 [1985], p. 336).

51. As Beard notes, "This idea of an almost physical invasion of the mind and of the seeing eye as a barrier to intrusion and the guardian of privacy and self is a nice symbol of the related ideas of control, awareness and aggression. The people in Revok's head are trampling him, tripping him out of control. To keep them out he must establish an appearance of awareness and vigilance (the 'eye'). Thus is established the notion of gazing as a weapon—awareness as an aggressive tool. Revok the monster scanner, using the 'eye' in his head to control and destroy others, is born in this act of his younger self" (William Beard, "The Visceral Mind: The Major Film of David Cronenberg," Canada Council, ed., p. 44).

52. In particular, by Studlar (*In the Realm of Pleasure*); Silverman (especially "Too Early/Too Late"; "White Skin, Brown Masks: The Double Mimesis, or with Lawrence in Arabia," *Differences* 1 [1989], 3–54; "Masochism and Male Subjectivity," and "Fassbinder and Lacan"); Rodowick, "The Difficulty of Difference"; Neale, "*Halloween*"; Doane, *The Desire to Desire* and "Misrecognition and Identity," Ciné-Tracts 11 (1980), 25–32; Jacqueline Rose, "Paranoia and the Film System," *Screen* 17 (1976–1977), 85–104 (via a consideration of paranoia); Paul Smith, "Action Movie Hysteria,", or Eastwood Bound," *Differences* 1 (1989), 88–107; and Linda Williams, "Power, Pleasure, and Perversion: Sadomasochistic Film Pornography," *Representations* 27 (1989), 37–65 (an expanded version of chapter 7 of her *Hard Core* (Berkeley and Los Angeles: University of California Press, 1989). Lynne Kirby's remarks on male hysteria also bear on the subject of masochism ("Male Hysteria and Early Cinema," *Camera Obscura* 17 [1988], 112–31). Leo Bersani's work, while only occasionally about film, suggests ways of theorizing masochistic representations; see especially *The Freudian Body* (New York: Columbia University Press, 1986) and "Is the Rectum a Grave?" (October 43 [1989], 194–222) and, with Ulysse Dutoit, *The Forms of Violence: Narrative in Assyrian Art and Modern Culture* (New York: Schocken, 1985). More generally, see Gayle Rubin, "Thinking Sex: Notes for a Radical Theory of the Politics of Sexuality," in Carole S. Vance, ed., *Pleasure and Danger: Exploring Female Sexuality* (Boston: Routledge & Kegan Paul,) and Gilles Deleuze, *Masochism: Coldness and Cruelty*. (New York: Zone Books, 1989).

53. The point has been underscored by Silverman ("Masochism and Male Subjectivity"), who also quotes Freud in *Three Essays* to the effect that sadism "would correspond to an aggressive component of the sexual instinct," the biological significance of which "seems to lie in the need for overcoming the resistance of the sexual object by means other than the precess of wooing" ("Masochism and Male Subjectivity," pp. 33–34).

54. Silverman, especially "Masochism and Male Subjectivity." For a critical summary of Freud's views, see Laplanche, *Life and Death in Psychoanalysis*, pp. 85–102.

55. Laplanche and Pontalis, *The Language of Psycho-Analysis*, s.v. "Compulsion to Repeat," p. 78.

56. Recall Mark's anguish (in *Peeping Tom*) when he sees, on watching the projected film of the murder of Vivian, that the lighting was off (the implication being that he must

try again, with yet another woman, as he has been trying all his adult life, to get it right). See also Greenberg's brief remarks in The Movies on Your Mind, pp. 196–97, and, on repetition in film in general, Heath, Questions of Cinema ("Repetition Time"), pp. 165–75.

57. Laplanche and Pontalis, The Language of Psycho-Analysis, s.v. "Compulsion to Repeat," p. 78; Edward Bibring, "The Conception of the Repetition Compulsion" (Psycho-analytic Quarterly 12 [1943], 486–519); Laplanche, Life and Death in Psychoanalysis, pp. 85–102; Sigmund Freud, Beyond the Pleasure Principle (1920, Standard Edition 18:1–64); and "The Economic Problem of Masochism" (1924, Standard Edition 19: 157–70).

58. Freud, "The Economic Problem of Masochism," pp.164–65.

59. Ibid., p. 162.

60. Silverman, "Masochism and Male Subjectivity," p. 36. See also Parveen Adams, "Per Os(cillation)," Camera Obscura 17 (1988), 7–29.

61. Silverman argues that the girl's fantasy may in fact be more "perverse" than Freud recognized. See her "Masochism and male Subjectivity," especially pp. 48–50.

62. Laplanche and Pontalis, The Language of Psycho-Analysis, s.v. "Masochism," p. 245. Several commentators have objected to the locution feminine masochism not least because of the implication that it corresponds to masochism in women. Theodor Reik suggests dropping the term altogether or, failing that, reserving its use of "the perverted inclination of the man" and making clear its distinctness from "the masochism of the woman" (Masochism in Modern Man [New York: Grove Press, 1981], p. 212). As I shall suggest in the remarks that follow, I have retained it here because of its obvious appropriateness to the sort of male-to-female transvestite or transsexual imaginings that are so central to modern horror cinema.

It is crucial, in parsing Freud on masochism, to distinguish between femininity as it manifests itself in female sexuality (a vexed and interesting topic, but not one on the table here) and femininity as it manifests itself in male fantasy. For Freud, male fantasies of being "gagged, bound, painfully beaten, whipped, in some way maltreated, forced into unconditional obedience, dirtied, and debased" place the subject "in a characteristically female situation" insofar as the "signify...being castrated, or copulated with, or giving birth to a baby." The word signify may give pause here as suggesting a natural relation between Set A and Set B (between debasement and being sexually penetrated, for example), but if we keep in mind the conventional homosexual taboo that hovers about such fantasies in the male, a taboo that may moreover understand the vagina in anal terms, feelings of degradation or debasement come into focus as a form of psychic camouflage. That taboo may also help to account for what is claimed by Reik and freud to be the flamboyant and self-shattering character of male masochistic fantasies and practices in comparison with the rather more restrained ones of the female. In either case, the very fact that feminine masochism is a male affliction attests to its artifactual status. Also worth remembering in this connection is the fact that, according to psychoanalytic testimony, men fantasize about receptive copulation, being pregnant, and giving birth in pleasant as well as unpleasant terms.

63. The possibility of bisexual spectatorship has been widely entertained. See especially Mulvey, "Afterthoughts on 'Visual Pleasure'" Wood, "Repression, the Other, the Monster," in "An Introduction to the American Horror Film", in Andrew Britton et al., eds., American Nightmare: Essays on the Horror Film (Toronto: Festival of Festivals, 1979), rpt. in Bill Nichols, ed., Movies and Methods, vol. 2 (Berkeley and Los Angeles: University of California Press, 1985); and de Lauretis, especially "The Technology of Gender," in Technologies of Gender.: Theories of Theory, Film, and Fiction (Bloomington: Indiana University Press, 1987). performative gender, see Judith Butler, Gender Trouble.: Feminism and the Subversion of Identity (New York Routledge, 1990).

64. As Beard suggests, the female body is virtually the *only* site of sexual feeling for David Cronenberg. "It is notable that none of Cronenberg's male protagonists before *Videodrome* is at all sexual....Sex in these films is in fact vested in the female for the most part" ("Visceral Mind," p. 75). The case could be made that the sexuality of even *Videodrome*'s protagonist is contingent on his feminization and that powerful or trans-formative sexual feeling is, for Cronenberg, very much associated with masochistic experience and very little with sadism. Beard hints at the homoerotic implications in his discussion of *Videodrome* ("The Visceral Mind," pp.60–62). Mention should also be made of Rose's analysis of paranoia in the film system, in particular her remarks on the complex paranoia/femininity. "The woman is centered in the clinical manifestation of paranoia as position. Paranoia is characterized by a passive homosexual current, and hence a 'fem-inine' position in both man and woman. In the case of Schreber, the attack actually transforms his body into that of a woman; this is necessary because the 'state of voluptuousness,' which in his delusion is demanded of Schreber by God, is not restricted for the woman to the genitals but is dispersed over the whole body...and is constant (extension in time and space as a reference to woman's relation to a non-genital, i.e., un-normativised sexuality). The attack itself is sexually ambivalent-apparition of the foreclosed phallus in the real (Schreber is to be inseminated by God) but also the penetration of the body by feminine tissue" ("Paranoia and the Film System," p. 102). See also Doane, *The Desire to Desire,* especially pp. 129–34, and Christopher Craft, "'Kiss Me with Those Red Lips': Gender and Inversion in Bram Stoker's *Dracula,*" *Representations* 8 (1984), pp. 114–15). See also chapter 1, n. 55.

65. Freud, "Analysis Terminable and Interminable" (1973, *Standard Edition* 23: 216–53), especially p. 252.

66. Twitchell has argued that the organizing fear of horror is incest, by which he means that horror texts play out a version of the patricidal scenario outlined by Freud in *Totem and Taboo,* trans. James Strachey, (New York: W. W. Norton, 1950). For Twitchell, the "horror of incest" comes down to this: "We humans have developed a code...to inform the prepotent males of the consequences *before* they can choose. This information is embedded into both the brain matter and the rites and myths of initiation with one simple message: have intercourse with a 'taken' woman and you will be cast out. It is as simple as that—make a mistake and you will not breed for a while" (*Dreadful Pleasures,* pp. 103–4; see also his *Forbidden Partners.: The Incest Taboo in Modern Culture* [New York: Columbia University Press, 1987]). Although Twitchell must be right that horror trades in incest, I fail to see how his selective and "vanilla" version of the Freudian scenario works as a universal key (it seems inapplicable, or subsidiary, to most horror plots), or how it might work for the female viewer (of whose presence in the audience Twitchell insists that the woman in question is to be understood not as a mother or a sister but as any woman in another man's possession), and thus reduced, as Twitchell himself acknowl-edges, to a lesson in social history, it accounts for the play of transgressive desire that manifestly animates most horror texts.

67. Although not all horror films are equally suspenseful and although the suspense may take different forms (including the hesitation between natural and supernatural explanations of horror that Todorov takes as the defining feature of the fantastic), I take suspense to be a hallmark of horror. Carroll writes that "although suspense and horror are distinct—there may be suspense stories without horror and horror stories without sus-pense—they also have a natural, though contingent, affinity" (Noël Carroll, *The Philoso-phy of Horror,: Or, Paradoxes of the Heart* [New York: Routledge, 1990], p. 144).

68. Reik, *Masochism in Modern Man,* p. 184. In his close analysis of *Halloween,* Neale notes the imbrication of suspense in the sadomasochistic aesthetic, which he in turn relates to the traffic in looks: "In moments of suspense...the spectator's loss of a

position of control is translated either into an acute anxiety or eventually into an act of extreme diegetic violence" (p. 342).

69. Silverman, *"Masochism and Male Subjectivity,"* p. 52. For a summary of Freud's views on "subjectivization" in conscious and unconscious fantasy, see Laplanche and Pontalis, *"Fantasy and the Origins of Sexuality,"* in Victor Burgin et al., eds., *Formations of Fantasy* (London: Methuen, 1986), especially p. 22. On the relation of dreams to folktales, see Bruno Bettelheim's brief-but-to-the-point remarks in *The Uses of Enchantment,: The Meaning and Importance of Fairy Tales* (New York: Random House, 1989), p. 36.

70. Of *Halloween*'s episodic stalk-and-kill structure, Tudor writes, "The essence of our involvement, then, is of the 'Where is he?' 'When will he strike next?' 'Will she get away?' type, and the movie works as a series of tension-building sequences culminating in moments of intense shock and economically portrayed violence....All the films [that follow the *Halloween*'s formula] climax with the pursuit of the solitary surviving female" (Andrew Tudor, *Monsters and Mad Scientists,: A Cultural History of the Horror Movie* [Oxford: Blackwell, 1989], pp. 68–69).

71. Reik, *Masochism in Modern Man*, p. 42. For an exploration of the psychosexual dynamics of story at the mythic level, see de Lauretis, "Desire in Narrative" in *Alice Doesn't.: Feminism, Semiotics, Cinema* (Bloomington: Indiana University Press, 1984).

72. John Ellis, *Visible Fictions,: Cinema, Television, Radio* (London: Routledge & Kegan Paul, 1982), p. 44 (italics mine); see also Gaylyn Studlar and David Desser, "Never Having to Say You're Sorry: *Rambo*'s Rewriting of the Vietnam War," in Linda Dittmar and Gene Michaud, eds., *From Hanoi to Hollywood: The Vietnam War in American Film* (New Brunswick, N.J.: Rutgers University Press, 1990). Carroll also reminds us that it is not so much the scary embedded. "Indeed, I think it is fair to say that in our culture, horror thrives above all as a narrative form. Thus, in order to account for the interest we take in and the pleasure we take from horror, we may hypothesize that, in the main, the locus of our gratification is not the monster as such but the whole narrative structure in which the presentation of the monster is staged" (*The Philosophy of Horror*, p. 181).

73. Paul Comisky and Jennings Bryant, "Factors Involved in Generating Suspense." *Human Communication Research* 9 (1982), pp. 57–58. See also Noël Carroll, "Toward a Theory of Film Suspense," *Persistence of Vision* 1 (1984), 65–89.

74. Comisky and Bryant, "Factors Involved in Generating Suspense," especially p. 54.

75. Carroll dismisses the masochistic motivation of horror spectatorship on grounds that it presupposes an "illusion theory", whereby "theatrical, or alternatively, cinematic techniques of verisimilitude so overwhelm us that we are deceived into believing that a monster really looms before us....Were the illusion theory true, horror would be too unnerving for all save heroes, consummate masochists, and professional vampire killers" (*The Philosophy of Horror*, pp. 63–64).

76. My view here is conditioned by folklore studies and the textual and narratological study of medieval texts. Laura Mulvey has moved in the same direction in her "Changes: Thoughts on Myth, Narrative and Historical Experience," *History Workshop Journal* (1987), 3–19; rpt. in Laura Mulvey, *Visual and Other Pleasures*. Bettelheim, *The Uses of Enchantment*, introduction. Smith, however, wants to reprivilege endings; see his "Action Movie Hysteria." Linda Williams sums up the issue nicely when she remarks of *Stella Dallas* that "although the final moment of the film 'resolves' the contradiction of Stella's attempt to be a woman *and* a mother by eradicating both, the 108 minutes leading up to this moment present the heroic attempt to live out the contradiction" ("'Something Else besides a Mother,': *Stella Dallas* and the Maternal Melodrama," *Cinema Journal* [1984], p. 24). Although endings are obviously important (enough for studios to present alternative ones to test audiences), their importance is just as obviously contingent on what came before—what it is that needs resolving and sealing off. Because endings are

generically overdetermined (one reason they are so often misremembered), it is to middles one should look for the meanings that are being contested in the text.

77. Doane (*The Desire to Desire*, pp. 94–95 and passim) has suggested that "weepies" offer an essentially masochistic experience to their audiences. She takes the fact that the object of the weepie address is female to suggest that women viewers are more susceptible to masochistic spectatorship than males. It seems to me equally possible that, in the same way horror exploits male masochistic fantasies, weepies exploit female ones. In either case, the markers of these films go about jerking tears in ways manipulative enough to be compared with the sadistic tactics of horror. For a literary perspective, Kirby's summary remarks about the positioning of the spectator of early train films are worth quoting here: "In theoretical terms, the assaulted spectator is the hysterical spectator. The fantasies of being run over and assaulted, penetrated, produce a certain pleasure of pain—beyond the pleasure principle and in the realm of repetition compulsion—which is as much about will-to-submission, to loss-of-mastery, as it is about will-to-master/control" ("Male Hysteria and Early Cinema," p. 128).

78. I assume this is what Raymond Bellour has in mind when he opines that a woman "can love, accept and give a positive value to these films [American cinema] only from her own masochism, and from a certain sadism that she can exercise in return on the masculine subject, within a system loaded with traps" (As quoted in Janet Bergstrom, "Alternation, Segmentation, Hypnosis,: Interview with Raymond Bellour," *Camera Obscura* 3-4 [1979], p. 84). Judith Butler's suggestion that "it may well be more frightening to acknowledge and identification with the one who debases than with the one who is debased" ("The Force of Fantasy",: Feminism, Mapplethorpe, and Discursive Excess," *Differences* 2 [1990], p. 114) may be true for female spectators (for whom sadistic desire is more severely repressed), but it is hardly true of male ones.

79. This is not to deny the displacement value of a female in a male-homoerotic drama—a possibility I have discussed at length in the previous chapters. It is, however, to suggest that displacement value is an insufficient explanation for the phenomenon.

80. Of Silverman's several pronouncements on the subject, I quote only one here-one that proceeds from her reading of Deleuze's reading of Freud on masochism: "In inviting the mother to beat and/or dominate him, he [the male who fantasizes himself in the "feminine masochistic" position] transfers power and authority from the father to her, remakes the symbolic order, and 'ruins' his own paternal legacy. And that is not all. As Freud remarks of those two [male] patients in" 'A Child Is Being Beaten'" (1919, *Standard Edition* 17:177–204), the conscious phantasy of being disciplined by the mother 'has for its content a feminine attitude without a homosexual object-choice.' It thereby effects another revolution of sorts, and one whose consequences may be even more socially transforming than eroticism between men—it constitutes a 'feminine' yet heterosexual male subject" ("Masochism and Male Subjectivity," p. 57). See, more generally, her *Male Subjectivity at the Margins*. (New York: Routledge, 1992). In his remarkable essay "Is the Rectum a Grave?" Bersani suggests that rather than denying the association, in the public mind and in private fantasy, of the (gay male) anus with the vagina, gay men accept it and embrace its implication."'AIDS,' [Simon] Watney writes, 'offers a new sign for the symbolic machinery of repression, making the rectum a grave.' But if the rectum is a grave in which the masculine ideal (an ideal shared-differently-by men *and* woman) of proud subjectivity is buried, then it should be celebrated for its very potential for death. Tragically, AIDS has literalized that potential as the certainty of biological death and has therefore reinforced the heterosexual association of anal sex with a self-annihilation originally and primarily identified with the fantasmatic mystery of an insatiable, unstoppable female sexuality. It may, finally, be in the gay man's rectum that he demolishes his own perhaps otherwise uncontrollable identification with a murderous judgment against him." Bersani continues, "That judgment, as I have been suggesting, is grounded in the

sacrosanct value of selfhood, a value that accounts for human beings' extraordinary willingness to kill in order to protect the seriousness of their statements. The self is a practical convenience; promoted to the status of an ethical ideal, it is a sanction for violence....Gay men's 'obsession' with sex, far from being denied, should be celebrated—not because of its communal virtues, not because of its subversive potential for parodies of machismo, not because it offers a model of genuine pluralism to a society that at once celebrates and punishes pluralism, but rather because it never stops re-presenting the internalized phallic male as an infinitely loved object of sacrifice. Male homosexuality advertises the risk of the sexual itself as the risk of self-dismissal, of *losing sight* of the self, and in so doing it proposes and dangerously represents *jouissance* as a mode of ascesis" (p. 222). See also Bersani's *Baudelaire and Freud* (in which, however, he does not pursue the feminine dimension, (Berkeley and Los Angeles: University of California Press, 1977), especially pp. 67–89, and his and Dutoit's *Forms of Violence*, especially pp. 110–25 ("The Restlessness of Desire"); Christopher Newfield, "The Politics of Male Suffering: Masochism and Hegemony in the American Renaissance," Differences 1 (1989), 55–87; Adams, "Per Os(cillation)"; and Tania Modleski, "Three Men and Baby M." *Camera Obscura* 17 (1988), especially 73–74. It is also important to consider the possibility that masochistic fantasy (or masochistic acting out in a sexual relationship) may work to enable the man to take command in other parts of his life; consider, for example, the phenomenon, repeatedly attested by prostitutes, of the captain of industry (say) with a taste for being beaten. See also Lynne Segal, *Slow Motion,: Changing Masculinities, Changing Men* (New Brunswick, N.J.: Rutgers University Press, 1990), especially chapter 8.

81. As Deleuze notes, the work of Leopold von Sacher-Masoch "has suffered from unfair neglect, when we consider that Sade has been the object of such penetrating studies both in the field of literary criticism and in that of psychoanalytic interpretation, to the benefit of both *Masochism*, p. 133).

82. Tania Modleski, "A Father Is Being Beaten: Male Feminism and the War Film," *Discourse* 10 (1988), especially pp. 66–67.

83. Modleski makes the related point, apropos Anthony Wilden's argument in *Man and Woman, War and Peace* (New York: Methuen, 1987) to the effect that women can never challenge male supremacy by standing outside war culture: "Feminism has now paradoxically become the last alibi for the liberal male's fascination with war: (ibid., p. 67).

84. These instances of one-way vision are, of course, part and parcel of the longstanding and wholesale assumption, in cultural thought, that people in general identify upward, toward power and prestige. Thus blacks identify with whites, poor with rich, women with men—and either not the reverse or the reverse only for purposes of appropriation. A psychoanalytically informed analysis of such territories as horror and pornography (to name just two obvious cases) suggests not only the existence of a downward movement but a more nuanced understanding of it. See Silverman's remarks on the correspondence in chapter 1 of *The Acoustic Mirror*, "Lost Objects and Mistaken Subjects."

85. I note that although Silverman and Bersani claim to be making their case on strictly psychoanalytic grounds, both of them are acutely conscious of, and seem to an extent driven by, the "cultural secret" aspect of male masochism. Both of them, that is, take the silence surrounding the subject as evidence of its importance.

86. Greenson's "Dis-Identifying from Mother: Its Special Importance for the Boy," *International Journal of Psycho-Analysis* 49 (1968), 370–74, makes the intriguing suggestion that the boy can "dis-identify" with his mother only by first enjoying the phase of identification with her—a phase of which the generations after Freud have become particularly intolerant. If that is so, horror comes into focus as the site of the repressed femininity.

87. In Silverman's formulation, woman is made to bear "double lack". See chapter 1 of *The Acoustic Mirror*.

88. I am referring especially to the slasher and the rape-revenge film here. The possession film does not evacuate the male in the same way, but as I suggested at some length in chapter 2, "Opening Up," it has its own, only slightly less obvious, ways of "admitting" male engagement with the feminine position.

89. Thus a film like *Henry: Portrait of a Serial Killer*, which plays definitively on sadistic impulses, does not in my view qualify as horror. The reviews I saw simultaneously classified it as and distinguished it from horror. ("This low-budget film is gory and chilling, but not exploitative in the way of most slasher movies. Unrated" [*San Francisco Examiner*, Pink Section, 13 May, 1989], and so on).

90. This is not to say that all higher or mainstream cinema is so muted or minimally masochistic. See Studlar's analyses of von Sternberg's films (*In the Realm of Pleasure*) and Doane's of woman's films of the 1940's (*The Desire to Desire*). I should also acknowledge some useful discussions with Richard Hutson on a (significantly) "unremembered" genre of forties films he refers to as "male melodramas."

Rhona J. Berenstein

Spectatorship-as-Drag: The Act of Viewing and Classic Horror Cinema

If Looks Could Kill

The performative dimensions of gender, race, and sexual identity-formation have been the focus of significant theoretical and creative work in the past few years. Writers such as Judith Butler and Marjorie Garber have loosened gender and sexuality from binary poles and argued for unstable notions of sexual identity. With the exception of a few recent works, such as Steven Cohan's and Ina Rae Hark's *Screening the Male*, film analyses of identity as performance have used precisely the binaries that Butler and Garber seek to overturn.[1] Film theory, especially work on sex, gender, and spectatorship, has relied on a male-versus-female spectator, and limited concepts of amorphous sexuality (e.g., pre-Oedipal bisexual viewing).

Since the 1970s, film spectatorship has occupied three categories: (1) Lacanian-ideological approaches that posit a textual position into which the subject is inserted, (2) Freudian readings that propose viewing positions that correspond to the behavior of heroes and heroines (e.g., either a sadistic or a masochistic point of view), and (3) multiple positions

This is an adaptation of a chapter from the forthcoming book *Attack of the Leading Ladies: Gender and Performance in Classic Horror Cinema*. Printed by permission of the author and Columbia University. Copyright © 1995 by Columbia University Press.

that conceive of cinema as a phantasy-terrain or discursive site upon which spectators access shifting subject-positions.

The first and second approaches have dominated the analysis of genres—horror movies in particular (e.g., James B. Twitchell [*Dreadful Pleasures*] and Carol J. Clover [*Men, Women, and Chain Saws*]).[2] The second model has also held sway in a significant segment of feminist work on spectatorship. Yet the conflation of spectatorship with sadism or masochism provides too simplistic an evaluation of the spectator-genre relationship. The paradigm also limits the imputed spectator's identification with and desire for on-screen characters, as some feminist scholars have pointed out (e.g., Miriam Hansen [Babel and Babylon]).[3]

What has yet to be accomplished in feminist film studies is the detailed investigation of the third category of spectatorship, which conceives of multiple viewing positions, with recourse to theoretical frameworks beyond the psychoanalytic pale and with a view to dislodging the field's favorite dualities: male/female and heterosexual/homosexual. Such a project is important for its commitment to theorizing the sex and gender permutations of spectatorship in a manner that takes into account historical and generic specificity and does not reduce viewing to a masochistic-sadistic duality.

This chapter is devoted to interrogating the ways in which Hollywood's 1930s horror films, usually thought to be home to sadistic and male forms of viewing pleasure, allow fluid subject-positions and invite spectators to engage in roles similar to those appropriated by actors in the performance of drag. In this context, drag is understood as the theatrical adoption of sex and gender behavior, with the term *sex* referring to biological sex and *gender* to the display of behaviors culturally conceived as either feminine or masculine. I argue that classic horror has been misinterpreted by most critics as a representational venue for the promotion of solely patriarchal mores, which in turn elicit sexually differentiated spectatorial responses.

The multiplicity of identifications and desires available to film spectators has been addressed, primarily, in terms of psychoanalytic phantasies, especially Freud's work on beating fantasies. In this context I too will appeal to Freud's oeuvre in order to expand prior analyses of horror viewing. However, the model of spectatorship proffered by the beating fantasies provides only part of horror's viewing puzzle and is best augmented by a theory that can account for horror's confusion of categories of sexual identity, biological sex, and gender. Drag offers such a model not only because it provides a framework for addressing gender behaviors as modes of performance but also because it throws into question the notion of an authentic spectating self. From this perspective, then, identity politics remain a crucial mode of action in the political arena, but spectators seated in a movie theater, especially those who watch classic horror, are likely to engage in and exhibit a more fluid and malleable range of social and sexual identities than they would in their everyday lives.

Studying imputed spectatorship is never a purely theoretical endeavor, as Judith Mayne has recently pointed out: "[T]he analysis of spectatorship is an analysis of one's *own* fascination and passion. Unless this is acknowledged, then we are left with a series of fuzzily defined 'ideal readers' in whom it is difficult to know how much of their responses are displaced representations of the critic's own."[4] While theorists may describe an ideal viewer promoted by textual systems, that claim is always informed by their personal investment in describing the specificities of spectatorial patterns.

As a lesbian film scholar and spectator living in a late-twentieth-century culture in which heterosexuality is the norm, I delight in classic horror's transgression of dominant renditions of sexual difference and gender traits. While I may experience fear (although historical hindsight offers much in the way of critical distance), I also derive pleasure from viewing a monster that toys with the requisites of sexual identity as either male or female and that American patriarchy deems a threat to its mores. Thus, from a personal perspective, one of the draws of evaluating classic horror cinema is to address imputed spectatorship in a genre that may do little to unhinge the workings of patriarchy outside the theater but plays havoc with conventional identifications and roles behind closed doors.

Classic horror provides textual and extratextual terrains imbricated in the adoption of disguises and role-playing—the masking and unmasking of creatures and characters. For example, in the publicity materials distributed by Paramount for its 1933 possession film, *Supernatural,* one poster proclaimed of the heroine/monster: "Beneath Her Mask of beauty [sic] . . . . . . Lurks The [sic] Spirit of a Demon" (Library of Congress Collection). The publicity campaign for *Daughter of the Dragon* (Paramount, 1931), a film about the monstrous evils of a Chinese doctor and his daughter, employed similar tactics: "Fu Manchu's Daughter, a Fascinating Beauty Whose Beauty Masks the Vengeful Heart of a Serpent About to Strike" (Library of Congress Collection). The appeal to role-play as a selling ploy was not limited to female fiends, as one byline for *The Crime of Dr. Crespi* (Republic, 1935), a mad-doctor film, suggests: "Great Surgeon—or Inhuman Fiend?" (Library of Congress Collection).

While it would be imprudent to draw a one-to-one correspondence between publicity ploys and spectatorial positions, it would be equally unwise to ignore the influence of textual and extratextual forms of disguise on audiences. As I argue in a more sustained fashion elsewhere, classic horror relishes "gender-bending."[5] Not only are heroines the monster's victims, but they also often desire the fiends and are visually and narratively doubled with them; male leads not only valiantly attempt to save heroines from monsters but also often fail in their heroic efforts, are portrayed as effeminate and helpless, and exhibit homoerotic inclinations; and, finally, monsters are not only male aggressors but sometimes female, and, by being creatures that defy ontological categories such as humanness, they trouble the stability of biological sex and gender. Thus, monsters that are coded male also exhibit strikingly feminine characteristics and often adopt narrative roles traditionally reserved for heroines.

Here, Marjorie Garber's recent work on cross-dressing lends a useful parallel: "[O]ne of the most important aspects of cross-dressing is the ways in which it offers a challenge to easy notions of binarity, putting into question the categories of 'female' and 'male,' whether they are considered essential or constructed, biological or cultural."[6] And she continues: "The transvestite . . . is both terrifying and seductive precisely because s/he incarnates and emblematizes the disruptive element that intervenes, signaling not just another category crisis, but . . . a crisis of 'category' itself."[7] Garber's description of the transvestite is consonant with the role of monsters in horror, since they too are interstitial creatures. They repeatedly transgress conventional categories of sexual and human identity, and they incite fear and desire in those they encounter.

While classic horror spectatorship is not equivalent to the textual manifestations of role-playing and disguise, there is much to suggest that horror's investment in a multiplicity of roles resonates with spectators. Yet the specific impact on viewers, though transgressive of conventional readings of the genre, may not be disruptive of the social sphere per se. Although horror promotes the adoption of multiple positions, sometimes aligning those positions with gender-bending, it is unclear to what degree spectatorial identifications and desires can be attributed progressive ideological significance outside the viewing context. This is especially true from the perspectives of identity politics and spectator subjectivity, for what classic horror may offer is a temporary release from the requisites of everyday identities while at the same time relying upon those identities as a fall-back position. Classic horror's dynamics suggest that cinematic spectatorship may generate multiple and sometimes transgressive positions from within a culture committed to the maintenance of rigid sex roles and gender behavior.

Mayne introduces this possibility when she writes of cinema's "safe zone": "Film theory has been so bound by the heterosexual symmetry that supposedly governs Hollywood cinema that it has ignored the possibility, for instance, that one of the distinct pleasures of the cinema may well be a 'safe zone' in which homosexual as well as heterosexual desires can be fantasized and acted out" (p. 97). In other words, cinema may allow heterosexual spectators to perform homosexual desires and vice versa. Classic horror, as the following arguments indicate, is one genre in which spectators are invited to play it safe, in Mayne's terms.

Sadism, Masochism, and Spectating Travails

In her now-classic contribution to feminist film theory "Visual Pleasure and Narrative Cinema," Laura Mulvey asserts that Hollywood's spectatorial pleasures are sadistic.[8] She also maintains that those pleasures find extratextual support in the heterosexual male viewer who identifies with the hero's dominant point-of-view and objectifying gaze. Mulvey's estimation of male spectatorship has been entrenched in feminist film analysis and implicitly embraced in a range of classic horror criticism (e.g., that by Roger Dadoun).[9]

The most striking challenge to Mulvey's estimation of sadistic male viewership comes from Gaylyn Studlar, who asserts the primacy of masochism: "Mulvey's deterministic, polarized model . . . cannot admit that the masculine look contains passive elements and can signify *submission to* rather than *possession of* the female."[10] Relying on Gilles Deleuze's work, Studlar aligns masochism with the male subject's pre-Oedipal identification with and subjection to a powerful mother.[11] Studlar believes that much of this male-maternal bond is replicated in the spectator's relationship to the cinema screen and endures, to a degree, in the Oedipal phase.

Mulvey and Studlar offer two primary approaches to spectatorship in feminist film theory—approaches that have been applied to horror cinema with varying degrees of theoretical complexity. The importance of sadism and masochism to horror film analysis cannot be overestimated. Perhaps more than any other genre, horror's narratives of monster attacks and human victimization appear to be perfect homes to sadism and masochism. That said, the degree to which models of sadistic and masochistic viewing can be easily applied to horror has yet to be determined. This section will evaluate film theories of sadism and masochism and their applicability to spectatorship.

Unlike Mulvey, Studlar proposes the viability of male opposite-sex identification.[12] However, problems remain. First, Studlar's outright rejection of sadism is an awkward inversion, versus negotiation, of Mulvey's work. Second, although she argues that opposite-sex desire and identification coexist in the Oedipal phase, Studlar's privileging of the pre-Oedipal relegates mature sexual desire to a later time—one that favors the father and not the mother. As in Mulvey's schema, the paternal realm accounts for sexual desire. Since Studlar claims that the pre-Oedipal is marked by a form of bisexuality that accommodates male identification with the maternal, male opposite-sex and female same-sex identifications are given preeminence.

As a result, male same-sex and female opposite-sex identification and desire are relegated to the Oedipal stage. Although Studlar does not go so far as to call the pre-Oedipal better, she privileges its relevance for spectatorship. By focusing on masochism, Studlar forecloses the dual operation of masochism and sadism in cinema spectatorship. In fact, she is at pains to argue that Freud's "supposition of a sadomasochistic duality" is wrong and that sadism and masochism are incontrovertibly distinct.[13] As I argue in the next section, Freud's claims, and not Studlar's, better approximate classic horror.

Here, I would like to address a film briefly in order to underscore the constraints of foregrounding either a sadistic Oedipal model or a masochistic pre-Oedipal paradigm of viewing pleasure. Tod Browning's classic vampire film *Dracula* (Universal, 1931) lends support to Mulvey's sadistic schema. Not only does the male-coded fiend possess an aggressive gaze, which he uses with panache, but he also assumes a distinctly paternal role. For example, in a scene at the symphony, Dracula enters the box occupied by Dr. Seward, his heroine-daughter Mina, her friend Lucy, and Mina's fiancé John. Dracula causes Mina's father to leave (on the pretext that he is wanted on the telephone) and takes up Seward's vacated paternal position next to Mina.

In a later sequence, in which Professor Van Helsing discovers that Dracula's image is not reflected in a mirror, the count occupies a paternal position again. At the end of the scene in question, Seward expresses concern for his daughter's frail health and urges her to her room. Only after Dracula reiterates Seward's command, however, does Mina heed the request. That is, Dracula too becomes her father—the man who bids her do his will. The conflation of Dracula with Mina's father is reinforced by shot alternations between three-shots, in which Mina, Seward, and Dracula appear, and two-shots, reflected in the mirror of a cigarette case, from which Dracula disappears. In a good portion of the images, therefore, we are aware of Dracula's presence (we hear his voice), but he is visually conflated with Seward, Mina's real father.

While this description of Dracula's Oedipal role is compelling and reinforces associations among classic horror, paternity, and sadism, it provides a partial description of the count's function. In both the symphony and mirror sequences, Dracula also occupies a maternal position. As in a range of other classic horror movies, such as *The Mummy* (Universal, 1932) and *The Old Dark House* (Universal, 1932), the maternal role is associated with death and absence in *Dracula*. Mina's mother never appears in the film, is never directly mentioned, and is not depicted in a portrait or photograph. Instead, the maternal is located in the roles the count assumes and the narrative fissures that populate this film.

For example, Dracula's entry into Seward's symphony box is precipitated by his hypnotism of an usher, whom he commands to inform Seward of a phone call. Before Seward departs, Mina notes: "If it's from home, will you say I'm spending the night in town with Lucy?" Mina's rather vague phrase, "If it's from home," suggests that the caller may be her mother, for who else would she need to alert that she is spending the night in town? After all, her other parental caretaker, her father, is in her company. If it is true that the caller is Mina's mother, however, it is also Dracula; for there is no real caller except him, except his hypnotically manufactured one.

That Mina's rapport with Dracula invokes her mother reinforces a point made by Linda Williams in "When the Woman Looks," namely, the rapports between horror's male-coded monsters and heroines signify repressed female sexuality.[14] In the context of *Dracula*, a film marked by a maternal absence, the erotic powers attributed to monsters by Williams may connote maternal *potency*. In fact, Dracula's alignment with the maternal is reinforced by the very lack of a mother figure in the film and by his ability to give birth to his victims. For the count serves as an object of fear and desire (Mina and Lucy are fascinated with and by him) of a rather different sort from the conventional men who populate the movie. Thus, while Dracula may be the film's sadistic father, he is also a mysterious and deadly mother.

The visual fluctuation between Dracula's presence and absence in the mirror scene reinforces the vampire's dual positioning as a maternal and paternal signifier; like Mina's father we see him; like her mother he disappears into narrative space. Dracula is, therefore, a familial icon, a role attributed to him by a number of horror critics.[15] In his analysis of the vampire in cinema, for example, Dadoun argues for the count's sexual and parental prowess by aligning him with the "phallic mother," a maternal figure entrenched in Oedipal configurations: a woman who fulfills the father's castrating powers.[16] In "Horror and the Monstrous-Feminine," Barbara Creed posits a more expansive version of maternal monstrosity and takes issue with Dadoun's reading. More than the phallic mother of the Oedipal stage, argues Creed, the monster signifies an "archaic mother," one who is powerful not in a castrating but in a regenerative sense.[17] Creed's version of the maternal reminds us of Studlar's masochistic schema; the mother/monster is a pre-Oedipal source of fascination and anxiety. She is not, as Dadoun would argue, a father in disguise.

Both Dadoun's and Creed's analyses of monstrosity are compelling, yet each alone is inadequate to account for the fluctuation of parental roles that characterizes Browning's *Dracula*. In contrast to theories intent on positing a temporal separation between the maternal and paternal, or the conflation of maternal functions with Oedipal or pre-Oedipal concerns, *Dracula* suggests the simultaneity of pre-Oedipal and Oedipal configurations and the conflation of sadism and masochism in a single character.

The separation of the maternal from the paternal is, therefore, a poor mode of accounting for horror's textual and extratextual fascination for viewers. Moreover, *Dracula* indicates that the pre-Oedipal/Oedipal distinction reduces the genre to parent-focused psychoanalytic configurations of identification and desire, and elides one of horror's most insistent terrors: the lures of that which lies outside the familial domain. From this perspective, Mulvey's Oedipal and Studlar's pre-Oedipal biases may each account for important identifications, but foreclose malleable sexual identities, especially those that depend on the rejection of familial relations.

Like Studlar's theory, Carol J. Clover's recent work on contemporary horror is a notable effort to move beyond the confines of Mulvey's model and is the only sophisticated study of horror to reject the primacy of sadism. According to Clover, neither masochism nor sadism is cinema's sole mode of operation. Horror, however, is more closely related to the former function: "The masochistic aesthetic is and always has been the dominant one in horror. . . . the fantasies in which horror cinema trades are particular (though not exclusively) tailored to male forms of masochistic experience (accounting for the disproportionate maleness of the audience).[18,19] Like Studlar, Clover expands male spectatorship beyond sadism. However, by turning the conventional estimation of viewing relations on its head, that is, by privileging masochism over sadism, she limits the genre's investment in both conditions. Moreover, Clover privileges a spectatorial model—masochism—which may be transgressive for male spectators, to whom she applies it, but is highly conventional and confining for women.

There is every indication that classic horror's theaters were filled with women as well as men. If the genre's contemporary texts are oriented primarily toward male forms of masochism and male subject-positions, as Clover argues, is there another model to account for female viewing pleasures in classic films—films to which female spectators were drawn?

S/he Loves Me, S/he Loves Me Not

In a compelling article, Lawrence S. Kubie notes that "from childhood, and throughout life . . . in varying proportions or emphases, the human goal seems almost invariably to be *both* sexes, with the inescapable consequence that we are always attempting in every moment and every act both to affirm and deny our gender identities."[20] Kubie provides us with an important entry into spectatorship. For if he is correct in proclaiming a human desire to be both sexes, a most important and undertheorized aspect of cinematic spectatorship may well be that viewing pleasures are derived as much from the unleashing of mechanisms of sexual similarity as difference.

In the context of classic horror, the drive to become both sexes, as the title of Kubie's article claims, is developed not only via an ontologically and biologically liminal monster but also by the very fact that the monster is a source of dread and fascination for protagonists and viewers alike. The monster often signifies the dissolution of sexual difference and stable gender traits, threatening to dislodge a range of patriarchal structures upon which characters and spectators depend. The monster also personifies the viewer's desire, as Kubie's work suggests, to blur conventional divisions within categories of biological sex and gender.

Here we must remember that in classic horror, the desire to be both sexes occurs in a narrative inflected by sadism and masochism and in which the monster is usually assumed to be male. The dual operations of these conditions in other types of films have been noted by theorists. For example, Hansen argues that Rudolph Valentino was an icon of female spectatorial ambivalence.[21] Spectatorial pleasure for women, argues Hansen of Valentino, is imbricated with sadomasochistic intimations: Valentino's persona, like viewer identifications and desires, oscillates between sadism and masochism.[22]

The concept of oscillation, often grounded in Freud's work on beating fantasies, comes closer than prior efforts to theorizing a model of spectatorship that can account for malleable subject-positions, such as those deployed in classic horror. But absent from previous analyses has been a recognition of the degree to which Freud is at pains to shut down a fluid definition of subjectivity in spite of the evidence provided by fantasies to the contrary.

Freud's analysis of male and female beating fantasies in "A Child Is Being Beaten" (1919) is useful for our consideration of classic horror not only because of what it may tell us about the coexistence of sadism and masochism in a viewing context but also because of what Freud fails to address in terms of viewing pleasures.[23] The bulk of "A Child Is Being Beaten" is devoted to four fantasies experienced by female patients. The fantasies are composed of three phases: two articulated by patients and one articulated by the analyst. The first phase—"a child is being beaten"—is noteworthy because the child who has the phantasy is not the one being struck. Freud concludes that the distance between the fantasizing child and the one appearing in it confirms that the phantasy "is certainly not masochistic."[24] He hesitates to call it sadistic, however, because the patient is not doing the beating herself.

Another crucial component of this phase is that the sex of the adults meting out the punishment is ambiguous. Although Freud asserts that "Later on this indeterminate grown-up person becomes recognizable clearly and unambiguously as the (girl's) *father*," Freud never indicates whether that recognition is articulated by the female patients themselves or the analyst. In fact, patients often refer to the adult as a teacher, a sexually ambiguous figure that is not necessarily a stand-in for the father. Moreover, in his analysis of male fantasies, Freud literally replaces the mother with the father. His insistence upon naming the sex of the adult and his assertion that the mother in males' fantasies is actually a father may reflect Freud's keen analytic mind, but also reveals Freud's propensity to shut down adult sexual ambiguity in the first instance and elevate a paternal signifier in both types of fantasies.

The second phase of the phantasy is articulated by Freud as "I am being beaten by my father."[27] Despite the fact that Freud admits that this phase "never had a real existence" and "is a construction of analysis," it is the most important stage and the linchpin of his interpretations.[28] Through his own constructions Freud arrives at the masochistic segment of the patient's phantasy, links it to her father, and consolidates a heterosexual incest motif.

Passing through the second stage, Freud phrases the final one as follows: "I am probably looking on." Freud contends that the little girl sees children (often boys) being beaten by her father. Yet, as the patient remembers it, she watches children being punished by a nonsexed adult. Of the third phase, Freud notes that in its passage through the unconscious second stage, it becomes attached to sexual excitement and sadism.[29] Although Freud implies that the female patient identifies with the adult doing the beating, he never articulates this point. Instead he focuses on the excitations aroused and on tracing the girl's attraction to her father.

In lieu of further examining the girl's responses, I would like to stop here in order to address the coextensive relationships among sadism, masochism, and multiple-sexed identifications that exist in the phantasies. Although Freud wavers between calling the phases sadistic, the very imaginary and unconscious quality of the second phase underscores his belief that sadism and masochism inform each other. For Freud to manufacture the second stage, that is, to align the patient with masochism, he depends on a sadistic buffer created by the first and third phases. Freud allows sadism and masochism to oscillate in female phantasies, and he suggests that they occupy central positions in a female experience similar to spectatorship.[30]

The patterns of identification and desire unleashed in the phantasies are shifting and complex. Since Freud notes that the sex of the child being beaten in the first and third phases is unimportant and since the second phase figures the phantasizing child in the positions previously occupied by boys and girls, cross-sex identification with a masochistic role is implied. What Freud overlooks, or chooses not to explore, is that cross-sex identification with sadistic adults is also possible on the part of the phantasizing child. This child-adult, cross-sex identification is implied when Freud refers to the third stage as sadistic. Yet in refusing to articulate that aspect, Freud insists on limiting the child's identificatory pattern to other children and confines her relationship with the adult to a perverse daughter-father link.

While Freud allows the children's sexes to fluctuate, he does not confer the same freedoms upon adults. By naming the adult a father, Freud creates sex where there is none and manufactures a social role—the parent—where there is none. Freud's maneuver is not surprising considering his theoretical reliance on the Oedipal family structure.[31] The effect is a streamlining of identification patterns, thus reducing the patient's sexual excitation to heterosexual incest. However, not only does a cross-sexed reading of the phases reveal that identification and desire may exceed the confines of heterosexuality (little girls identify with and desire other little girls), but it also throws into question the very parameters of identification and desire.

If the beating phantasies generate pleasure for the patients experiencing them and if the identifications and desires deployed fluctuate among sexes, ages, and social roles, then part of the pleasure may be that the phantasies generate and facilitate cross-sexed or nonspecified identifications and desires. That Freud is at pains to attribute the patient's excitation to a heterosexual framework consonant with the Electra complex does little to silence the plausibility that his analytic maneuvers disguise as much as they reveal. Freud masks the possibility that sexual excitation may result from the very fact that the identities of the adults and children are shifting. That possibility has significant implications for classic horror.

A malleable approach to the phantasies allows us to envision oscillations between sadism and masochism for male and female viewers. Although the phantasies mentioned belong to female patients, Studlar's recent claim is important: "Instead of suggesting a direct parallel between female patients and female spectators, the situation of Freud's female subjects more exactly duplicates cinema's positioning of *all* spectators."[32] Whereas Studlar sees that positioning as masochistic, an oscillation between sadism and masochism more fully approximates the phantasies. But cross-sex identification of females with males and adults, and nonsexed identification of females with adults allow for an expanded definition of viewing that accommodates the ambiguities of horror's characters, especially monsters.

This revised reading of "A Child Is Being Beaten" allows identifications and desires to be conferred upon those committing sadistic acts and those in receipt of punishment. Although in Freud's view the range of identifications available to females and males differ, his article allows for a fluid conceptualization of identificatory positions based on sex, gender, and sexual orientation (e.g., in the male phantasies, Freud attributes a homosexual object-choice to men whose mothers are read as fathers). Since the monster is an aggressor, an object of desire and identification, and a sufferer at once, an expanded view of the beating phantasies accommodates movements between sadism and masochism and between identification and desire in horror films.

Victor Halperin's *Supernatural* (Paramount, 1933) is a good example of a classic horror film that facilitates shifting identifications and desires. *Supernatural* traces Roma's travails after her twin brother John dies. Willing to believe anyone who promises her the chance to communicate with John, Roma is taken in by a fake spiritual guide. In the midst of her psychic explorations, Roma is possessed by the spirit of Ruth Rogen, a murderess executed at the film's start. Through metonymic devices, such as parallel editing, Ruth's and John's deaths are aligned, suggesting that it is no coincidence that Roma channels a dead woman's soul while trying to communicate with a dead man.

By the film's end, Roma's internalization of the fiend renders her status as the innocent heroine precarious: she begins to act sexually aggressive; she becomes monstrous. Roma's fiendish exploits are eventually compounded by the mystical appearance of John's face—without the psychic's intervention—late in the narrative. Like Ruth's migrating soul, John too travels among the living and stays close to Roma. While Ruth literally occupies Roma's body, John is not far behind—he is bonded to his twin in death as in life. In a sense, therefore, when Roma channels Ruth, John also participates in that transmigration of souls.

On the one hand, Roma is the movie's appealing and innocent heroine—an object of desire for the hero, Grant Wilson, a suitable locus of identification and (potentially) desire for viewers and a prime victim in Ruth's vengeful postmortem plans. On the other hand, Roma internalizes a monstrous figure—a woman framed for the mass murder of a group of men found dead in her Greenwich Village apartment. Furthermore, the ghost of John lurks nearby, revealing his translucent visage in the same manner that Ruth appears to the spectator. Like other classic monsters, Roma crosses boundaries: she is at once a heroine, a fiend, and a signifier of her male twin. Ruth and John too are liminal figures: they move easily between the realms of the visible and invisible, the living and the dead.

Roma's contradictory on-screen role suggests that she is an equally complex object of identification and desire for spectators. Alternately exhibiting behavior that connotes passivity, femininity, masculinity, sexual depravity, and danger, Roma is a fluctuating center of attention. A good part of her fascination resides in her ability to move among her roles with ease. That she is an object of desire in spite of or, perhaps, because of her monstrosity is suggested by her name, which spelled backward reads *Amor*. That she is intended to elicit the spectator's fear is indicated by her association with Ruth, a calculating woman who is anything but sympathetic. And that Roma allows for cross-sex identification and desire is hinted at by both her intimate rapport with her dead brother and the doubling that is inherent in their status as twins.

This reading of *Supernatural* expands the spectatorial options available to viewers in previous writing on horror. However, in an attempt to confer oscillating positions upon female and male viewers, I have neatly removed the specificity of biological sex from the visual realm. By describing Roma as a contradictory figure, I explore the multiple identifications and desires she may inspire in sexually unspecified viewers. In other words, by accepting Studlar's claim that the female patient's oscillating experience can be applied to men, the sex and gender traits that may well differentiate viewers and their experiences of classic horror are overlooked.

While one of my projects is to challenge a polarized model of spectatorship, it would be imprudent to discard altogether the relationships between biological sex, gender, and horror. This is especially true since culture often invites differential responses to the genre (e.g., heterosexual women are expected to scream, and heterosexual men are called upon to prove their mettle and calm their female companions). In order to develop mechanisms to more comprehensively account for forms of subjective specificity such as biological sex and sexual orientation, the remainder of this chapter is devoted to an evaluation of theories of spectatorship that address sexual identity and to the introduction of spectatorship-as-drag.

There is yet another reason to move beyond the beating fantasies. Although the fantasies depict fluctuating sexual and social identities (the adults are alternately nonsexed, fathers, mothers, teachers, and parents), they still rely on the ontological category of humanness. Classic horror relishes the transgression of that category by introducing that which is nonhuman into the family. By being more-than-human and more-than-a-man and/or a-woman, monsters highlight the constructed aspects of sexual identity. As a result, a trope aligned with theatrical display and the performance of roles provides an important addition to the sadomasochistic paradigm.

Horror is Such a Drag

"Clothing typical of one sex worn by a person of the opposite sex" is how Merriam Webster defines the term *drag*. It is a sartorial inversion, a reversal of the cultural relationship between biological sex and sex-role displays. The transvestite is in drag whenever she or he wears men's or women's clothing, as the case may be. As noted earlier, drag's relationship to classic horror includes its transgression of sex roles, as well as connotations of terror and allure. Cross-dressing, like monstrosity, poses a crisis of categories for those who perform and watch it.

Drag provides a sartorial scenario that engages fluid identifications and desires. For example, despite the fact that most male transvestites are heterosexual, drag is associated with homosexual performances, thus troubling the boundary between heteroperformance and homoperformance practices. Drag also allows us to situate classic horror's preoccupation with the adoption of disguises and theatrical displays in a more explicit framework. Like the form of drag defined by Merriam Webster, the monster often invokes both sexes at once. For example, when Ling Moy agrees to continue her father's reign of terror in the Fu Manchu film *Daughter of the Dragon*, she tells the dying patriarch that she will become his son. The fiend personifies a theoretical movement past the binaries of biological sex. In being like men and women, but not being men and women, monsters disrupt categories of sexual difference and humanness. They pose the threat that sexual identities are unstable and that so-called essential identities, which are assumed to lie beneath the drag costume, are manufactured.

Writing about underlying messages in transvestite self-help magazines, Marjorie Garber comments, "The social critique performed by these transvestite magazines for readers who are not themselves cross-dressers is to point out the degree to which *all* women cross-dress as women when they produce themselves as artifacts."[33] In order to construct the signifier *woman* via accoutrements such as clothing, jewelry, and makeup, Garber confirms that many women engage in drag. They performsexual identity and adopt a costumed role.

Performance is a privileged trope in recent gay and lesbian writing. Noting that the homosexual/heterosexual binary creates a tension between the concepts of original and copy, Judith Butler intones, "if it were not for the notion of the homosexual *as* copy, there would be no construct of heterosexuality as *origin*. . . . the entire framework of copy and origin proves radically unstable as each position inverts into the other."[34] If sexual identities cannot be traced to an origin, Butler argues, *"gender is a kind of imitation for which there is no original."*[35] Butler uses drag to focalize the imitative and manufactured qualities of gender and identity. Although, in its popular guise, drag refers to a sex and gender performance enacted by gay men, it is also part of a more complex sex and gender continuum, as Garber's cross-dressing comment reinforces.[36] From the perspective of classic horror, drag is a useful means of highlighting the precarious status of sexual identity and opens a door to theories of spectatorship that move beyond the dualities male/female and homosexual/heterosexual.

In her book on female impersonators of the 1960s and 1970s, *Mother Camp,* Esther Newton describes drag's disruption of binaries:

> [Drag] symbolizes two somewhat conflicting statements concerning the sex-role system. The first statement is that the sex-role system is really natural: therefore homosexuals are unnatural. . . . The second symbolic statement of drag questions the "naturalness" of the sex-role system *in toto;* if sex-role behavior can be achieved by the "wrong" sex, it logically follows that it is in reality also achieved, not inherited, by the "right" sex.[37]

The symbolism of drag resonates for classic horror, for the monster poses the tension between Newton's symbolic statements: (1) as a monster, a figure who transgresses ontological classifications of humanness and sexual difference, s/he confirms the normalcy of those categories, and (2) the fiend is a reminder that monstrosity and normalcy are interdependent, that the unnatural resides within the natural and vice versa, and that both are constructed.

Newton argues that one of the most compelling aspects of female impersonators is that "they do not consider themselves to be females and neither do audiences. So if one is *really* male, it is even more of a feat to look like a glamorous and exciting woman."[38] A similar interaction between knowledge and disavowal characterizes spectators' relationships to horror. While viewers may, on one level, accept the male-coding of most classic monsters and be convinced of their humanness, on another level audiences know that fiends are monstrous and that they defy ontological categories. Spectators trade in a process of disavowal by denying that fiends are inhuman and attributing stable sex and gender traits to them. Yet the terms of horror demand that disavowal be subtended by the acceptance of monstrosity. In a sense, viewers practice reverse fetishism; in lieu of devising elaborate means to disguise the creature's monstrosity—its "lack" of humanness—they encounter narrative and visual tropes intended to unmask monsters. Instead of revealing an inner core, however, unmasking provides more layers of drag, and instead of positing the stability of humanness, heroes and heroines are implicated in the realm of monstrosity.[39]

Michael Curtiz's *Mystery of the Wax Museum* (Warner Bros., 1933), for example, relishes and underplays the removal of the fiend's face mask. Having been burned in a fire that destroyed his first wax museum, Ivan traverses the film wearing and removing a mask that hides his molten features. Although a series of narrative cues builds toward the act of unmasking, that gesture is anticipated by the audience. Viewers already know that beneath the veneer of Ivan's mask lies a disfigured visage, a face that itself has an artificial look. Furthermore, the disguise that Ivan wears to hide his burns is identical to his appearance before he was maimed. If his original features are the essence of his visage, that essence is aligned with the constructed mask that Ivan later discards. Like Butler's arguments, this suggests there is no real Ivan, no original, but only a series of appearances.

The question that arises is: what effect do textual forms of drag and role-playing have on spectators? As a sexually ambiguous figure, the monster prevents a rigid one-to-one pattern with female or male viewers; male viewers may identify with a male-coded monster, but not on the basis of a stable sexual identity. Here the concept of drag makes an important contribution to classic horror criticism by introducing a schism between character and role. The necessary theoretical leap is the assumption that that schism can be transposed, to varying degrees, to the realm of viewing. Just as horror's characters highlight both the strength and artificiality of conventional sex roles, so too may spectatorial reactions play out traditional identifications and desires while also lending a performative and transgressive dimension to viewer responses.

Conceiving of spectatorship-as-drag provides the means with which to conceptualize conventional and more malleable reactions to on-screen characters. The first of these is promoted by dominant culture. "[Gender] is *performative* in the sense that it constitutes as an effect the very subject it appears to express," writes Butler. "It is compulsory performance in the sense that acting out of line with heterosexual [and other] norms brings with it ostracism, punishment, and violence, not to mention the transgressive pleasures produced by those very prohibitions."[40] The performance of gender is often constrained by traditional cultural norms; however, the viewing sphere—a locale aligned with a phantasy scenario—seems a likely place in which those norms may, if only temporarily, break down or oscillate. Thus, a female spectator viewing a classic horror film may respond as culture dictates, with screams, but she may also aggressively identify with and desire the monster whose exploits transgress the sex role she usually assumes.

The Sex and Gender Limits of Spectatorship

The reigning feminist models of spectatorship have centered on familiar binaries such as male/female and heterosexual/homosexual. Even those theories that propose the dissolution of oppositions (e.g., models of bisexual viewing) eventually return to bifurcated concepts, reminding us of the need to theorize spectatorship differently—performatively.

In the introduction to her book *The Women Who Knew Too Much*, Tania Modleski notes that Alfred Hitchcock's films portray a feminine ambivalence that undermines male mastery. Modleski asserts that one of her "intent[s] is to problematize *male* spectatorship and masculine identity in general"; she explores the concept of double identification, in which men identify with characters of both sexes.[41] According to Modleski, male identification with and desire for Hitchcock's heroines aligns men with female bisexuality and reminds "man of his *own* bisexuality . . . a bisexuality that threatens to subvert his 'proper' identity."[42]

Modleski's alignment of male ambivalence with female bisexuality is a noteworthy attempt to loosen male spectatorship from the sadistic, heterosexual confines of Mulvey's model. However, Modleski's version of bisexuality is circuitous: it reveals itself to men only via women and therefore via a woman's, and not a man's, inherent bisexuality. One of the limitations of this concept, in addition to its equation of male spectatorship with female viewing (a refreshing reversal of sexist claims that posit males as the norm), is that the form of bisexuality alluded to by Modleski is one in which identification is privileged over desire. Shared by a number of feminist critics, this model depends on the female infant's identification with the mother and, therefore, does little to trouble heterosexuality. It follows, then, that the male spectator's brand of bisexuality in Modleski's schema is as constrained as that of the bisexual female, that is, he may be "bi" in terms of identification, but can remain heterosexual in terms of desire.

In an article on Hitchcock's *Strangers on a Train*, Robert J. Corber grapples with the often unintended heterosexist biases of much feminist film theory. In response, Corber urges for a closer look at psychoanalysis: "the male spectator's identification with the hero *always* involves the repression of a homosexual object-cathexis that recalls his pre-Oedipal attachment to the father."[43] Like Modleski, Corber appeals to the pre-Oedipal to account for same-sex forms of identification. Unlike female bisexuality, however, Corber explicitly eroticizes the male spectator's identification with on-screen heroes. Yet as I noted earlier of Studlar's masochistic model, the valorization of the pre-Oedipal limits the re-visionist scope of theories of viewing.

Corber's article returns us to the problems inherent in theories of spectatorship that privilege either Oedipal or pre-Oedipal configurations. As J. Laplanche and J.-B. Pontalis note of the pre-Oedipal/Oedipal division in Freud's work: "one may either accentuate the exclusiveness of the dual relationship [between the pre-Oedipal and the Oedipal] or else identify signs of the Oedipus complex so early on that it becomes impossible to isolate a strictly preoedipal phase."[44] If Oedipus indeed intervenes in the pre-Oedipal, as Laplanche and Pontalis suggest he might, then Corber, Modleski, and Studlar are wrong to privilege the earlier temporal mode and attribute all malleable sexual identities and identifications to it.

By relying upon the pre-Oedipal phase, Corber's theory treads close to the limitations he critiques. He reduces the field of sexual identity to a pitched battle between homosexuality and heterosexuality. Although I sympathize with the lure of discussing homosexual desire as both central and preexistent to heterosexuality, theorizing the primacy of homosexuality manufactures a whole new set of constraints.[45] Surely Corber is wrong when he assumes that all male gazes are marked by homosexual identification and desire. The question remains: how can we account for the specificity of male homosexual and heterosexual gazing?

Ellis Hanson inadvertently provides a preliminary response in his article "The Undead." Unlike Corber, when Hanson addresses male viewing patterns, he asks some important questions: "Is the gaze the gays? What could it mean for a man to engage the gaze of another man? In psychoanalytic terms, such a gaze would be a form of madness. . . . The gay male gaze is the gaze of the male vampire: he with whom one is forbidden to identify."[46] Instead of beginning with a consideration of men in toto, as Corber attempts, Hanson focuses on gay men.

Hanson's proposal that homosexual gazing is analogous to the look of a male vampire fits neatly with a consideration of classic horror. For Hanson implies a theorization of viewing patterns based on social and not only sexual categories. If a gay male gaze is horrifying, part of its horror resides in the recognition by gay man and monster of their similar status within patriarchy. In other words, while not all male gazes are informed by homosexuality, some are, and, in the realm of horror, homosexuality (a culturally monstrous identity) fosters desire for and identification with a socially marginalized fiend on the basis of shared marginalization.

Moving beyond the realm of homosexuality, this approach indicates that viewer identification may be forged on the basis of shared social status. In other words, if a homosexual viewer's identifications exceed the traits of sex, gender, and sexual orientation by including social standing, then it follows that other groups may also identify via means other than biological sex and gender. Thus, identification and desire on the basis of race, class, ethnicity, nationality, and so on, may be as strong as sexual identity.

The concept of viewing based on social categories raises an important question: to what degree do the sexual and social identities of viewers determine the identifications and desires deployed in viewing? Although gay and lesbian work has focused on homosexual subjectivity, the thorny question of the equivalence of a spectator's everyday identity with viewing positions has yet to be fully addressed. Having raised the issue, queries emerge. Is it possible for a male homosexual viewer to identify with and desire a female character? Or, for that matter, is it possible for a heterosexual male to both identify with and desire a hero?[47] While it is important to theorize a space in which gays and lesbians access same-sex desire, that approach does not exhaust all venues of viewer identification.

The theories that dominate the field describe viewing pleasures via similarities (e.g., women identify with heroines on the basis of biological sex) and sexual drives (e.g., straight women are romantically invested in heroes due to heterosexual desire). What is left out is the possibility that spectators also identity against themselves. Viewing patterns depend as much on the dissolution of a one-to-one viewer-character relationship as they do on its perpetuation.[48] In fact, as Mayne notes of cinema's "safe zone," identification in opposition may be one of cinema's primary pleasures—viewers may relish the ability to escape their everyday social, racial, sexual, and economic identities.[49] This concept, thus, reminds us of narrative cinema's importance as a phantasy scenario, as both a confirmation of and temporary release from the subjectivities engaged in by spectators in their everyday lives.

The ability to identify against oneself—spectatorship as a form of drag—is invoked by Mulvey in "Afterthoughts on 'Visual Pleasure and Narrative Cinema.'" Female spectators, Mulvey argues, oscillate between passivity and transvestitism. In the first role they are allied with on-screen women; in the second they adopt a male point-of-view. While the latter approach includes cross-sex connotations, Mulvey views it as conventional. Nowhere does she allow for the fact that spectatorial transvestitism may offer women the pleasures of identifying against their socially prescribed roles. She asserts that to give men what they want, and to access male powers, women imagine themselves into male positions.[50] Doing so offers female spectators little more than the elusive experience of wearing the emperor's clothes.[51]

In "Film and the Masquerade," Mary Ann Doane tried to theorize a way out of the constrictions posed by Mulvey. As she notes, the passive position introduced by Mulvey constructs female viewing as over-identification with women and images. Female overidentification is generated by women's pre-Oedipal alignment with their sexually alike mothers; overidentification is, thus, a side effect of bisexuality. Lacking the ability to fetishize their mothers, according to Doane, women cannot assume a position of difference, as can men, and thereby engage in overidentification and masochism.[52]

As an alternative to Mulvey's spectatorial options—transvestitism and masochism—Doane suggests that female viewing may also be a masquerade, a performance in which the spectator creates distance from the image. That distanced position is not unlike the form of drag mentioned earlier vis-à-vis transvestite self-help magazines; Doane's masquerading woman, as we will see in the next section, constructs her femininity as a role.[53]

Doane's theorization of female overidentification is based on the model of bisexuality mentioned previously. Female bi*sexuality* is, in a sense, a misnomer in that it functions as the means with which to articulate pre-Oedipal identifications between women and their mothers at the expense of addressing adult, female, same-sex desire. Despite this limitation, female bisexuality has been mobilized as a progressive means of theorizing spectatorship. As noted earlier, Modleski's work on Hitchcock is, like Doane's, based on a pre-Oedipal valorization of the maternal. Modleski, however, goes an important step further when she addresses lesbianism and asserts that "the desire of women for other women" sends a subversive ripple through culture.[54] Yet, ultimately, Modleski and Doane suggest that the desire of one woman for another is explicable either as a form of regression or as an idealized relationship, both of which are part of a mother-daughter dyad.

This approach is replicated by Williams in her work on horror cinema. By noting that the monster and the heroine are sexually alike in their shared difference from the male, Williams repeats the core argument of female bisexuality; she accentuates identification with the monster while downplaying an attraction based on similarity: "The strange sympathy and affinity that often develops between the monster and the girl may thus be less an expression of sexual desire . . . and more a flash of sympathetic identification."[55] Desire based on sexual sameness is not only rendered secondary but is almost effaced.

These feminist approaches have, therefore, utilized bisexuality as a theoretical way out of the dead end offered by heterosexual models of spectatorship. But the form of bisexuality employed confirms the primacy of heterosexual desire. Not surprisingly, this approach has come under attack by lesbian theorists such as Sue-Ellen Case, who argues that "the queer" occupies an ontological and social position between the living and the undead. Case uses this perspective to critique heterosexist feminist theory:

> This "woman," then, in Doane, Williams, and others, is really heterosexual woman. Though her desire is aroused vis-à-vis another woman (a monstrous occasion), and they are totally proximate, they identify with rather than desire one another. . . . What melds monster to woman is not lesbian desire . . . [but] daughter emulating mother in the Oedipal triangle with the absent male still at the apex.[56]

Case is correct to highlight the heterosexism of feminist theory; despite her use of a vampire trope in the remainder of the article, however, her work is limited for classic horror spectatorship.

In addressing the vampire of folklore, Case notes that "proximity is a central organizing principle—not only in the look, but also in the mise en scène."[57] While I do not take issue either with Case's use of the vampire as a queer icon or with her attempts to theorize "queerly," her valorization of proximity is troubling. Case fails to articulate how queer proximity is different from Doane's, Modleski's, and Williams's bisexual proximity. In her argument, queer proximity is a departure only insofar as it insists on same-sex desire. Case's use of proximity to transgress ontology and valorize same-sex desire creates a system in which sameness occupies a complementary role to that held by sexual difference in Freudian psychoanalysis. Homosexuality, then, is the monstrous invert to heterosexuality.[58]

Whereas some heterosexist theories of spectatorship privilege the importance of difference and distance to spectatorial pleasures or valorize overidentification to articulate a nonsexual female bisexuality, homosexist accounts valorize sameness for the purpose of sexualizing identification, (i.e., rendering desire and identification alike). All of these approaches center on familiar binaries: male/female and heterosexual/homosexual. Thus Case's focus on proximity and sameness cuts out the play of differences in homosexual relationships. Like theories that favor overidentification, Case also eliminates the role of similarity in heterosexuality and the potential play of sameness and difference in relationships that fall outside the hetero/homo divide.

In *Epistemology of the Closet*, Eve Kosofsky Sedgwick argues that the conflation of homosexual desire with identification is an old one in our culture:

> [T]he fact that "homosexuality," being . . . posited on definitional similarity, was the first modern piece of sexual definition that simply took as nugatory the distinction between relations of identification and relations of desire, meant that it posed a radical question to cross-gender relations and, in turn, to gender discourse in which a man's desire for a woman could not guarantee his difference from her—in which it might even, rather, suggest his likeness to her.[59]

According to Sedgwick, one of the dangers of homosexuality is that its assumed conflation of identification with desire throws into question the conventional separation of those responses in heterosexuality. But what Sedgwick fails to articulate is that the reverse might also be true. The assumed separation of identification and desire—the belief that heterosexual desire is based on difference—also troubles the focus on sameness in homosexual rapports. There is every indication that both homosexual and heterosexual relations engage processes of identification and desire that rely on differences as well as similarities. Addressing that possibility, however, runs the risk of shifting the balance of politics, as well as of desire. For if both homosexual and heterosexual desires engage processes of similarity and difference, then the social and political separation of those orientations may be forced in a more profound sense than previously acknowledged.

Masquerading Horrors

Theories of spectatorship that propose the performative dimensions of viewing, such as masquerade and transvestitism, provide a first step in extricating film studies from favored binaries. By aligning viewing processes with performance, with the adoption of sex, gender, and, potentially, other disguises (e.g., race), we can locate a starting point from which to expand theories of classic horror spectatorship and allow for the simultaneity of similarity and difference.[60]

Spectatorship-as-drag accommodates aspects of viewing previously deemed mutually exclusive. For example, drag suggests that proximity to the image (usually aligned with female masochism or lesbianism) and distance from the image (conventionally associated with male viewing) are potential components of all spectatorship. Drag serves as a viable spectating paradigm in that female overidentification can be explained as the internalization of dominant norms, and distance from the image is explicable as the generation of schisms among the subject, his or her social roles, and his or her relationship to characters. Drag acknowledges the constructed aspects of role acquisition, points out the space between actor and costume, and accounts for the lures of both conventional and unconventional on- and off-screen performances.

When Esther Newton argues that drag "implies *distance* between the actor and the role or 'act,'" she describes a process similar to Mary Ann Doane's arguments in "Film and the Masquerade."[61] Noting that conventional concepts of female identity formation rely on overidentification, Doane mobilizes masquerade to separate the woman from the screen. According to her, a more liberating female spectatorship depends on distance. Relying on Joan Riviere's case study, Doane offers a paradigm aligned with performance.

In her 1929 article "Womanliness as a Masquerade," Riviere describes the travails of a patient who performs femininity in response to her professional success with men. According to Riviere, the patient's display of her intellectual skills to men signifies her possession of powers conventionally deemed masculine and male. (In psychoanalytic terms, Riviere phrases this as the patient's "exhibition of herself in possession of the father's penis, having castrated him.")[62] In order to compensate for her male attributes, womanliness is "assumed and worn as a mask, both to hide the possession of masculinity and to avert the reprisals expected if she was found to possess it."[63] In this schema, masculinity is dangerous to the woman who displays it (she risks retribution from men) and to the men whom she encounters (they risk castration from women).

Masquerade is a reaction-formation that provides protection and disguises a female threat to men under the veneer of a socially prescribed role. As a mask, femininity generates distance between the patient and the behavior she adopts. As a form of drag, the woman who performs her femininity is, through her performance, separated from the conventional female role.[64] Doane utilizes the distance between actor and role to loosen female spectatorship from overidentification. Although, as I noted earlier, privileging proximity or distance in any theory is problematic, Doane's work on masquerade remains important for its introduction of a performative trope into spectatorship and for its focus on Riviere's article. However, whereas Doane relies on Riviere to analyze the heterosexual woman's masquerading options, I prefer to use the case study, and the concept of masquerade, to address a range of viewing positions.

In classic horror, masquerade provides a productive means of explaining the popularity and performativity of conventional male and female responses to the genre. The traditional reactions of the female spectator (e.g., screams and eye-covering) can be explained in part as a function of masquerade. Although some women may be truly horrified by on-screen images, it is likely that others experience more than terror. Here, Riviere's case study is instructive. The patient uses her femininity to mask threatening qualities: her accession to male roles, identification with masculinity and men, possible danger to men, and potential desire for women.[65] Each of these variables is fostered at the textual level in many classic horror films and, in the context of patriarchal culture, may well demand a form of spectatorial masking that disguises gender-bending.

This is especially true in terms of sexual orientation, for Western patriarchy assumes that displays of femininity and heterosexuality are synonymous for women. Again, Riviere's article provides an alternative lesson. Although Riviere's patient is said to be heterosexual (she is married) and though masquerade aids her in attaining male sexual interest, hints of homosexuality persist. In writing of research conducted by S. Ferenczi (1916), Riviere notes, "homosexual men exaggerate their heterosexuality as a 'defence' against homosexuality." Riviere implies that heterosexuality is donned as a mask, a gendered disguise (i.e., it involves the conventional display of masculinity). Riviere continues, "I shall attempt to show that women who wish for masculinity may put on a mask of womanliness to avert anxiety and the retribution feared from men."[66]

Whereas Riviere shifts easily from male sexual orientation to female gender behavior, her second comment literally follows the first, implying a rhetorical and logical connection between them. In other words, if, as Riviere claims, homosexual men sometimes exaggerate their masculinity to pass as heterosexual, it follows that female exaggeration of femininity may sometimes cover homosexuality. Although these arguments are not immutable (e.g., some homosexual men use masculinity to confirm masculinity and not cover femininity, and certain heterosexual women masquerade to disguise their interests in male powers and not to mask lesbian desire), they are possible examples of the masquerade.

Masquerade's mobility is reinforced by Riviere when she addresses male homosexuality a second time. Unlike her first example, which privileges heterosexuality and masculinity as disguises, in her second citation she elevates femininity and femaleness. In writing of a homosexual man who was excited by his image in a mirror, with his hair parted and wearing a bow tie, she notes, "These extraordinary 'fetishes' turned out to represent a *disguise of himself* as his sister; the hair and bow were taken from her. His conscious attitude was a desire to *be* a woman."[67] Whereas masquerade promotes the illusion of heterosexuality and masculinity in the first example, it simultaneously creates and masks the impression of femaleness in the second.

It is but a small leap from the examples of masquerade in Riviere's work to heterosexual men, for if some heterosexual women use womanliness as a masquerade of their accession to male-coded prerogatives, it follows that some men may well use "manliness" to disguise their investment in femininity. With that perspective in mind, let us turn to an example from classic horror. At the beginning of *Dracula* when the count tells his vampire-wives to leave his guest, Renfield, alone so that he can have him to himself, multiple identifications and desires may be experienced by heterosexual male spectators. Yet the invitation to identify with Renfield as a victim, Dracula as an attacker, and both as homosexual object-choices may very well take form in a straight male spectator's refusal to display signifiers of fear.[68] In other words, a heteromale spectator of *Dracula* may identify with and desire feminine and nonheterosexual positions beneath a conventional and brave response. The scenario becomes more complex when we acknowledge that a gay viewer may respond in the same manner (i.e., with bravery and a refusal to display fear). In both cases, identification with and desire for Dracula and Renfield may exist beneath society's expected and promoted spectatorial response.

Writing about Doane's theorization of the masquerade, Teresa de Lauretis inquires, "The question remains . . . whether this distance [between the woman and the image] can in fact be assumed by the straight female spectator in relation to the image of woman on the screen: how would a spectator 'flaunt' her femininity, in the dark of the movie theater?"[69] I would like to use de Lauretis's question as a point of departure not only to provide a tentative answer but also to reconfigure masquerade as a model of spectatorship that allows heterosexuals, homosexuals, and bisexuals to display similar behavior.

First, to suggest how classic horror's heterosexual female spectators flaunt their femininity in a movie theater, I need only reinvoke conventional responses to horror described earlier: namely, a woman can scream bloody murder, cower behind the shoulder of her date, and alternately cover and uncover her eyes in a visual game of masking and unmasking not unlike that which often occurs on-screen. Thus, female spectators who watch horror films are assumed to flaunt their femininity all the time. However, there may also be a performative dimension to their display of terror. Here, a marketing example from *The Motion Picture Herald* lends an important perspective. During each screening of *Mark of the Vampire* (MGM, 1935) in Bridgeport, Connecticut, in 1935, a female viewer was planted in the audience by the exhibitor.[70] At predetermined moments, she began to scream and feigned fainting. Ushers then removed her from the theater and whisked her away in an ambulance that waited at the curb outside the theater doors. As the Bridgeport ploy testifies, traditionally feminine responses to a horror film may be genuine for some female spectators, but they are also loaded cultural roles that are intentionally deployed in excessive and theatrical forms. The Bridgeport case is but an extreme example of the masquerade that some female viewers may exhibit in similar spectatorial contexts.

Second, de Lauretis's query raises a question linked to lesbian subjectivity: how can lesbian spectators access the masquerade if they are not as concerned with masquerading for men, as is Riviere's patient? There are a number of ways in which to respond. It can be argued that lesbian spectators cannot masquerade, because that process is put into play for the benefit of men.[71] Since, for argument's sake, lesbianism represents rejection of men as object-choices, lesbians would not need to masquerade. As a result, their access to the female image is necessarily more direct than that of the masquerading heterosexual woman and is destined to replicate bisexual overidentification. Or, conversely, lesbians cannot masquerade, precisely because they desire women, a fact that, according to enduring stereotypical assumptions, links lesbianism to masculinity. That is, lesbians cannot use womanliness as a masquerade, because they exhibit signs of manliness instead.

Despite the fact that lesbians' objects of desire are not men (a contestable definition of sexual orientation), living in a patriarchal culture requires that some lesbians either must or choose to masquerade (or "pass," to use another term) in order to access certain powers.[72] Masquerade is not only the heterosexual woman's means of disguising independence and a will-to-power beneath a mask of womanliness, or her opportunity to view an image of a woman at a greater distance; it also serves as some lesbians' and bisexual women's means of disguising their cinematic and everyday desires behind the same mask.[73]

Asking how the heterosexual woman gazing at a female image can flaunt her femininity in a darkened theater is only part of the point. The more pressing question is how do women either consciously or unconsciously access masquerade as a viewing position, i.e., how can their viewing responses be seen both as traditional and as generating a distance from traditional social and sexual roles? What is likewise crucial is analyzing texts that provide imputed positions in which female spectators are invited to masquerade, such as classic horror films.

The most telling question for some lesbians may not be how do female spectators masquerade, but what happens when a lesbian or bisexual woman flaunts her femininity not only as a signifier of her distance from the image, or as a means of protecting herself from patriarchal wrath, but also as a disguise of her erotic investment in the image (an investment that is not equivalent to overidentification because it is motivated by same-sex desire)? The lesbian or bisexual woman who flaunts her femininity in response to the sight of an on-screen woman engages in masquerade in as performative a manner as the heterosexual woman described by Doane. In assuming a feminine position vis-à-vis the female image, or the image of her monstrous double, the lesbian or bisexual woman assumes a role that patriarchal culture and psychoanalysis deem impossible: she surveys a female object of desire from a position of femininity. Whereas that variation of masquerade can by no means account for all viewing positions, it poses a more expansive means of conceptualizing masquerade as the dual operation of distance (the lesbian flaunts femininity) and proximity (one woman desires another).

A scene from Tod Browning's *Mark of the Vampire* (MGM, 1935) provides a case in point about the potential variations of female masquerade. The first attack/seduction scene in this vampire tale occurs on a terrace outside the heroine's home. In a suggestive sequence, shots of the vampire Luna walking toward the camera are intercut with images of the heroine, Irena, who rises to meet the fiend. Inserts of a male vampire looking on are interspersed throughout the sequence. Irena arrives at the terrace and sits down in a trancelike state, all the while staring at the approaching Luna. Just before Luna bends over the heroine, Irena swoons.

One type of lesbian spectator watching this scene may well flaunt her femininity by gasping at the horrifying sight of the monster's advances. But beneath that feminine veneer she may simultaneously harbor both a masculine-connoted identification with the aggressive fiend and a homosexual desire for the women engaged in an erotic embrace. In fact, a heterosexual woman watching this scene may display and experience the same masquerading and illicit responses, thereby expanding the applicability of drag beyond the confines of lesbianism and bisexuality, i.e., beyond the sexual orientations that spectators live out when not in a movie theater. Here, we are reminded of Mayne's characterization of cinema as a safe zone: a space in which a good dose of spectatorial pleasure may be grounded in viewers' accession to identifications and desires that contrast with their everyday identity.

Masquerade provides a useful spectatorial position for classic horror. Not only does it allow for the simultaneity of multiple identifications and desires, it also accommodates an interplay between difference and similarity (e.g., gay male masquerade may involve identification with and/or against masculinity). As a genre that trades in patriarchal dictums (women are often victimized by monstrous males) and that disrupts those expectations (women are aligned with monsters, and fiends possess ambiguous sexual traits), masquerade serves as an appropriate description of the genre's dual operations of convention and transgression,

As a disguise that connotes resistance to traditional behavior, masquerade accounts for many of classic horror's textual and extra-textual operations. It is an apt response to the images of a genre that consistently trades in ambiguous sexual identities and represents the concept of disguise as a narrative, visual, and marketing trope. Although direct relationships do not always exist between images and viewers, masquerade allows spectators to maintain the illusion of traditional displays while disguising unconventional ones.

In terms of drag, masquerade and transvestitism are similar processes: they both foreground the constructed quality of sex roles. Yet Doane, like Mulvey, quickly discards the usefulness of transvestitism.[74] She argues that whereas it is logical for a woman in a patriarchal culture to want to pose as a man, patriarchy cannot account for "why a woman might flaunt her femininity, [and] produce herself as an excess of femininity."[75] Although Doane is correct in assuming that patriarchy can more easily incorporate female adoptions of male personae than female personae, a degree of transgression inheres in any activity that foregrounds the manufactured quality of roles. Furthermore, by describing a process in which identification runs counter to the subject's social position, transvestitism allows us to systematically conceive of identification-in-opposition.

For example, if a heterosexual woman identifies with a heterosexual hero, she identifies against her own constructed identity on the basis of sex (she is not a man) and sexual orientation (in her everyday life, she is not lesbian). This notion is even more striking if we shift the terms of the participants and position a heterosexual man identifying with a heterosexual woman's point of view. Like the female spectator, the man may identify against his own identity on the basis of sex and sexual orientation. The pattern continues to shift if we posit a lesbian viewer identifying with a heterosexual male. Although the lesbian may identify against herself on the basis of biological sex, she identifies with the hero through the operations of desire. As a mode of spectating, these examples suggest that transvestitism not only depends on differences but also accommodates similarities.

In Karl Freund's *The Mummy* (Universal, 1932), for example, identification with the heroine is reinforced by point-of-view structures and narrative events. In the case that a male spectator identifies with Helen's terrified reactions at the film's conclusion, when the fiend threatens to kill the heroine and transform her into his undead partner, the spectator has at least two options available to him: either he can masquerade his accession to femininity behind a masculine display, or he can shiver in his seat. Though the second approach may not be as culturally promoted as the first, the display of terror is not reserved for women. In fact, Clover asserts that even though a masochistic viewing position may be coded feminine, it is also available to male viewers.[76] The example from *The Mummy* suggests how transvestitism may be adopted as a viewing strategy: the man "wears" a spectatorial response aligned with women.

In the context of classic horror cinema, the drag components of spectatorship (either as masquerade or as transvestitism) are not implicitly progressive or conservative. Instead, spectatorship-as-drag allows for viewing patterns that accommodate classic horror's textual machinations. I have no doubt that viewing relations that take the form of drag are transgressive of conventional spectator positions. I am less certain of whether they have a progressive ideological impact outside the theater doors. But what remains clear is that the masquerade involves distance from the image not only because womanliness is performed (by the monster, the heroine, and the spectator) but also because the sight of the monster (a figure who resembles a woman but is not one) generates a schism between the performer and the sex role adopted.

In a sense, therefore, the threat that resides behind the mask of womanliness is not confined to the danger of female appropriations of masculinity and maleness. Masquerade does not indicate that behind a feminine veneer lies a woman who is a man but that behind the mask resides someone who is not a man and who is terrifying and powerful precisely because she resembles a man but does not possess her father's penis—to use Riviere's terms. Conversely, the terrors offered by the masquerade of manliness are that behind the mask resides a man who is not a woman but who is feminine nonetheless. Both of these options are monstrous according to the terms of dominant culture, and one of the venues in which they emerge as engaging spectatorial positions is in response to classic horror's images of monstrosity.

Spectatorship-as-drag, therefore, transposes classic horror's sex and gender ambiguities to the spectating domain. Part of horror's and drag's draw for spectators is opening a space for an attraction to figures that revel in sex and gender fragmentation, and posit something more than the conventional sex-role and gender options available to men and women in American patriarchy. As a framework for spectatorship, drag suggests both that transgressive identifications and desires lurk beneath or on the surface of gender displays and that the lure of conventional roles does not counteract social expectations. That is, classic horror's transgressive spectatorial pleasures are intimately connected to the genre's simultaneous support of conventional desires.

Forming part of the genre's appeal is its designation of the monster as repulsive and threatening to women, and the obstacle that heroes and male spectators must overcome in order to assume their proper places within patriarchy. Yet as the preceding arguments indicate, another part of the appeal resides in the on- and off-screen malleability that classic horror celebrates, that is, the invitation to identify with and desire against everyday modes of behavior and to play with the masks that Western culture asks us to treat as core identities. Amidst signifiers of fear and desire and of loathing and longing, classic horror celebrates malleable spectatorial positions, the dissolution of conventional sex and gender categories, the fragility of the heterosexual couple and the family, and the precariousness of Western patriarchal institutions and values. Convention may win out in the end, and often the straight couple parades away, but the bulk of these films invite viewers to witness an alternative world: one in which they can oscillate between sadism and masochism, experience the transgressive pleasures of drag, and still wear their street clothes.

Many thanks to Carol J. Clover, Kate Davy, Anne Friedberg, Alison McKee, and Linda Williams for their insights during the development of this article.

NOTES

1. Steven Cohan and Ina Rae Hark, eds., *Screening the Male: Exploring Masculinities in Hollywood Cinema* (London: Routledge, 1993).

2. James B. Twitchell, *Dreadful Pleasures: An Anatomy of Modern Horror* (New York: Oxford University Press, 1985), and Carol J. Clover, *Men, Women and Chain Saws: Gender in the Modern Horror Film* (Princeton, N.J.: Princeton University Press, 1992).

3. Miriam Hansen, *Babel and Babylon: Spectatorship in American Silent Film* (Cambridge, Mass., and London: Harvard University Press, 1991).

4. Judith Mayne, *Cinema and Spectatorship* (London: Routledge, 1993), p. 84.

5. Rhona J. Berenstein, "Frightening Women: An Introduction to Classic Horror's Marketing Strategies," *Framework* 5:2/3 (1992), pp. 42–45.

6. Marjorie Garber, *Vested Interests: Cross-Dressing and Cultural Anxiety* (New York: Routledge, 1992), p. 10.

7. Ibid., p. 32.

8. Laura Mulvey, *Visual and Other Pleasures* (Bloomington and Indianapolis: Indiana University Press, 1989).

9. Roger Dadoun, "Fetishism in the Horror Film," in *Phantasy and the Cinema,* ed. James Donald (London: British Film Institute, 1989), pp. 39–62.

10. Gaylyn Studlar, "Masochism and the Perverse Pleasures of the Cinema," in *Movies and Methods: Volume II,* ed. Bill Nichols (Berkeley, Los Angeles, and London: University of California Press, 1985), p. 611.

11. Gilles Deleuze, *Masochism: An Interpretation of Coldness and Cruelty,* tr. Jean McNeil (New York: George Braziller, 1971), pp. 55–56.

12. Studlar, "Masochism and the Perverse Pleasures of the Cinema," p. 615.

13. Gaylyn Studlar, *In the Realm of Pleasure: Von Sternberg, Dietrich, and the Masochistic Aesthetic* (Urbana and Chicago: University of Illinois Press, 1988), pp. 12–13.

14. Linda Williams, "When the Woman Looks," in *Re-Vision: Essays in Feminist Film Criticism,* eds. Mary Ann Doane, Patricia Mellencamp, and Linda Williams (Frederick, Md.: American Film Institute Monograph Series, University Publications of America, 1984), p. 88.

15. In *The Old Dark House* (1932), James Whale's humorous foray into horror-mystery narratives, the paternal and maternal realms are also conflated, and the latter is represented in an indirect way. Although composed primarily of men, the family that lives in the house possesses the surname *Femm.* Signifying the effete components of the clan that dwells in the "old dark house," the surname also throws into question the masculine and, ultimately, paternal status of the Femm patriarch, a 102-year-old father who spends the course of the film locked in a room in the upper reaches of the house. When we finally meet Sir Roderick, the Femm father, there is something mysterious and disturbing about him. Laying bare that disturbing component requires a bit of research and, eventually, situates us within classic horror's conflation of the paternal and maternal realms, as well as the genre's fondness for gender-bending. Although the credits note that the role was played by John Dudgeon, Hollywood has no record of that actor. Instead, as James Curtis reveals in his biography of Whale, the part of Sir Roderick was played by Elspeth Dudgeon, a character actress known by the director (*James Whale* [Metuchen, N.J.: Scarecrow Press, 1982], p. 97). "'Jimmy couldn't find a male actor who looked old enough to suit him,' said David Lewis [Whale's longtime lover]. 'So he finally used an old stage actress he knew called Elspeth Dudgeon. She looked a thousand'" (Lewis quoted in Curtis, p. 97). Although the maternal is not directly represented within the film, the patriarch of *The Old Dark House* can be read as a disguised mother figure in that Sir Roderick was played by a woman.

16. Dadoun, "Fetishism in the Horror Film," pp. 39–62.

17. Barbara Creed, "Horror and the Monstrous-Feminine: An Imaginary Abjection," *Screen* 27:1 (1986), p. 59.

18. Clover, *Men, Women and Chain Saws,* p. 222.

19. In writing of the cycle of stalker films that appeared between 1978 and 1981, Vera Dika makes the following claim regarding audience composition: The audience . . . is overwhemingly young: these R-rated films . . . were frequented by adolescents between the ages of twelve and seventeen, and these films of excessive violence against women found an audience that was 55 percent female" ("The Stalker Film, 1978–81," in *American Horrors,* ed. Gregory Waller [Urbana and Chicago: University of Illinois Press, 1987], p. 87). Although the demographics of slasher films may have changed during the late 1980s and though video rentals have altered studios' abilities to chart audience composition, Dika's findings force us to look beyond male forms of masochism to account for horror spectatorship.

20. Lawrence S. Kubie, "The Drive to Become Both Sexes," in *Symbols and Neurosis: Selected Papers of L. S. Kubie,* ed. Herbert J. Schlesinger (New York: International University Press, 1978), p. 202.

21. Hansen, *Babel and Babylon,* p. 277.

22. Miriam Hansen, "Pleasure, Ambivalence, Identification: Valentino and Female Spectatorship," *Cinema Journal* 25:4 (Summer 1986), p. 19.

23. "A Child Is Being Beaten" has been a favorite resource in film studies. In her introduction to *The Desire to Desire,* for example, Mary Ann Doane uses Freud's article to address female spectatorship. However, Doane privileges masochism, and sexual pleasure is evacuated from the female spectatorial position (*The Desire to Desire: The Woman's Film of the 1940s* [Bloomington and Indianapolis: Indiana University Press, 1987], p. 19). In her work on Valentino, Miriam Hansen also appeals to "A Child Is Being Beaten" to explain female viewing relations. Unlike Doane, however, Hansen maintains that sadism and masochism oscillate, the fantasies illustrate shifting sex and gender identities, and female spectatorship and pleasure are entwined. According to Hansen, the punishment of males in female beating fantasies finds textual correspondence in Valentino's films, in which women view the hero's oft-whipped physique (Hansen, Pleasure, Ambivalence, Identification," p. 19). David N. Rodowich also addresses the importance of the fantasies to film spectatorship in his book *The Difficulty of Difference.* Rodowick takes note of the fantasizing girls' autoeroticism (D. N. Rodowick, *The Difficulty of Difference* [New York: Routledge, 1991], p. 77). Freud's article has recently been applied to literature. In her book on women and the Gothic *In the Name of Love,* Michelle A. Massé analyzes the subject positions deployed in "A Child Is Being Beaten" to account for the fluidity of the female reader's relationship to literary heroines (*In the Name of Love: Women, Masochism, and the Gothic* [Ithaca, N.Y., and London: Cornell University Press, 1992], pp. 7–8 and 40–72).

24. Sigmund Freud, "A Child Is Being Beaten," in *Collected Papers,* vol. II, tr. Joan Riviere (New York: Basic Books, 1959), p. 179.

25. Ibid., p. 179.

26. Although Freud's article on the beating fantasies has been generously analyzed by film theorists, most have accepted his claim that the sex of the adult doing the beating is the father. In my opinion, this assumption is open to debate. First, Freud is not averse to making bold claims that are the result of his analysis; the second phase, as we will see, is never consciously articulated by the patient, yet it forms the nucleus of Freud's interpretation. Second, when Freud argues that the adult is the father, he never once quotes a female patient; instead, after noting that it later becomes clear that the adult is the father, he asserts, "This first phase of the beating-phantasy is therefore completely represented by the phrase: 'My father is beating the child'" (ibid., p. 179). The first stage is "completely represented" by Freud's phrase and, perhaps, by his, and not his patients', figuration of the father. In fact, when Freud later rewrites the female patients' third phase, in which they are watching the father beat boys, he asserts, "The person beating is never the father, but is either left undetermined just as in the first phase, or turns in a characteristic way into a representative of the father, such as a teacher" (ibid., p. 180). Freud indicates that an intervention, his act of naming the adult a father, occurs in the first and third phases. Exactly when the adult becomes "clearly and unambiguously" equated with the father remains unspecified, but all clues point to Freud himself as the origin of and repository for that claim.

27. Freud, "A Child Is Being Beaten," p. 179.

28. Ibid., pp. 179–80.

29. Ibid., p. 180.

30. The power of female sadism was articulated in the 1930s by Dr. R. Allendy in "Sadism and Women" (1933): "The tactics of woman seem not only predatory and

primitive, but monstrous; because she is conscious of her weakness she destroys what is weak. . . . Woman plunders, castrates, dishonors, destroys. In contrast to male sadism woman's sadism is chronic, lasting, and unappeasable" (Allendy quoted in Tama Starr, *The "Natural Inferiority" of Women: Outrageous Pronouncements by Misguided Males* [New York and London: Poseidon Press, 1991] p. 83).

31. Freud's tendency to rely on a heterosexual model to account for identification and desire and his manufacture of the sex of the parent in the female fantasies are not unlike his interpretive maneuvers in other areas. In his analysis of his patient in "The Psychogenesis of a Case of Homosexuality in a Woman" (1920), for example, he is at pains to replace the lesbian's female object-choice with opposite-sex desire. As Judith Roof asserts, "[The patient's] shift in object-choice from male to female is accompanied by her assumption of a masculine attitude toward the object. In both cases her object-choices clearly stand in for inaccessible males, presenting a lesbian gloss for an underlying heterosexual desire" ("Freud Reads Lesbians: The Male Homosexual Imperative," *Arizona Quarterly* 46:1 [Spring 1990], p. 22). By deeming his patient's female object-choice a heterosexual cover and claiming that in order to effect that cover a woman must adopt a masculine position, Freud ensures that opposite-sex desire is paramount. In a similar vein, his transformation of the nonsexed adult into the father in the girls' fantasies confirms the Oedipal scenario, bestows primacy on heterosexuality, and limits the girls' play of identifications and desires. That the males' fantasies exceed the heterosexual model (they too are unconsciously beaten by their fathers, according to Freud) provides men with an extra degree of fluidity, rendering their sexualities less easily containable than women's.

32. Studlar, *In the Realm of Pleasure*, p. 47.

33. Garber, *Vested Interests*, p. 49.

34. Judith Butler, "Imitation and Gender Insubordination," in *Inside/Out: Lesbian Theories, Gay Theories*, ed. Diana Fuss (New York: Routledge, 1991), p. 22.

35. Ibid., p. 21.

36. Although drag is defined as a gay male practice, the definition highlights the constructed components of this type of performance. When Esther Newton asked a female impersonator in the 1960s whether there are any heterosexual impersonators, he responded, "In practice there may be a few, but in theory there can't be any" (*Mother Camp: Female Impersonators in America* [Englewood, N.J.: Prentice-Hall, 1972], p. 6). According to this performer's logic, the very act of transgressing gender roles and gender expectations exceeds heterosexuality; the latter is that which is transgressed and, therefore, cannot theoretically be that which does the transgressing.

37. Ibid., p. 103.

38. Ibid., p. 57.

39. In writing of the drag striptease, Newton takes note of a process that applies to classic horror: "The trick in stripping is to look and move as much like a 'real' stripper as possible and create the same erotic effects on the audience, to sustain the illusion of 'reality' down to the bra and g-string, and then, as a climax, to 'pull' (slip off) the bra, revealing a perfectly flat chest" (ibid., p. 45. One of the ways in which this is different from horror is that whereas the striptease moves toward a final moment of revelation— when the bra is removed—horror often traces multiple "stripping" scenes. Whereas the monstrous Mr. Hyde transforms back into the romantic young doctor only twice in *Dr. Jekyll and Mr. Hyde* (Paramount, 1931), Jekyll becomes Hyde at regular intervals. The repetition of transformations is a constant reminder of the presence of the hero's dual roles, as well as those roles' interdependence. In other words, horror's striptease alternates between revealing the "flat chest" and the "padded bra."

40. Butler, "Imitation and Gender Insubordination," p. 24.

41. Tania Modleski, *The Women Who Knew Too Much: Hitchcock and Feminist Theory* (New York and London: Methuen, 1988), p. 5.

42. Ibid., p. 42.

43. Robert J. Corber, "Reconstructing Homosexuality: Hitchcock and the Homoerotics of Spectatorial Pleasure," *Discourse* 13:2 (Spring-Summer 1991), p. 81.

44. J. Laplanche and J.-B. Pontalis, *The Language of Psycho-Analysis*, tr. Donald Nicholson-Smith (New York and London: W. W. Norton, 1973), p. 329.

45. Lee Edelman and Paul Willeman have made similar arguments for the importance of homosexuality. In his description of the primal scene from the case study of the Wolf Man, Edelman notes, "the primal scene as Freud unpacks it presupposes the imaginary priority of a sort of proto-homosexuality, and it designates male heterosexuality, by contrast, as a later narcissistic compromise that only painfully and with difficulty represses its identification with the so-called 'passive' position in that scene." (Lee Edelman, "Seeing Things: Representation, the Scene of Surveillance, and the Spectacle of Gay Male Sex," in *Inside/Out: Lesbian Theories, Gay Theories*, p. 101). Willeman's valorization of homosexuality appears in his discussion of fetishistic scopophilia. He notes that Mulvey's definition of that process ignores its autoerotic origin: "Mulvey doesn't allow sufficient room for the fact that in patriarchy the direct object of scopophilic desire can also be male. If scopophilic pleasure relates primarily to the observation of one's sexual like . . . then the two looks distinguished by Mulvey are in fact varieties of one single mechanism: the repression of homosexuality" (Paul Willeman, "Voyeurism, the Look and Dwoskin," in *Narrative, Apparatus, Ideology: A Film Theory Reader*, ed. Philip Rosen [New York: Columbia University Press, 1986], pp. 212–13).

46. Ellis Hanson, "Undead," in *Inside/Out: Lesbian Theories, Gay Theories*, p. 328.

47. Whereas psychoanalysis can conceive of these identifications and desires by rewriting homosexual object-choices as displaced heterosexual ones—a lesbian may desire another woman insofar as that desire disguises her desire for men—subjects are locked within the confines of sexual difference and heterosexuality.

48. A note of thanks is due to Anne Friedberg, who, in listening to my qualms about the conventional theorizations of a one-to-one correspondence between viewers and their on-screen counterparts, offered the notion of "identifying against oneself" as a means of better conceptualizing spectatorship. Although the concept has not been addressed in any detail in existing theories of spectatorship, it appears in its embryonic form in Mayne's new work *Cinema and Spectatorship* (see her fourth chapter, "Paradoxes of Spectatorship") and in Friedberg's book on the flâneuse, *Window Shopping*. As Friedberg writes, "[T]heories of spectatorship which imply a one-to-one correspondence between the spectator position and gender, race, or sexual identity . . . do not consider the pleasures of escaping this physically-bound subjectivity. Isn't cinema spectatorship pleasurable precisely because new identities can be 'worn' and discarded?" (*Window Shopping* [Berkeley and Los Angeles: University of California Press, 1993], pp. 184–185). Clover also introduces an identification-in-opposition motif, although she confines her analysis to biological sex and gender: "No one who has read 'Red Riding Hood' to a small boy or attended a viewing of, say, *Deliverance* . . . or, more recently, *Alien* and *Aliens* . . . can doubt the phenomenon of cross-gender identification" (Clover, *Men, Women, and Chain Saws*, p. 46).

49. Clues to this component of spectatorship can be found in a number of historical accounts of movie going. For example, Garth Jowett notes that the cinema provided early twentieth-century immigrants with "extra relief" amidst a difficult life of labor (*Film: The Democratic Art* [Boston: Little, Brown, 1976], p. 39). According to both Jowett and Russell Merritt, the fantasy elements of the movies were an escape from the drab and difficult conditions of the American immigrant's everyday reality (Russell Merritt, "Nickelodeon Theaters 1905–1914: Building an Audience for the Movies," in *The American Film Industry*, ed. Tino Balio [Madison: University of Wisconsin Press, 1985], p. 88).

50. Mulvey, *Visual and Other Pleasures*, p. 33.

51. Although more recently engaged with expanding spectatorship beyond a paradigm of sexual difference, de Lauretis revises Mulvey's model in *Alice Doesn't*. De Lauretis offers a paradigm that is more complex than Mulvey's but just as theoretically constrained. She argues for the sexed operations of narrative cinema's constructions of story movement and space. De Lauretis rephrases Mulvey's schema as a double identification: women identify with active male and passive female narrative positions (*Alice Doesn't: Feminism, Semiotics, Cinema* [Bloomington: Indiana University Press, 1984], p. 143). In *Alice Doesn't*, de Lauretis overlooks forms of spectatorship that defy a heterosexual journey toward Oedipus.

52. Mary Ann Doane, "Film and the Masquerade: Theorising the Female Spectator," *Screen*, 23:3-4 (Fall 1982), p. 80.

53. In a recent article on Sheila McLaughlin's *She Must Be Seeing Things* (1987), de Lauretis makes the following claim: "The notions of masquerade, transvestitism, and cross-dressing have been recurrent figures of feminist discourse in the 1980s and in the theorization of female spectatorship in particular" ("Film and the Visible," in *How Do I Look? Queer Film and Video*, eds. Bad Object-Choices [Seattle: Bay Press, 1991], p. 244). Focusing on Case's contribution to the field in "Towards a Butch-Femme Aesthetic," de Lauretis rejects the heterosexist theorizations of masquerade and transvestitism that have appeared thus far in feminist film studies (Sue-Ellen Case, "Towards a Butch-Femme Aesthetic," *Discourse* 11:1 [1988–89], pp. 55–73). De Lauretis privileges lesbian subjectivity in butch and femme roles as modes of ideological resistance and political discourse. As my arguments in the forthcoming sections indicate, not only do I think it imprudent to align the transgressive spectatorial positions of drag solely with a homosexual subject, but so too do I contend that Joan Riviere's original article on masquerade opens spaces in which to theorize a range of subjectivities not limited to heterosexuality or homosexuality.

54. Modleski, *The Women Who Knew Too Much*, p. 51.

55. Williams, "When the Woman Looks," p. 88.

56. Sue-Ellen Case, "Tracking the Vampire," *Differences* 3:2 (1992), p. 11.

57. Ibid., p. 13.

58. In a recent piece on the "homo/hetero" binary, Diana Fuss asks, "What gets left out of the inside/outside, heterosexual/homosexual opposition, an opposition which could at least plausibly be said to secure its seemingly inviolable dialectical structure only by assimilating and internalizing other sexualities (bisexuality, transvestitism, transsexualism . . .) to its own rigid polar logic?" (Diana Fuss, "Inside/Out," in *Inside/Out: Lesbian Theories, Gay Theories*, p. 2) Whereas Fuss notes that the danger of the homo is that s/he "codifies the very real possibility and ever-present threat of a collapse of boundaries, an effacing of limits," she also notes that it is unclear to what extent the homo confirms the primacy of the hetero, instead of disturbing it (ibid., p. 6). Part of what limits the powers of the homo in our culture is that s/he is confined to the homo/hetero binary and is, therefore, often locked within a model that depends on a struggle between the two terms in order to maintain the primacy of the second.

59. Eve Kosofsky Sedgwick, *Epistemology of the Closet* (Berkeley and Los Angeles: University of California Press, 1990), pp. 159–60.

60. Although my focus is on drag's impact on spectatorship in terms of biological sex, gender, and sexual orientation, the notions of identifying against oneself and performing identity also inflect the relationships between spectatorship and race and ethnicity, especially in classic horror cinema. For the genre is replete with monsters who, from the perspective of white America, are racial and ethnic Others. For example, the fiend in *The Mummy*, is an Egyptian Arab; the eponymous monster in *The Mysterious Dr. Fu Manchu* (Paramount, 1929) is Chinese; and the over-grown ape in *King Kong* (RKO, 1933) is textually conflated with African natives. While these films may, in the end, ask viewers to disavow their identification with and desire for monsters, many horror narratives

encourage spectators to bond with fiends through most of the films. Identification and desire may take, therefore, cross-racial or cross-ethnic form (e.g., a white viewer may identify with and desire Dr. Fu Manchu, or a black viewer may identify with and desire the mummy). As in the case of the vampiric status of the gay gaze, the relationship between viewers of color and monsters may include recognition of shared social status. Although on the one hand this confirms the marginalization of viewers and monsters alike, the fact that monsters are often objects of fascination that attempt to disrupt American institutions of power (e.g., the law, the family, and medicine) also lends an unconventional element to those identifications and desires. Unfortunately, the performative dimensions of viewing, from the perspectives of race and ethnicity, may be harder to pinpoint than gender (i.e., screaming is more readable as feminine than as a sign of a particular race or ethnic group). Although race may be more resistant to the types of performance cues and analyses outlined in the following pages, further research needs to be done in this area.

61. Newton, *Mother Camp*, p. 109.

62. Joan Riviere, "Womanliness as a Masquerade," in *Formations of Phantasy*, eds. Victor Burgin, James Donald, and Cora Kaplan (London: Methuen, 1986), p. 37.

63. Ibid., p. 38.

64. There may be yet another layer to the patient's masquerade in Riviere's article. A number of critics have speculated that the patient is none other than the analyst Joan Riviere. If this claim is true, then not only does the patient's masquerade disguise her accession to male-associated behavior, but it also disguises a tenuous distinction between the roles of analyst and analysand.

65. The assertion that Riviere's masquerade allows for multiple identifications and orientations is an important one, especially since Doane does not address masquerade from that perspective. Both Roof and de Lauretis complain of the heterosexism of Doane's model. According to de Lauretis, Doane's masquerade is intended to "find a position in heterosexuality from which the woman (spectator) can see and signify her desire in her distance from the image" ("Film and the Visible," p. 248). Roof notes, "While masquerade could destabilize the essential gendermentof viewing alignments if it shook up the certain heterosexual premises of desire—if, for example, it were admitted that no one's desire is strictly for the opposite sex—Doane's version of masquerade repeats the gender essentialism it tries to avoid" (*A Lure of Knowledge: Lesbian Sexuality and Theory* [New York: Columbia University Press, 1991], p. 49). Although Doane's discussion of masquerade may be heterosexist, the case study on which Doane's work is based does allow for mobility.

66. Riviere, "Womanliness as a Masquerade," p. 35.

67. Ibid., p. 40.

68. Of the extensive writings on horror literature and film, only Christopher Craft's article "Kiss Me with Those Red Lips" provides a sustained analysis of the homosexual components of Bram Stoker's original work ("'Kiss Me with Those Red Lips': Gender and Inversion in Bram Stoker's *Dracula*," *Representations* 8 [Fall 1984], pp. 107–33). Although some film critics briefly note that Lambert Hillyer's sequel to Browning's *Dracula—Dracula's Daughter* (Universal, 1936)—suggests lesbianism, the depiction of male homosexuality, according to critical reviews, is absent from the classic vampire movies. Literary critic Elaine Showalter is one of the few scholars to assert the endurance of homosexual connotations in film adaptations from the 1930s: "While most film versions of *Dracula* have been heterosexual, nevertheless, homosexuality is strongly represented in the films, coded into the script and images in indirect ways" (Elaine Showalter, *Sexual Anarchy: Gender and Culture at the Fin de Siècle* [New York: Penguin, 1990], pp. 182–83).

69. de Lauretis, "Film and the Visible," p. 248.

70. *Motion Picture Herald*, 29 June 1935, n. pag.

71. Critics have argued that the masquerade is a female performance enacted for the benefit of men. Stephen Heath, for example, notes, "The masquerade is the woman's thing, hers, but is also exactly *for the man, a male presentation, as he would have her.*" (Stephen Heath, "Joan Riviere and the Masquerade," in *Formations of Fantasy*, p. 50). De Lauretis, who notes the heterosexism of Doane's version of masquerade, argues, "It is not only inscribed within a male-defined and male-dominant heterosexual order, but more inexorably, in the current struggle for women's 'equal access' to pleasure in heterosexuality, the masquerade of femininity is bound to reproduce that order by addressing itself—its work, its effects, its plea—to heterosexual men" ("Film and the Visible," pp. 249–50). While de Lauretis is correct to point to a heterosexual limit-point for heterosexually deployed versions of the masquerade within a broader cultural context, it is unclear to what degree the same rules apply in cinematic spectatorship. If one of the pleasures of viewing is identifying against one's identity, then the ideological effects de Lauretis speaks of may be that much more complex and, perhaps, that much less applicable to viewing.

72. When I question the concept that lesbians' objects of desire are not men, I mean to suggest two variations on that statement. First, there are some lesbians who define their identity as a political or personal choice independent of and sometimes in spite of their sexual desire for men. Second, a desire for men may be considered a component of some lesbian desires. As Butler notes of one femme's object of desire, "she likes her boys to be girls, meaning that 'being a girl' contextualizes and resignifies 'masculinity' in a butch identity. As a result that 'masculinity,' if it can be called that, is always brought into relief against a culturally intelligible 'female body'" (*Gender Trouble* [New York and London: Routledge, 1990] p. 123). By liking her boys to be girls, the femme's boys are unlike other boys. But, to a degree, a desire for boys who are girls brings a desire for males into play.

73. By using the term *masquerade* to describe the feminine behavior of some lesbians and bisexual women, I do not mean to suggest that their feminine gender displays are always consciously mobilized or do not seem normal to those who experience them. Rather, I want to propose that in the example of a femme lesbian, especially a femme whose objects of desire are other femmes, the performative quality of sex-role behavior and object-choices is heightened, and masquerade functions as a means of disguising desires and identifications that run contrary to patriarchal culture. Other concepts that masquerade accommodates are that femininity may be donned as a mask for varying reasons and that the desires and identifications disguised behind the masquerade of womanliness are potentially unstable. As a spectatorial response, masquerade may also be the means by which some straight female spectators disguise their desire for on-screen women.

74. In writing of female spectatorship and Valentino, Hansen critiques Mulvey's and Doane's rather simple marginalizations of the transvestite. "The very figure of the transvestite," notes Hansen, "suggests that the difference of female spectatorship involves more than the opposition of activity and passivity, that it has to be conceptualized in terms of a greater degree of mobility and heterogeneity, including a sense of theatricality and selectivity" ("Pleasure, Ambivalence, Identification," p. 8).

75. Doane, "Film and the Masquerade," p. 81.

76. Clover, *Men, Women and Chain Saws,"* p. 60.

Annotated Bibliography

The following bibliography represents an attempt to draw together some of the philosophically foundational texts most important to spectatorship in cinema in conjunction with more recent reconsiderations of the relation of viewers to images.

Adams, Parveen. "Per Os(cillation)," *Camera Obscura* 17(1988):7–29.
    Through close readings resulting in new interpretations of Freud's examples, this article demonstrates that even within Freudian psychoanalysis, object-choice and identification are not necessarily linked.

Altman, Rick. 1989. "Dickens, Griffith, and Film Theory Today," *South Atlantic Quarterly* 88:2, 321–59.
    Questions the "classicism" of the classical realist film and, by implication, the unified and unitary perspectives of the spectator by introducing the notion of a submerged melodramatic subtext in some of the most apparently classical of films.

Barthes, Roland. 1970, tr. 1974. *S/Z*. Paris: Seuil; New York: Hill & Wang, tr. Richard Miller.
    A detailed analysis of Balzac's tale *Sarrasine*, which reveals a "limited plurality"—the multiple and even contradictory meanings—of classical realist writing.

Baudry, Jean-Louis. 1970, rpt. 1986. "Ideological Effects of the Basic Cinematographic Apparatus," in Philip Rosen, ed., *Narrative, Apparatus, Ideology*. New York: Columbia University Press, pp. 286–98.
    Baudry argues that the cinematic apparatus of camera and projector emerges from the subject's innate desire to see itself as whole and unified. The spectator identifies less with the content of a film per se than the apparatus that (re)produces the images.

——. 1975, rpt. 1986. "The Apparatus: Metapsychological Approaches to the Impression of Reality in Cinema," in Philip Rosen, ed., *Narrative, Apparatus, Ideology*. New York: Columbia University Press, pp. 299–318.
    Locates cinema's conceptual and psychic roots in the projected images and bound spectators of Plato's cave, developing an analogy between

dream and cinema. Like sleep, cinema suspends the secondary process of revision and satisfies desire through the transfer of perception to (near) hallucination. In cinema's "representations mistaken for perceptions," Baudry identifies the imaginary lure of the cinematic apparatus.

Benjamin, Walter. Tr. 1969. "The Work of Art in the Age of Mechanical Reproduction," in *Illuminations*, tr. Harry Zorn. New York: Schocken Books, pp. 217–251.

> Benjamin analyzes the changed cultural and political status of the art object stripped of its aura of uniqueness through the reproductive technology of printing, photography, film, and mass production. Of particular interest to film theory is his discussion of the distance afforded by the apparatus, the fragmentation of performance, and the reality effect produced through elaborate artifice.

Berger, John. 1977. *Ways of Seeing*. New York: Penguin Books.

> In this popular book, Berger blurs the distinction between high and low art by showing how the two appeal to similar desires and the common perspective of the masculine gaze. Much of the book draws on Benjamin's "Work of Art in the Age of Mechanical Reproduction," to which it adds a gender critique of popular culture summed up in the expression *men act, women appear.*

Bordwell, D., J. Staiger, and K. Thompson. 1985. *The Classical Hollywood Cinema: Film Style and Mode of Production to 1960* (New York: Columbia University Press, 1985).

> A historical elucidation of the dominant styles and modes of production of the Hollywood film. The authors are interested in demonstrating a theoretical approach to film history that links formal elements to conditions of production.

Bruno, Giuliana. 1993. *Streetwalking on a Ruined Map*. Princeton, N.J.: Princeton University Press.

> Bruno investigates spectatorship as a kinetic affair, which can include the *flâneries* of spectators through space and time.

Butler, Judith. 1991. "Imitation and Gender Insubordination," in *Inside/Out; Lesbian Theories, Gay Theories*, ed. Diana Fuss. New York: Routledge.

> Butler examines the epistemological, linguistic, philosophical, and scientific structures that define and naturalize gender. Defining signification and hence gender as a repetition of particular acts (i.e., a performative process), she opens up the possibility of subverting the traditional binaries.

Camera Obscura. The Spectatrix (1989) 20–21.

> This issue presents a survey of research on and theories of the female spectator in film and television, culled internationally from a wide variety of feminist film theorists as a guide to past and current work on the topic.

Clover, Carol J. 1992. *Men, Women, and Chain Saws: Gender in the Modern Horror Film.* Princeton, N.J.: Princeton University Press.

An original study of several subgenres of the contemporary horror film from a perspective that argues for the masochistic pleasures of a viewer's engagement with the plight of the genre's various victim-heroes.

Corrigan, Timothy. 1991. *A Cinema without Walls: Movies and Culture after Vietnam.* New Brunswick, N.J.: Rutgers University Press.

An examination of the ways modern advertising, VCR, cable TV, and media coverage of the Vietnam war changed the ways we watch movies.

Cowie, Elizabeth. 1984. "Fantasia," *m/f* 9, 70–105.

An influential essay adopting Laplanche's and Pontalis's notion that fantasy does not so much represent an object of desire as its setting or *mise-en-scène.* Cowie urges an approach to film that adopts the analogy of fantasy rather than that of dream or hallucination.

Crary, Jonathan. 1992. *Techniques of the Observer: On Vision and Modernity in the Nineteenth Century.* Cambridge, Mass.: Massachusetts Institute of Technology Press.

In this reexamination of many assumptions about nineteenth-century visual culture, Crary argues that the rupture with classical forms of vision occurred not in modern art and representation but much earlier— through a massive reorganization of knowledge, social practices, and techniques of observation.

Creed, Barbara. 1993. *The Monstrous Feminine: Film, Feminism, Psychoanalysis.* London and New York: Routledge.

Challenging the conventional wisdom that horror cinema is about female victims terrorized by male monsters, Creed argues that the fundamental prototype of the monstrous is the female body and that man's fear of that body derives not from her castrated state but from her power to castrate.

de Lauretis, Teresa. 1991. "Film and the Visible," in *How Do I Look? Queer Film and Video,* eds. Bad Object-Choices. Seattle: Bay Press, pp. 225–84.

Through an analysis of Sheila McLaughlin's *She Must Be Seeing Things* (1987), de Lauretis articulates how a film's work with and against narrative codes and conventional forms of enunciation may alter the standard frame of reference and visibility for lesbians.

Deleuze, Gilles. 1983. tr. 1986. *Cinema 1: The Movement-Image,* tr. Hugh Tomlinson and Barbara Habberjam. Minneapolis: University of Minnesota Press.

———. 1985, tr. 1989. *Cinema 2: The Time-Image,* tr. Hugh Tomlinson and Robert Galeta. Minneapolis: University of Minnesota Press.

Taking as his starting point Bergson's theses on movement and drawing upon Peirce's semiotics, Deleuze intercuts philosophy and cinema in order to produce a taxonomy of cinematic signification based on the movement-image and the time-image.

Doane, Mary Ann. 1982. "Film and the Masquerade: Theorising the Female Spectator," *Screen* 23:3-4, 74–87.

An early attempt, following Mulvey, but applying Riviere's "Womanliness as Masquerade" to theorize what for Doane and Mulvey is nevertheless ultimately the near impossibility of female spectatorship.

———. 1987. *The Desire to Desire: The Woman's Film of the 1940s.* Bloomington: Indiana University Press.

An extended study of the 1940s woman's film, which stresses the many ways that classical cinema and the cinematic apparatus are aligned with patriarchal ways of seeing.

Elsaesser, Thomas, and Adam Barker, eds. 1990. *Early Cinema: Space, Frame, Narrative.* London: British Film Institute.

This anthology turns to the roots of cinema to explore the varieties of spectatorial pleasures in the years before narrative became the dominant cinematic form. Includes Tom Gunning's "Cinema of Attractions: Early Film, Its Spectator and the Avant-Garde."

Freud, Sigmund. 1974. "'A Child Is Being Beaten,'" in *The Standard Edition of the Complete Psychological Works of Sigmund Freud,* vol. 17, James Strachey, ed., pp. 177–204. London: Hogarth Press.

Freud's extended analysis of fantasy examines beating fantasies collected and reconstructed from his patients.

Friedberg, Anne. 1993. *Window Shopping: Cinema and the Post-modern Condition.* Berkeley and Los Angeles: University of California Press.

Situates spectatorship within the historical development of the practices of shopping and tourism, which permit a "mobile virtual gaze" that travels to representations rather than to "the real." Friedburg concludes that the postmodern is more usefully considered not as a style but as a state produced by the apparatus, with psychic and social effects.

Gledhill, Christine. 1988. "Pleasurable Negotiations," in *Female Spectators,* ed. E. Deidre Pribram. New York and London: Verso, pp. 12–27.

In order to avoid the bipolarization of readings that artificially fix meaning as they label a text subversive or reactionary, Gledhill proposes an approach to spectatorship and textual analysis based on Gramsci's notion of hegemony as continually reestablished through negotiation between conflicting perspectives rather than forced on the spectator.

Gunning, Tom. 1989. "An Aesthetic of Astonishment: Early Film and the Incredulous Spectator," *Art & Text* 34, 31–45.

Habermas, Jurgen. 1962, tr. 1989. *The Structural Transformation of the Public Sphere,* tr. Thomas Burger. Cambridge, Mass.: Massachusetts Institute of Technology Press.

Traces the literary and political self-consciousness of the bourgeois class beginning with the rise in the eighteenth century of a newly conceived public sphere and continuing to the demise of that public space during the twentieth century in the face of mass culture, which renders us consumers, not producers, of culture.

Hansen, Miriam. 1991. *Babel and Babylon: Spectatorship in American Silent Film.* Cambridge, Mass.: Harvard University Press.

A study of early American film, which examines the ways that cinema could sometimes function as an alternative public sphere where women could enjoy visual pleasures to which they had no access in normal social life.

Jameson, Fredric. 1984. "Postmodernism, or the Cultural Logic of Late Capitalism," *New Left Review* 146 (July-August), 59–92.

Claims that post–World War II fragmentation of the subject has produced similarly decentered, postmodern cultural products. A new depthlessness and loss of historicity find expression in the nostalgia film and cultural pastiche.

Jay, Martin. 1993. *Downcast Eyes: The Denigration of Vision in Twentieth-Century French Thought.* Berkeley: University of California Press.

A groundbreaking work in the history of visuality, with important implications for cinema spectatorship. Offering a survey of "ocularcentric discourse" from the Greeks to the present, Jay's special focus is on the shift in French thought from ocularcentrism to ocularphobia: "the gaze," as seen from the long view of intellectual history.

Kaplan, E. Ann. 1983. "The Case of the Missing Mother: Maternal Issues in Vidor's *Stella Dallas*," *Heresies* 16, 81–85.

Argues that this maternal melodrama so entirely marginalizes and vilifies even the mother who tries to be good that the audience watching the film can only accede to the necessity of the mother's self-sacrificing assumption of the role of spectator of, rather than participant in, her daughter's life.

Laplanche, Jean, and Jean-Bertrand Pontalis. 1964, tr. 1986. "Fantasy and the Origins of Sexuality," in Victor Burgin, James Donald, and Cora Kaplan, eds., *Formations of Fantasy.* London and New York: Methuen, pp. 5–34.

Traces the development of Freud's often contradictory work on fantasy and develops a schema in which (1) fantasy is the setting—not the object—of desire, a point of transition between the unconscious and the conscious, whose fantasies are strikingly similar in content and activation, and, most important for cinema, (2) fantasy does not fix a single subject position.

Mayne, Judith. 1993. *Cinema and Spectatorship.* London: Routledge.

Organizing the topic through a continual tension between hypothetical subjects constructed by texts and actual historical viewers, Mayne offers the first systematic, book-length study of the role of the spectator in film studies. Case studies of particular films complement the theoretical overview.

Metz, Christian. 1975, tr. 1982. *The Imaginary Signifier: Psychoanalysis and the Cinema*, tr. Celia Britton, Annwyl Williams, Ben Brewster, and Alfred Guzzetti. Bloomington: Indiana University Press.

The first extended, systematic application of psychoanalytic theory to cinema. Metz accounts for the reality effect of cinema with a model that uses the psychoanalytic concept of the imaginary exemplified in Lacan's mirror stage. Metz argues that the experience of viewing a film draws on similarities to an imaginary recognition that is inherently a misrecognition.

Modleski, Tania. 1988. *The Women Who Knew Too Much: Hitchcock and Feminist Theory.* New York and London: Methuen.

Modleski refuses to claim either that Hitchcock is unequivocally misogynistic or progressively critical of patriarchy. Rather, she points to a crucial ambiguity in the films' attitudes, which reveals a fascination with femininity from both masculine and feminine positions. This fascination and covert identification place all spectators in a feminine position, thus throwing masculine identification into crisis.

Mulvey, Laura. 1975. "Visual Pleasure and Narrative Cinema," *Screen* 16:3, 6–18. Reprinted in *Visual and Other Pleasures.* Bloomington: Indiana University Press, 1989.

This article established the psychoanalytic groundwork for feminist theory of spectatorship. Mulvey argues that cinematic spectatorship is divided along lines of gender. In a world ordered by sexual imbalance, pleasure in looking has been split between active/male and passive/female. A male gaze either voyeuristically investigates or fetishizes a female object. Narrative and spectacle are determined by the demands of a patriarchal unconscious.

Penley, Constance. 1985. "Feminism, Film Theory and the Bachelor Machines," *m/f* 10, 39–59. Reprinted in *The Future of an Illusion: Film, Feminism, and Psychoanalysis.* Minneapolis: University of Minnesota Press, 1989.

Penley surveys and critiques apparatus theory as defined by Baudry and Metz and revised by Joan Copjec and Mary Ann Doane. She argues that countering the exclusive masculinization of cinema need not reintroduce the feminine body, but should instead include sexual difference, which she proposes to do through a consideration of fantasy.

Silverman, Kaja. 1988. "Masochism and Male Subjectivity," *Camera Obscura: A Journal of Feminism an Film Theory* 17, 31–63. Reprinted in *Male Subjectivity at the Margins.* New York and London: Routledge, 1992.

Explores the concepts of feminine masochism and moral masochism in men while surveying the literature on masochism from Freud to Deleuze. Concludes that male subjectivity is far more heterogeneous and divided than most theoretical models have heretofore suggested.

Sobchack, Vivian. 1992. *The Address of the Eye: A Phenomenology of Film Experience.* Princeton, N.J.: Princeton University Press.

Sobchack challenges psychoanalytic film theories that reduce film to an object of vision and the spectator to a victim of a deterministic apparatus. She proposes a phenomenological perspective that sees spectator and film each existing as subject and object of vision.

Studlar, Gaylyn. 1988. *In the Realm of Pleasure: Von Sternberg, Dietrich, and the Masochistic Aesthetic.* Urbana and Chicago: University of Illinois Press.

Suggests that cinematic pleasure stems from similarities to the pre-Oedipal realm of infant sexuality characterized by helplessness and fusion with the mother. Masochism's active construction of such scenarios renders masochism more apt an explanation than sadism.

Williams, Linda. 1984. "'Something Else besides a Mother': *Stella Dallas* and the Maternal Melodrama," *Cinema Journal* 24:1, 2–27.

Arguing against Kaplan's position that the melodrama *Stella Dallas* forces the female spectator to accede to a necessary maternal sacrifice, Williams maintains that the film conjures up a variety of subject positions and draws on women's reading competence.

———. 1989. *Hard Core: Power, Pleasure, and the "Frenzy of the Visible."* Berkeley: University of California Press.

Sketches the history of hard-core pornography in the interest of delimiting its characteristics as a genre. Williams examines how the genre configures power and desire and finds it, contrary to received opinion, a site of great spectatorial instability.

Contributors

RHONA J. BERENSTEIN is Assistant Professor of Film Studies at the University of California, Irvine, where she teaches film and television. She is the author of *Attack of the Leading Ladies: Masks of Race, Gender and Sexuality in the Classic Horror Film*, forthcoming with Columbia University Press.

CAROL J. CLOVER is Professor of Rhetoric and Comparative Literature at the University of California at Berkeley. She is the author of *Men, Women and Chain Saws: Gender in the Modern Horror Film* and *The Medieval Saga*.

JONATHAN CRARY is Associate Professor of Art History at Columbia University. He is the author of *Techniques of the Observer: On Vision and Modernity in the Nineteenth Century* and a founding editor of Zone and Zone Books.

ANNE FRIEDBERG is Associate Professor of Film Studies at the University of California, Irvine. She is the author of *Window Shopping: Film and the Postmodern Condition*, University of California Press.

TOM GUNNING is Associate Professor of Radio/Film/Television at Northwestern University. He is the author of *D. W. Griffith and the Origins of American Narrative Film: The Early Years at Biograph*.

MIRIAM HANSEN is Professor of English and Director of the Film Studies Center at the University of Chicago. Her most recent book is *Babel and Babylon: Spectatorship and American Silent Film*. She is currently writing a book on the Frankfurt School's debates on Film and Mass Culture.

JUDITH MAYNE is Professor of French and of Women's Studies at Ohio State University. Her books include *Cinema and Specatorship* and *The Woman at the Keyhole: Feminism and Women's Cinema*.

VANESSA R. SCHWARTZ is Assistant Professor of History at American University. She is coeditor, with Leo Charney, of the collection of essays *Cinema and the Invention of Modern Life*, forthcoming from the University of California Press.

VIVIAN SOBCHACK is Professor in the Department of Film and Television at the University of California, Los Angeles. Her books include *The Address of the Eye:*

A Phenomenology of Film Experience and *Screening Space: The American Science Fiction Film.*

LINDA WILLIAMS is Professor of Film Studies and of Women's Studies at the University of California, Irvine. She is the author of *Hard Core: Power, Pleasure and the "Frenzy of the Visible"* and *Figures of Desire: A Theory and Analysis of Surrealist Film,* both with the University of California Press.

Index